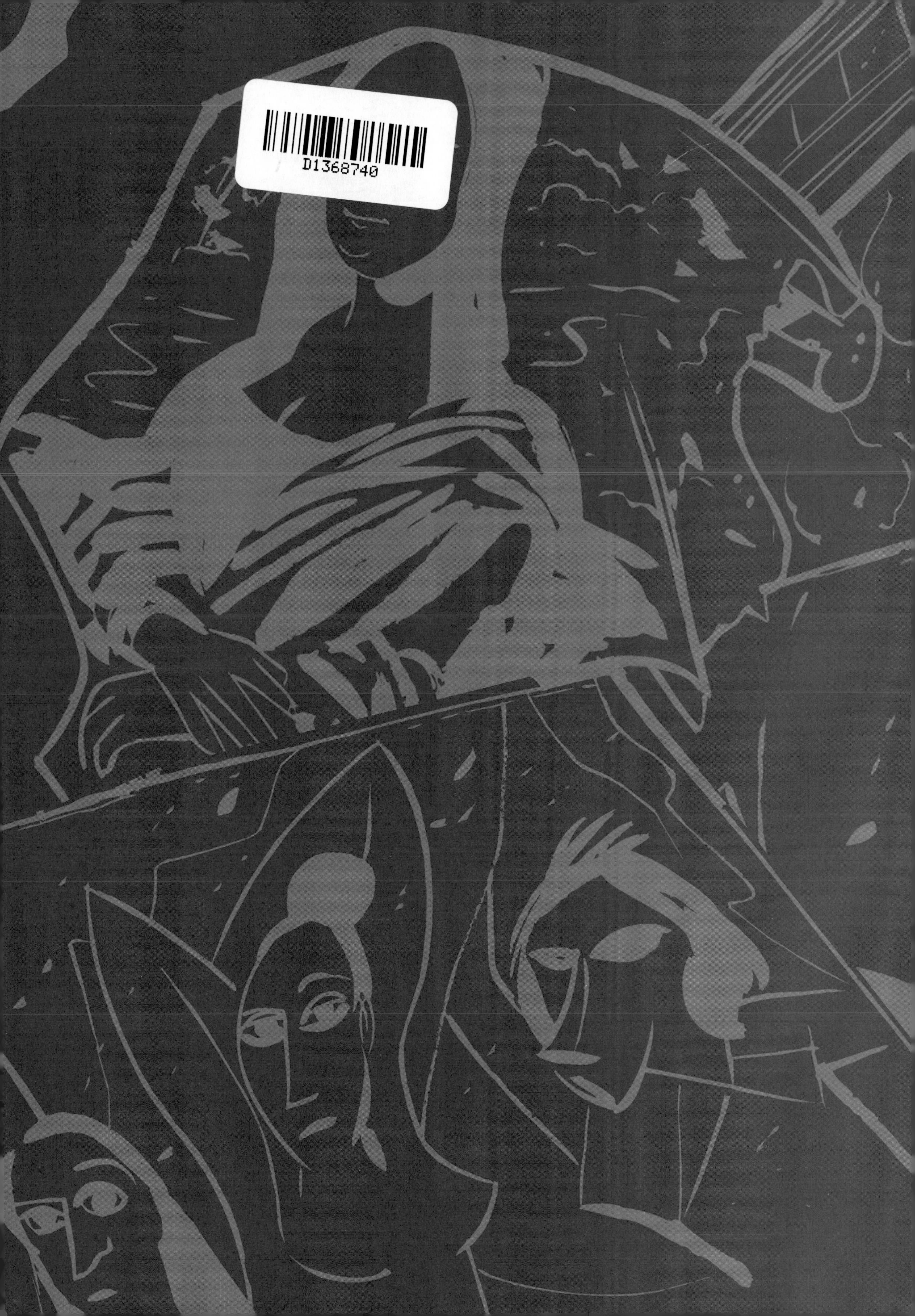

RASL

BY

JEFF SMITH

CARTOON BOOKS
COLUMBUS, OHIO

RASL Volume 4: The Lost Journals of Nikola Tesla

The chapters in this book were originally published in the comic book RASL
RASL™ is © 2012 by Jeff Smith.

For Cartoon Books:
Cover Art by Jeff Smith
Cover Color & Logo/Design by Steve Hamaker
Published by Vijaya Iyer
Production Manager: Kathleen Glosan
PrePress/Design: Tom Gaadt

For information write:
Cartoon Books
P.O. Box 16973
Columbus, OH 43216

Softcover ISBN-10: 1-888963-32-8
Softcover ISBN-13: 978-1-888963-32-8

10 9 8 7 6 5 4 3 2 1

Printed in the U.S.A

"THE DAY WHEN WE KNOW WHAT EXACTLY ELECTRICITY IS, WILL CHRONICLE AN EVENT PROBABLY GREATER,
MORE IMPORTANT THAN ANY OTHER RECORDED IN THE HISTORY OF THE HUMAN RACE."

"SOMEDAY - - BUT NOT AT THIS TIME - - I SHALL MAKE AN ANNOUNCEMENT
OF SOMETHING THAT I NEVER ONCE DREAMED OF."
-NIKOLA TESLA

12.
SYNCHRONICITY

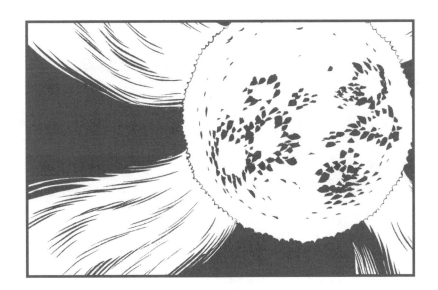

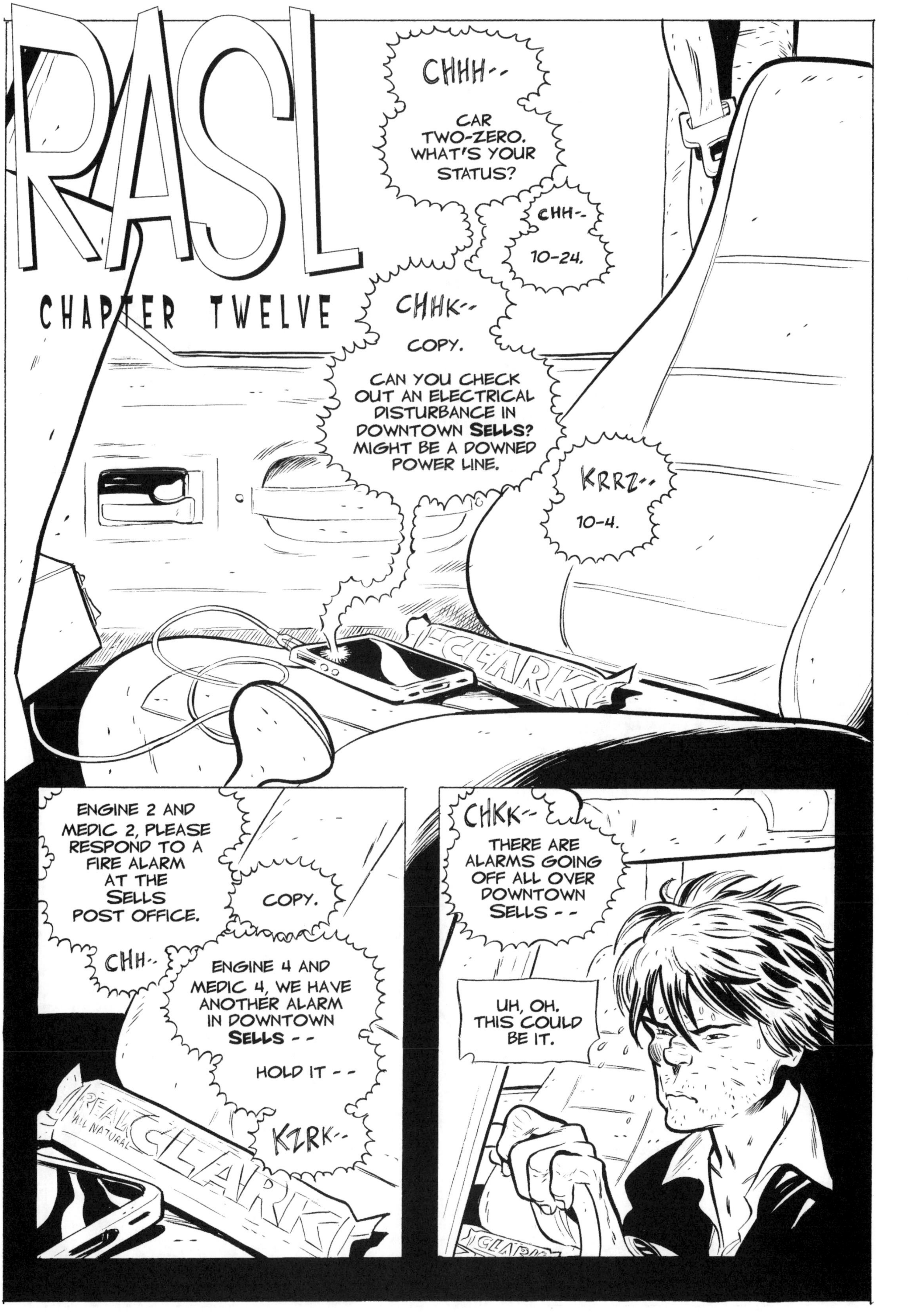
RASL
CHAPTER TWELVE
CHHH--
CAR TWO-ZERO. WHAT'S YOUR STATUS?
CHH--
10-24.
CHHK--
COPY.
CAN YOU CHECK OUT AN ELECTRICAL DISTURBANCE IN DOWNTOWN **SELLS?** MIGHT BE A DOWNED POWER LINE.
KRRZ--
10-4.
CLARK
ENGINE 2 AND MEDIC 2, PLEASE RESPOND TO A FIRE ALARM AT THE SELLS POST OFFICE.
COPY.
CHH--
ENGINE 4 AND MEDIC 4, WE HAVE ANOTHER ALARM IN DOWNTOWN **SELLS** --
HOLD IT --
KZRK--
REAL ALL NATURAL CLARK
CHKK--
THERE ARE ALARMS GOING OFF ALL OVER DOWNTOWN SELLS --
UH, OH. THIS COULD BE IT.

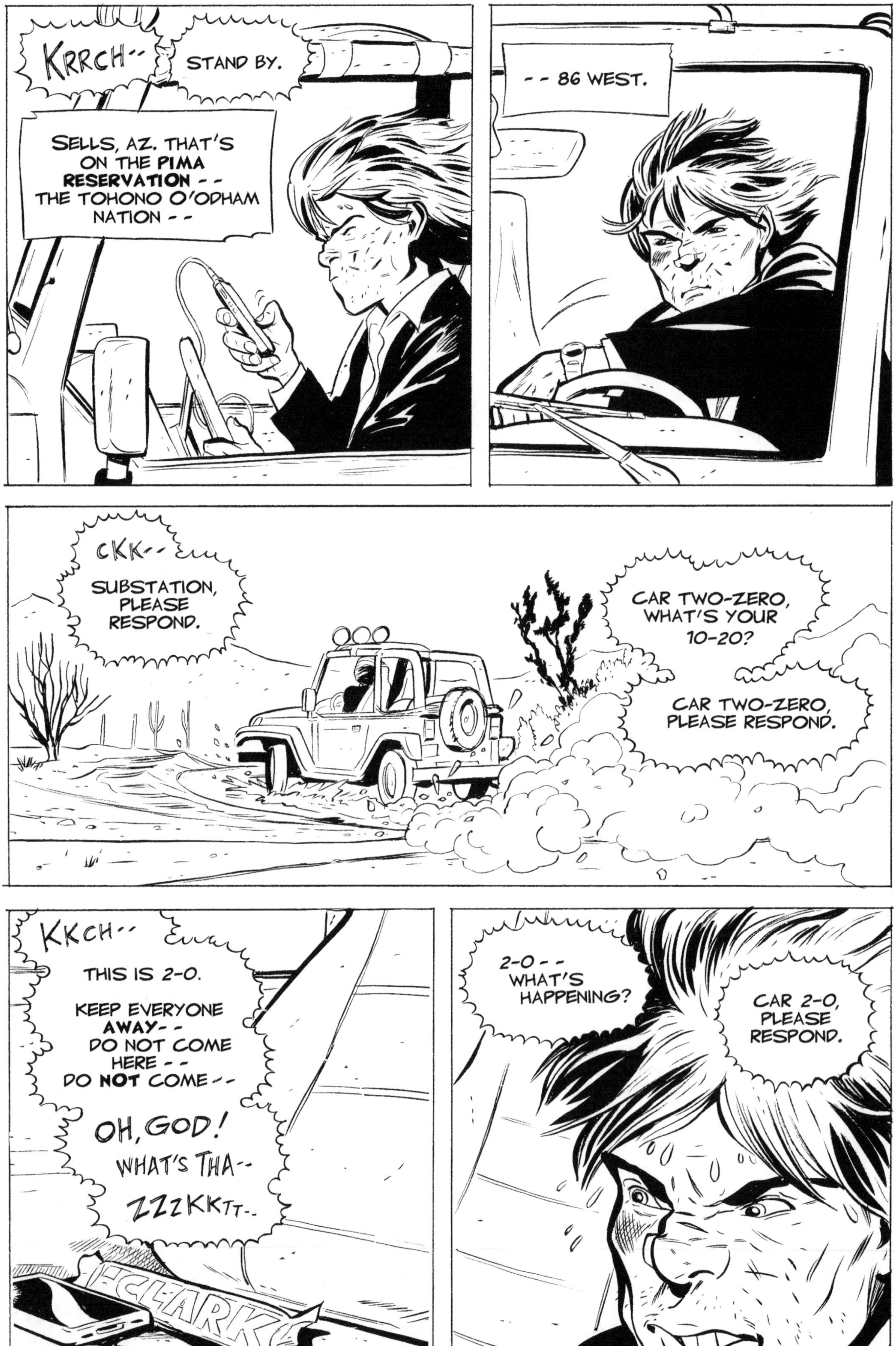
KRRCH--
STAND BY.
SELLS, AZ. THAT'S ON THE **PIMA RESERVATION** -- THE TOHONO O'ODHAM NATION --
-- 86 WEST.
CKK-- SUBSTATION, PLEASE RESPOND.
CAR TWO-ZERO, WHAT'S YOUR 10-20?
CAR TWO-ZERO, PLEASE RESPOND.
KKCH-- THIS IS 2-0. KEEP EVERYONE **AWAY**-- DO NOT COME HERE -- DO **NOT** COME--
OH, GOD! WHAT'S THA-- ZZZKKTT--
CLARK
2-0 -- WHAT'S HAPPENING?
CAR 2-0, PLEASE RESPOND.

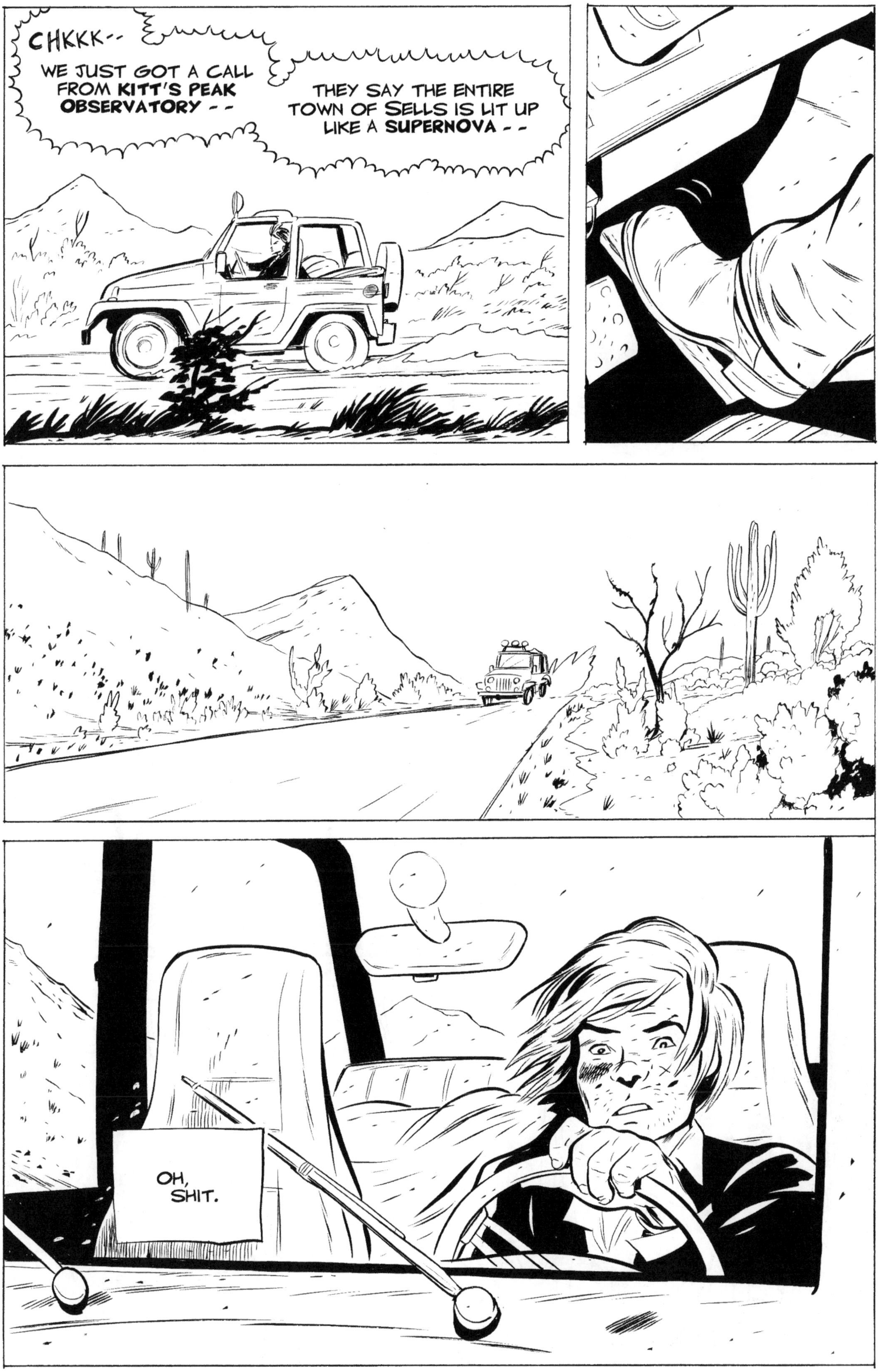
CHKKK--
WE JUST GOT A CALL FROM KITT'S PEAK OBSERVATORY --
THEY SAY THE ENTIRE TOWN OF SELLS IS LIT UP LIKE A SUPERNOVA --
OH, SHIT.

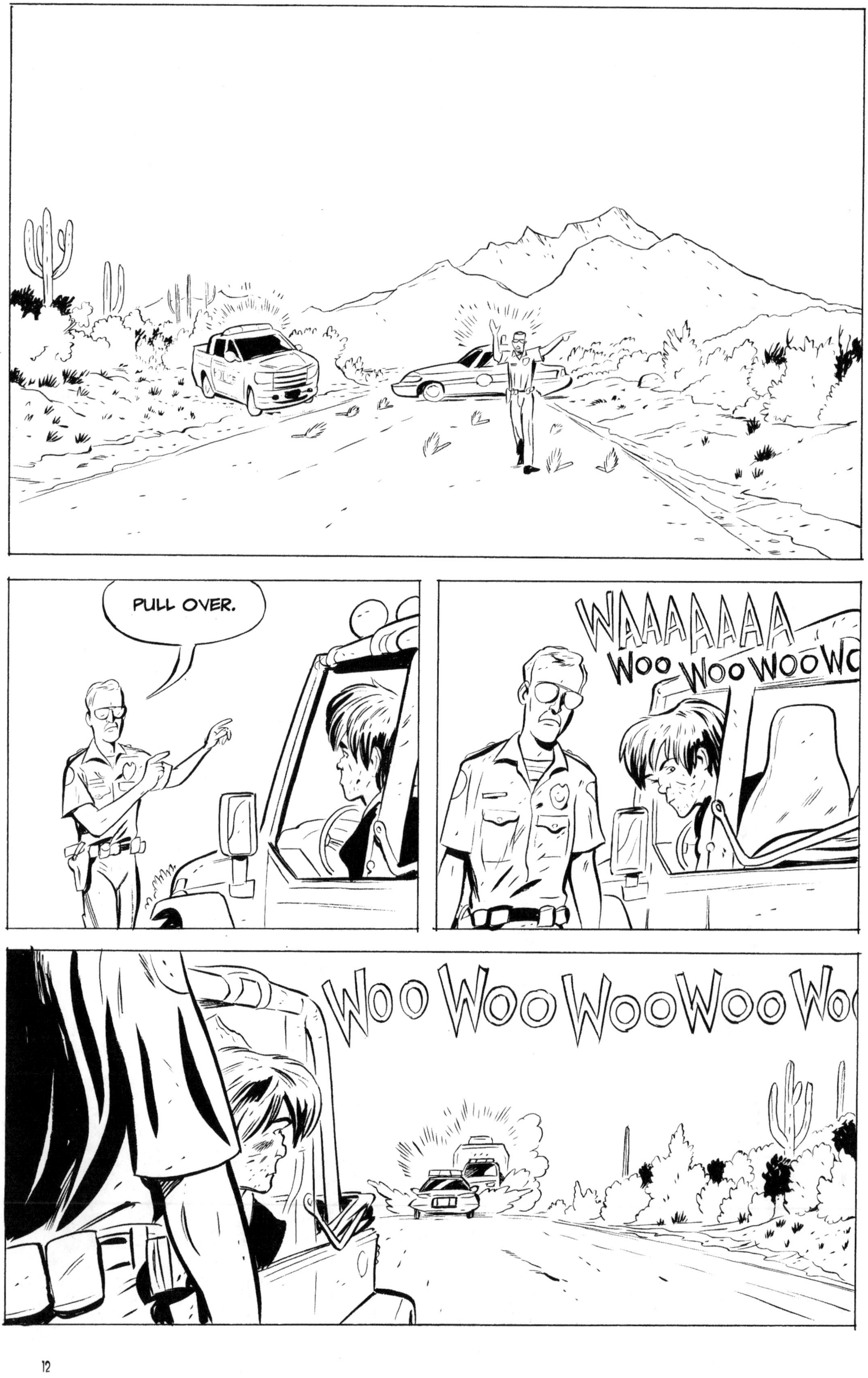
PULL OVER.
WAAAAAAA
Woo Woo Woo Wo
Woo Woo Woo Woo Wo

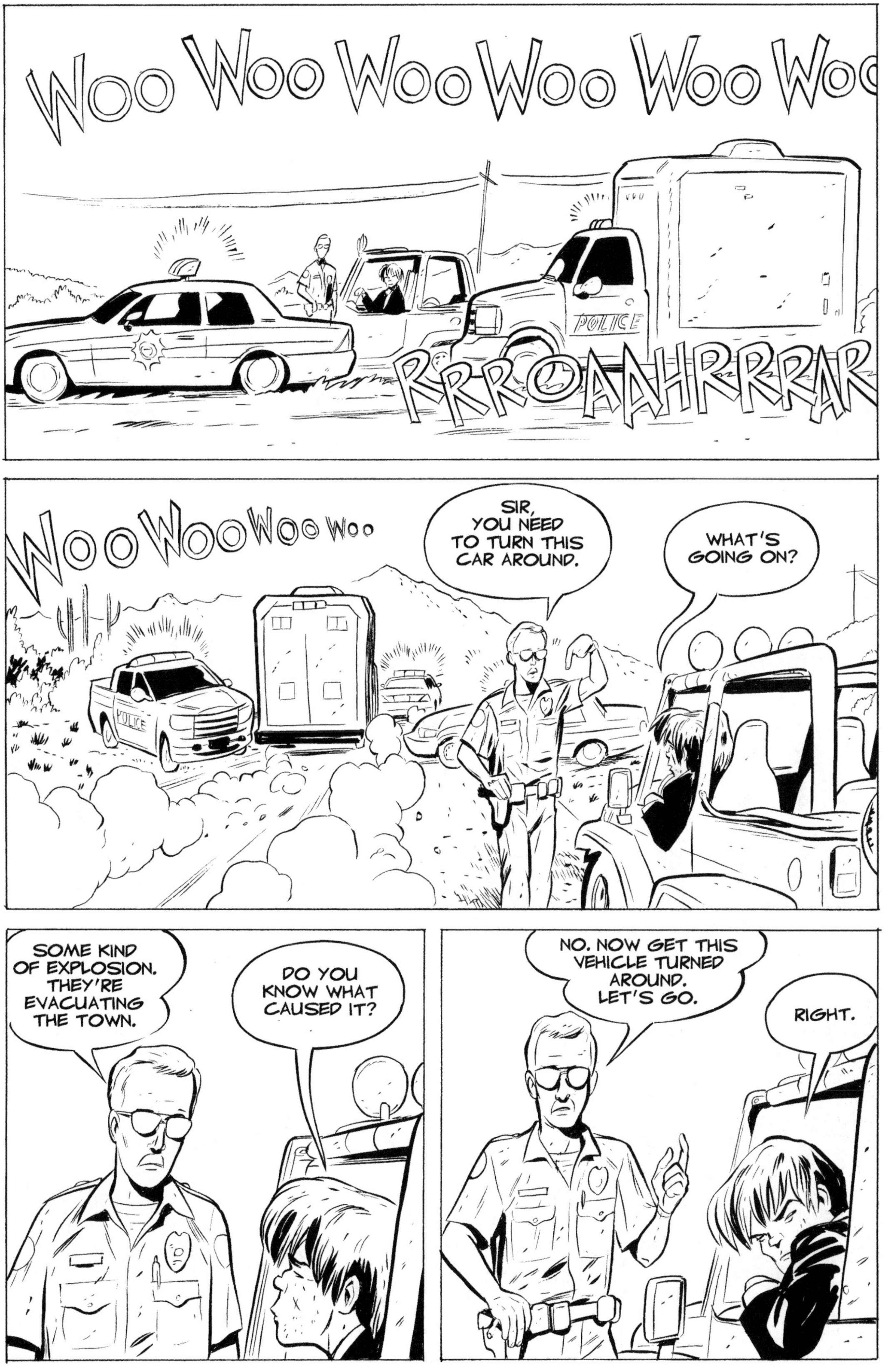
WOO WOO WOO WOO WOO WOO
POLICE
RRROAAHRRRAR
WOO WOO WOO WOO
POLICE
SIR, YOU NEED TO TURN THIS CAR AROUND.
WHAT'S GOING ON?
SOME KIND OF EXPLOSION. THEY'RE EVACUATING THE TOWN.
DO YOU KNOW WHAT CAUSED IT?
NO. NOW GET THIS VEHICLE TURNED AROUND. LET'S GO.
RIGHT.

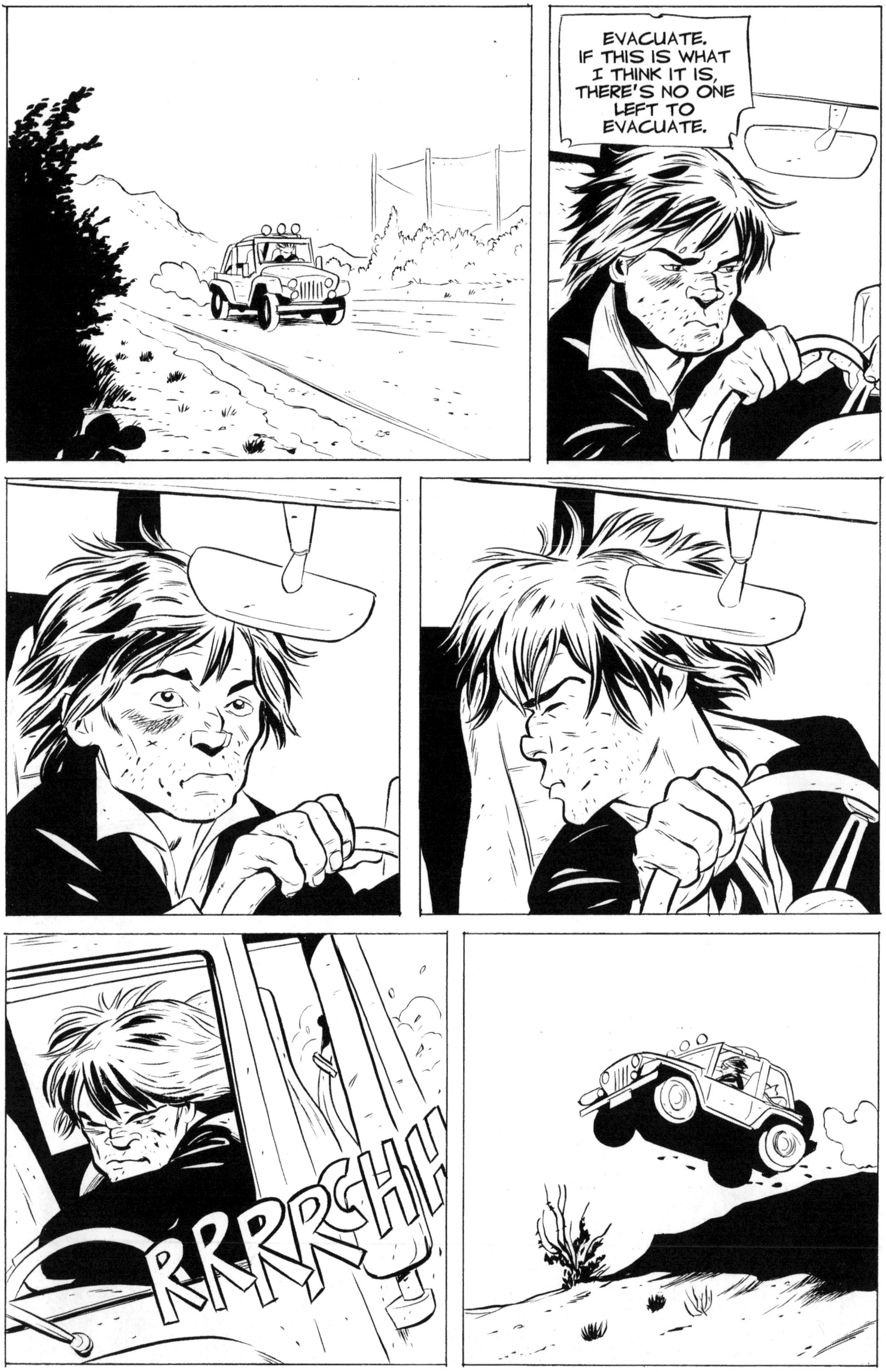
EVACUATE. IF THIS IS WHAT I THINK IT IS, THERE'S NO ONE LEFT TO EVACUATE.
RRRRCHHH

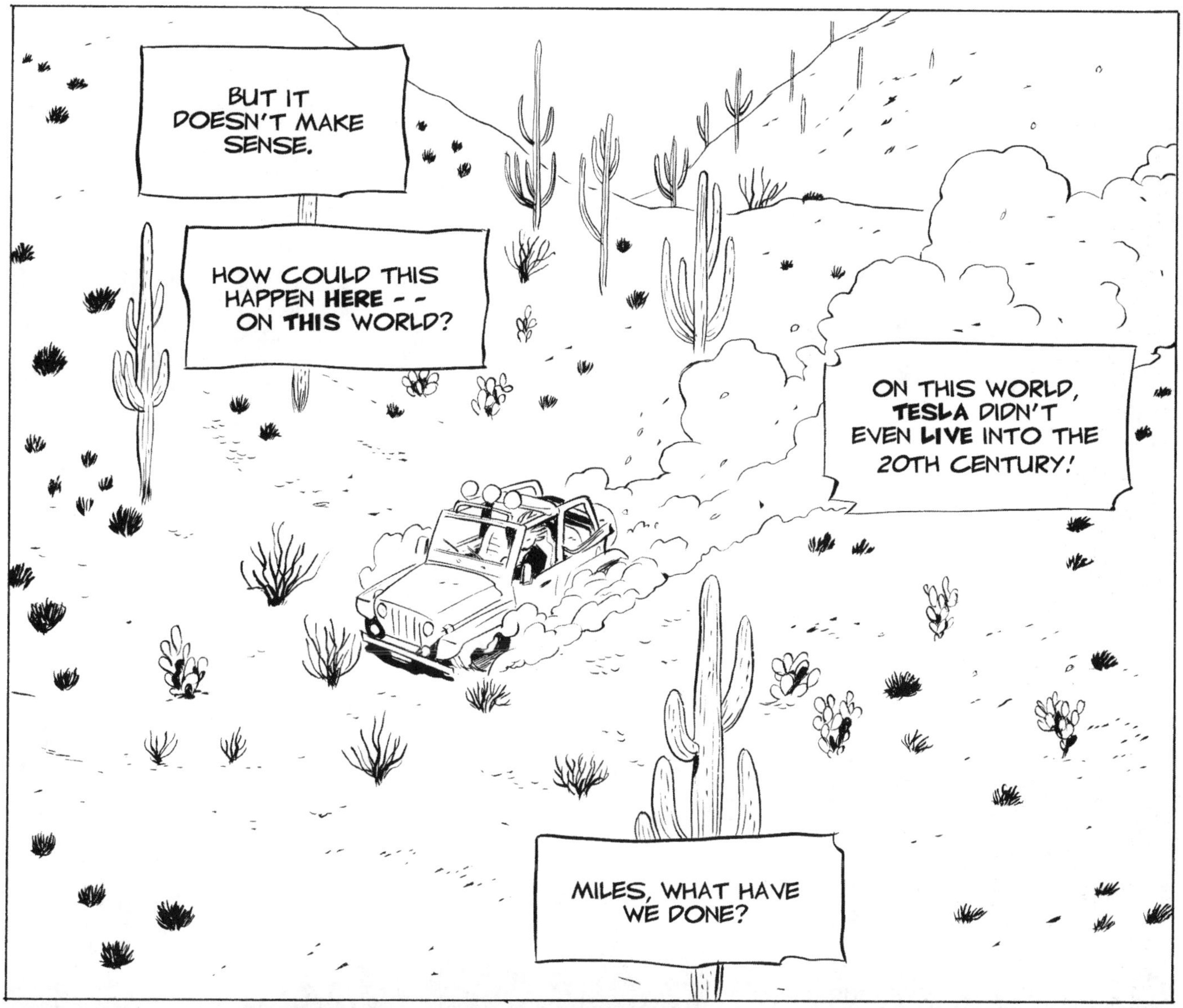
BUT IT DOESN'T MAKE SENSE.
HOW COULD THIS HAPPEN HERE -- ON THIS WORLD?
ON THIS WORLD, TESLA DIDN'T EVEN LIVE INTO THE 20TH CENTURY!
MILES, WHAT HAVE WE DONE?

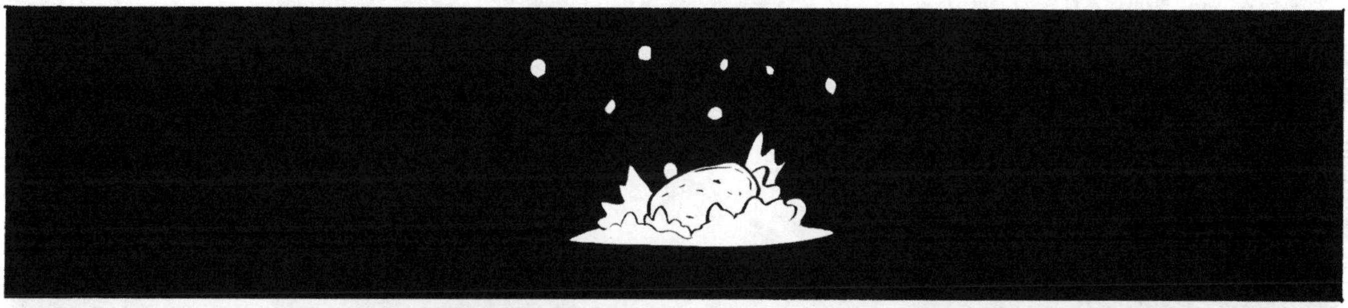

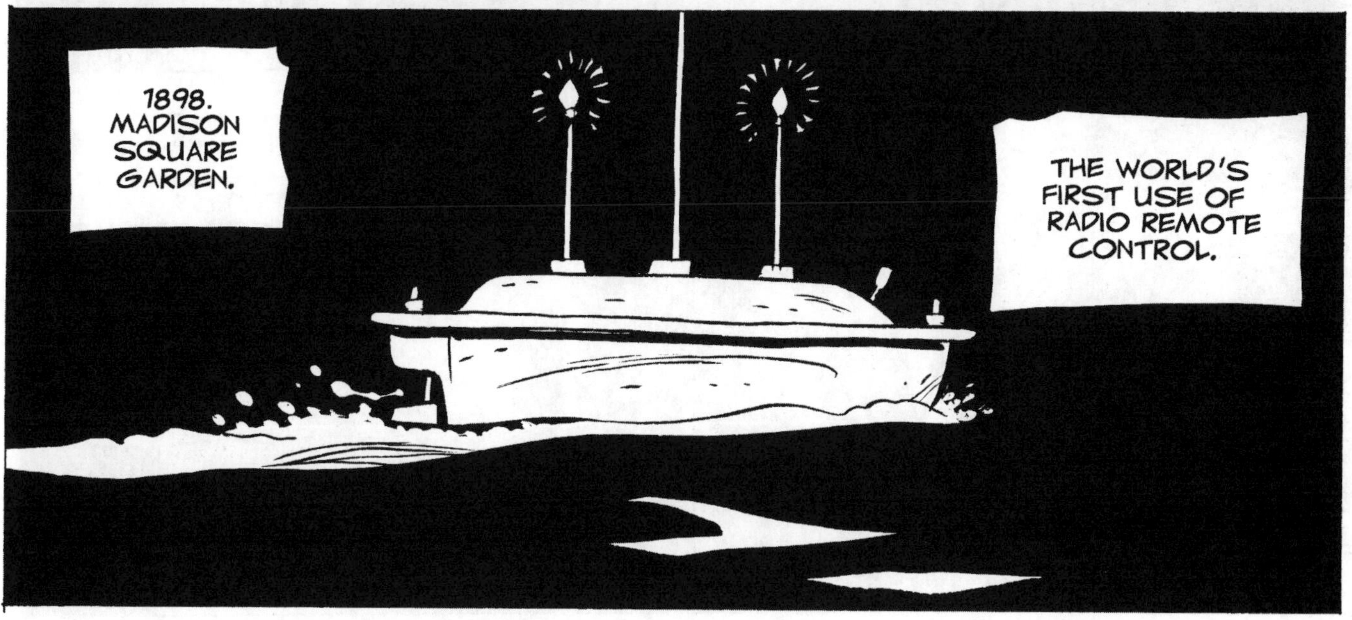
1898. MADISON SQUARE GARDEN.
THE WORLD'S FIRST USE OF RADIO REMOTE CONTROL.

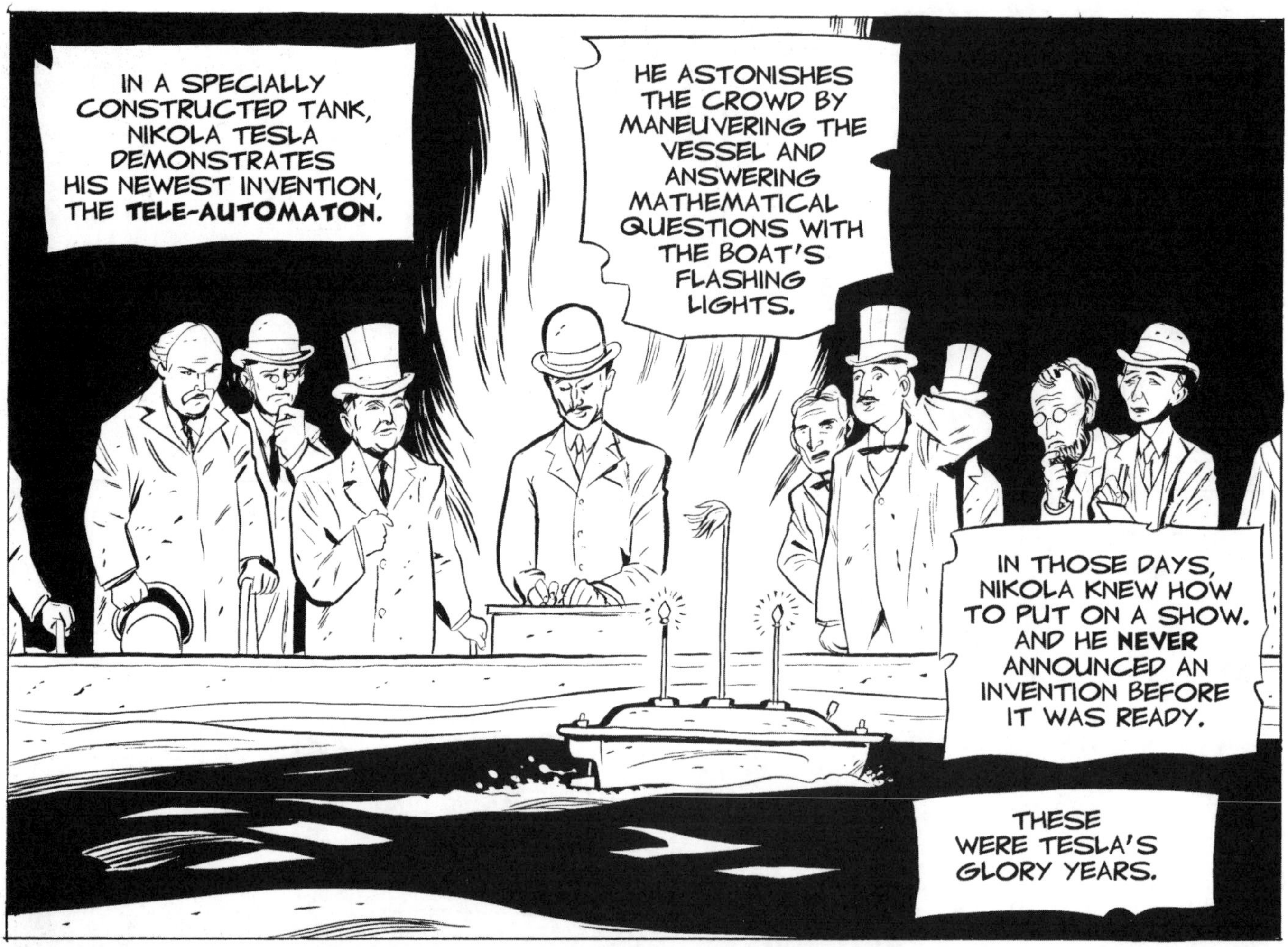
IN A SPECIALLY CONSTRUCTED TANK, NIKOLA TESLA DEMONSTRATES HIS NEWEST INVENTION, THE **TELE-AUTOMATON.**
HE ASTONISHES THE CROWD BY MANEUVERING THE VESSEL AND ANSWERING MATHEMATICAL QUESTIONS WITH THE BOAT'S FLASHING LIGHTS.
IN THOSE DAYS, NIKOLA KNEW HOW TO PUT ON A SHOW. AND HE **NEVER** ANNOUNCED AN INVENTION BEFORE IT WAS READY.
THESE WERE TESLA'S GLORY YEARS.

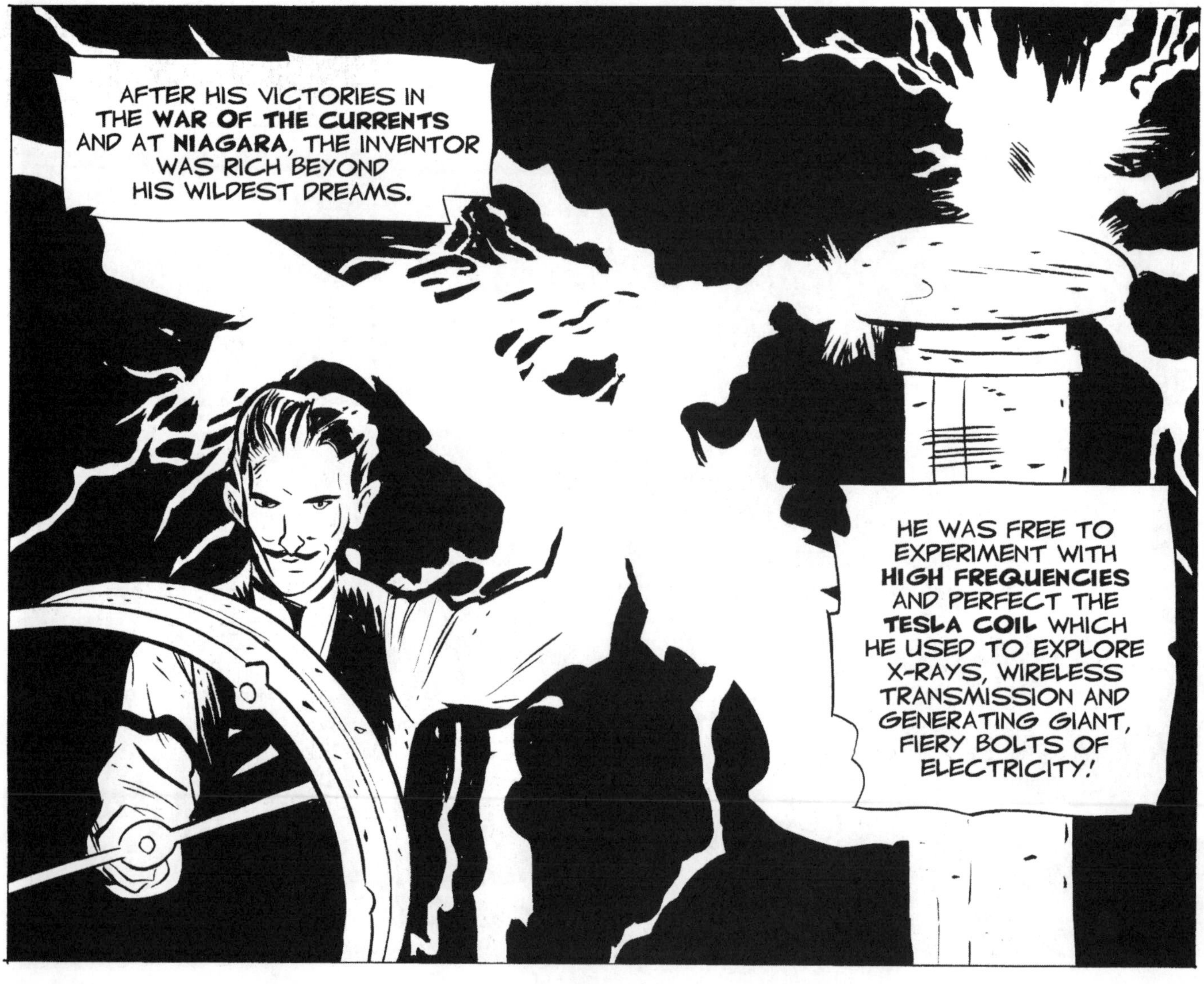
AFTER HIS VICTORIES IN THE **WAR OF THE CURRENTS** AND AT **NIAGARA**, THE INVENTOR WAS RICH BEYOND HIS WILDEST DREAMS.
HE WAS FREE TO EXPERIMENT WITH **HIGH FREQUENCIES** AND PERFECT THE **TESLA COIL** WHICH HE USED TO EXPLORE X-RAYS, WIRELESS TRANSMISSION AND GENERATING GIANT, FIERY BOLTS OF ELECTRICITY!

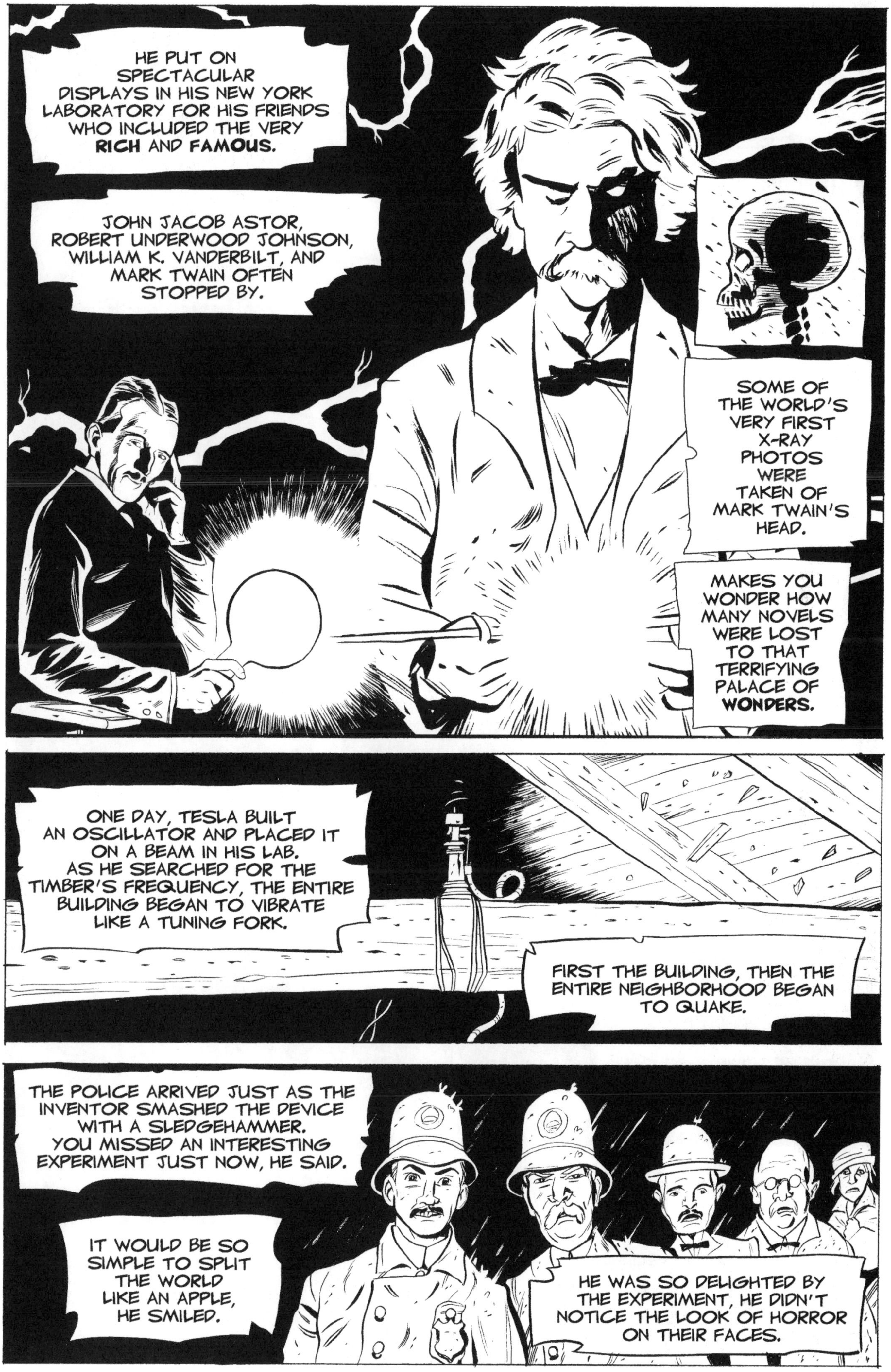
HE PUT ON SPECTACULAR DISPLAYS IN HIS NEW YORK LABORATORY FOR HIS FRIENDS WHO INCLUDED THE VERY **RICH** AND **FAMOUS.**
JOHN JACOB ASTOR, ROBERT UNDERWOOD JOHNSON, WILLIAM K. VANDERBILT, AND MARK TWAIN OFTEN STOPPED BY.
SOME OF THE WORLD'S VERY FIRST X-RAY PHOTOS WERE TAKEN OF MARK TWAIN'S HEAD.
MAKES YOU WONDER HOW MANY NOVELS WERE LOST TO THAT TERRIFYING PALACE OF **WONDERS.**
ONE DAY, TESLA BUILT AN OSCILLATOR AND PLACED IT ON A BEAM IN HIS LAB. AS HE SEARCHED FOR THE TIMBER'S FREQUENCY, THE ENTIRE BUILDING BEGAN TO VIBRATE LIKE A TUNING FORK.
FIRST THE BUILDING, THEN THE ENTIRE NEIGHBORHOOD BEGAN TO QUAKE.
THE POLICE ARRIVED JUST AS THE INVENTOR SMASHED THE DEVICE WITH A SLEDGEHAMMER. YOU MISSED AN INTERESTING EXPERIMENT JUST NOW, HE SAID.
IT WOULD BE SO SIMPLE TO SPLIT THE WORLD LIKE AN APPLE, HE SMILED.
HE WAS SO DELIGHTED BY THE EXPERIMENT, HE DIDN'T NOTICE THE LOOK OF HORROR ON THEIR FACES.

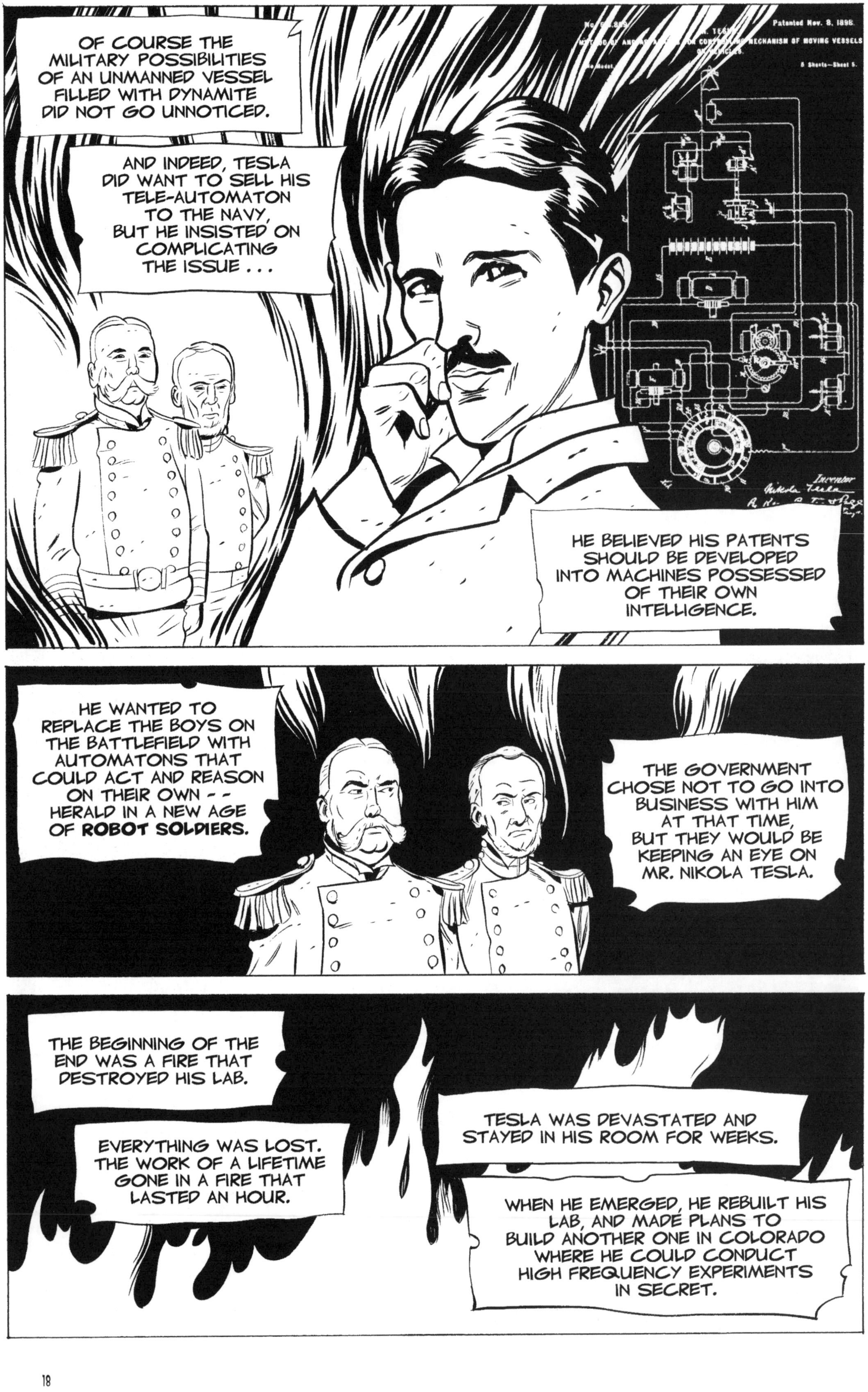
OF COURSE THE MILITARY POSSIBILITIES OF AN UNMANNED VESSEL FILLED WITH DYNAMITE DID NOT GO UNNOTICED.
AND INDEED, TESLA DID WANT TO SELL HIS TELE-AUTOMATON TO THE NAVY, BUT HE INSISTED ON COMPLICATING THE ISSUE . . .
Patented Nov. 8, 1898.
HE BELIEVED HIS PATENTS SHOULD BE DEVELOPED INTO MACHINES POSSESSED OF THEIR OWN INTELLIGENCE.
HE WANTED TO REPLACE THE BOYS ON THE BATTLEFIELD WITH AUTOMATONS THAT COULD ACT AND REASON ON THEIR OWN - - HERALD IN A NEW AGE OF **ROBOT SOLDIERS.**
THE GOVERNMENT CHOSE NOT TO GO INTO BUSINESS WITH HIM AT THAT TIME, BUT THEY WOULD BE KEEPING AN EYE ON MR. NIKOLA TESLA.
THE BEGINNING OF THE END WAS A FIRE THAT DESTROYED HIS LAB.
EVERYTHING WAS LOST. THE WORK OF A LIFETIME GONE IN A FIRE THAT LASTED AN HOUR.
TESLA WAS DEVASTATED AND STAYED IN HIS ROOM FOR WEEKS.
WHEN HE EMERGED, HE REBUILT HIS LAB, AND MADE PLANS TO BUILD ANOTHER ONE IN COLORADO WHERE HE COULD CONDUCT HIGH FREQUENCY EXPERIMENTS IN SECRET.

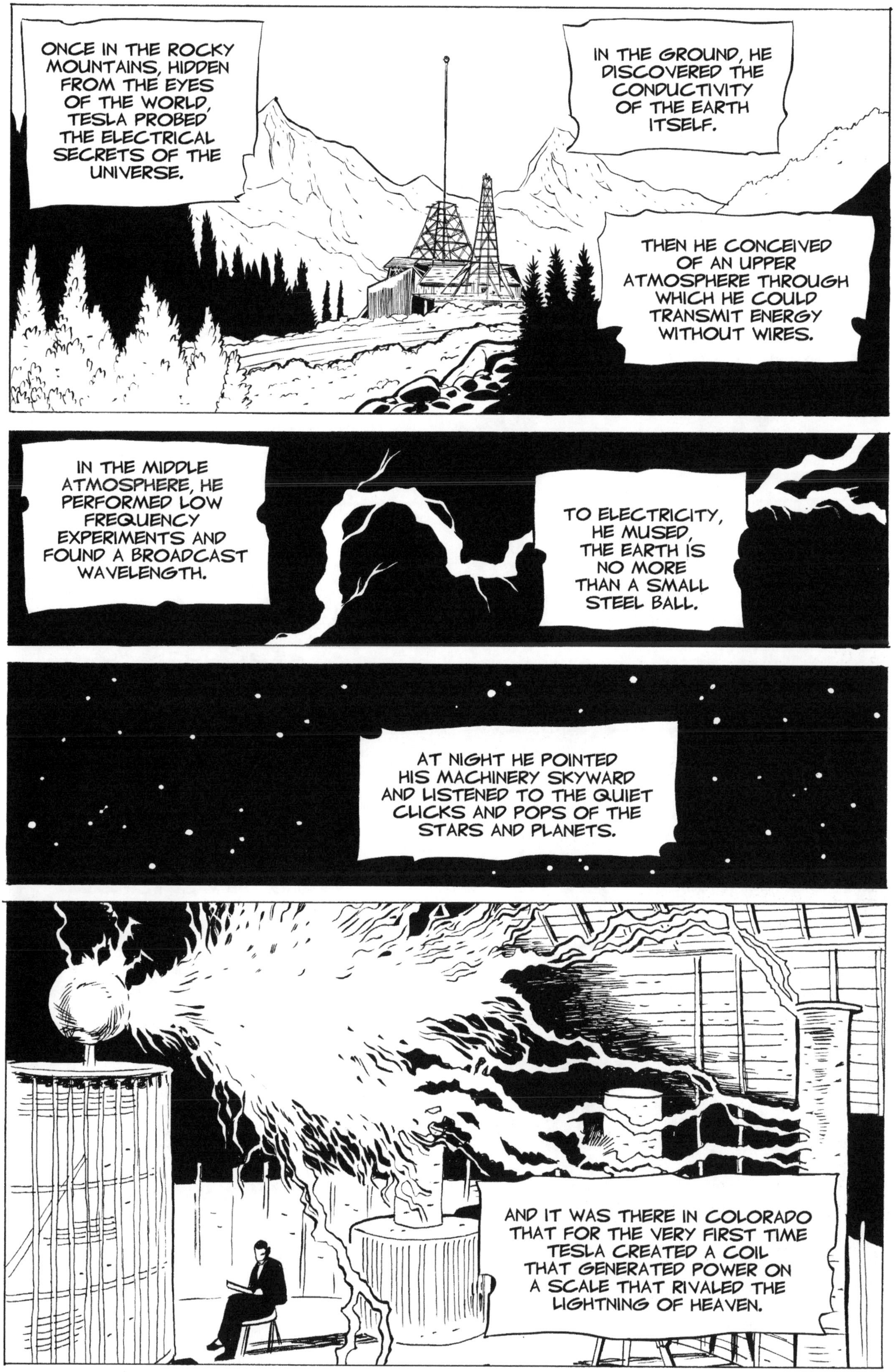
ONCE IN THE ROCKY MOUNTAINS, HIDDEN FROM THE EYES OF THE WORLD, TESLA PROBED THE ELECTRICAL SECRETS OF THE UNIVERSE.
IN THE GROUND, HE DISCOVERED THE CONDUCTIVITY OF THE EARTH ITSELF.
THEN HE CONCEIVED OF AN UPPER ATMOSPHERE THROUGH WHICH HE COULD TRANSMIT ENERGY WITHOUT WIRES.
IN THE MIDDLE ATMOSPHERE, HE PERFORMED LOW FREQUENCY EXPERIMENTS AND FOUND A BROADCAST WAVELENGTH.
TO ELECTRICITY, HE MUSED, THE EARTH IS NO MORE THAN A SMALL STEEL BALL.
AT NIGHT HE POINTED HIS MACHINERY SKYWARD AND LISTENED TO THE QUIET CLICKS AND POPS OF THE STARS AND PLANETS.
AND IT WAS THERE IN COLORADO THAT FOR THE VERY FIRST TIME TESLA CREATED A COIL THAT GENERATED POWER ON A SCALE THAT RIVALED THE LIGHTNING OF HEAVEN.

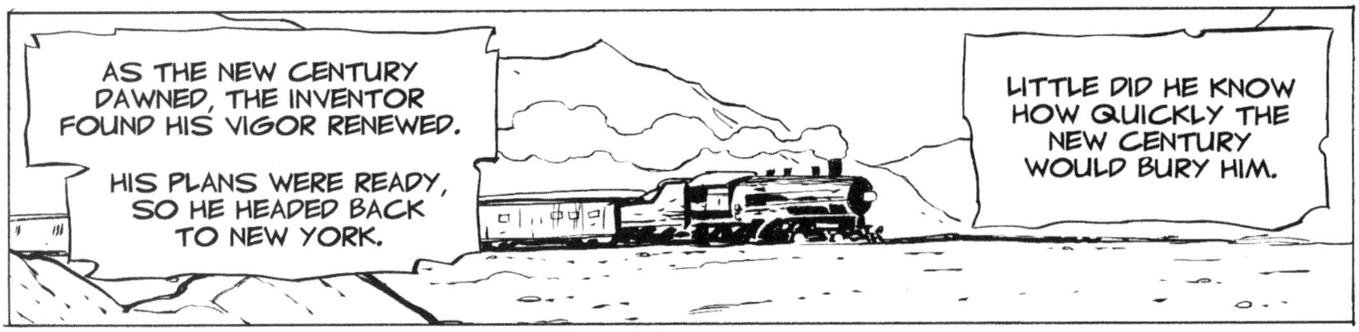
AS THE NEW CENTURY DAWNED, THE INVENTOR FOUND HIS VIGOR RENEWED.
HIS PLANS WERE READY, SO HE HEADED BACK TO NEW YORK.
LITTLE DID HE KNOW HOW QUICKLY THE NEW CENTURY WOULD BURY HIM.

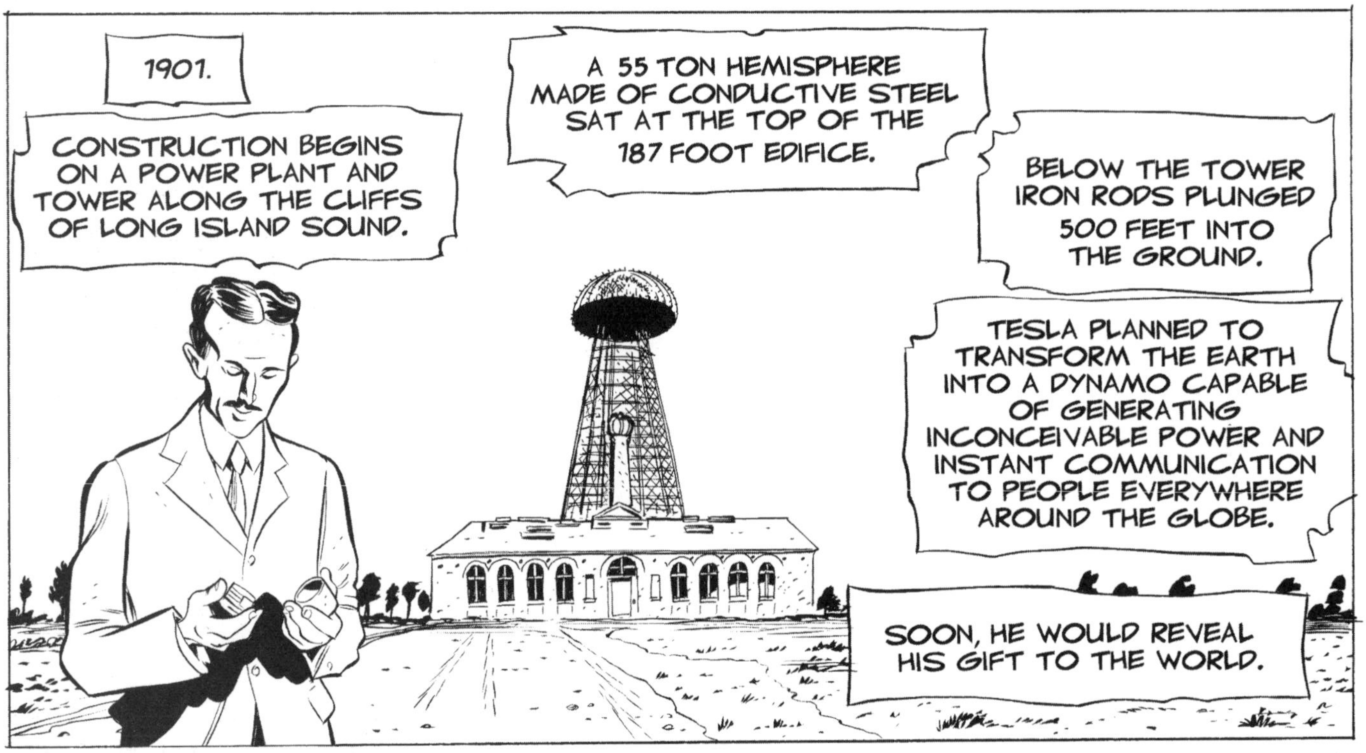
1901.
CONSTRUCTION BEGINS ON A POWER PLANT AND TOWER ALONG THE CLIFFS OF LONG ISLAND SOUND.
A 55 TON HEMISPHERE MADE OF CONDUCTIVE STEEL SAT AT THE TOP OF THE 187 FOOT EDIFICE.
BELOW THE TOWER IRON RODS PLUNGED 500 FEET INTO THE GROUND.
TESLA PLANNED TO TRANSFORM THE EARTH INTO A DYNAMO CAPABLE OF GENERATING INCONCEIVABLE POWER AND INSTANT COMMUNICATION TO PEOPLE EVERYWHERE AROUND THE GLOBE.
SOON, HE WOULD REVEAL HIS GIFT TO THE WORLD.

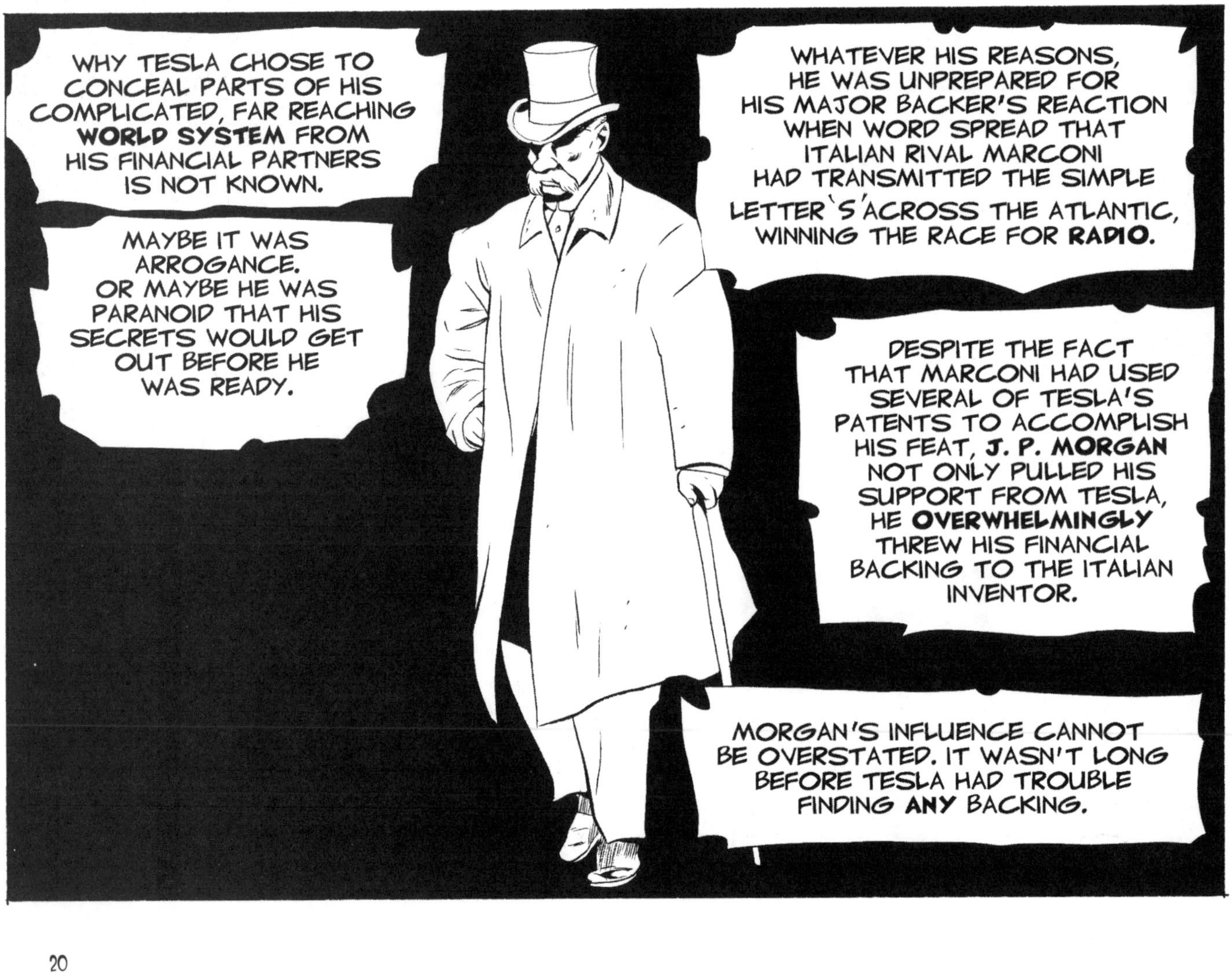
WHY TESLA CHOSE TO CONCEAL PARTS OF HIS COMPLICATED, FAR REACHING **WORLD SYSTEM** FROM HIS FINANCIAL PARTNERS IS NOT KNOWN.
MAYBE IT WAS ARROGANCE. OR MAYBE HE WAS PARANOID THAT HIS SECRETS WOULD GET OUT BEFORE HE WAS READY.
WHATEVER HIS REASONS, HE WAS UNPREPARED FOR HIS MAJOR BACKER'S REACTION WHEN WORD SPREAD THAT ITALIAN RIVAL MARCONI HAD TRANSMITTED THE SIMPLE LETTER 'S' ACROSS THE ATLANTIC, WINNING THE RACE FOR **RADIO**.
DESPITE THE FACT THAT MARCONI HAD USED SEVERAL OF TESLA'S PATENTS TO ACCOMPLISH HIS FEAT, **J. P. MORGAN** NOT ONLY PULLED HIS SUPPORT FROM TESLA, HE **OVERWHELMINGLY** THREW HIS FINANCIAL BACKING TO THE ITALIAN INVENTOR.
MORGAN'S INFLUENCE CANNOT BE OVERSTATED. IT WASN'T LONG BEFORE TESLA HAD TROUBLE FINDING **ANY** BACKING.

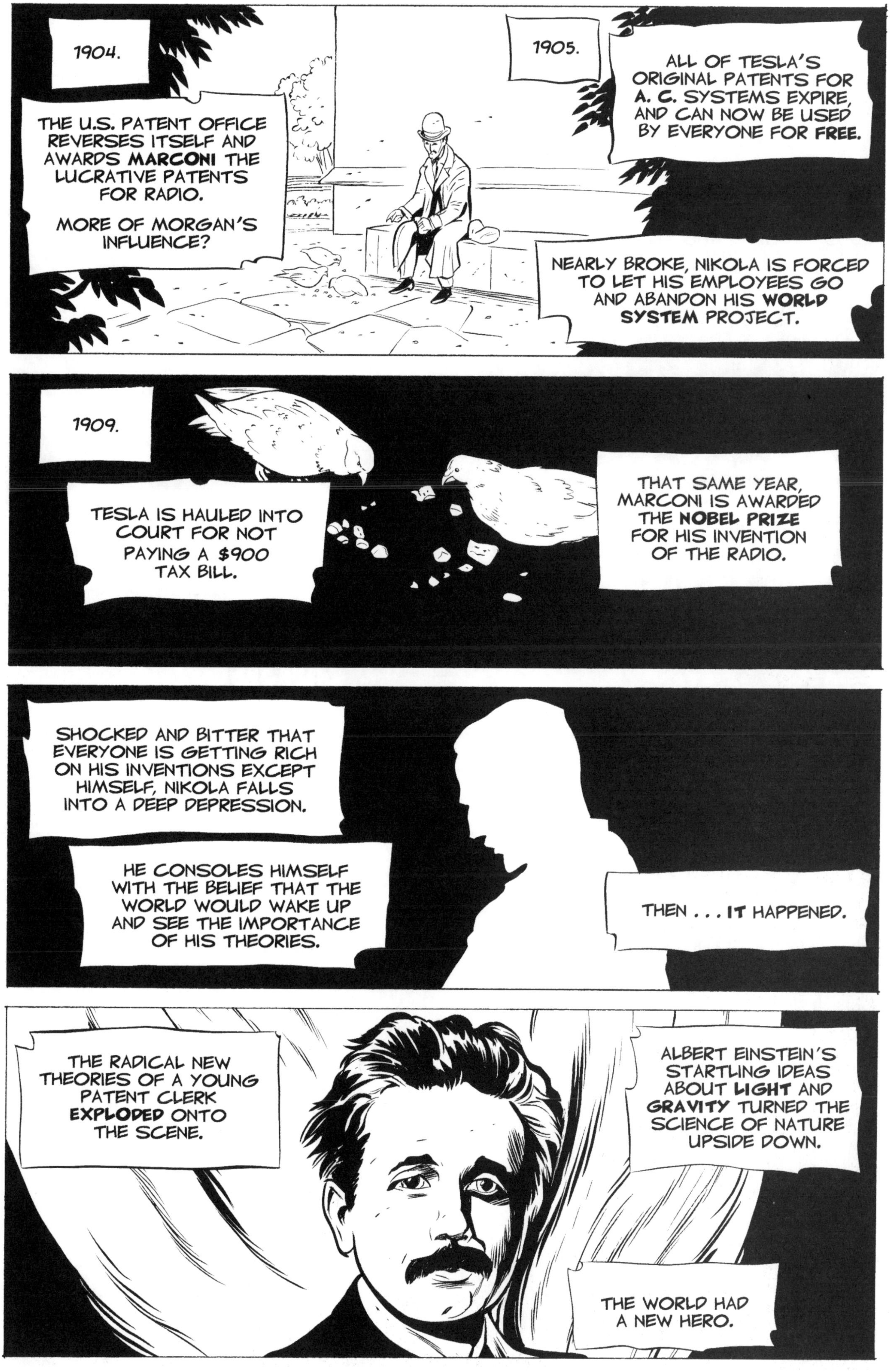
1904.
THE U.S. PATENT OFFICE REVERSES ITSELF AND AWARDS **MARCONI** THE LUCRATIVE PATENTS FOR RADIO.
MORE OF MORGAN'S INFLUENCE?
1905.
ALL OF TESLA'S ORIGINAL PATENTS FOR **A. C.** SYSTEMS EXPIRE, AND CAN NOW BE USED BY EVERYONE FOR **FREE.**
NEARLY BROKE, NIKOLA IS FORCED TO LET HIS EMPLOYEES GO AND ABANDON HIS **WORLD SYSTEM** PROJECT.
1909.
TESLA IS HAULED INTO COURT FOR NOT PAYING A $900 TAX BILL.
THAT SAME YEAR, MARCONI IS AWARDED THE **NOBEL PRIZE** FOR HIS INVENTION OF THE RADIO.
SHOCKED AND BITTER THAT EVERYONE IS GETTING RICH ON HIS INVENTIONS EXCEPT HIMSELF, NIKOLA FALLS INTO A DEEP DEPRESSION.
HE CONSOLES HIMSELF WITH THE BELIEF THAT THE WORLD WOULD WAKE UP AND SEE THE IMPORTANCE OF HIS THEORIES.
THEN . . . **IT** HAPPENED.
THE RADICAL NEW THEORIES OF A YOUNG PATENT CLERK **EXPLODED** ONTO THE SCENE.
ALBERT EINSTEIN'S STARTLING IDEAS ABOUT **LIGHT** AND **GRAVITY** TURNED THE SCIENCE OF NATURE UPSIDE DOWN.
THE WORLD HAD A NEW HERO.

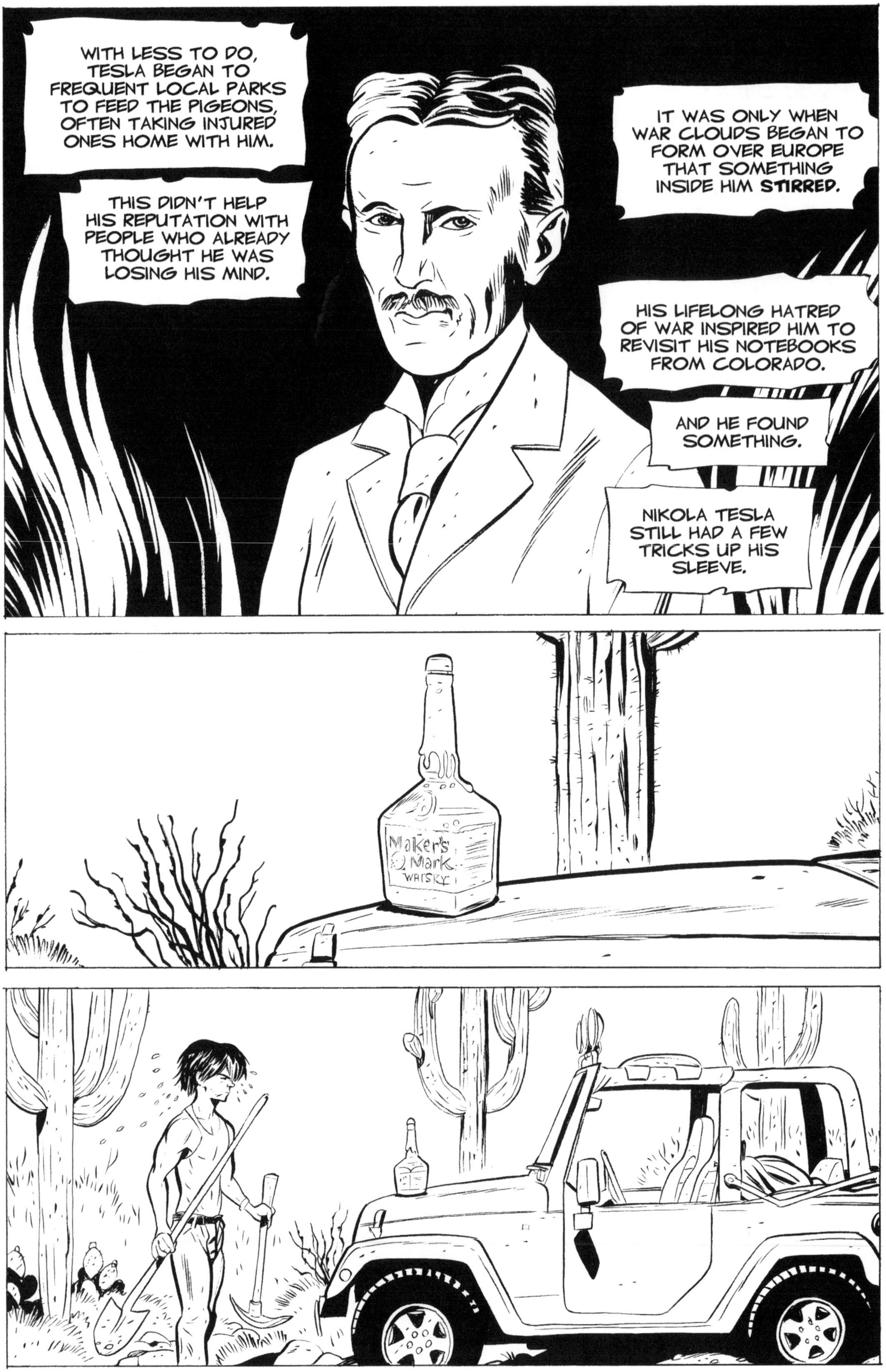
WITH LESS TO DO, TESLA BEGAN TO FREQUENT LOCAL PARKS TO FEED THE PIGEONS, OFTEN TAKING INJURED ONES HOME WITH HIM.
THIS DIDN'T HELP HIS REPUTATION WITH PEOPLE WHO ALREADY THOUGHT HE WAS LOSING HIS MIND.
IT WAS ONLY WHEN WAR CLOUDS BEGAN TO FORM OVER EUROPE THAT SOMETHING INSIDE HIM **STIRRED**.
HIS LIFELONG HATRED OF WAR INSPIRED HIM TO REVISIT HIS NOTEBOOKS FROM COLORADO.
AND HE FOUND SOMETHING.
NIKOLA TESLA STILL HAD A FEW TRICKS UP HIS SLEEVE.
Maker's Mark WHISKY

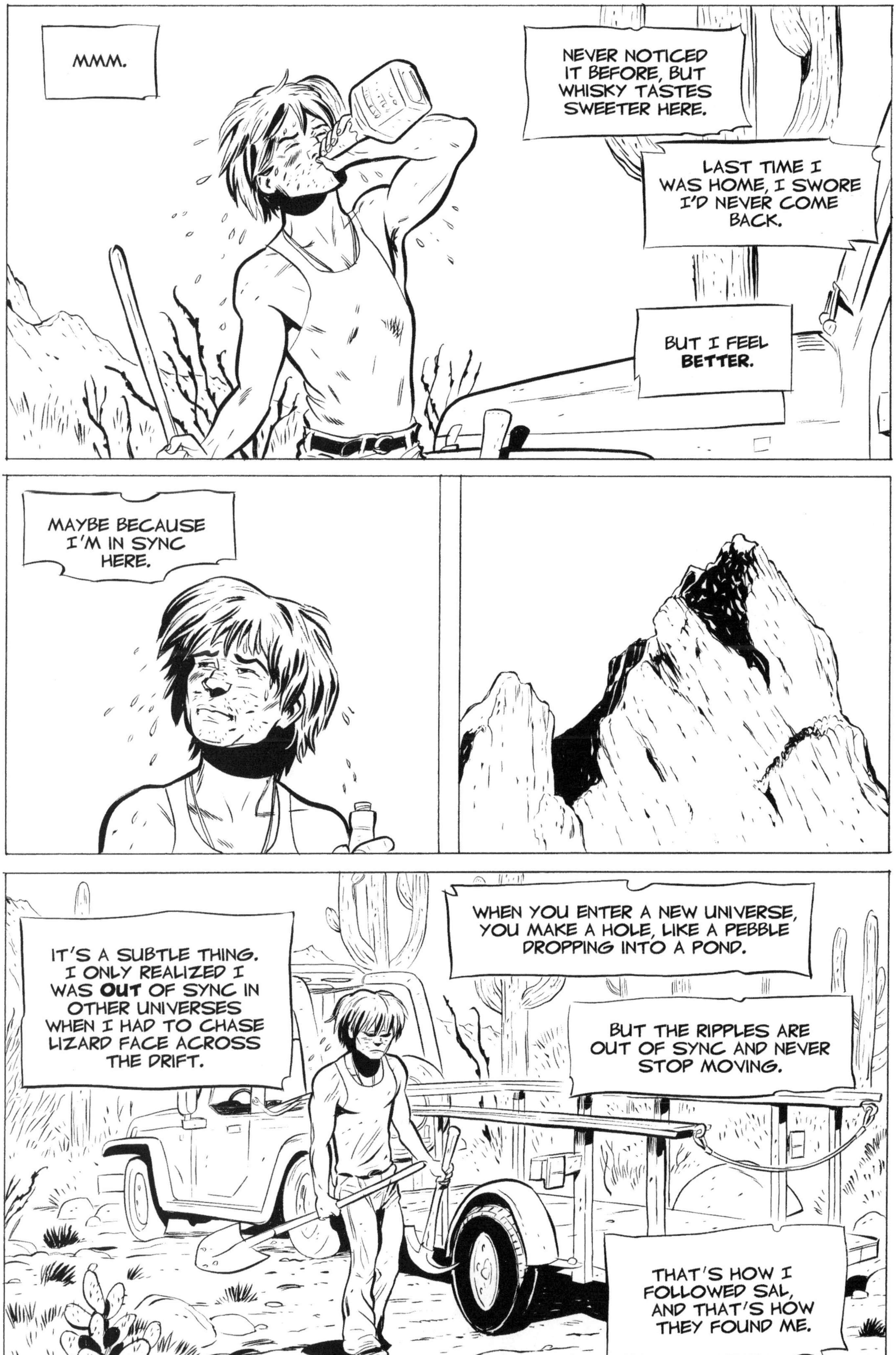
MMM.
NEVER NOTICED IT BEFORE, BUT WHISKY TASTES SWEETER HERE.
LAST TIME I WAS HOME, I SWORE I'D NEVER COME BACK.
BUT I FEEL **BETTER.**
MAYBE BECAUSE I'M IN SYNC HERE.
IT'S A SUBTLE THING. I ONLY REALIZED I WAS **OUT** OF SYNC IN OTHER UNIVERSES WHEN I HAD TO CHASE LIZARD FACE ACROSS THE DRIFT.
WHEN YOU ENTER A NEW UNIVERSE, YOU MAKE A HOLE, LIKE A PEBBLE DROPPING INTO A POND.
BUT THE RIPPLES ARE OUT OF SYNC AND NEVER STOP MOVING.
THAT'S HOW I FOLLOWED SAL, AND THAT'S HOW THEY FOUND ME.

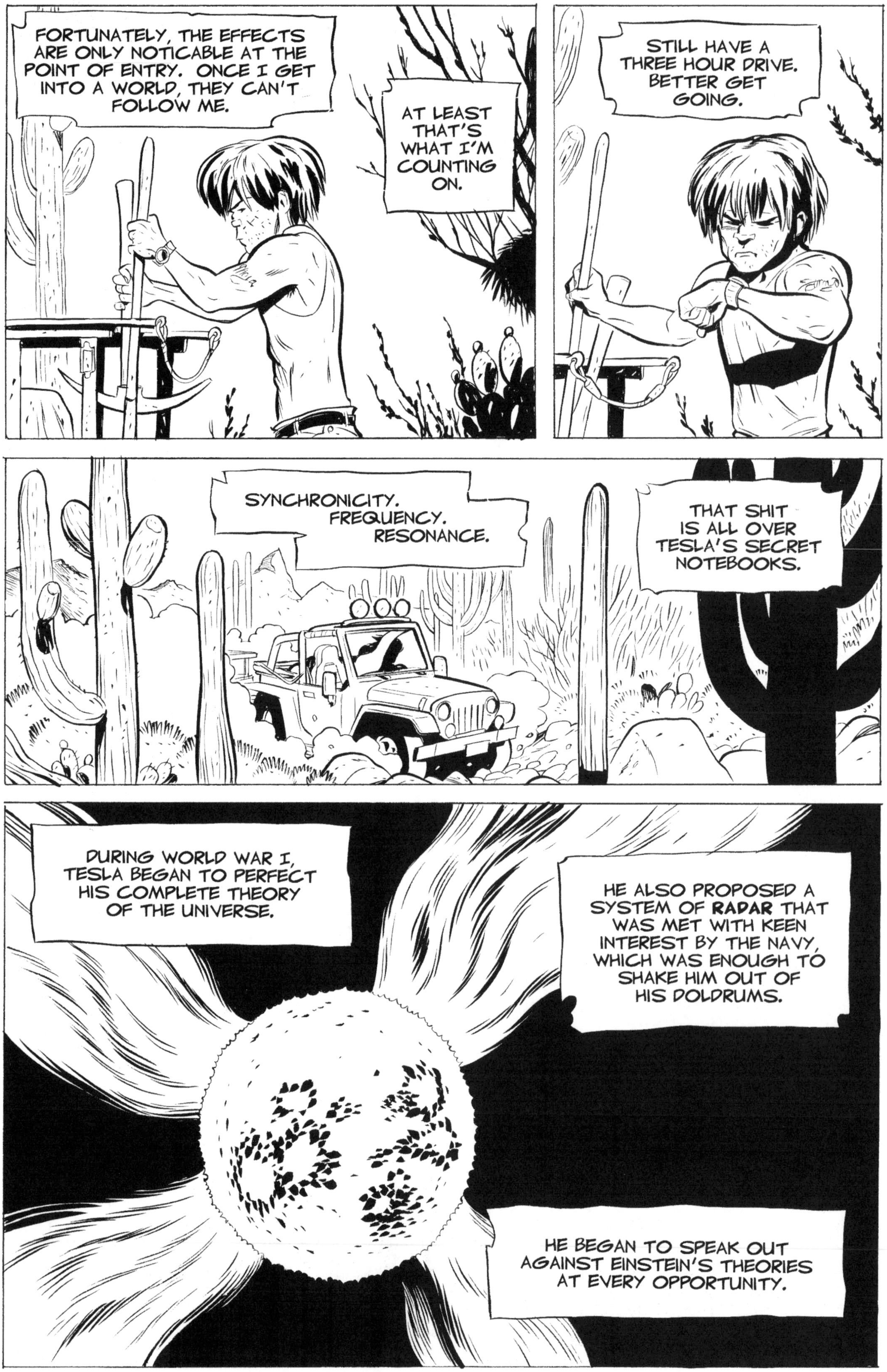
FORTUNATELY, THE EFFECTS ARE ONLY NOTICABLE AT THE POINT OF ENTRY. ONCE I GET INTO A WORLD, THEY CAN'T FOLLOW ME.
AT LEAST THAT'S WHAT I'M COUNTING ON.
STILL HAVE A THREE HOUR DRIVE. BETTER GET GOING.
SYNCHRONICITY. FREQUENCY. RESONANCE.
THAT SHIT IS ALL OVER TESLA'S SECRET NOTEBOOKS.
DURING WORLD WAR I, TESLA BEGAN TO PERFECT HIS COMPLETE THEORY OF THE UNIVERSE.
HE ALSO PROPOSED A SYSTEM OF RADAR THAT WAS MET WITH KEEN INTEREST BY THE NAVY, WHICH WAS ENOUGH TO SHAKE HIM OUT OF HIS DOLDRUMS.
HE BEGAN TO SPEAK OUT AGAINST EINSTEIN'S THEORIES AT EVERY OPPORTUNITY.

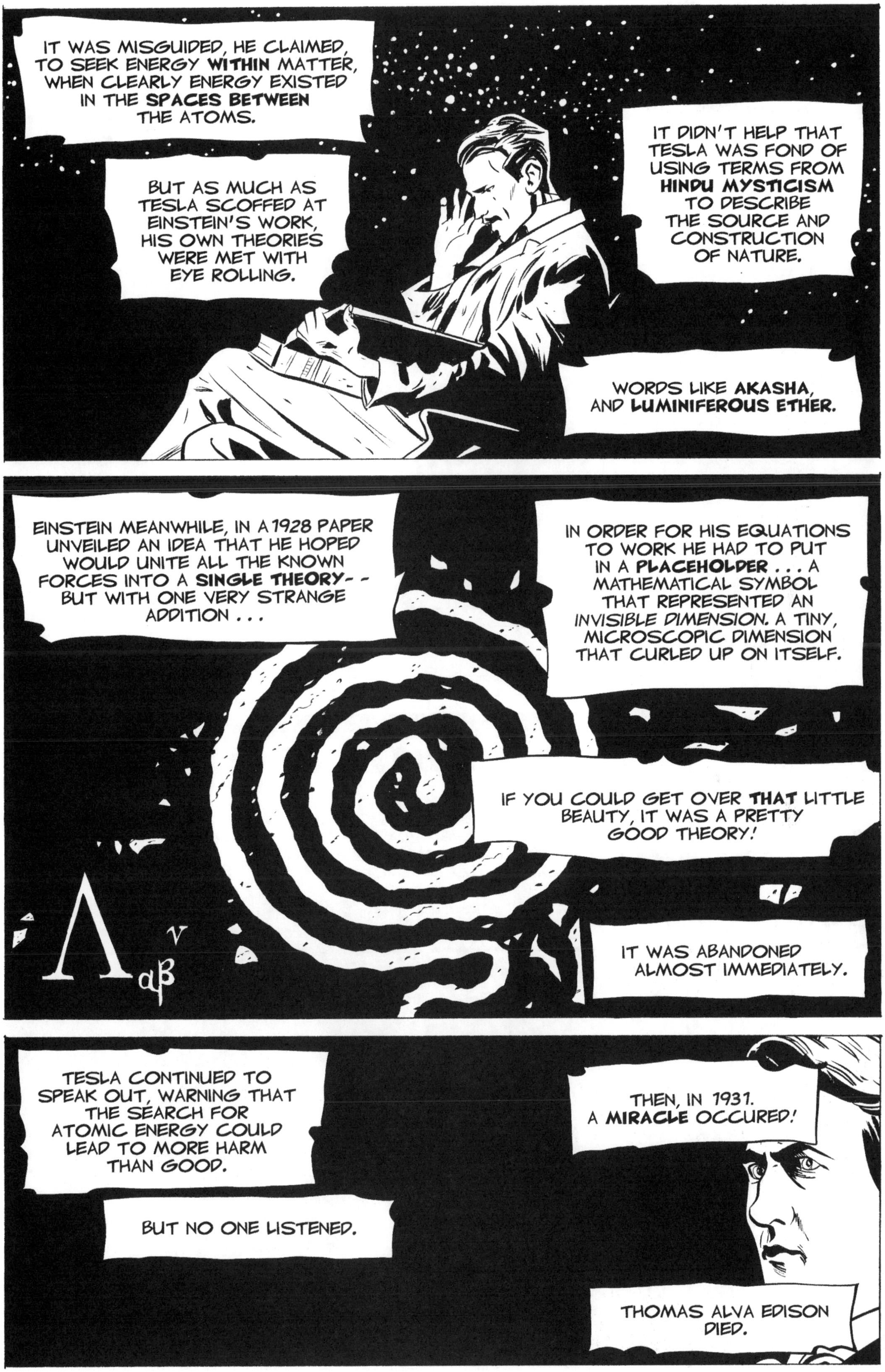
IT WAS MISGUIDED, HE CLAIMED, TO SEEK ENERGY WITHIN MATTER, WHEN CLEARLY ENERGY EXISTED IN THE SPACES BETWEEN THE ATOMS.
BUT AS MUCH AS TESLA SCOFFED AT EINSTEIN'S WORK, HIS OWN THEORIES WERE MET WITH EYE ROLLING.
IT DIDN'T HELP THAT TESLA WAS FOND OF USING TERMS FROM HINDU MYSTICISM TO DESCRIBE THE SOURCE AND CONSTRUCTION OF NATURE.
WORDS LIKE AKASHA, AND LUMINIFEROUS ETHER.
EINSTEIN MEANWHILE, IN A 1928 PAPER UNVEILED AN IDEA THAT HE HOPED WOULD UNITE ALL THE KNOWN FORCES INTO A SINGLE THEORY-- BUT WITH ONE VERY STRANGE ADDITION . . .
IN ORDER FOR HIS EQUATIONS TO WORK HE HAD TO PUT IN A PLACEHOLDER . . . A MATHEMATICAL SYMBOL THAT REPRESENTED AN INVISIBLE DIMENSION. A TINY, MICROSCOPIC DIMENSION THAT CURLED UP ON ITSELF.
IF YOU COULD GET OVER THAT LITTLE BEAUTY, IT WAS A PRETTY GOOD THEORY!
$\Lambda_{\alpha\beta}^{\nu}$
IT WAS ABANDONED ALMOST IMMEDIATELY.
TESLA CONTINUED TO SPEAK OUT, WARNING THAT THE SEARCH FOR ATOMIC ENERGY COULD LEAD TO MORE HARM THAN GOOD.
BUT NO ONE LISTENED.
THEN, IN 1931. A MIRACLE OCCURED!
THOMAS ALVA EDISON DIED.

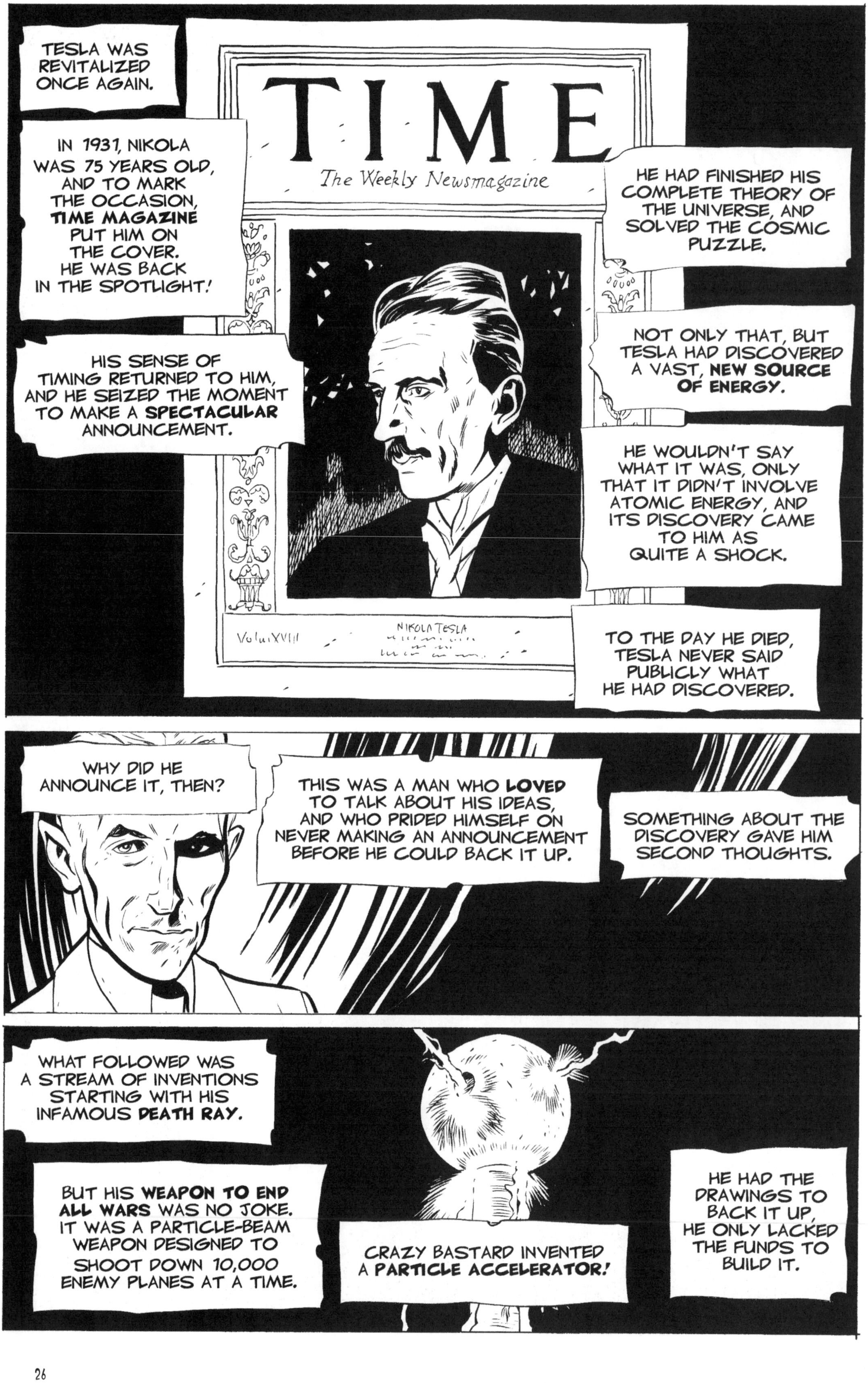
TESLA WAS REVITALIZED ONCE AGAIN.
IN 1931, NIKOLA WAS 75 YEARS OLD, AND TO MARK THE OCCASION, **TIME MAGAZINE** PUT HIM ON THE COVER. HE WAS BACK IN THE SPOTLIGHT!
TIME
The Weekly Newsmagazine
NIKOLA TESLA
HIS SENSE OF TIMING RETURNED TO HIM, AND HE SEIZED THE MOMENT TO MAKE A **SPECTACULAR** ANNOUNCEMENT.
HE HAD FINISHED HIS COMPLETE THEORY OF THE UNIVERSE, AND SOLVED THE COSMIC PUZZLE.
NOT ONLY THAT, BUT TESLA HAD DISCOVERED A VAST, **NEW SOURCE OF ENERGY.**
HE WOULDN'T SAY WHAT IT WAS, ONLY THAT IT DIDN'T INVOLVE ATOMIC ENERGY, AND ITS DISCOVERY CAME TO HIM AS QUITE A SHOCK.
TO THE DAY HE DIED, TESLA NEVER SAID PUBLICLY WHAT HE HAD DISCOVERED.
WHY DID HE ANNOUNCE IT, THEN?
THIS WAS A MAN WHO **LOVED** TO TALK ABOUT HIS IDEAS, AND WHO PRIDED HIMSELF ON NEVER MAKING AN ANNOUNCEMENT BEFORE HE COULD BACK IT UP.
SOMETHING ABOUT THE DISCOVERY GAVE HIM SECOND THOUGHTS.
WHAT FOLLOWED WAS A STREAM OF INVENTIONS STARTING WITH HIS INFAMOUS **DEATH RAY.**
BUT HIS **WEAPON TO END ALL WARS** WAS NO JOKE. IT WAS A PARTICLE-BEAM WEAPON DESIGNED TO SHOOT DOWN 10,000 ENEMY PLANES AT A TIME.
CRAZY BASTARD INVENTED A **PARTICLE ACCELERATOR!**
HE HAD THE DRAWINGS TO BACK IT UP, HE ONLY LACKED THE FUNDS TO BUILD IT.

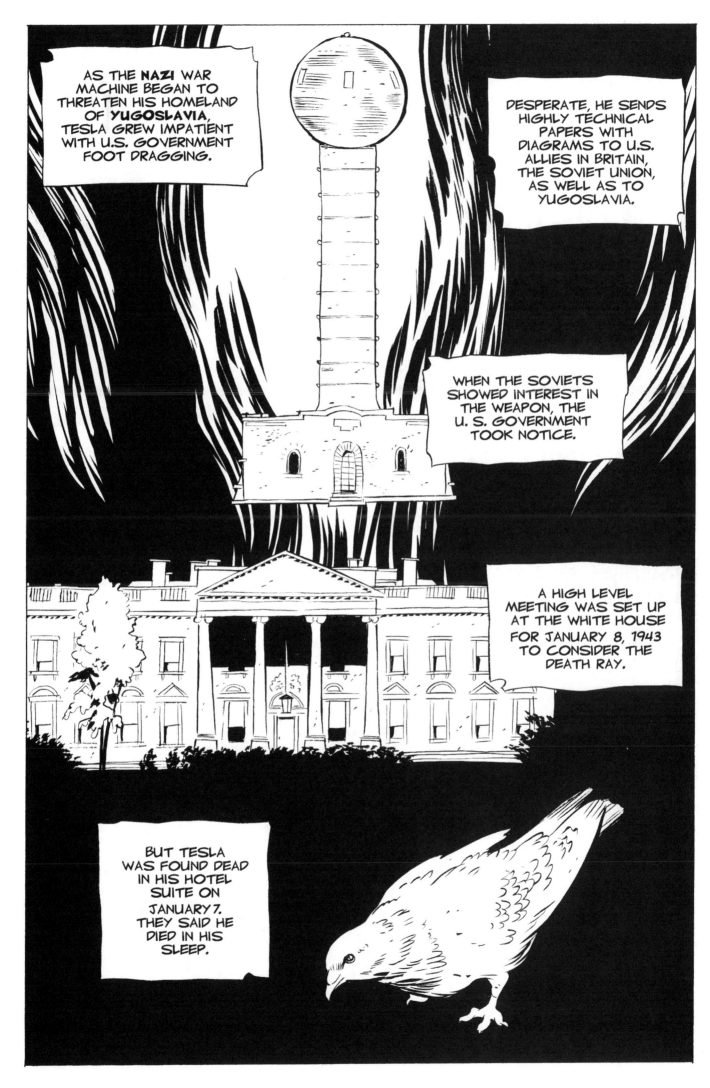

AS THE **NAZI** WAR MACHINE BEGAN TO THREATEN HIS HOMELAND OF **YUGOSLAVIA,** TESLA GREW IMPATIENT WITH U.S. GOVERNMENT FOOT DRAGGING.

DESPERATE, HE SENDS HIGHLY TECHNICAL PAPERS WITH DIAGRAMS TO U.S. ALLIES IN BRITAIN, THE SOVIET UNION, AS WELL AS TO YUGOSLAVIA.

WHEN THE SOVIETS SHOWED INTEREST IN THE WEAPON, THE U. S. GOVERNMENT TOOK NOTICE.

A HIGH LEVEL MEETING WAS SET UP AT THE WHITE HOUSE FOR JANUARY 8, 1943 TO CONSIDER THE DEATH RAY.

BUT TESLA WAS FOUND DEAD IN HIS HOTEL SUITE ON JANUARY 7. THEY SAID HE DIED IN HIS SLEEP.

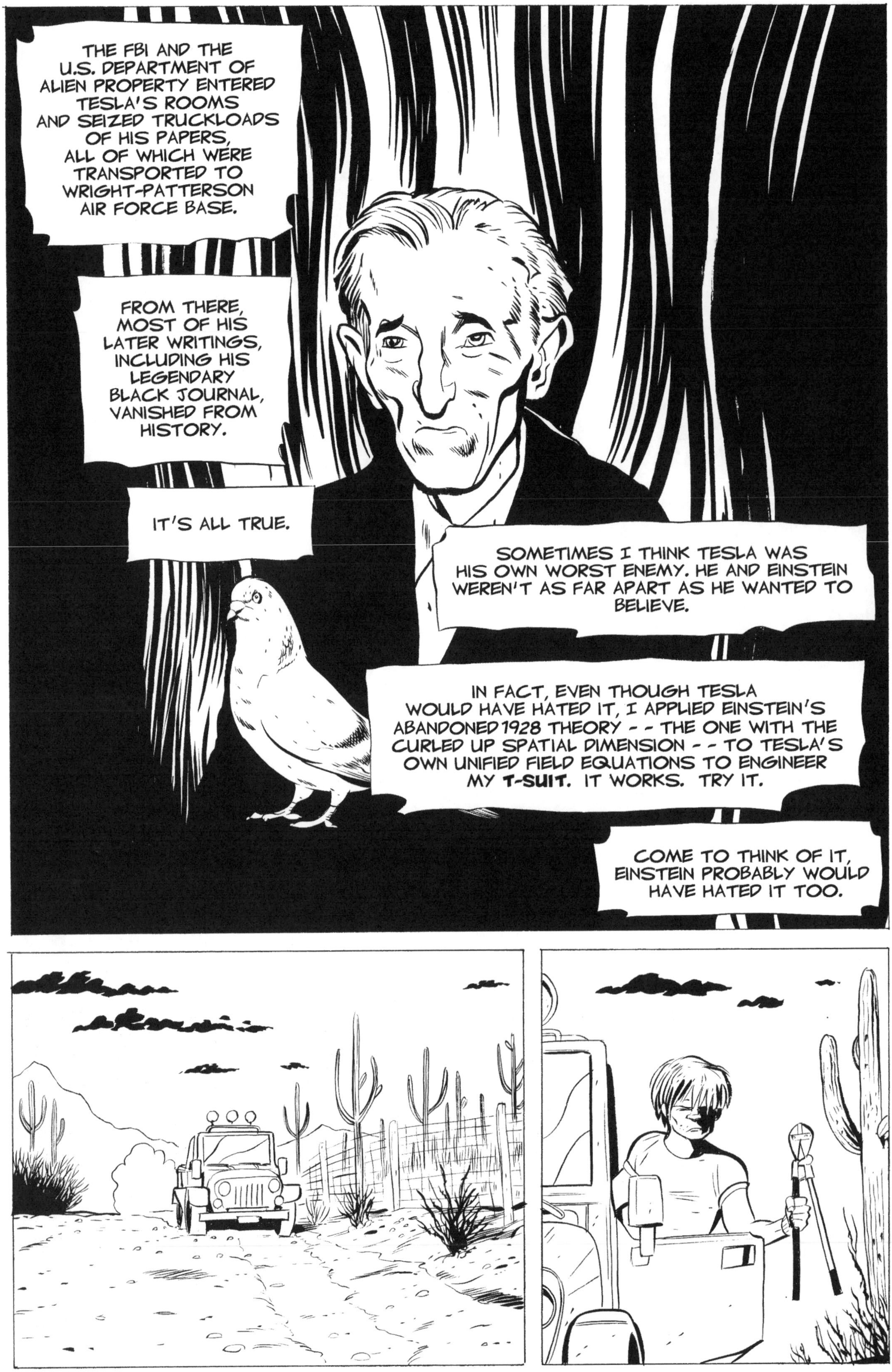
THE FBI AND THE U.S. DEPARTMENT OF ALIEN PROPERTY ENTERED TESLA'S ROOMS AND SEIZED TRUCKLOADS OF HIS PAPERS, ALL OF WHICH WERE TRANSPORTED TO WRIGHT-PATTERSON AIR FORCE BASE.
FROM THERE, MOST OF HIS LATER WRITINGS, INCLUDING HIS LEGENDARY BLACK JOURNAL, VANISHED FROM HISTORY.
IT'S ALL TRUE.
SOMETIMES I THINK TESLA WAS HIS OWN WORST ENEMY. HE AND EINSTEIN WEREN'T AS FAR APART AS HE WANTED TO BELIEVE.
IN FACT, EVEN THOUGH TESLA WOULD HAVE HATED IT, I APPLIED EINSTEIN'S ABANDONED 1928 THEORY -- THE ONE WITH THE CURLED UP SPATIAL DIMENSION -- TO TESLA'S OWN UNIFIED FIELD EQUATIONS TO ENGINEER MY **T-SUIT**. IT WORKS. TRY IT.
COME TO THINK OF IT, EINSTEIN PROBABLY WOULD HAVE HATED IT TOO.

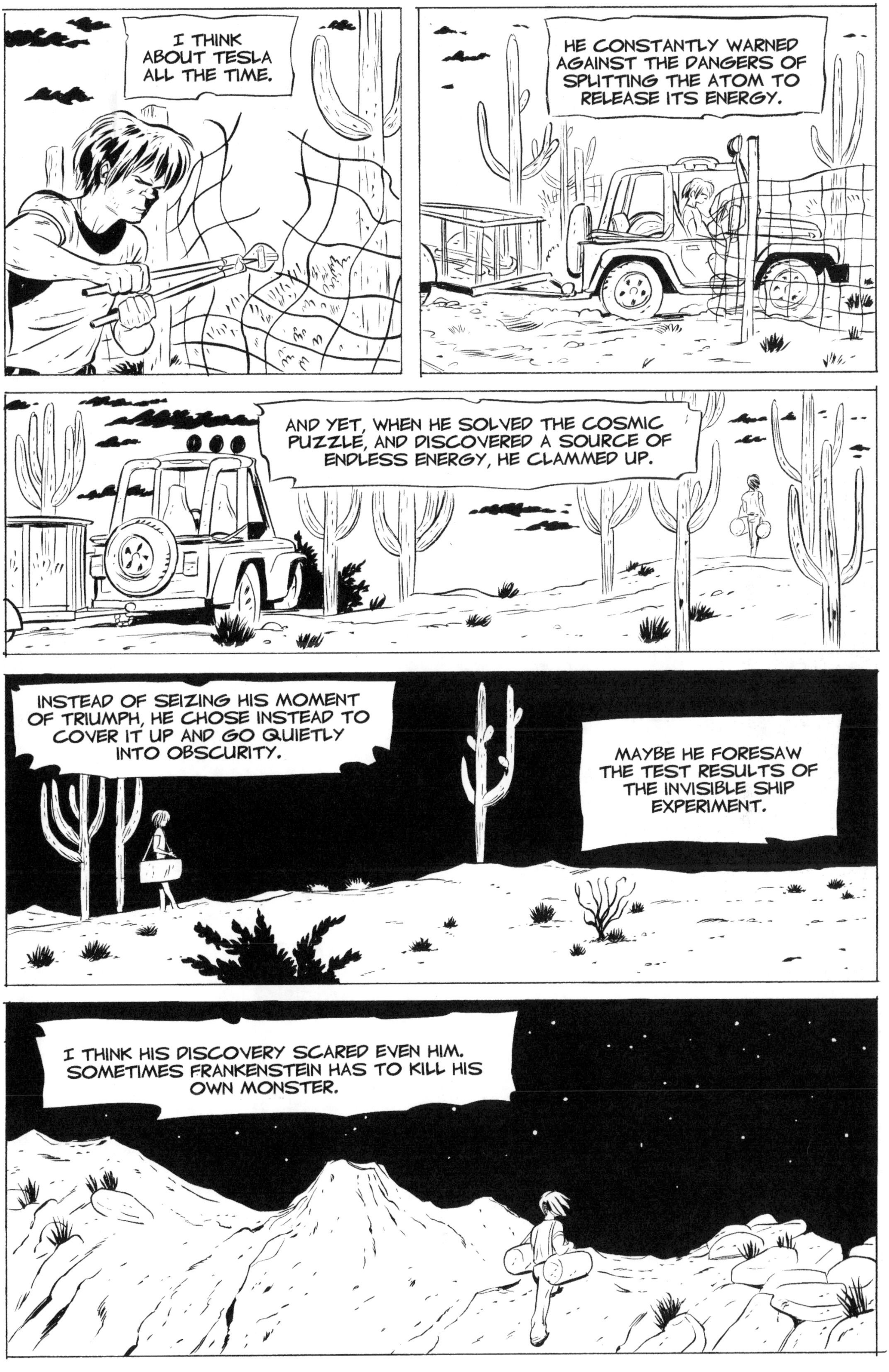
I THINK ABOUT TESLA ALL THE TIME.
HE CONSTANTLY WARNED AGAINST THE DANGERS OF SPLITTING THE ATOM TO RELEASE ITS ENERGY.
AND YET, WHEN HE SOLVED THE COSMIC PUZZLE, AND DISCOVERED A SOURCE OF ENDLESS ENERGY, HE CLAMMED UP.
INSTEAD OF SEIZING HIS MOMENT OF TRIUMPH, HE CHOSE INSTEAD TO COVER IT UP AND GO QUIETLY INTO OBSCURITY.
MAYBE HE FORESAW THE TEST RESULTS OF THE INVISIBLE SHIP EXPERIMENT.
I THINK HIS DISCOVERY SCARED EVEN HIM. SOMETIMES FRANKENSTEIN HAS TO KILL HIS OWN MONSTER.

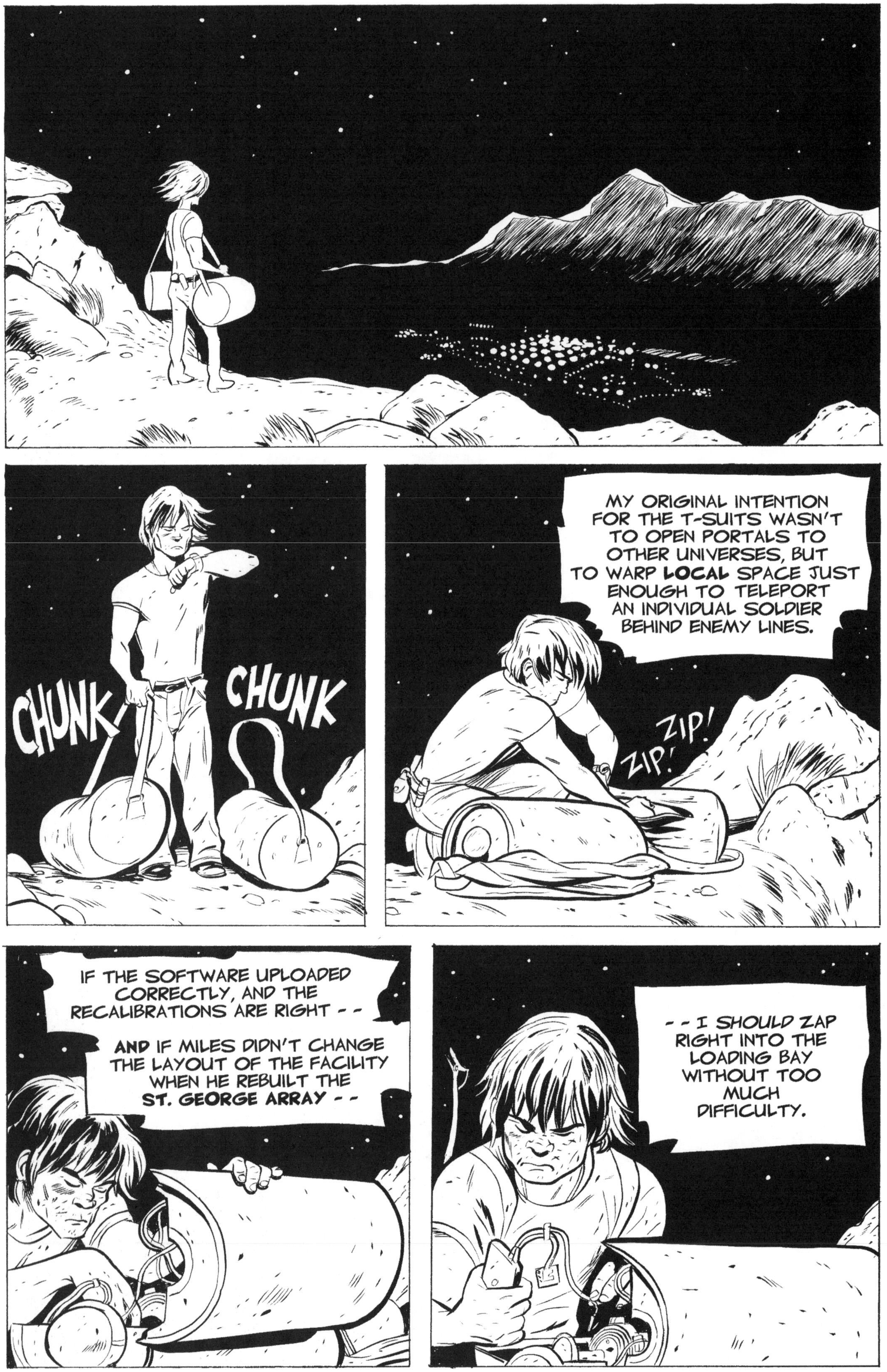

CHUNK!
CHUNK
MY ORIGINAL INTENTION FOR THE T-SUITS WASN'T TO OPEN PORTALS TO OTHER UNIVERSES, BUT TO WARP LOCAL SPACE JUST ENOUGH TO TELEPORT AN INDIVIDUAL SOLDIER BEHIND ENEMY LINES.
ZIP! ZIP!
IF THE SOFTWARE UPLOADED CORRECTLY, AND THE RECALIBRATIONS ARE RIGHT - -
AND IF MILES DIDN'T CHANGE THE LAYOUT OF THE FACILITY WHEN HE REBUILT THE ST. GEORGE ARRAY - -
- - I SHOULD ZAP RIGHT INTO THE LOADING BAY WITHOUT TOO MUCH DIFFICULTY.

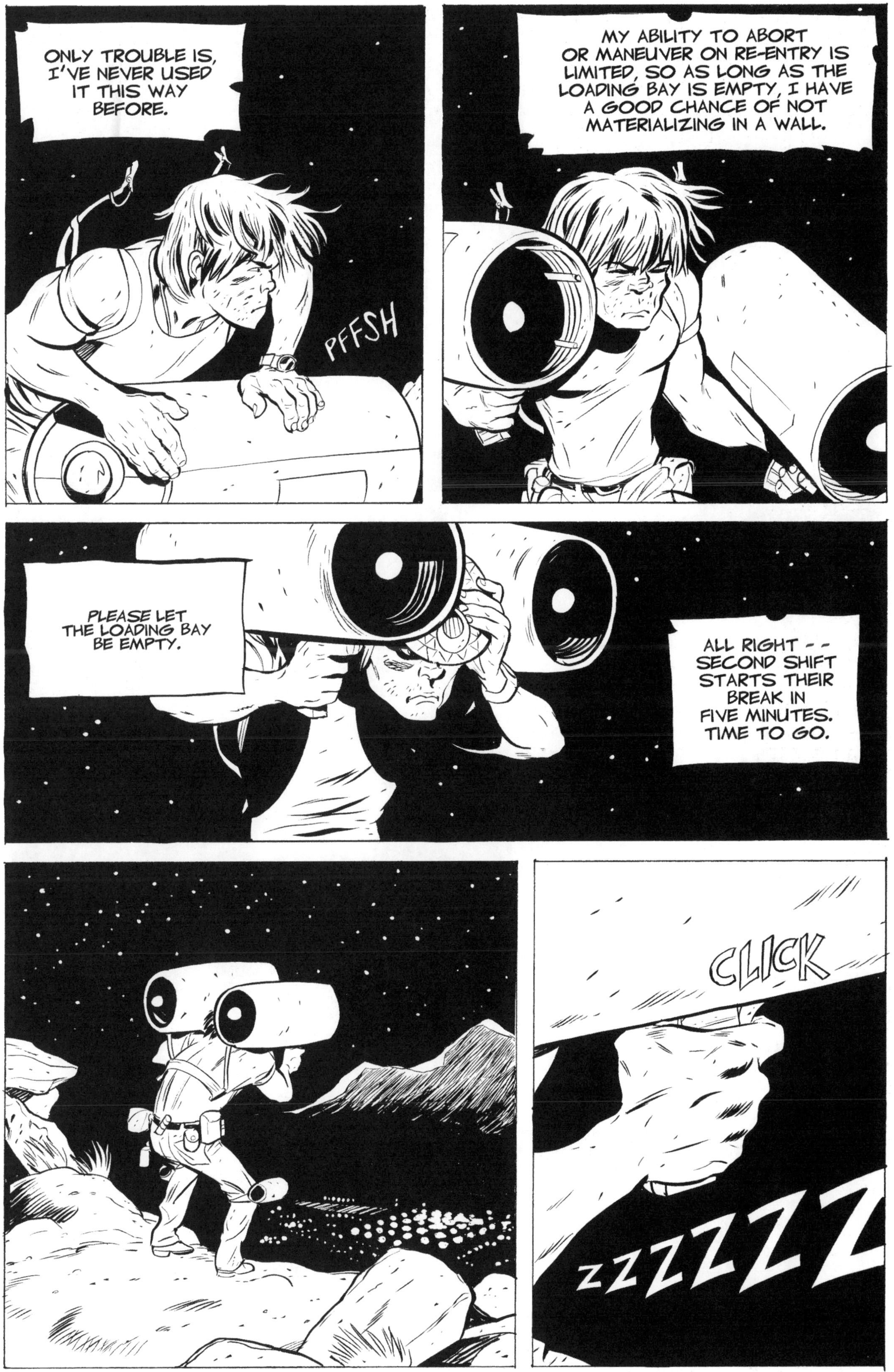
ONLY TROUBLE IS, I'VE NEVER USED IT THIS WAY BEFORE.
PFFSH
MY ABILITY TO ABORT OR MANEUVER ON RE-ENTRY IS LIMITED, SO AS LONG AS THE LOADING BAY IS EMPTY, I HAVE A GOOD CHANCE OF NOT MATERIALIZING IN A WALL.
PLEASE LET THE LOADING BAY BE EMPTY.
ALL RIGHT -- SECOND SHIFT STARTS THEIR BREAK IN FIVE MINUTES. TIME TO GO.
CLICK
ZZZZZZ

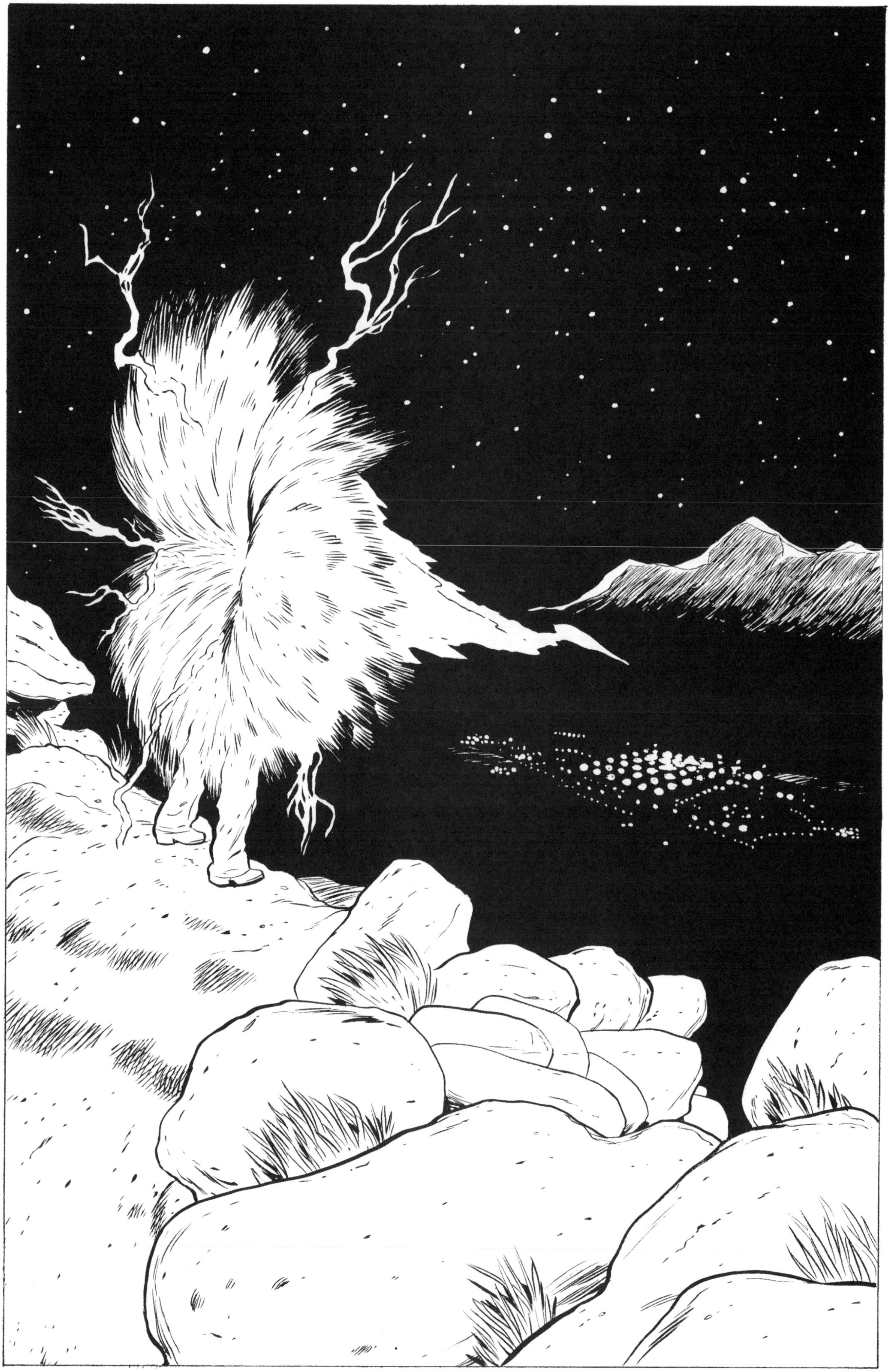

13.
MILES

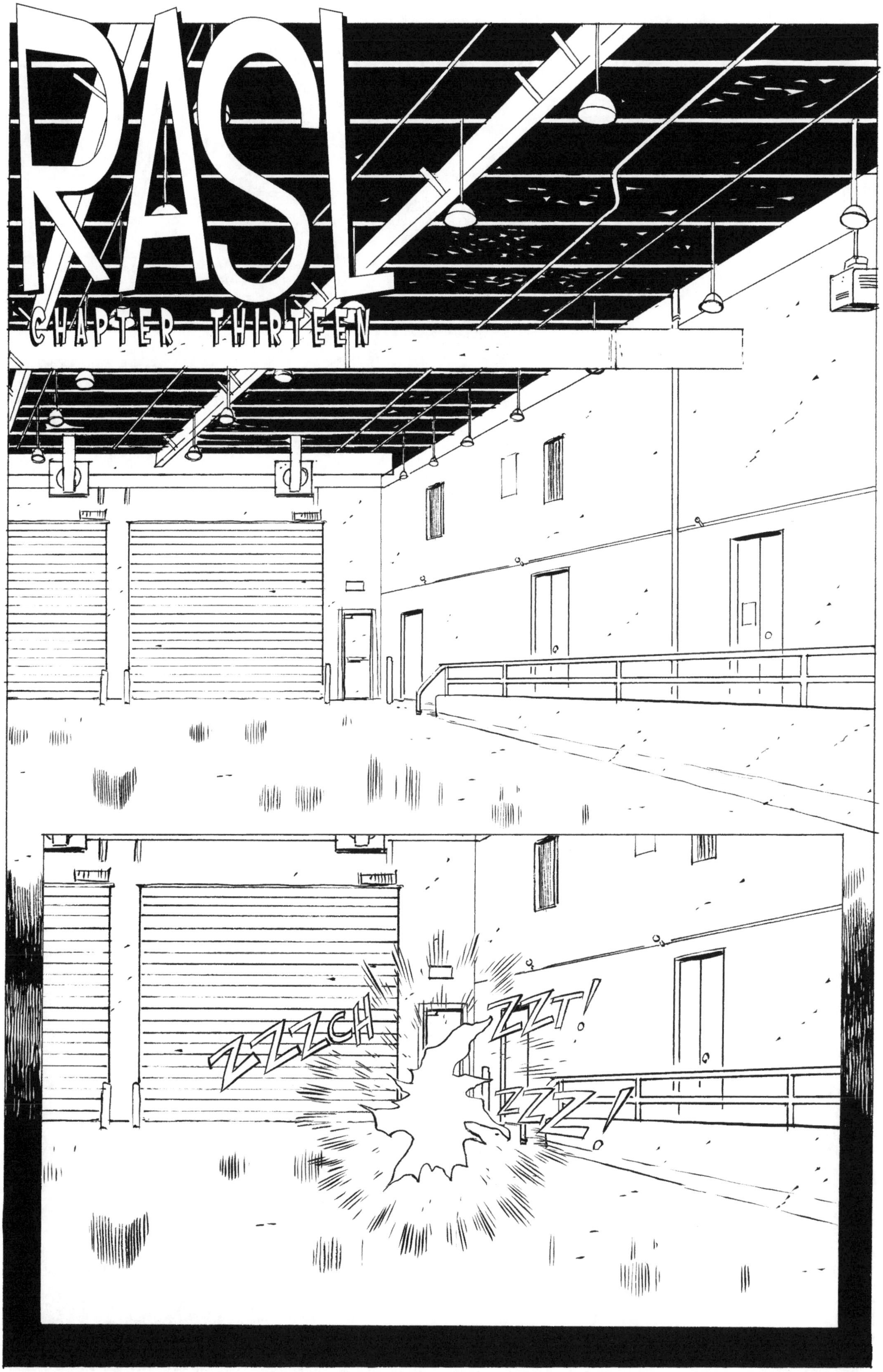
RASL
CHAPTER THIRTEEN
ZZZZCH
ZZT!
ZZZZ!

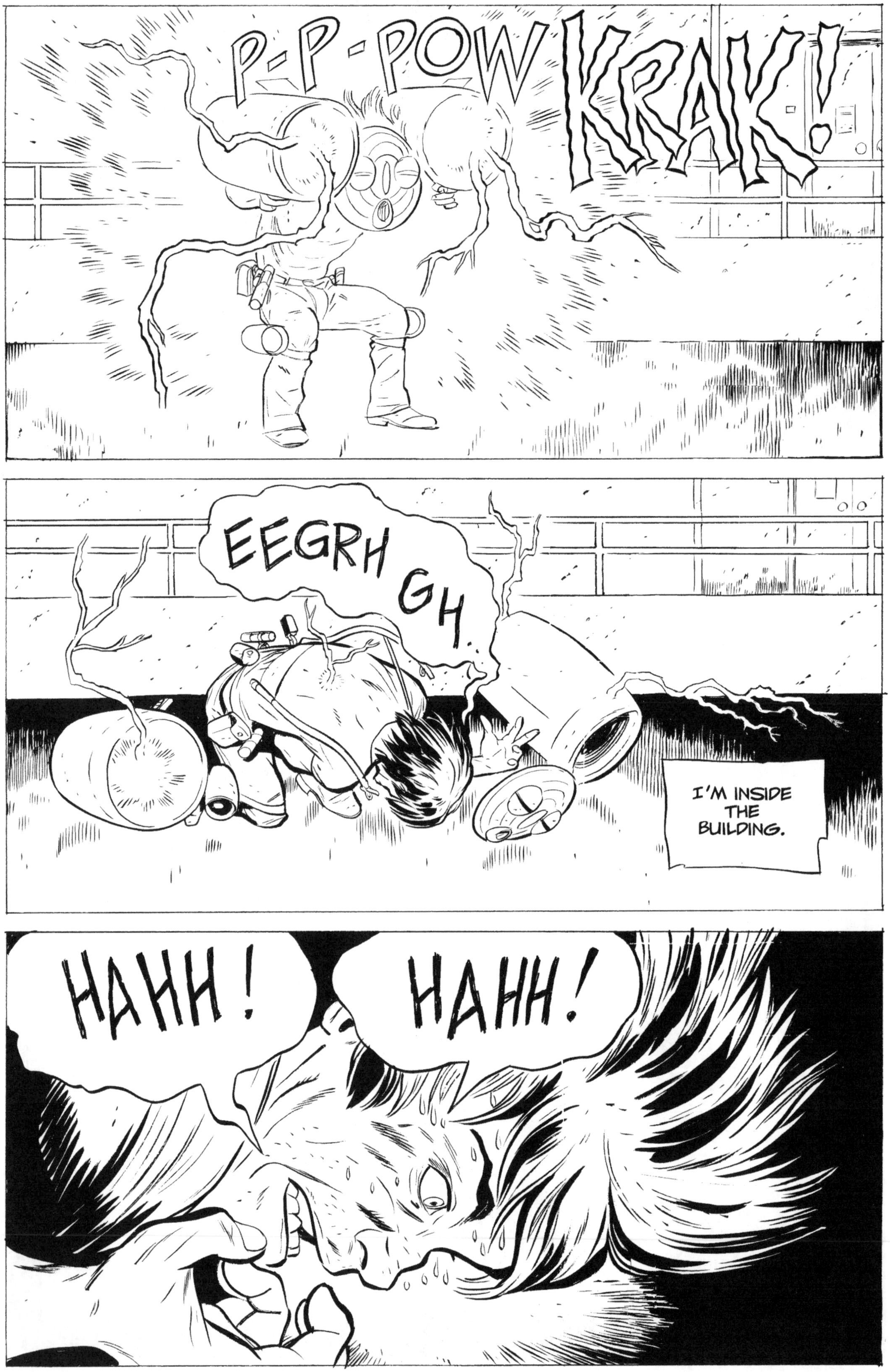
P-P-POW
KRAK!
EEGRH GH.
I'M INSIDE THE BUILDING.
HAHH!
HAHH!

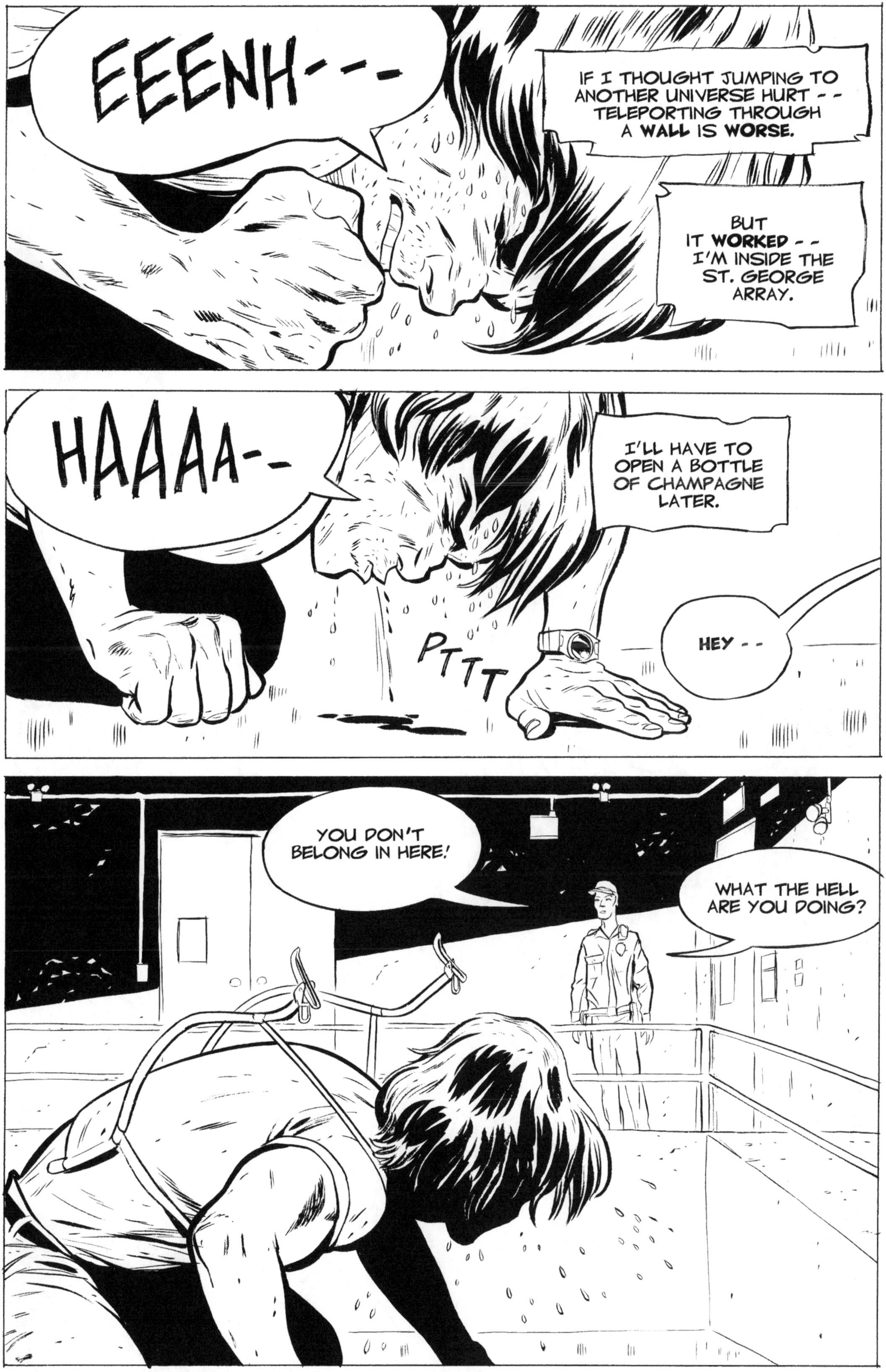
EEENH- - -
IF I THOUGHT JUMPING TO ANOTHER UNIVERSE HURT - - TELEPORTING THROUGH A **WALL** IS **WORSE.**
BUT IT **WORKED** - - I'M INSIDE THE ST. GEORGE ARRAY.
HAAAA- -
I'LL HAVE TO OPEN A BOTTLE OF CHAMPAGNE LATER.
PTTT
HEY - -
YOU DON'T BELONG IN HERE!
WHAT THE HELL ARE YOU DOING?

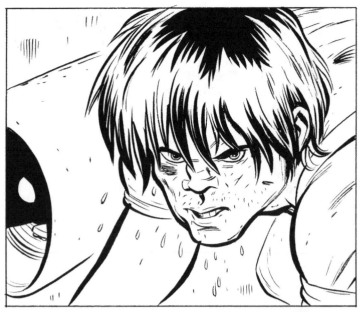

MOVE QUICK --

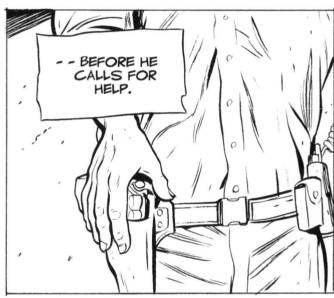

-- BEFORE HE CALLS FOR HELP.

CRACK!

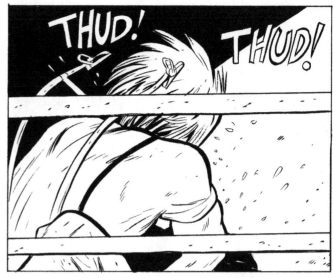

THUD! THUD!

BZZT...

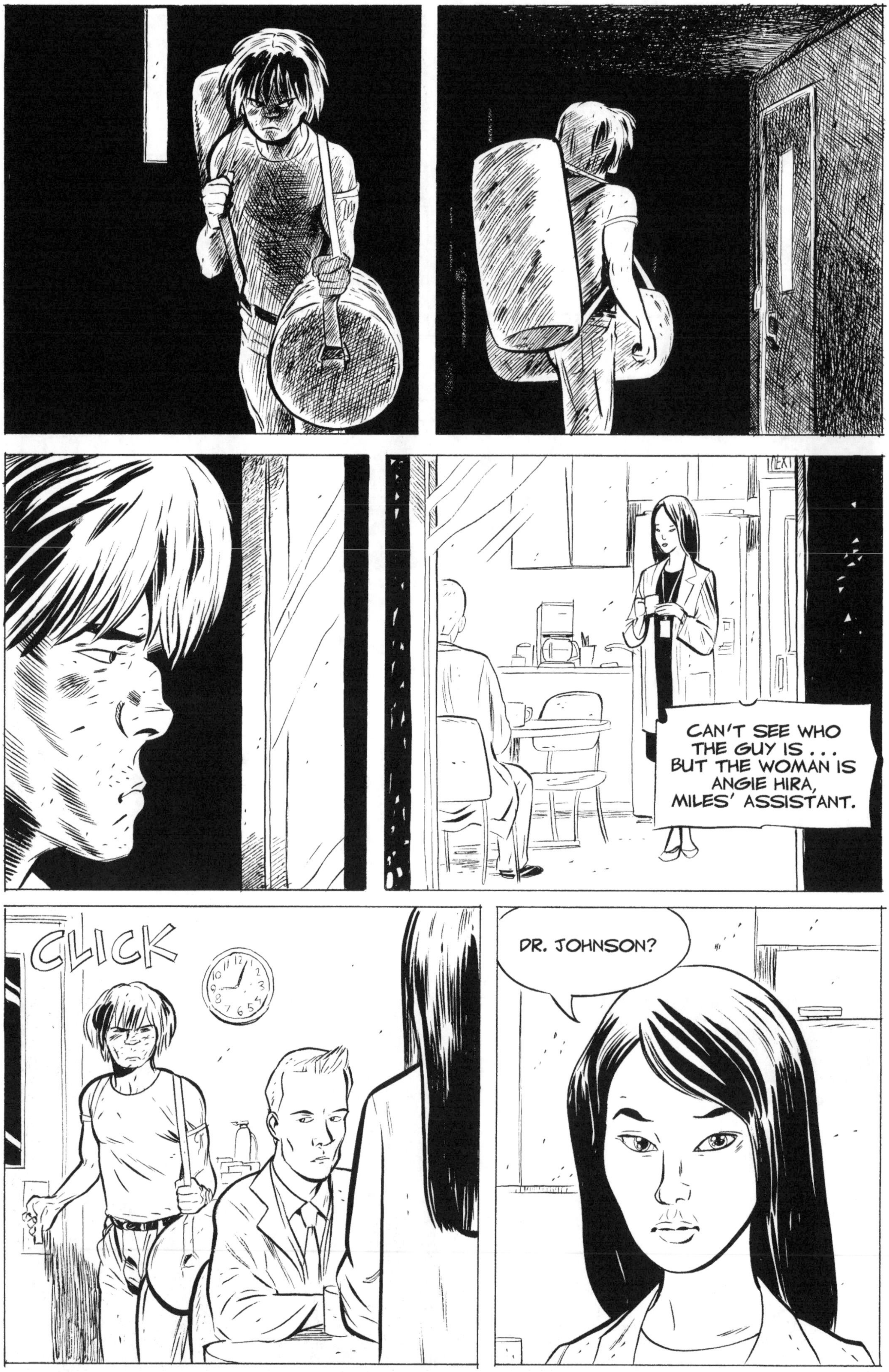
CAN'T SEE WHO THE GUY IS . . . BUT THE WOMAN IS ANGIE HIRA, MILES' ASSISTANT.
CLICK
DR. JOHNSON?

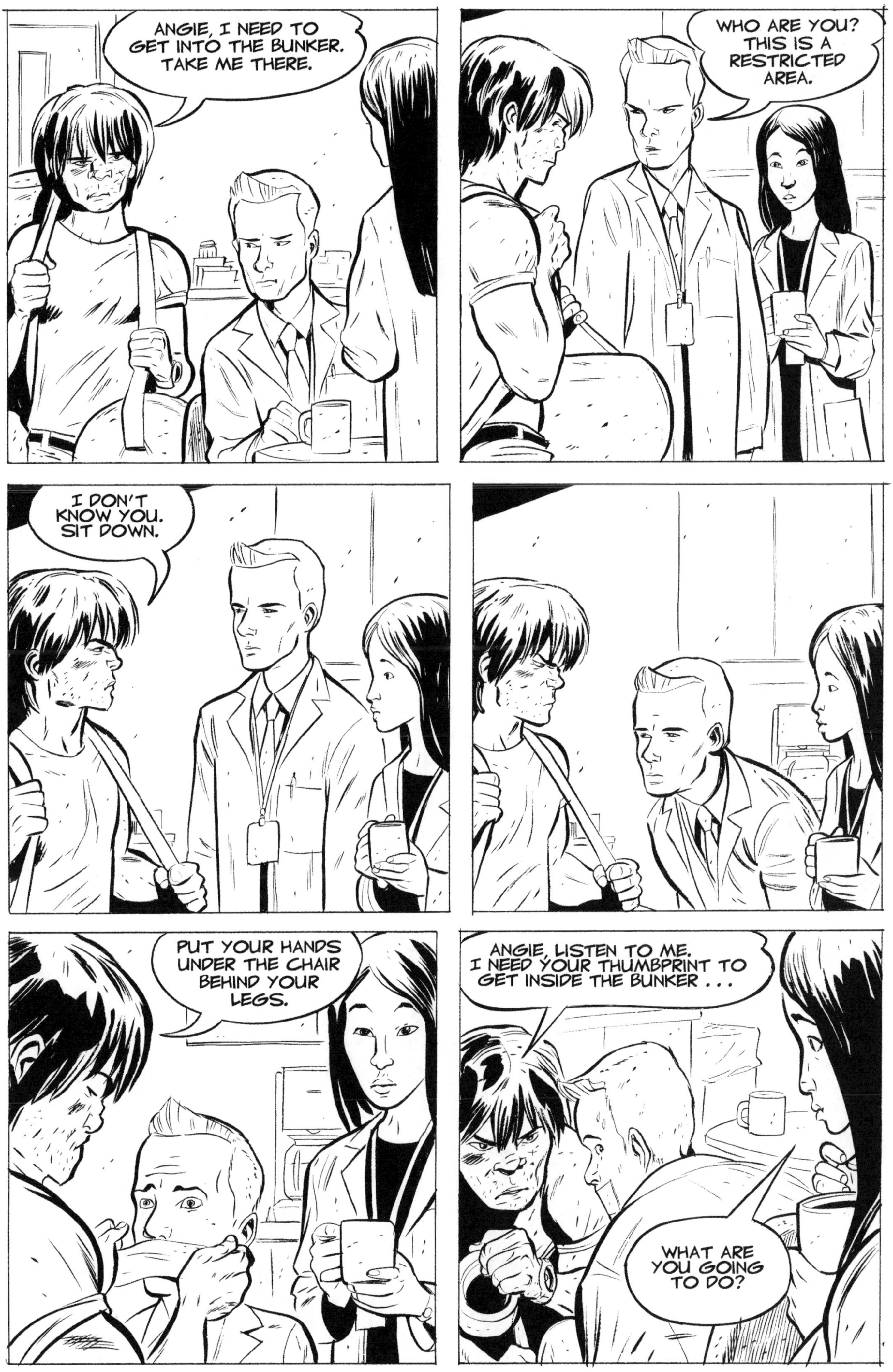
ANGIE, I NEED TO GET INTO THE BUNKER. TAKE ME THERE.
WHO ARE YOU? THIS IS A RESTRICTED AREA.
I DON'T KNOW YOU. SIT DOWN.
PUT YOUR HANDS UNDER THE CHAIR BEHIND YOUR LEGS.
ANGIE, LISTEN TO ME. I NEED YOUR THUMBPRINT TO GET INSIDE THE BUNKER . . .
WHAT ARE YOU GOING TO DO?

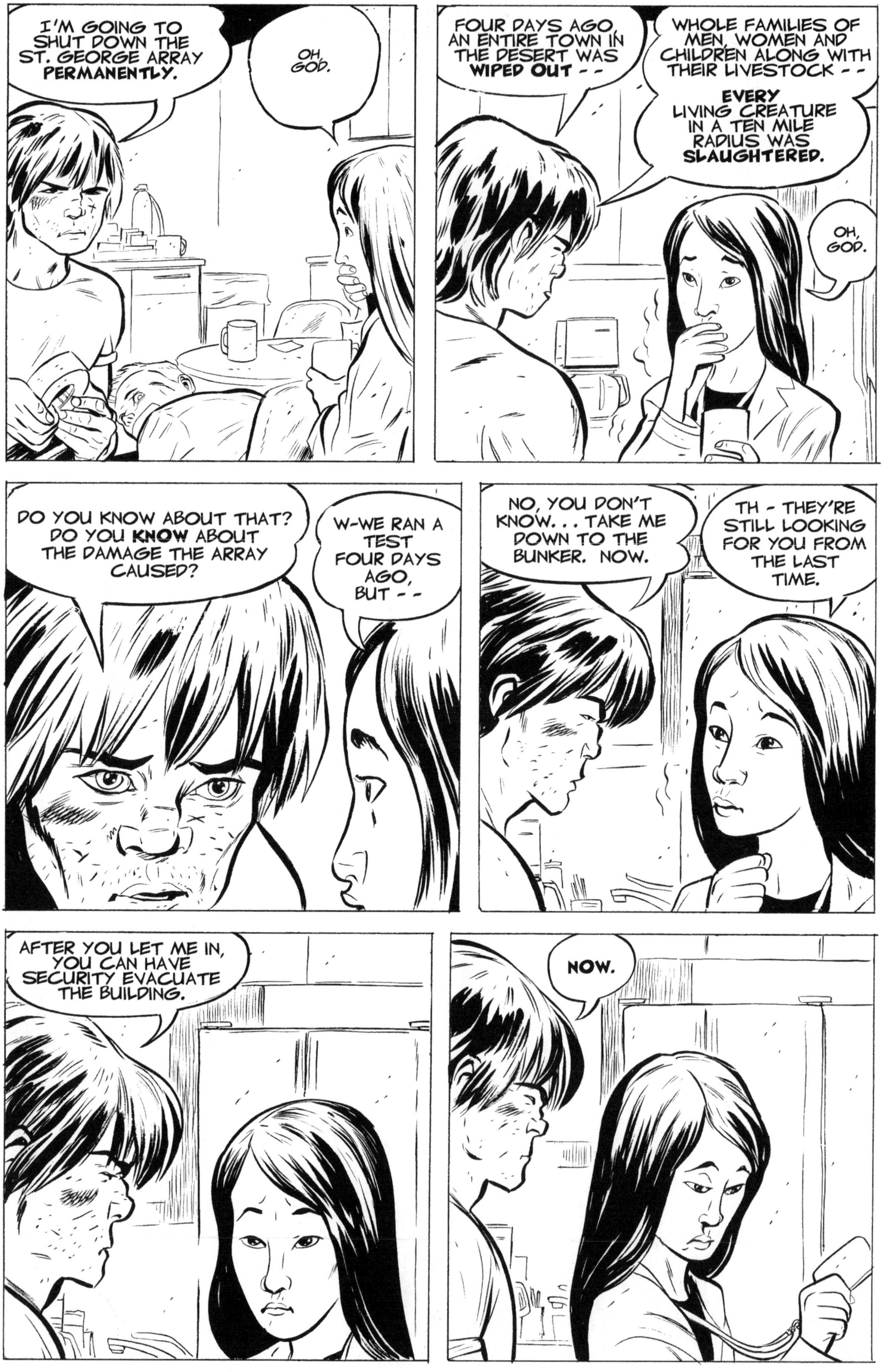
I'M GOING TO SHUT DOWN THE ST. GEORGE ARRAY **PERMANENTLY.**
OH, GOD.
FOUR DAYS AGO, AN ENTIRE TOWN IN THE DESERT WAS **WIPED OUT** - -
WHOLE FAMILIES OF MEN, WOMEN AND CHILDREN ALONG WITH THEIR LIVESTOCK - -
EVERY LIVING CREATURE IN A TEN MILE RADIUS WAS **SLAUGHTERED.**
OH, GOD.
DO YOU KNOW ABOUT THAT? DO YOU **KNOW** ABOUT THE DAMAGE THE ARRAY CAUSED?
W-WE RAN A TEST FOUR DAYS AGO, BUT - -
NO, YOU DON'T KNOW. . . TAKE ME DOWN TO THE BUNKER. NOW.
TH - THEY'RE STILL LOOKING FOR YOU FROM THE LAST TIME.
AFTER YOU LET ME IN, YOU CAN HAVE SECURITY EVACUATE THE BUILDING.
NOW.

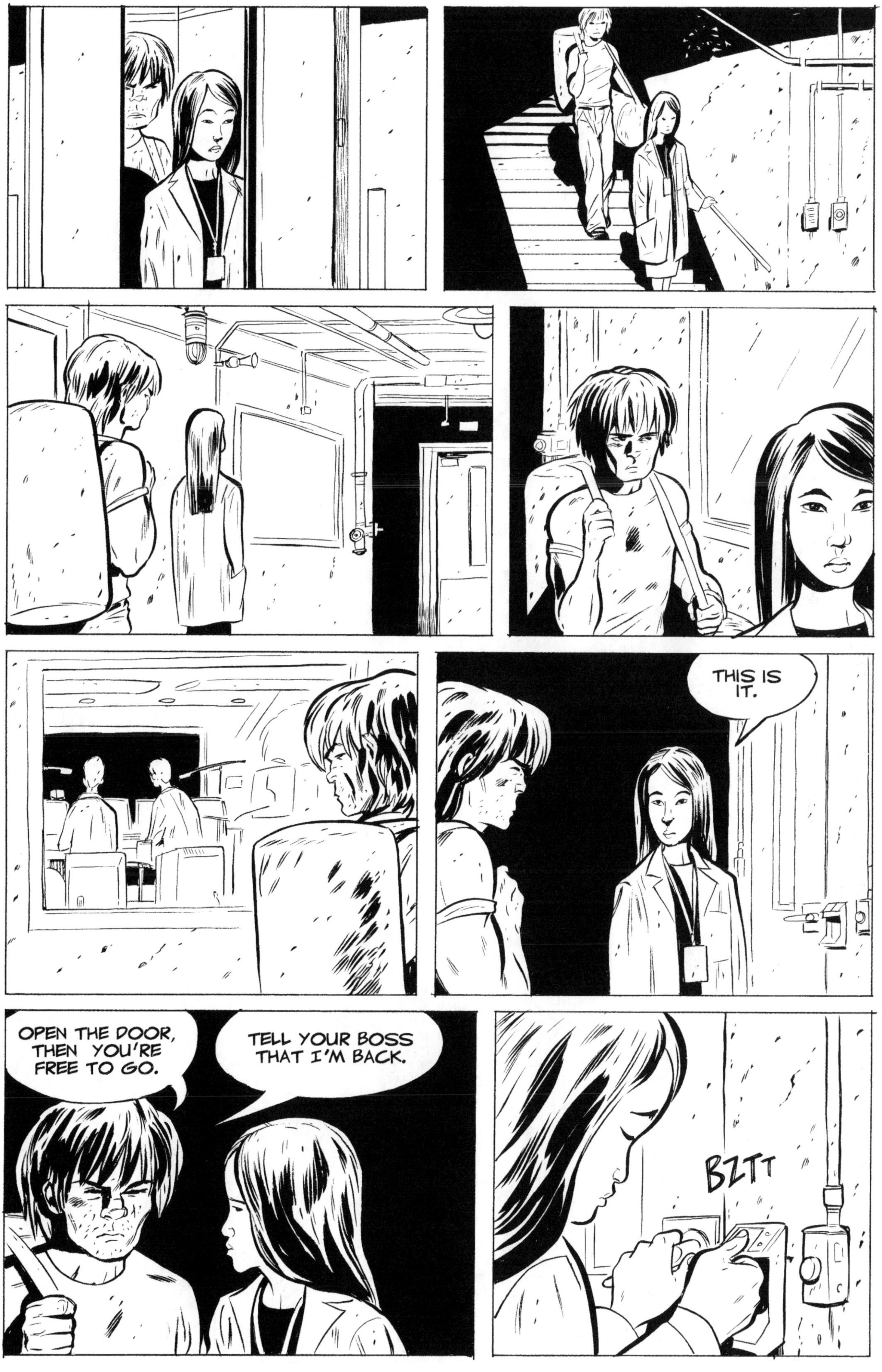

THIS IS IT.
OPEN THE DOOR, THEN YOU'RE FREE TO GO.
TELL YOUR BOSS THAT I'M BACK.
BZTT

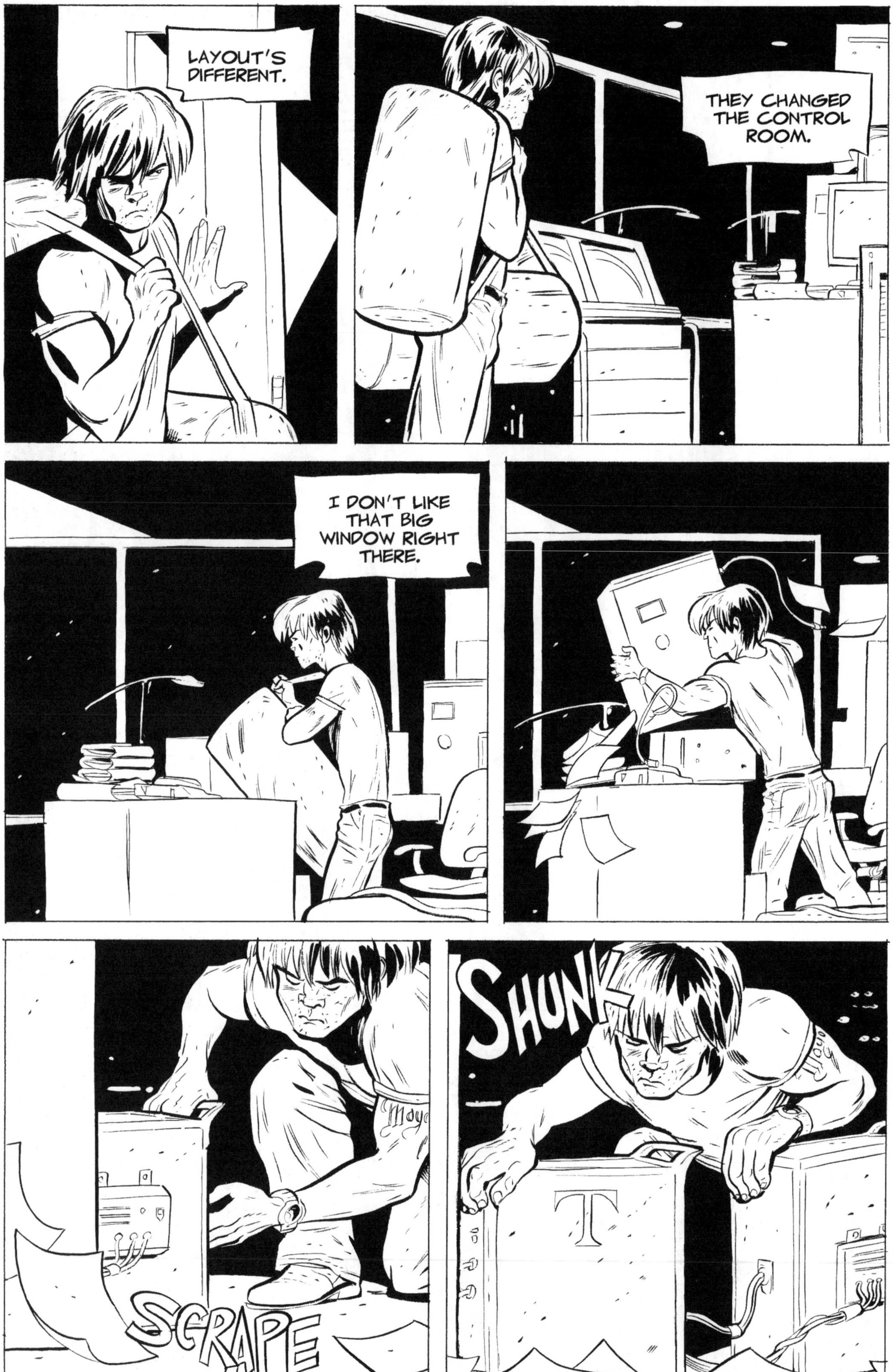
LAYOUT'S DIFFERENT.
THEY CHANGED THE CONTROL ROOM.
I DON'T LIKE THAT BIG WINDOW RIGHT THERE.
SCRAPE
SHUNK

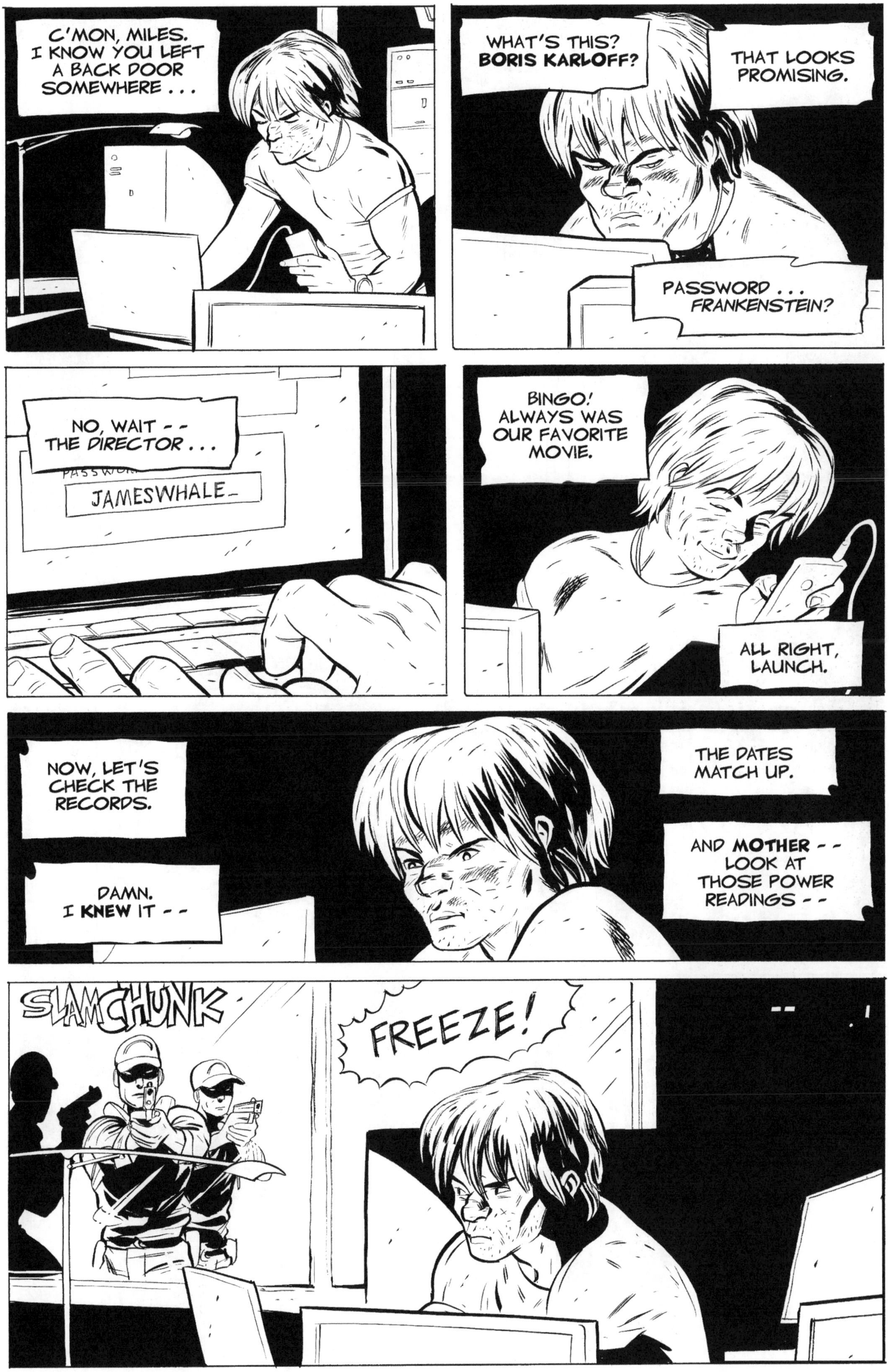
C'MON, MILES. I KNOW YOU LEFT A BACK DOOR SOMEWHERE . . .
WHAT'S THIS? BORIS KARLOFF?
THAT LOOKS PROMISING.
PASSWORD . . . FRANKENSTEIN?
NO, WAIT -- THE DIRECTOR . . .
JAMESWHALE_
BINGO! ALWAYS WAS OUR FAVORITE MOVIE.
ALL RIGHT, LAUNCH.
NOW, LET'S CHECK THE RECORDS.
DAMN. I KNEW IT --
THE DATES MATCH UP.
AND MOTHER -- LOOK AT THOSE POWER READINGS --
SLAMCHUNK
FREEZE!

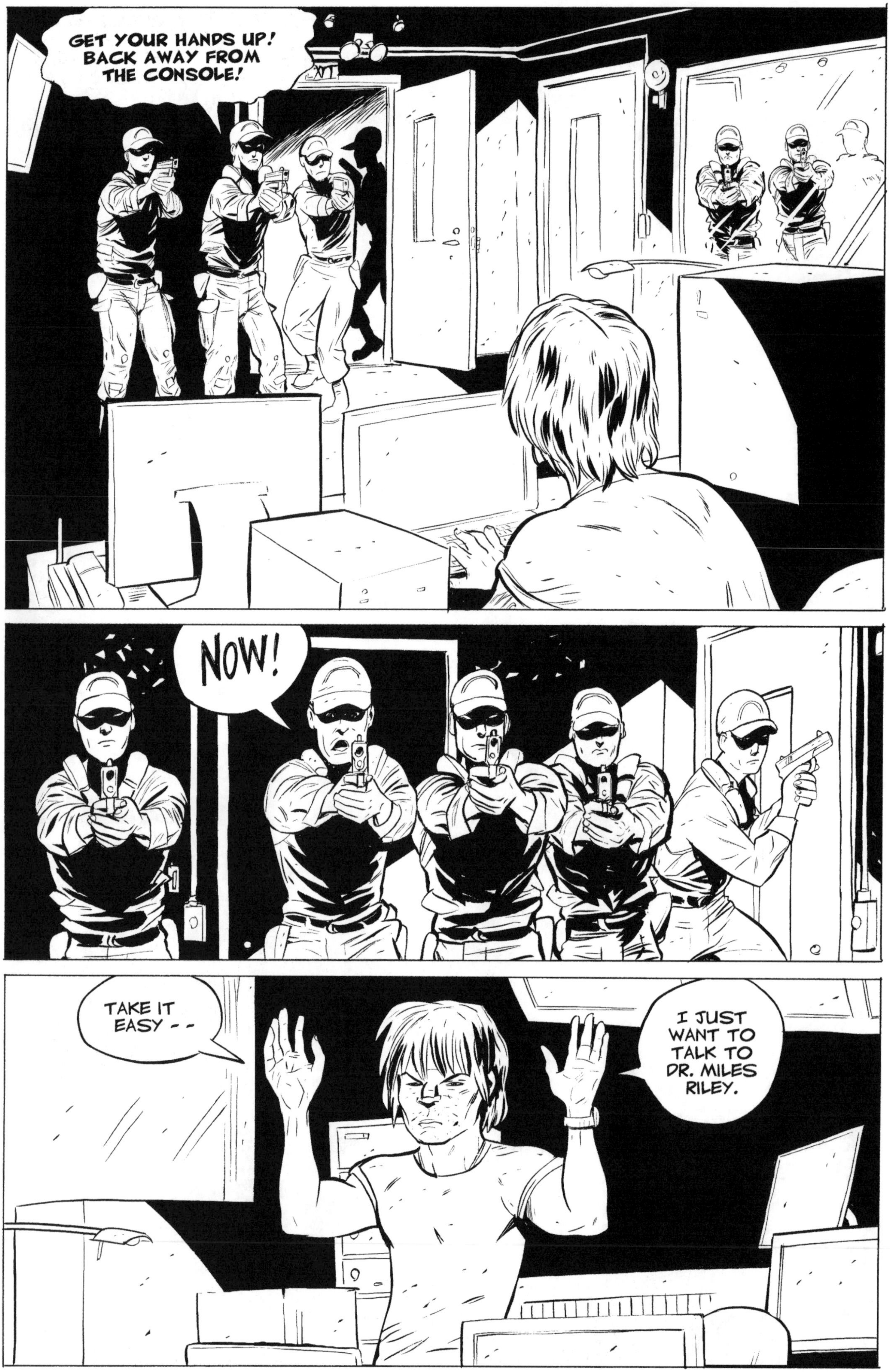
GET YOUR HANDS UP! BACK AWAY FROM THE CONSOLE!
NOW!
TAKE IT EASY --
I JUST WANT TO TALK TO DR. MILES RILEY.

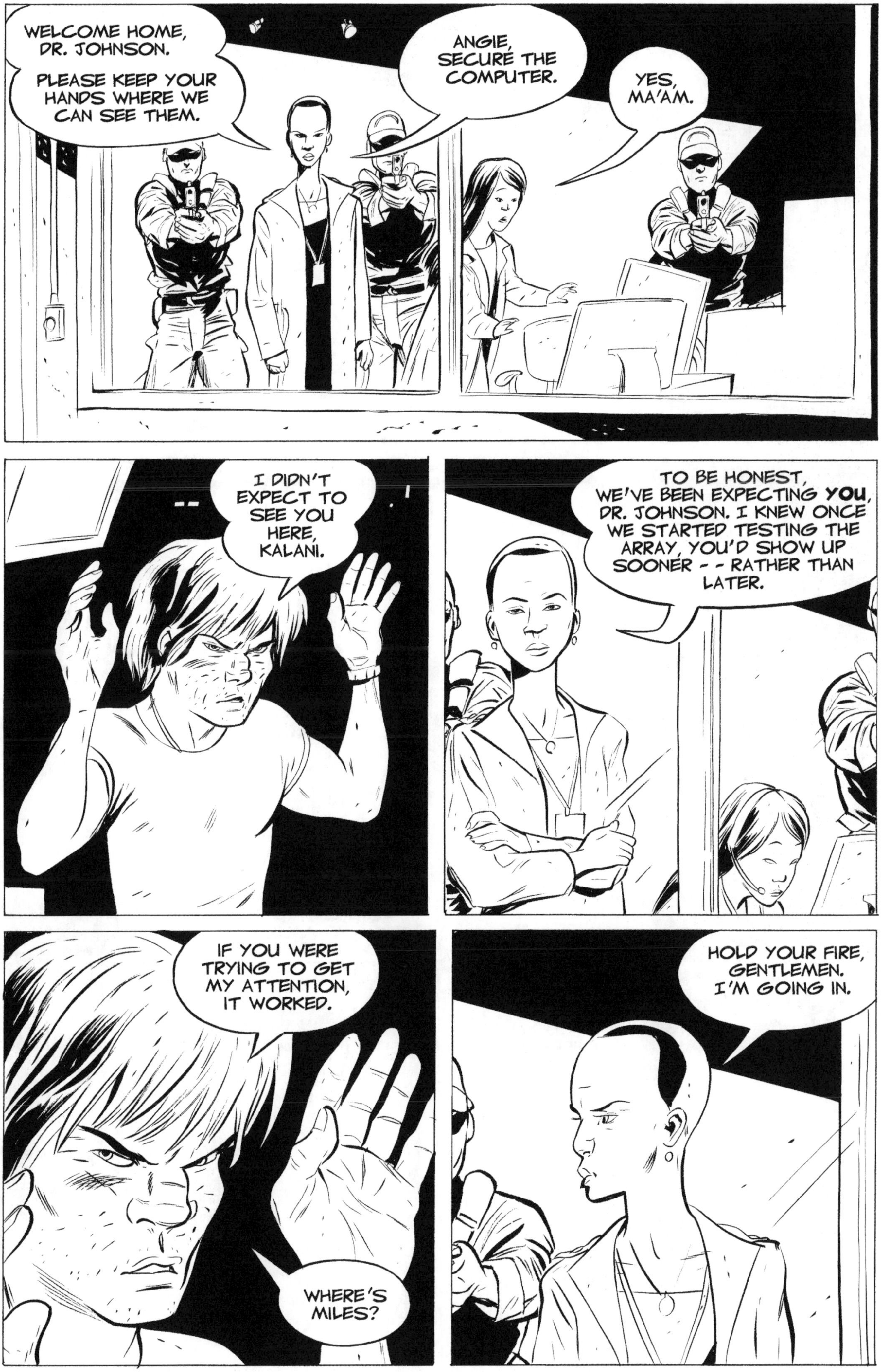
WELCOME HOME, DR. JOHNSON.
PLEASE KEEP YOUR HANDS WHERE WE CAN SEE THEM.
ANGIE, SECURE THE COMPUTER.
YES, MA'AM.
I DIDN'T EXPECT TO SEE YOU HERE, KALANI.
TO BE HONEST, WE'VE BEEN EXPECTING **YOU**, DR. JOHNSON. I KNEW ONCE WE STARTED TESTING THE ARRAY, YOU'D SHOW UP SOONER - - RATHER THAN LATER.
IF YOU WERE TRYING TO GET MY ATTENTION, IT WORKED.
WHERE'S MILES?
HOLD YOUR FIRE, GENTLEMEN. I'M GOING IN.

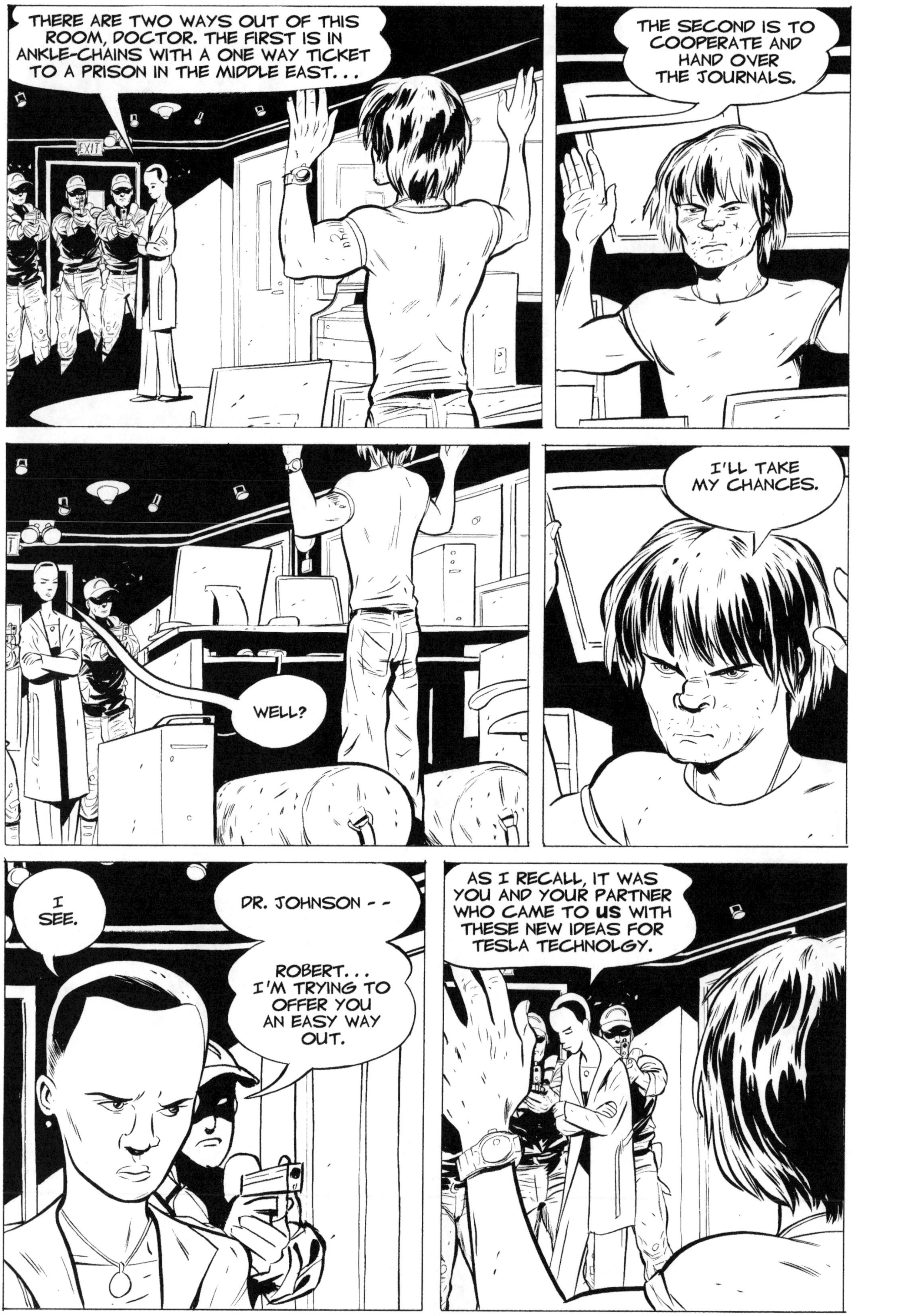
THERE ARE TWO WAYS OUT OF THIS ROOM, DOCTOR. THE FIRST IS IN ANKLE-CHAINS WITH A ONE WAY TICKET TO A PRISON IN THE MIDDLE EAST...
EXIT
THE SECOND IS TO COOPERATE AND HAND OVER THE JOURNALS.
WELL?
I'LL TAKE MY CHANCES.
I SEE.
DR. JOHNSON --
ROBERT... I'M TRYING TO OFFER YOU AN EASY WAY OUT.
AS I RECALL, IT WAS YOU AND YOUR PARTNER WHO CAME TO **US** WITH THESE NEW IDEAS FOR TESLA TECHNOLGY.

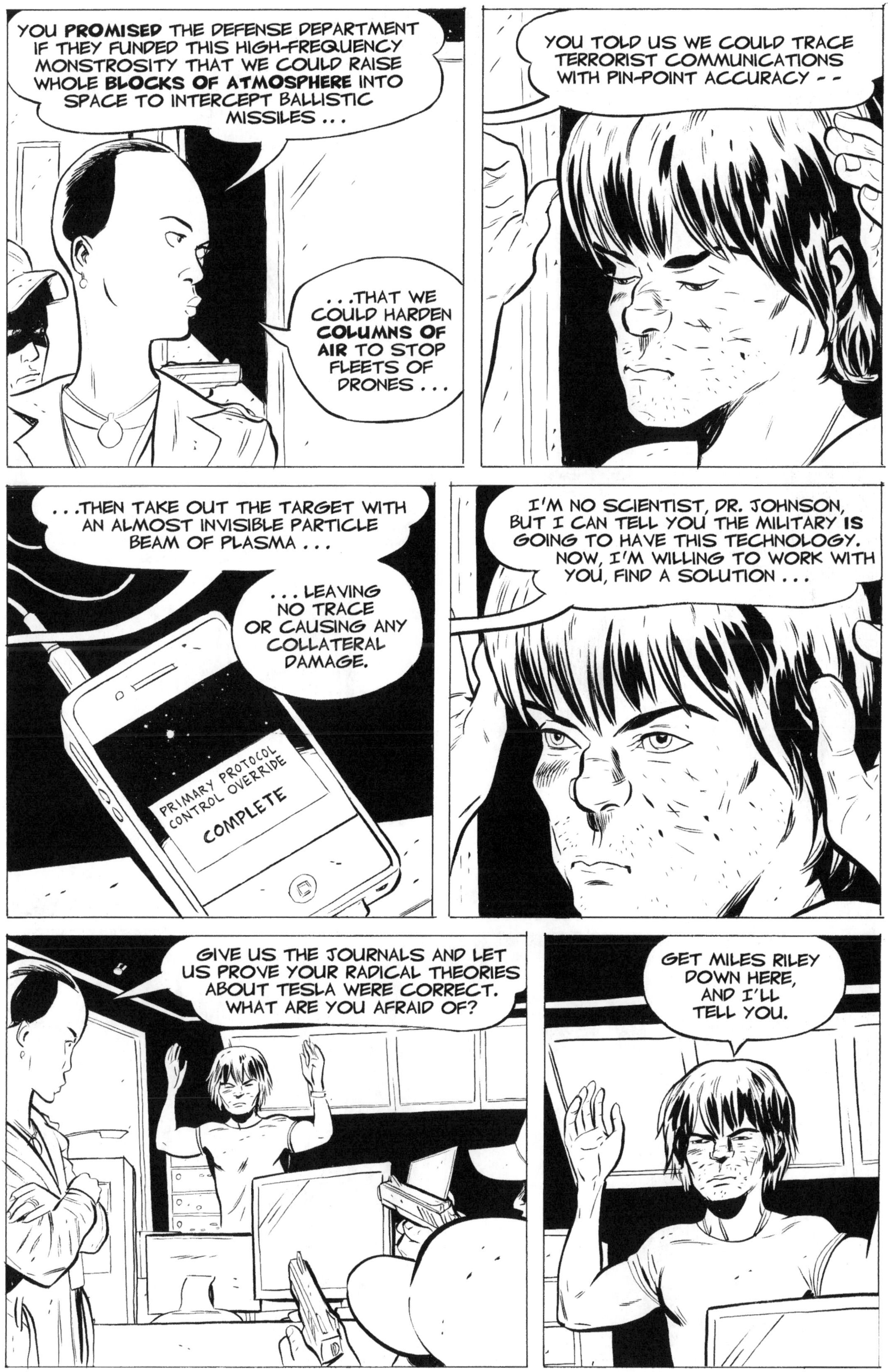
YOU **PROMISED** THE DEFENSE DEPARTMENT IF THEY FUNDED THIS HIGH-FREQUENCY MONSTROSITY THAT WE COULD RAISE WHOLE **BLOCKS OF ATMOSPHERE** INTO SPACE TO INTERCEPT BALLISTIC MISSILES ...
. . .THAT WE COULD HARDEN **COLUMNS OF AIR** TO STOP FLEETS OF DRONES . . .
YOU TOLD US WE COULD TRACE TERRORIST COMMUNICATIONS WITH PIN-POINT ACCURACY - -
. . .THEN TAKE OUT THE TARGET WITH AN ALMOST INVISIBLE PARTICLE BEAM OF PLASMA . . .
. . . LEAVING NO TRACE OR CAUSING ANY COLLATERAL DAMAGE.
PRIMARY PROTOCOL CONTROL OVERRIDE
COMPLETE
I'M NO SCIENTIST, DR. JOHNSON, BUT I CAN TELL YOU THE MILITARY **IS** GOING TO HAVE THIS TECHNOLOGY. NOW, I'M WILLING TO WORK WITH YOU, FIND A SOLUTION . . .
GIVE US THE JOURNALS AND LET US PROVE YOUR RADICAL THEORIES ABOUT TESLA WERE CORRECT. WHAT ARE YOU AFRAID OF?
GET MILES RILEY DOWN HERE, AND I'LL TELL YOU.

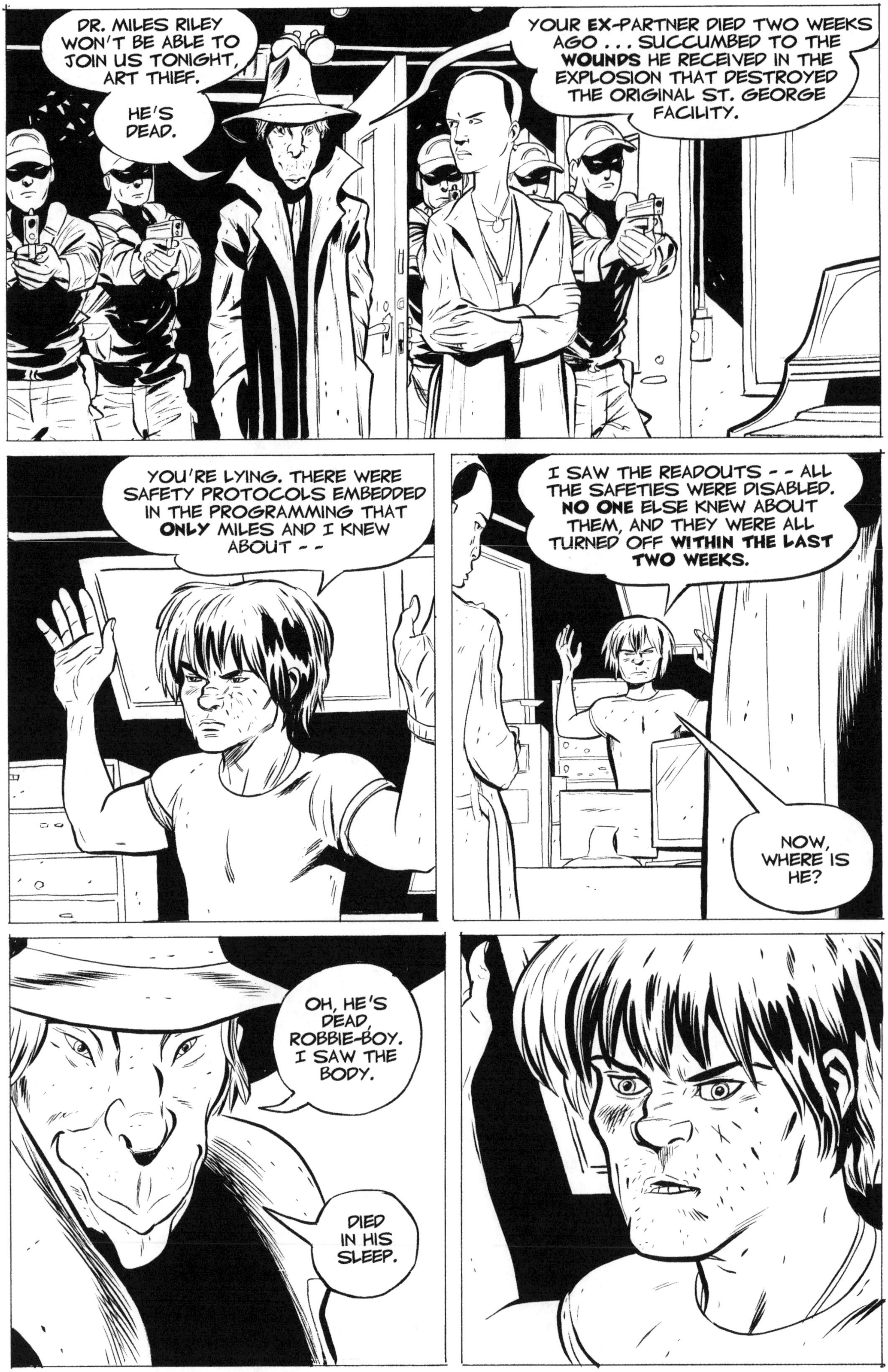
DR. MILES RILEY WON'T BE ABLE TO JOIN US TONIGHT, ART THIEF.
HE'S DEAD.
YOUR EX-PARTNER DIED TWO WEEKS AGO . . . SUCCUMBED TO THE WOUNDS HE RECEIVED IN THE EXPLOSION THAT DESTROYED THE ORIGINAL ST. GEORGE FACILITY.
YOU'RE LYING. THERE WERE SAFETY PROTOCOLS EMBEDDED IN THE PROGRAMMING THAT ONLY MILES AND I KNEW ABOUT - -
I SAW THE READOUTS - - ALL THE SAFETIES WERE DISABLED. NO ONE ELSE KNEW ABOUT THEM, AND THEY WERE ALL TURNED OFF WITHIN THE LAST TWO WEEKS.
NOW, WHERE IS HE?
OH, HE'S DEAD, ROBBIE-BOY. I SAW THE BODY.
DIED IN HIS SLEEP.

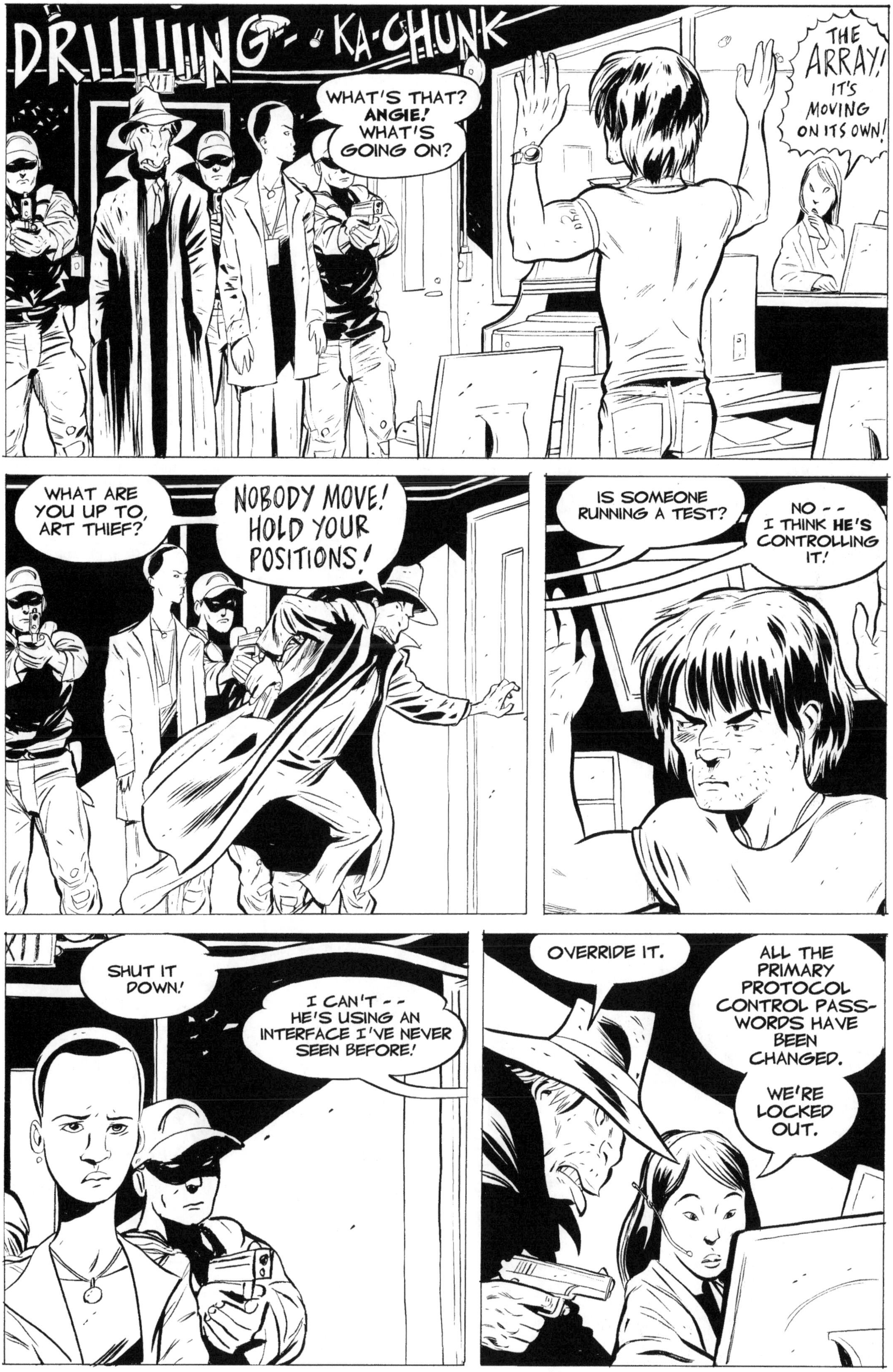
DRIIIIING - KA-CHUNK
WHAT'S THAT? ANGIE! WHAT'S GOING ON?
THE ARRAY! IT'S MOVING ON ITS OWN!
WHAT ARE YOU UP TO, ART THIEF?
NOBODY MOVE! HOLD YOUR POSITIONS!
IS SOMEONE RUNNING A TEST?
NO - - I THINK HE'S CONTROLLING IT!
SHUT IT DOWN!
I CAN'T - - HE'S USING AN INTERFACE I'VE NEVER SEEN BEFORE!
OVERRIDE IT.
ALL THE PRIMARY PROTOCOL CONTROL PASS-WORDS HAVE BEEN CHANGED.
WE'RE LOCKED OUT.

IT WILL ONLY TAKE A COUPLE OF MINUTES FOR THE ANTENNA ELEMENTS TO REALIGN.

AFTER THAT, YOU'LL HAVE THIRTY MINUTES TO EVACUATE THE BASE.

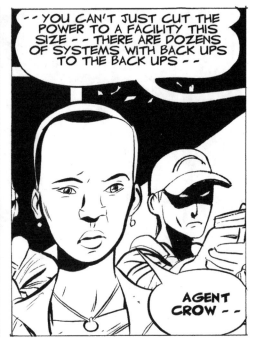

-- YOU CAN'T JUST CUT THE POWER TO A FACILITY THIS SIZE -- THERE ARE DOZENS OF SYSTEMS WITH BACK UPS TO THE BACK UPS --

AGENT CROW --

WE HAVE TO EVACUATE THE BASE IMMEDIATELY.

WHAT?

YOU! KEEP YOUR GUN ON THE ART THIEF -- IF HE MOVES, SHOOT HIM!

THE REST OF YOU GET UP TOP AND START CUTTING CABLES TO THE TOWERS -- JAM GEARS, USE EXPLOSIVES -- WE CAN REBUILD THE ELEMENTS!

THERE ARE FORTY-EIGHT TOWERS. YOU'LL NEVER DO IT IN TIME.

-- SON OF A -- I'LL SHOW YOU HOW TO CARE TAKE OF THIS --

AGENT CROW! LOWER YOUR WEAPON OR I'LL HAVE YOU ARRESTED.

BETTER LISTEN TO HER, SAL . . .

I'M THE ONLY ONE WHO CAN STOP IT NOW.

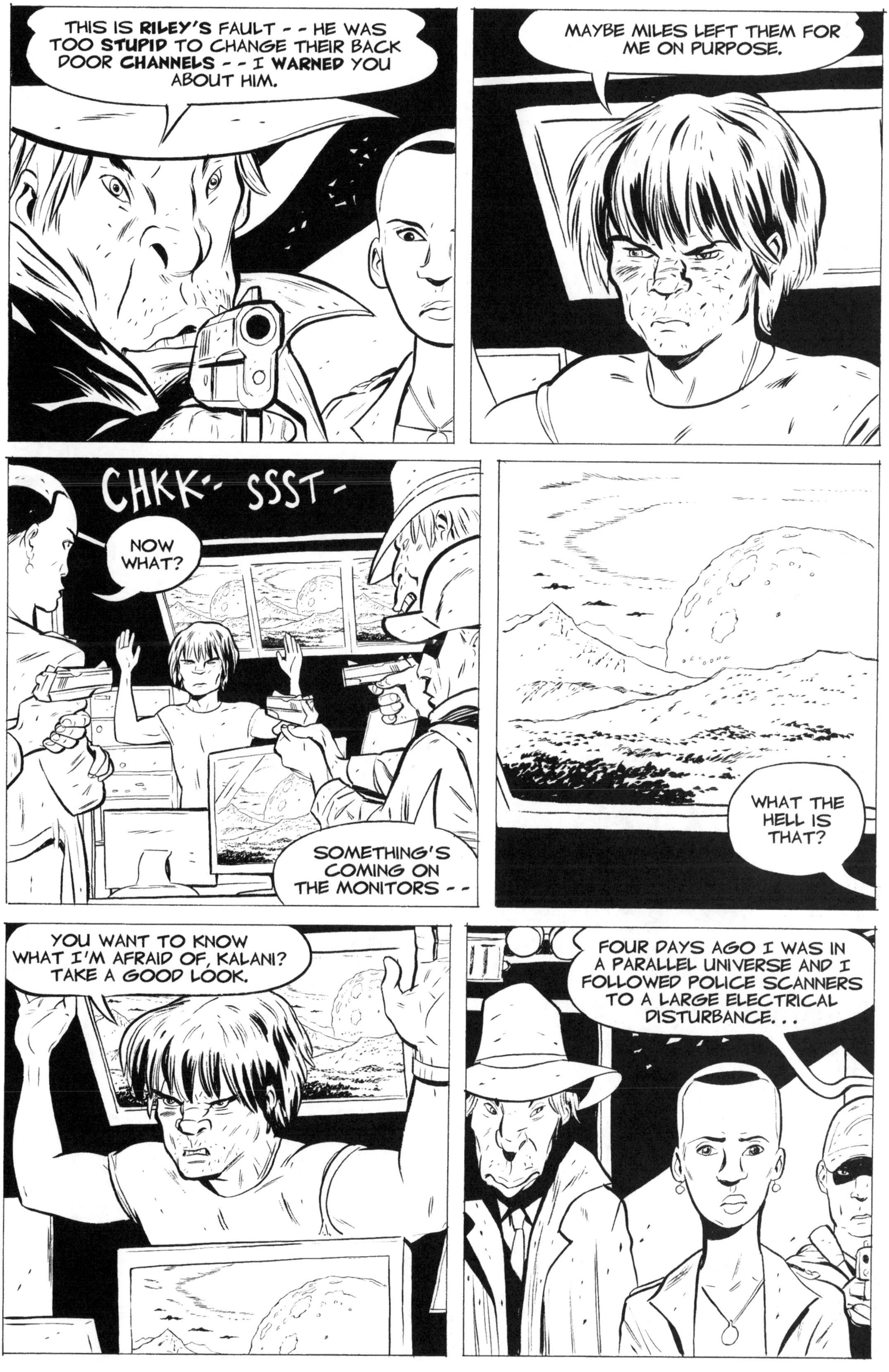
THIS IS RILEY'S FAULT - - HE WAS TOO STUPID TO CHANGE THEIR BACK DOOR CHANNELS - - I WARNED YOU ABOUT HIM.
MAYBE MILES LEFT THEM FOR ME ON PURPOSE.
CHKK - - SSST -
NOW WHAT?
SOMETHING'S COMING ON THE MONITORS - -
WHAT THE HELL IS THAT?
YOU WANT TO KNOW WHAT I'M AFRAID OF, KALANI? TAKE A GOOD LOOK.
FOUR DAYS AGO I WAS IN A PARALLEL UNIVERSE AND I FOLLOWED POLICE SCANNERS TO A LARGE ELECTRICAL DISTURBANCE. . .

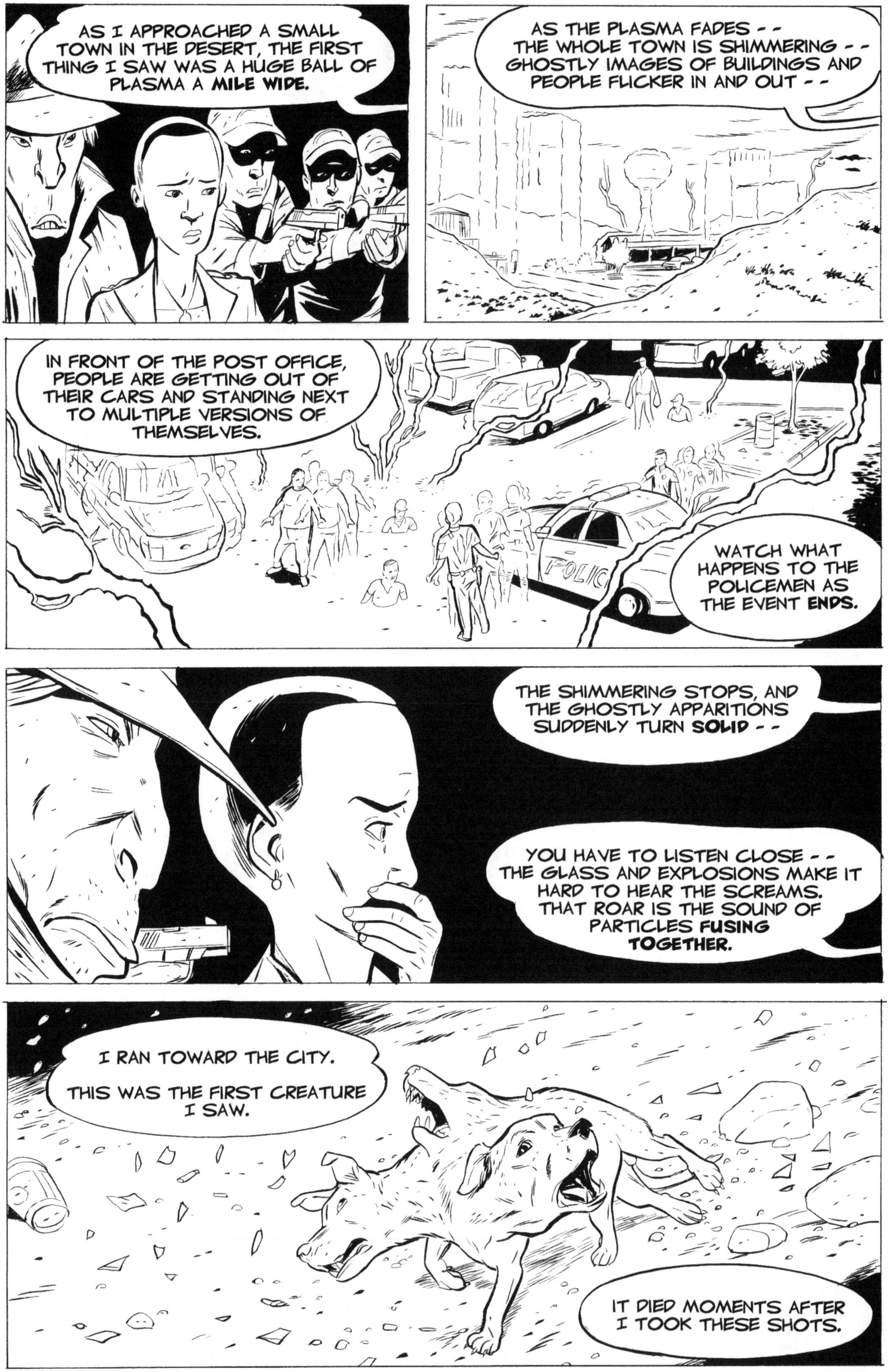
AS I APPROACHED A SMALL TOWN IN THE DESERT, THE FIRST THING I SAW WAS A HUGE BALL OF PLASMA A **MILE WIDE.**
AS THE PLASMA FADES -- THE WHOLE TOWN IS SHIMMERING -- GHOSTLY IMAGES OF BUILDINGS AND PEOPLE FLICKER IN AND OUT --
IN FRONT OF THE POST OFFICE, PEOPLE ARE GETTING OUT OF THEIR CARS AND STANDING NEXT TO MULTIPLE VERSIONS OF THEMSELVES.
POLIC
WATCH WHAT HAPPENS TO THE POLICEMEN AS THE EVENT **ENDS.**
THE SHIMMERING STOPS, AND THE GHOSTLY APPARITIONS SUDDENLY TURN **SOLID** --
YOU HAVE TO LISTEN CLOSE -- THE GLASS AND EXPLOSIONS MAKE IT HARD TO HEAR THE SCREAMS. THAT ROAR IS THE SOUND OF PARTICLES **FUSING TOGETHER.**
I RAN TOWARD THE CITY.
THIS WAS THE FIRST CREATURE I SAW.
IT DIED MOMENTS AFTER I TOOK THESE SHOTS.

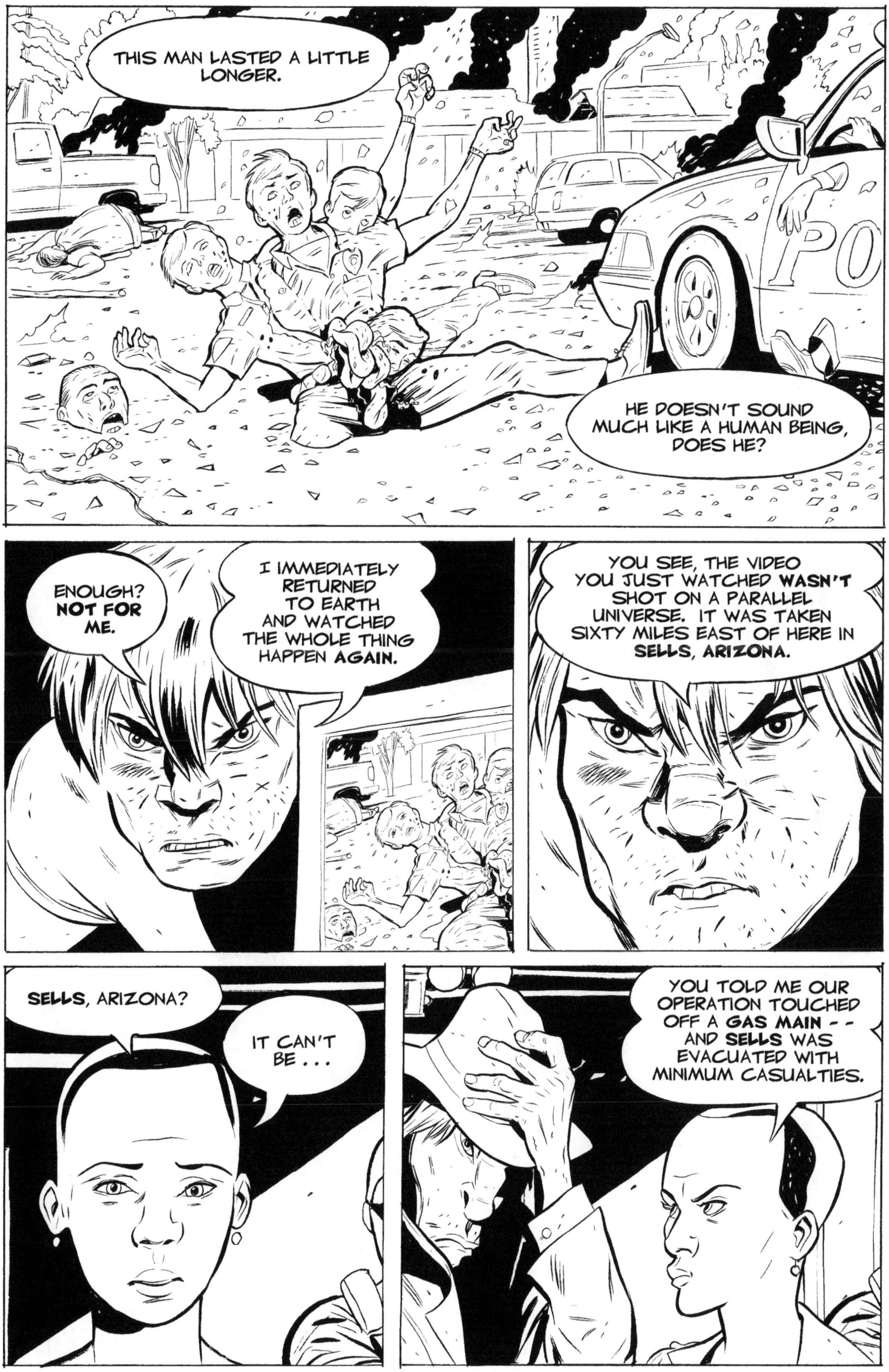

THIS MAN LASTED A LITTLE LONGER.
HE DOESN'T SOUND MUCH LIKE A HUMAN BEING, DOES HE?
ENOUGH? NOT FOR ME.
I IMMEDIATELY RETURNED TO EARTH AND WATCHED THE WHOLE THING HAPPEN AGAIN.
YOU SEE, THE VIDEO YOU JUST WATCHED WASN'T SHOT ON A PARALLEL UNIVERSE. IT WAS TAKEN SIXTY MILES EAST OF HERE IN SELLS, ARIZONA.
SELLS, ARIZONA?
IT CAN'T BE . . .
YOU TOLD ME OUR OPERATION TOUCHED OFF A GAS MAIN - - AND SELLS WAS EVACUATED WITH MINIMUM CASUALTIES.

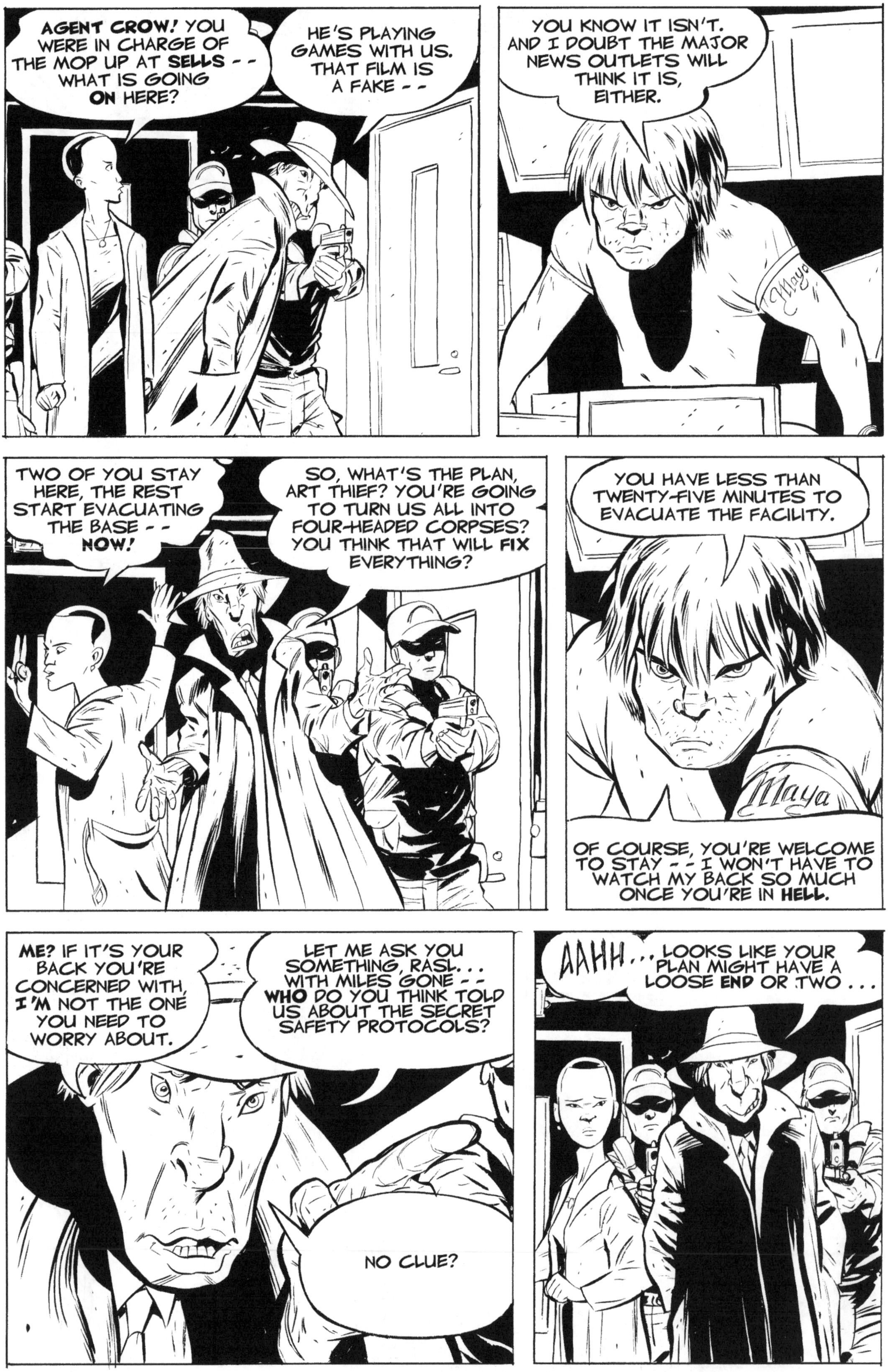
AGENT CROW! YOU WERE IN CHARGE OF THE MOP UP AT SELLS - - WHAT IS GOING ON HERE?
HE'S PLAYING GAMES WITH US. THAT FILM IS A FAKE - -
YOU KNOW IT ISN'T. AND I DOUBT THE MAJOR NEWS OUTLETS WILL THINK IT IS, EITHER.
Maya
TWO OF YOU STAY HERE, THE REST START EVACUATING THE BASE - - NOW!
SO, WHAT'S THE PLAN, ART THIEF? YOU'RE GOING TO TURN US ALL INTO FOUR-HEADED CORPSES? YOU THINK THAT WILL FIX EVERYTHING?
YOU HAVE LESS THAN TWENTY-FIVE MINUTES TO EVACUATE THE FACILITY.
Maya
OF COURSE, YOU'RE WELCOME TO STAY - - I WON'T HAVE TO WATCH MY BACK SO MUCH ONCE YOU'RE IN HELL.
ME? IF IT'S YOUR BACK YOU'RE CONCERNED WITH, I'M NOT THE ONE YOU NEED TO WORRY ABOUT.
LET ME ASK YOU SOMETHING, RASL... WITH MILES GONE - - WHO DO YOU THINK TOLD US ABOUT THE SECRET SAFETY PROTOCOLS?
NO CLUE?
AAHH... LOOKS LIKE YOUR PLAN MIGHT HAVE A LOOSE END OR TWO ...

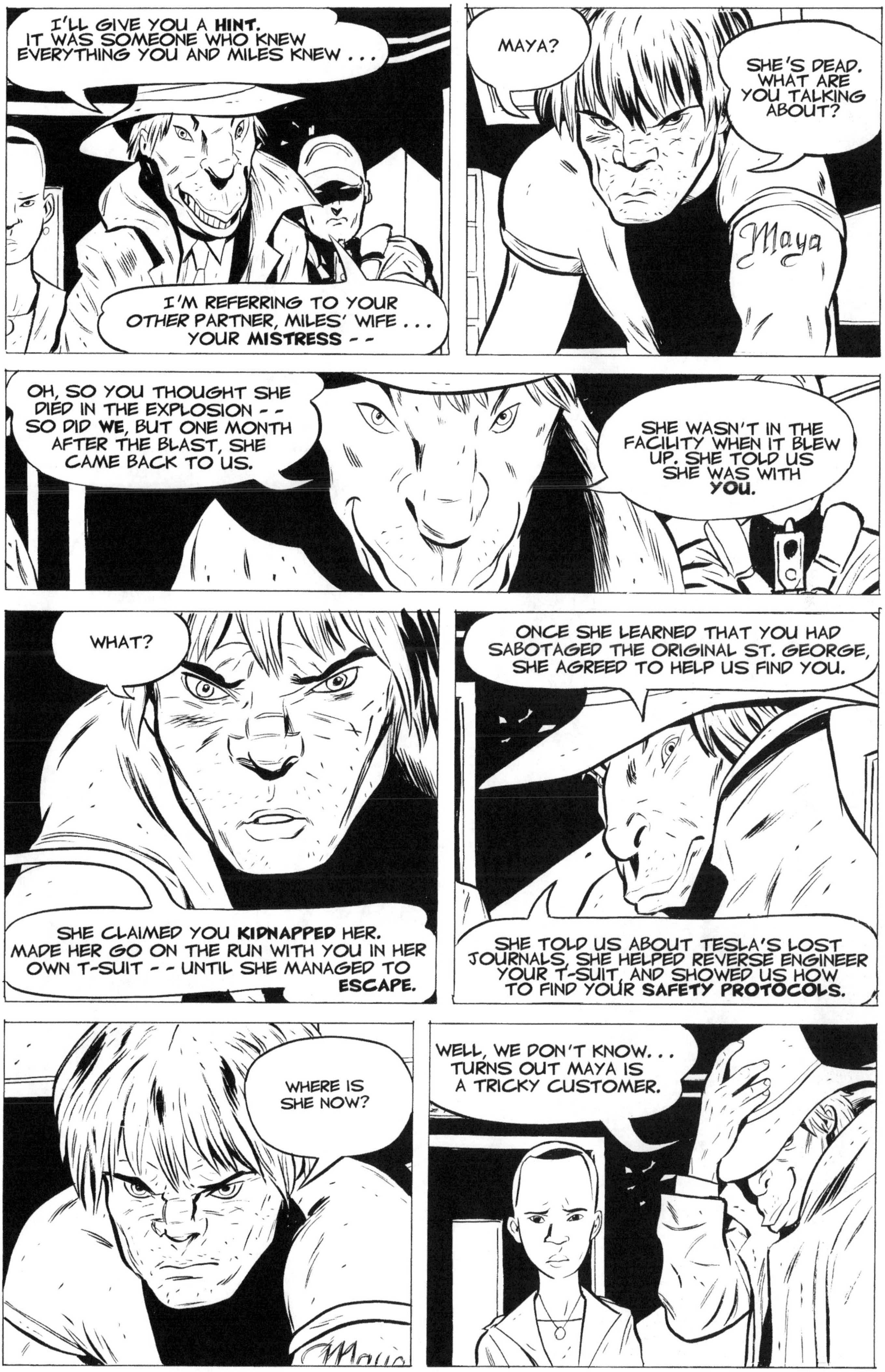
I'LL GIVE YOU A HINT. IT WAS SOMEONE WHO KNEW EVERYTHING YOU AND MILES KNEW . . .
I'M REFERRING TO YOUR OTHER PARTNER, MILES' WIFE . . . YOUR MISTRESS - -
MAYA?
SHE'S DEAD. WHAT ARE YOU TALKING ABOUT?
Maya
OH, SO YOU THOUGHT SHE DIED IN THE EXPLOSION - - SO DID WE, BUT ONE MONTH AFTER THE BLAST, SHE CAME BACK TO US.
SHE WASN'T IN THE FACILITY WHEN IT BLEW UP. SHE TOLD US SHE WAS WITH YOU.
WHAT?
SHE CLAIMED YOU KIDNAPPED HER. MADE HER GO ON THE RUN WITH YOU IN HER OWN T-SUIT - - UNTIL SHE MANAGED TO ESCAPE.
ONCE SHE LEARNED THAT YOU HAD SABOTAGED THE ORIGINAL ST. GEORGE, SHE AGREED TO HELP US FIND YOU.
SHE TOLD US ABOUT TESLA'S LOST JOURNALS, SHE HELPED REVERSE ENGINEER YOUR T-SUIT, AND SHOWED US HOW TO FIND YOUR SAFETY PROTOCOLS.
WHERE IS SHE NOW?
WELL, WE DON'T KNOW... TURNS OUT MAYA IS A TRICKY CUSTOMER.

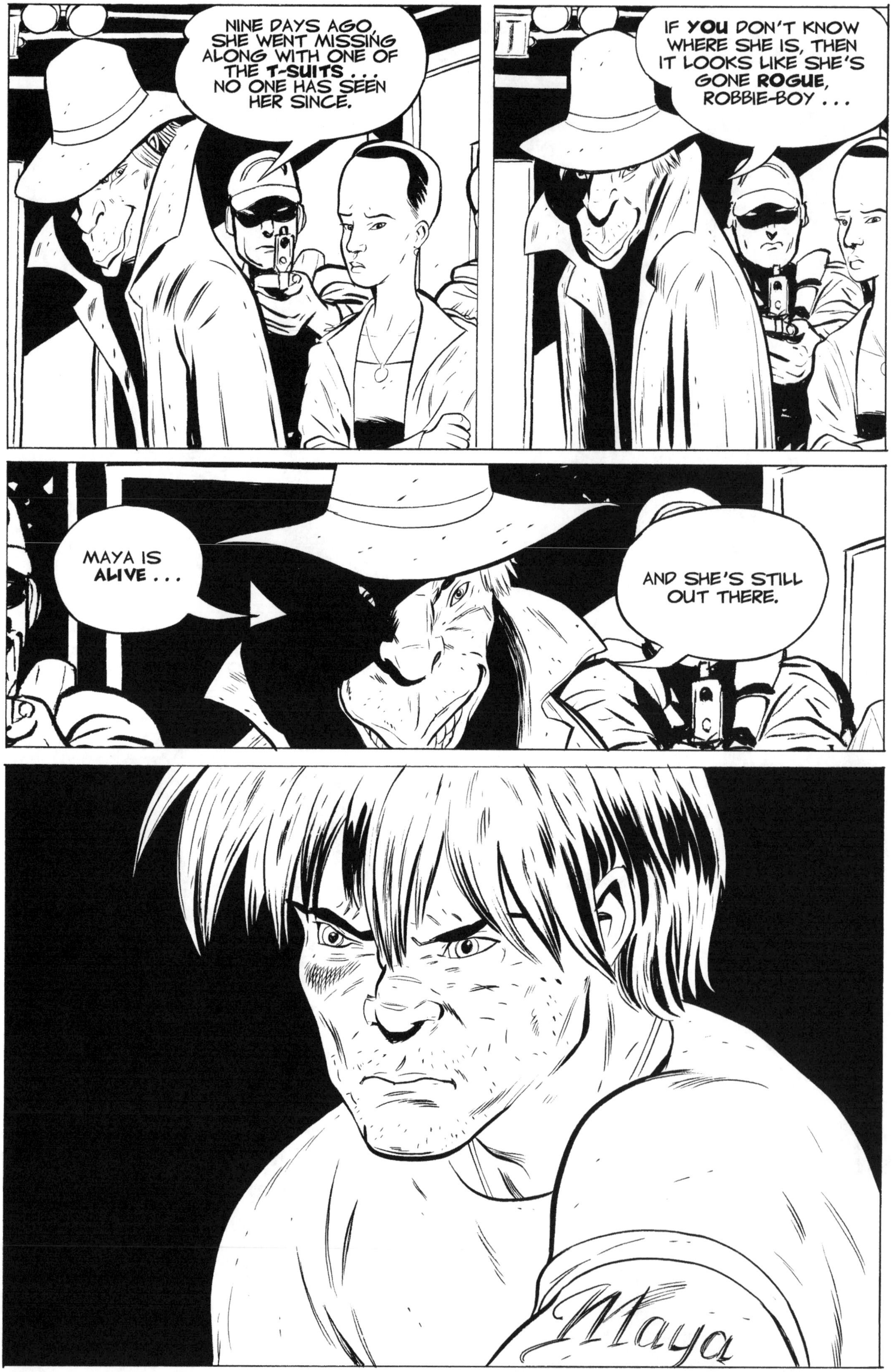
NINE DAYS AGO, SHE WENT MISSING ALONG WITH ONE OF THE **T-SUITS . . .** NO ONE HAS SEEN HER SINCE.
IF **YOU** DON'T KNOW WHERE SHE IS, THEN IT LOOKS LIKE SHE'S GONE **ROGUE**, ROBBIE-BOY . . .
MAYA IS **ALIVE . . .**
AND SHE'S STILL OUT THERE.
Maya

14.
CLOSER TO THE CENTER

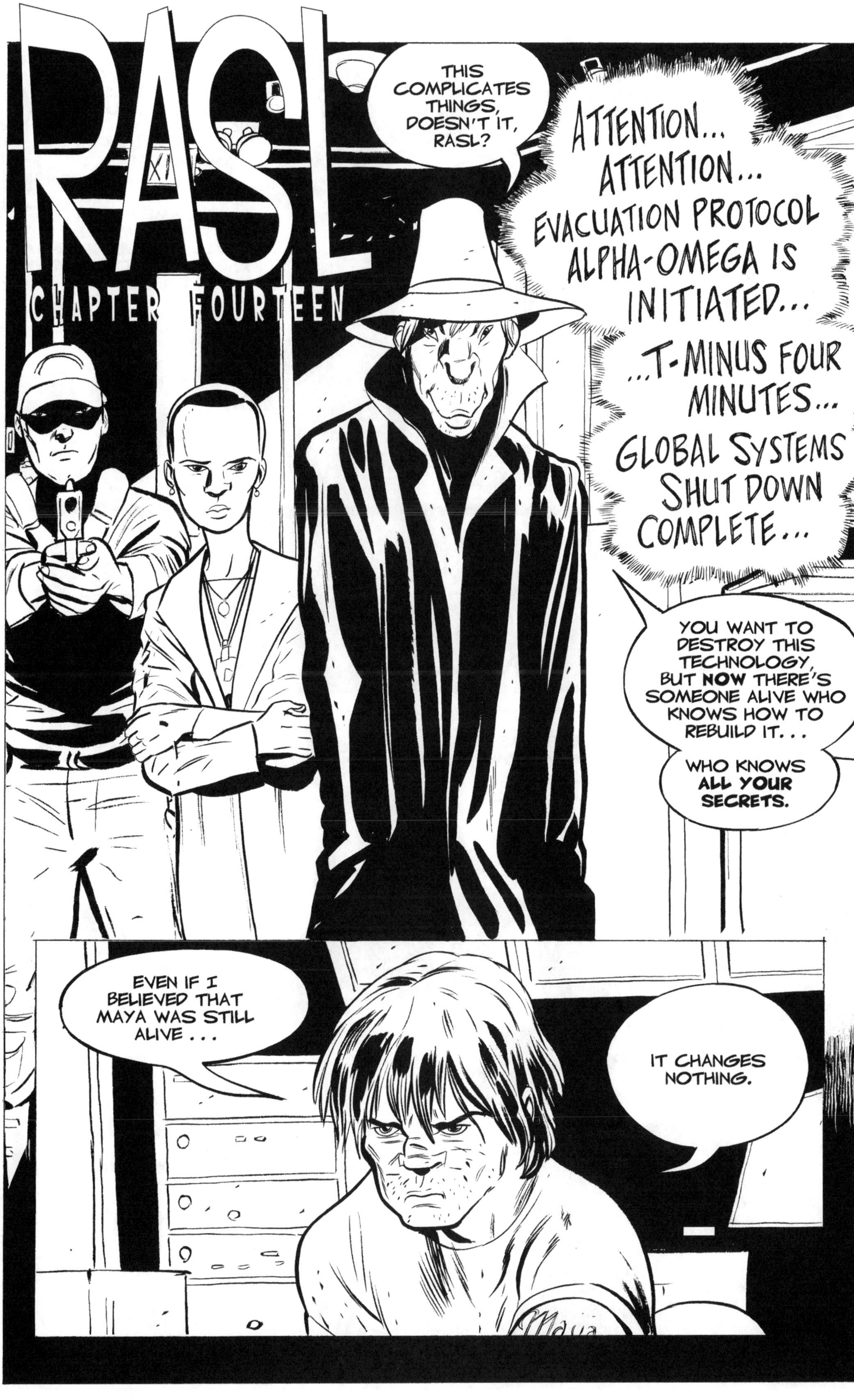
RASL
CHAPTER FOURTEEN
THIS COMPLICATES THINGS, DOESN'T IT, RASL?
ATTENTION... ATTENTION... EVACUATION PROTOCOL ALPHA-OMEGA IS INITIATED...
...T-MINUS FOUR MINUTES...
GLOBAL SYSTEMS SHUT DOWN COMPLETE...
YOU WANT TO DESTROY THIS TECHNOLOGY, BUT NOW THERE'S SOMEONE ALIVE WHO KNOWS HOW TO REBUILD IT...
WHO KNOWS ALL YOUR SECRETS.
EVEN IF I BELIEVED THAT MAYA WAS STILL ALIVE...
IT CHANGES NOTHING.
Maya

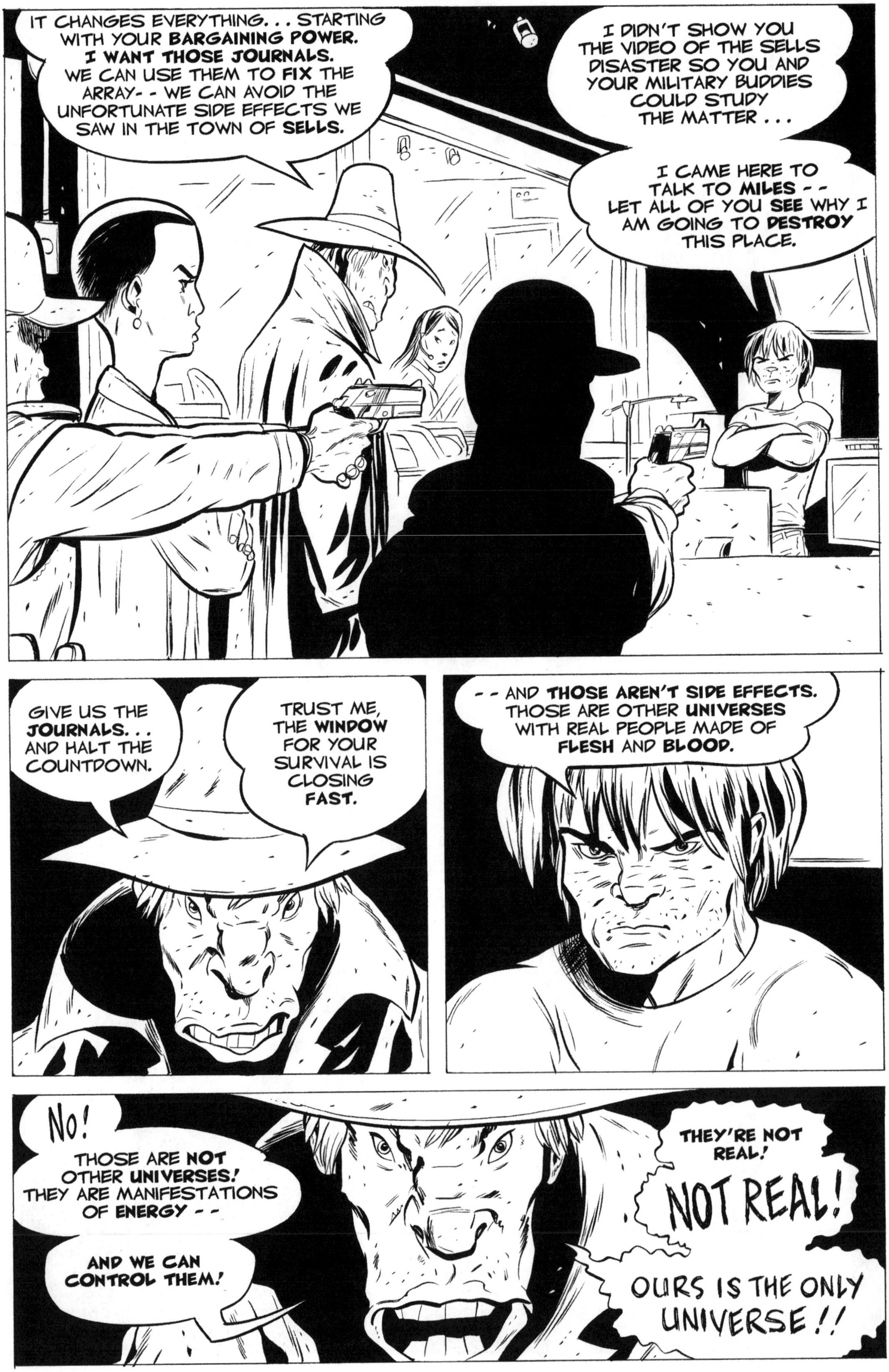

IT CHANGES EVERYTHING. . . STARTING WITH YOUR BARGAINING POWER. I WANT THOSE JOURNALS. WE CAN USE THEM TO FIX THE ARRAY- - WE CAN AVOID THE UNFORTUNATE SIDE EFFECTS WE SAW IN THE TOWN OF SELLS.
I DIDN'T SHOW YOU THE VIDEO OF THE SELLS DISASTER SO YOU AND YOUR MILITARY BUDDIES COULD STUDY THE MATTER . . .
I CAME HERE TO TALK TO MILES - - LET ALL OF YOU SEE WHY I AM GOING TO DESTROY THIS PLACE.
GIVE US THE JOURNALS. . . AND HALT THE COUNTDOWN.
TRUST ME, THE WINDOW FOR YOUR SURVIVAL IS CLOSING FAST.
- - AND THOSE AREN'T SIDE EFFECTS. THOSE ARE OTHER UNIVERSES WITH REAL PEOPLE MADE OF FLESH AND BLOOD.
No! THOSE ARE NOT OTHER UNIVERSES! THEY ARE MANIFESTATIONS OF ENERGY - -
AND WE CAN CONTROL THEM!
THEY'RE NOT REAL!
NOT REAL!
OURS IS THE ONLY UNIVERSE!!

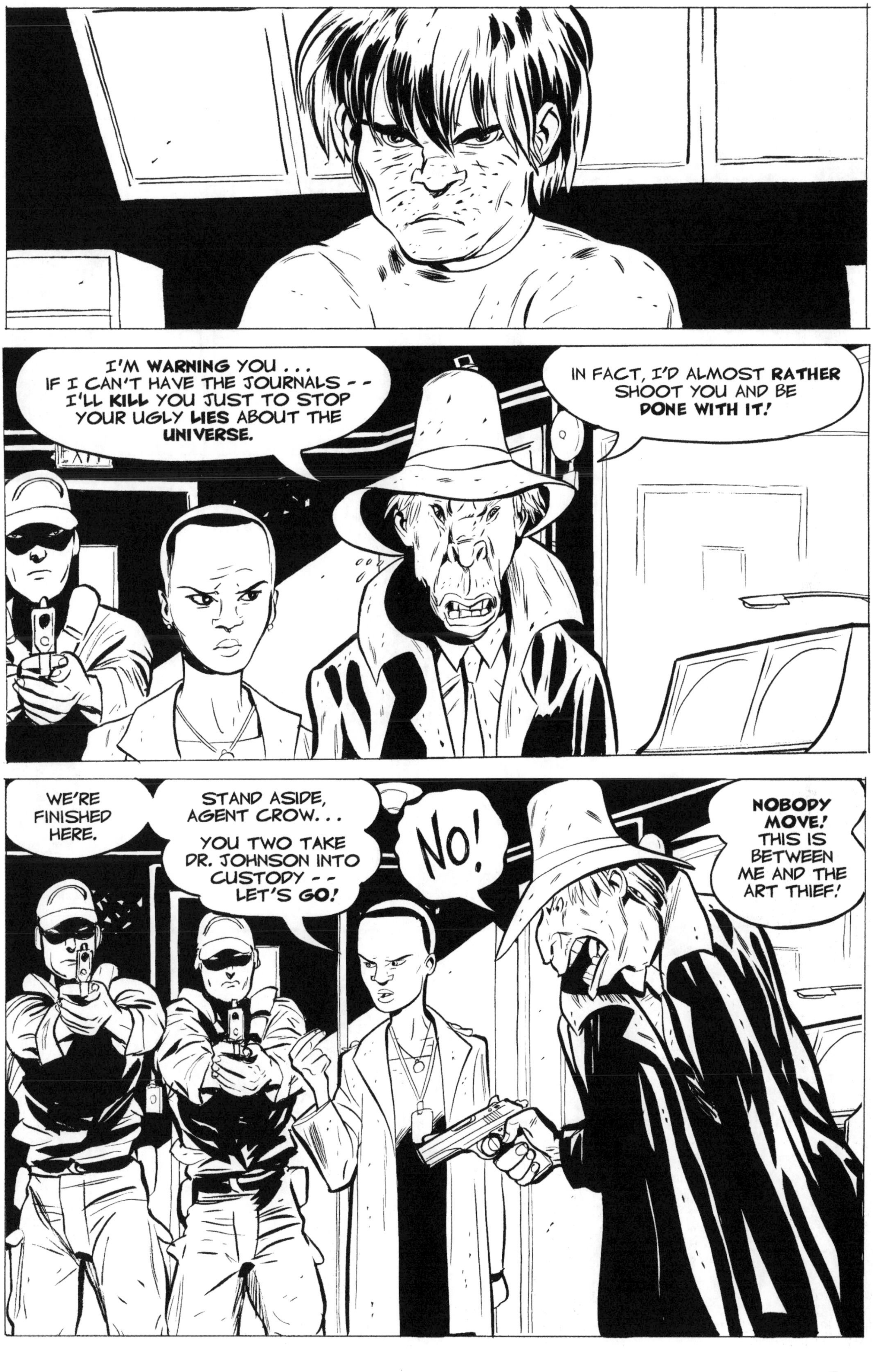
I'M WARNING YOU . . . IF I CAN'T HAVE THE JOURNALS - - I'LL KILL YOU JUST TO STOP YOUR UGLY LIES ABOUT THE UNIVERSE.
IN FACT, I'D ALMOST RATHER SHOOT YOU AND BE DONE WITH IT!
WE'RE FINISHED HERE.
STAND ASIDE, AGENT CROW. . .
YOU TWO TAKE DR. JOHNSON INTO CUSTODY - - LET'S GO!
No!
NOBODY MOVE! THIS IS BETWEEN ME AND THE ART THIEF!

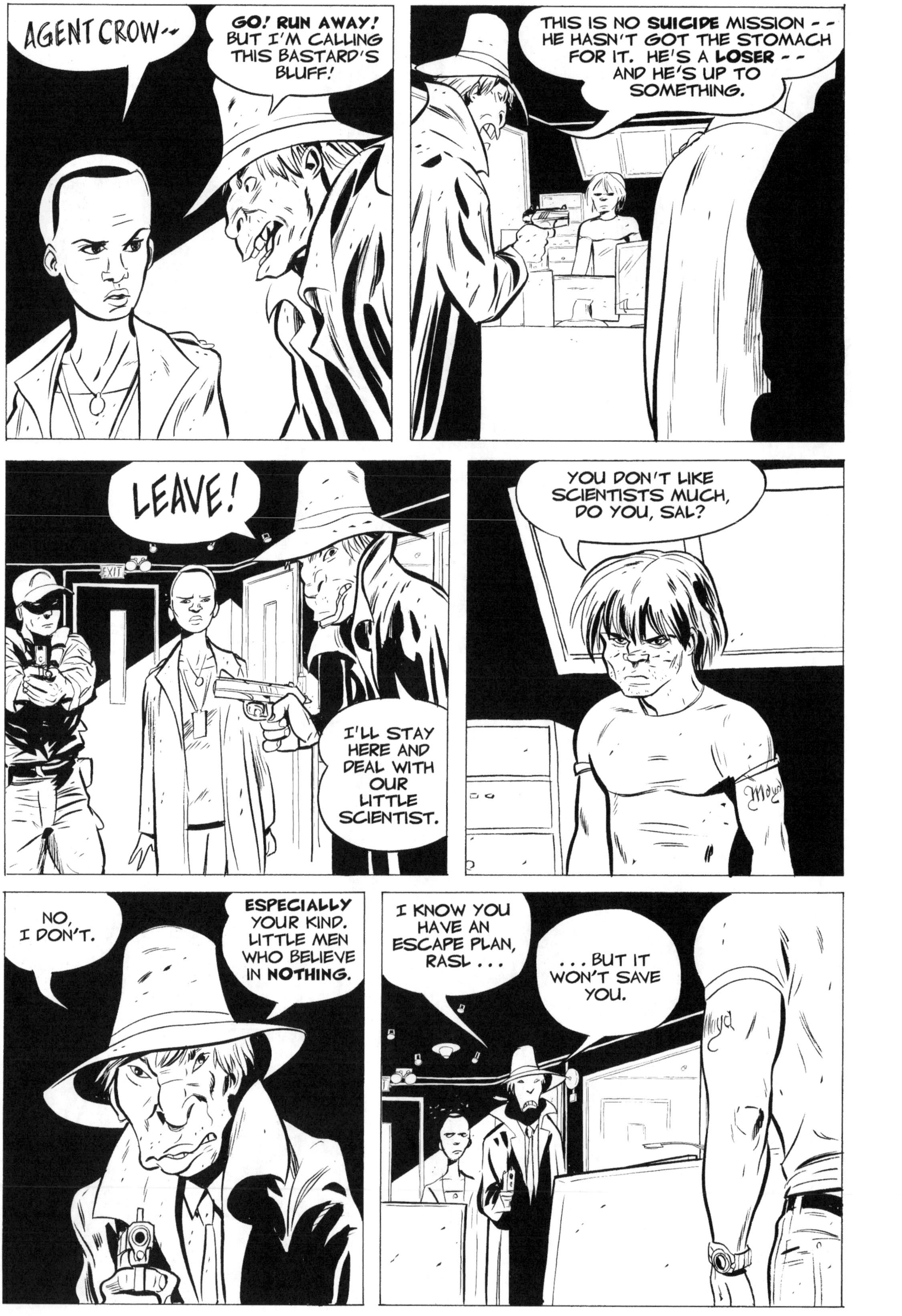
AGENT CROW--
GO! RUN AWAY! BUT I'M CALLING THIS BASTARD'S BLUFF!
THIS IS NO SUICIDE MISSION -- HE HASN'T GOT THE STOMACH FOR IT. HE'S A LOSER -- AND HE'S UP TO SOMETHING.
LEAVE!
EXIT
I'LL STAY HERE AND DEAL WITH OUR LITTLE SCIENTIST.
YOU DON'T LIKE SCIENTISTS MUCH, DO YOU, SAL?
NO, I DON'T.
ESPECIALLY YOUR KIND. LITTLE MEN WHO BELIEVE IN NOTHING.
I KNOW YOU HAVE AN ESCAPE PLAN, RASL . . .
. . . BUT IT WON'T SAVE YOU.

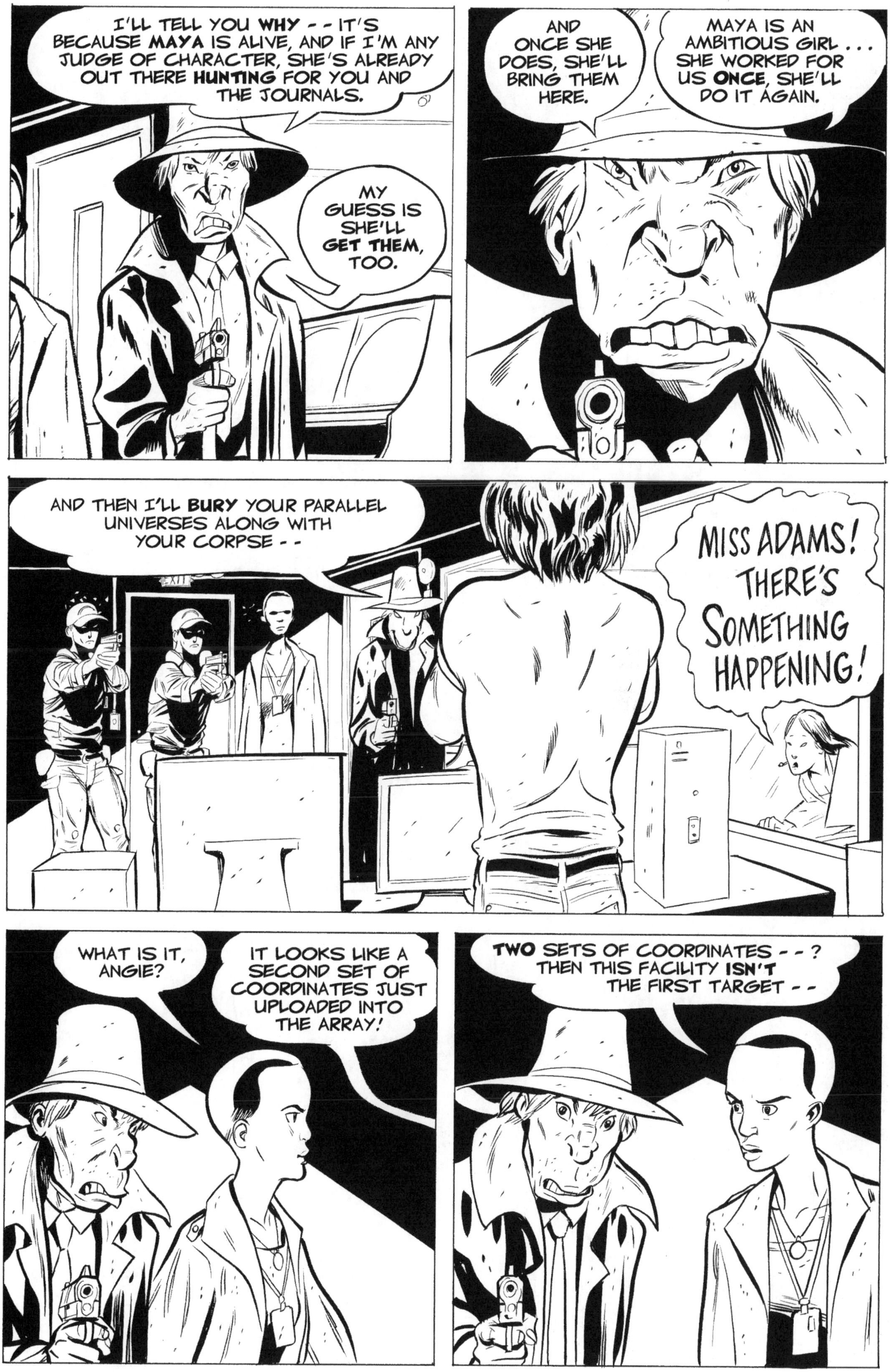
I'LL TELL YOU WHY - - IT'S BECAUSE MAYA IS ALIVE, AND IF I'M ANY JUDGE OF CHARACTER, SHE'S ALREADY OUT THERE HUNTING FOR YOU AND THE JOURNALS.
MY GUESS IS SHE'LL GET THEM, TOO.
AND ONCE SHE DOES, SHE'LL BRING THEM HERE.
MAYA IS AN AMBITIOUS GIRL . . . SHE WORKED FOR US ONCE, SHE'LL DO IT AGAIN.
AND THEN I'LL BURY YOUR PARALLEL UNIVERSES ALONG WITH YOUR CORPSE - -
EXIT
MISS ADAMS! THERE'S SOMETHING HAPPENING!
WHAT IS IT, ANGIE?
IT LOOKS LIKE A SECOND SET OF COORDINATES JUST UPLOADED INTO THE ARRAY!
TWO SETS OF COORDINATES - - ? THEN THIS FACILITY ISN'T THE FIRST TARGET - -

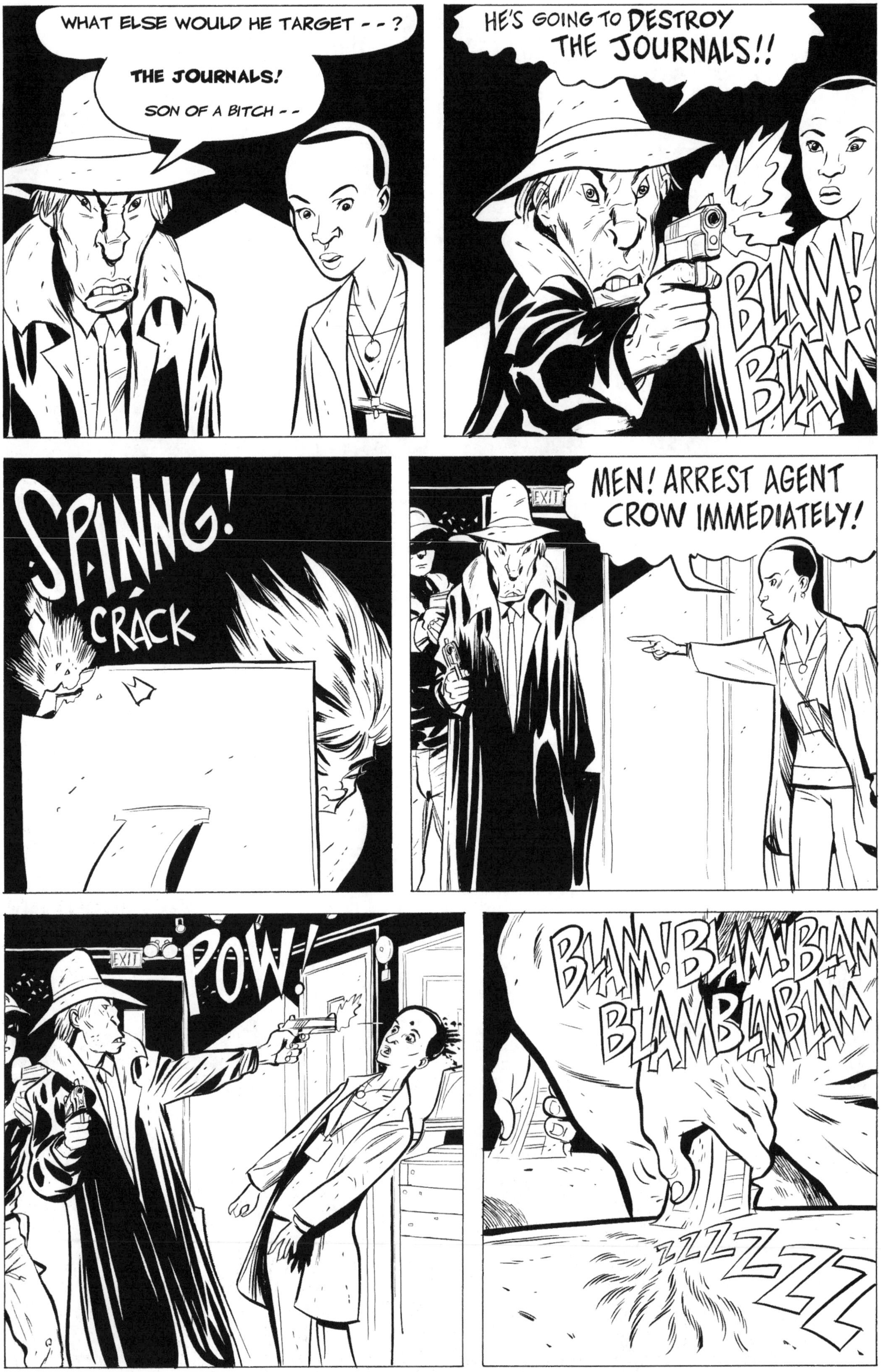
WHAT ELSE WOULD HE TARGET - - ?
THE JOURNALS! SON OF A BITCH - -
HE'S GOING TO DESTROY THE JOURNALS!!
BLAM! BLAM!
SPINNG!
CRACK
MEN! ARREST AGENT CROW IMMEDIATELY!
EXIT
POW!
EXIT
BLAM! BLAM! BLAM BLAM BLAM BLAM
ZZZZZZZ

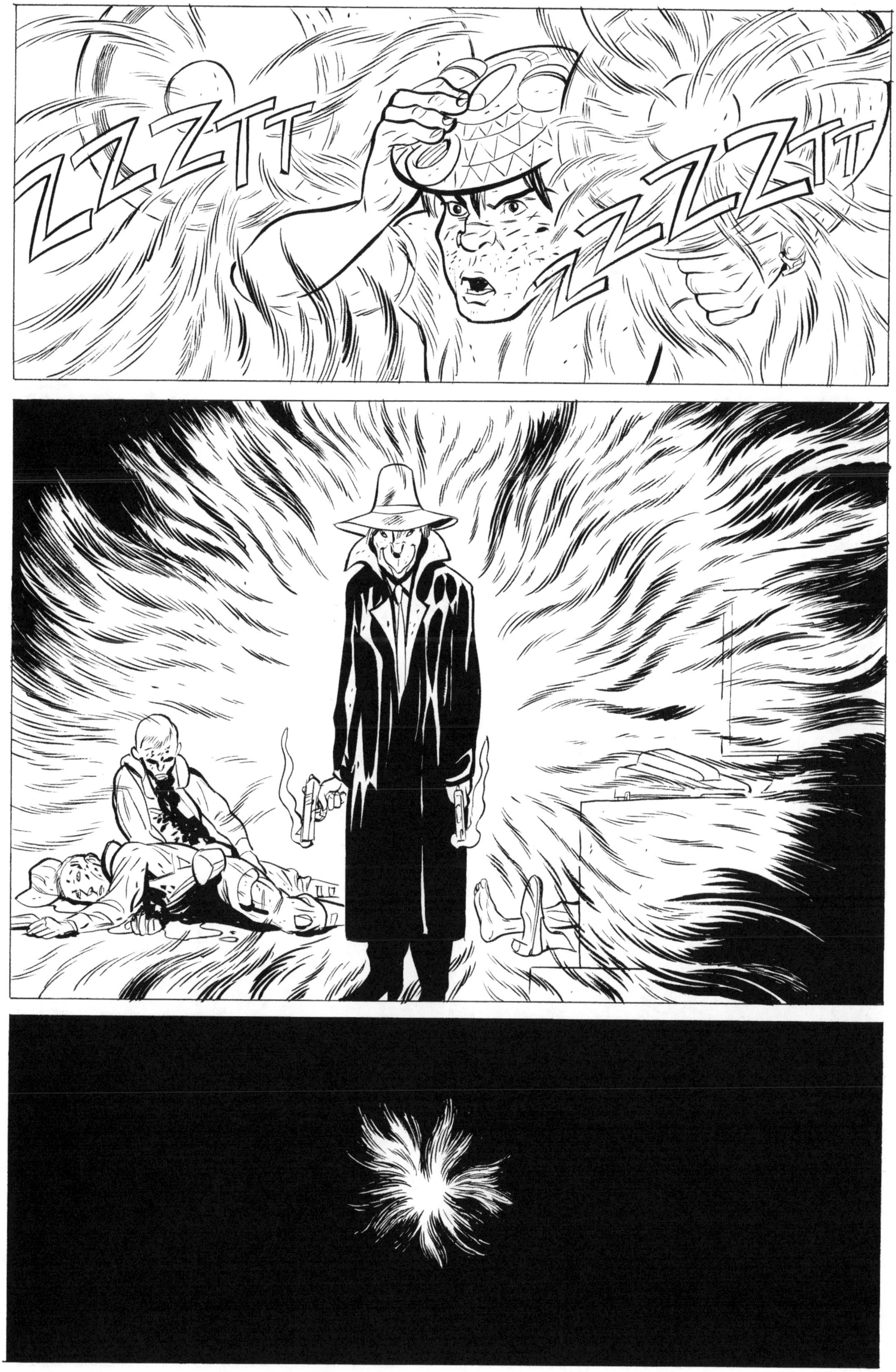
ZZZZTT
ZZZZZTT

CHUHF

AAAAAAAA--

UH, OH.
BLACKED
OUT --

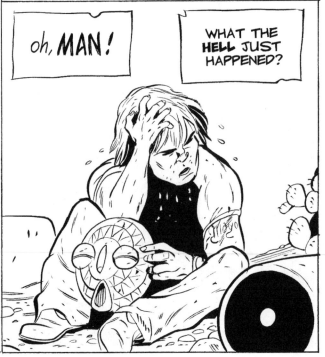

oh, MAN!

WHAT THE
HELL JUST
HAPPENED?

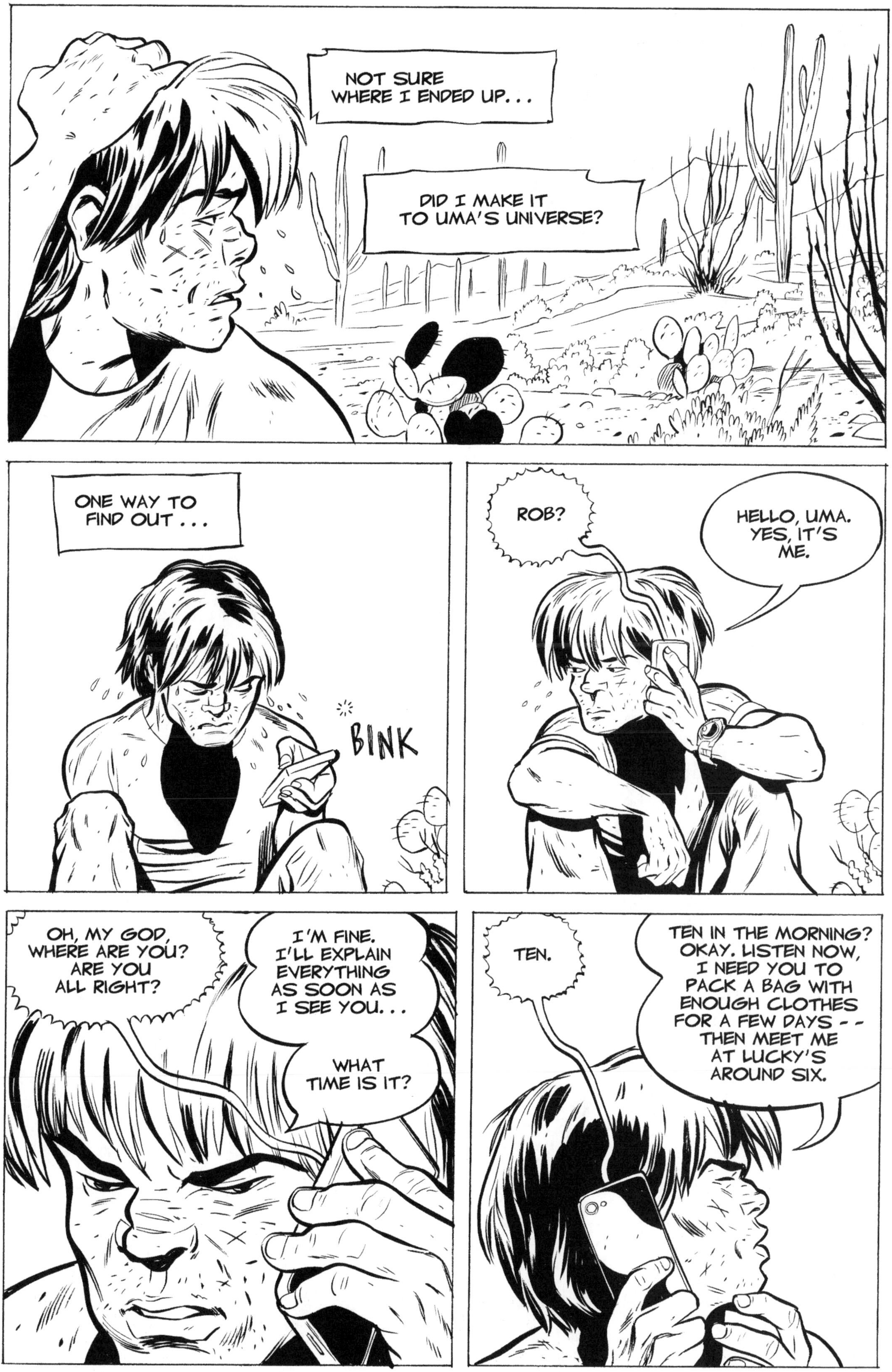
NOT SURE WHERE I ENDED UP...
DID I MAKE IT TO UMA'S UNIVERSE?
ONE WAY TO FIND OUT...
BINK
ROB?
HELLO, UMA. YES, IT'S ME.
OH, MY GOD, WHERE ARE YOU? ARE YOU ALL RIGHT?
I'M FINE. I'LL EXPLAIN EVERYTHING AS SOON AS I SEE YOU...
WHAT TIME IS IT?
TEN.
TEN IN THE MORNING? OKAY. LISTEN NOW, I NEED YOU TO PACK A BAG WITH ENOUGH CLOTHES FOR A FEW DAYS -- THEN MEET ME AT LUCKY'S AROUND SIX.

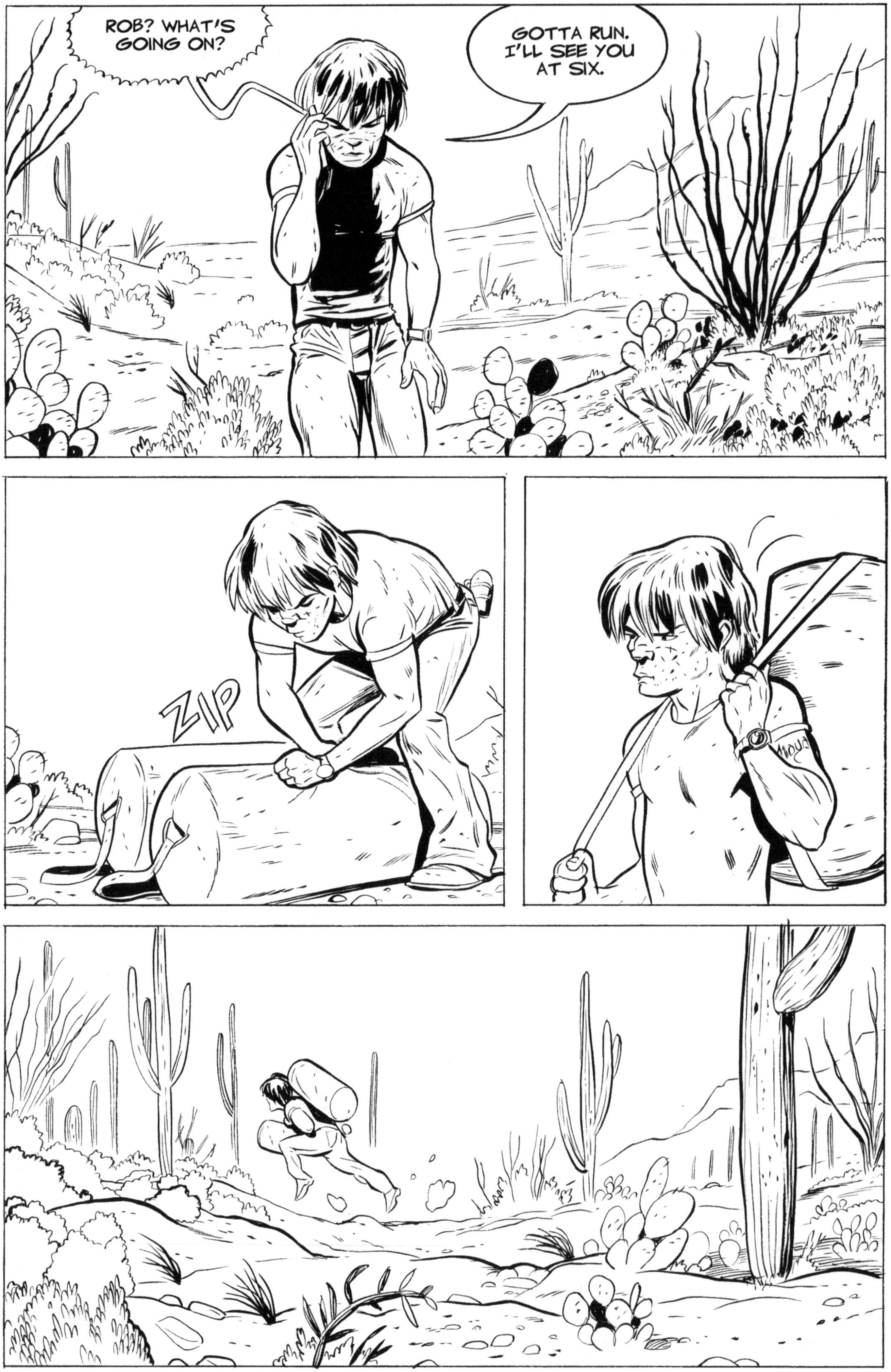
ROB? WHAT'S GOING ON?
GOTTA RUN. I'LL SEE YOU AT SIX.
ZIP

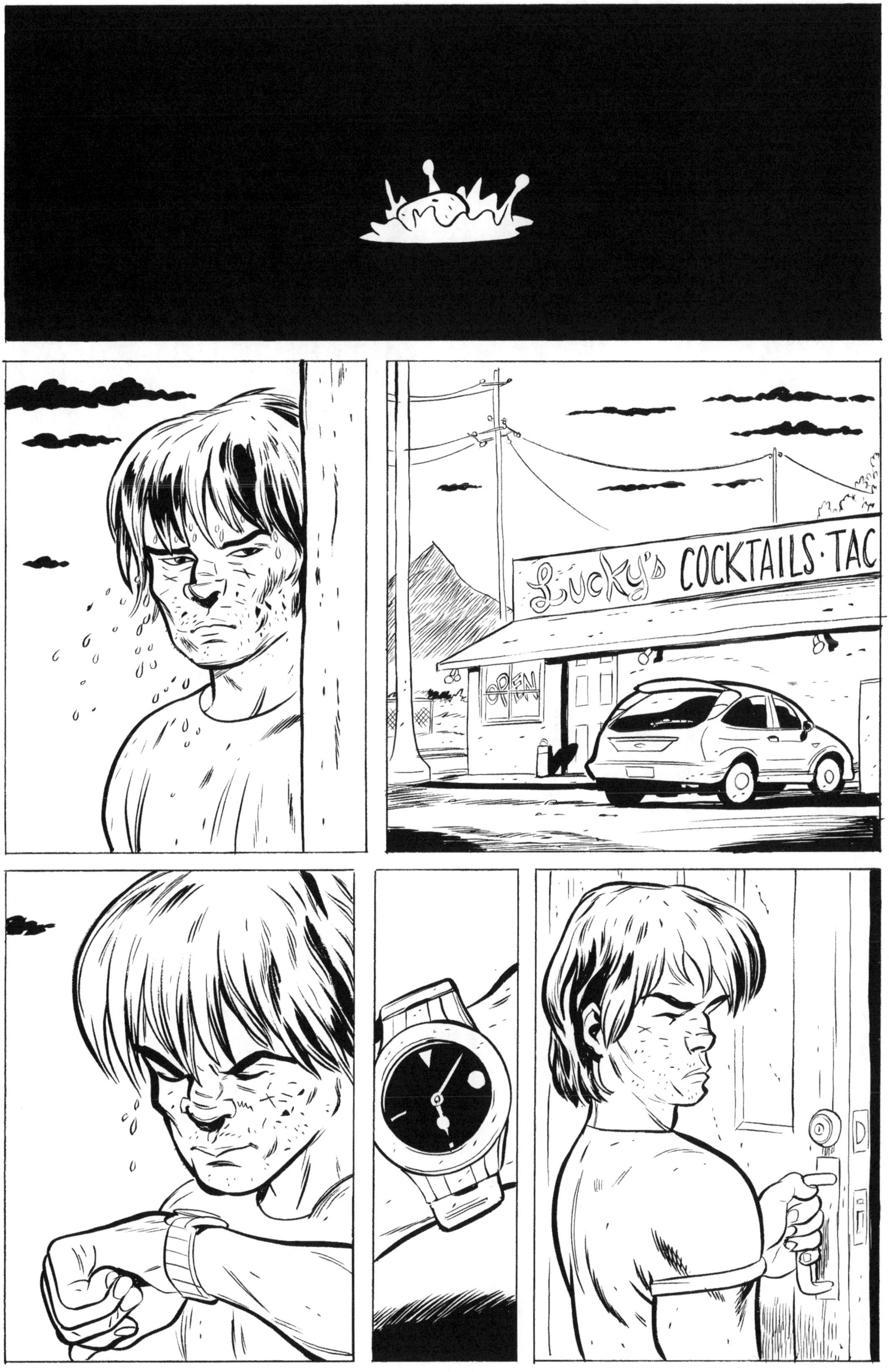
Lucky's COCKTAILS·TAC
OPEN

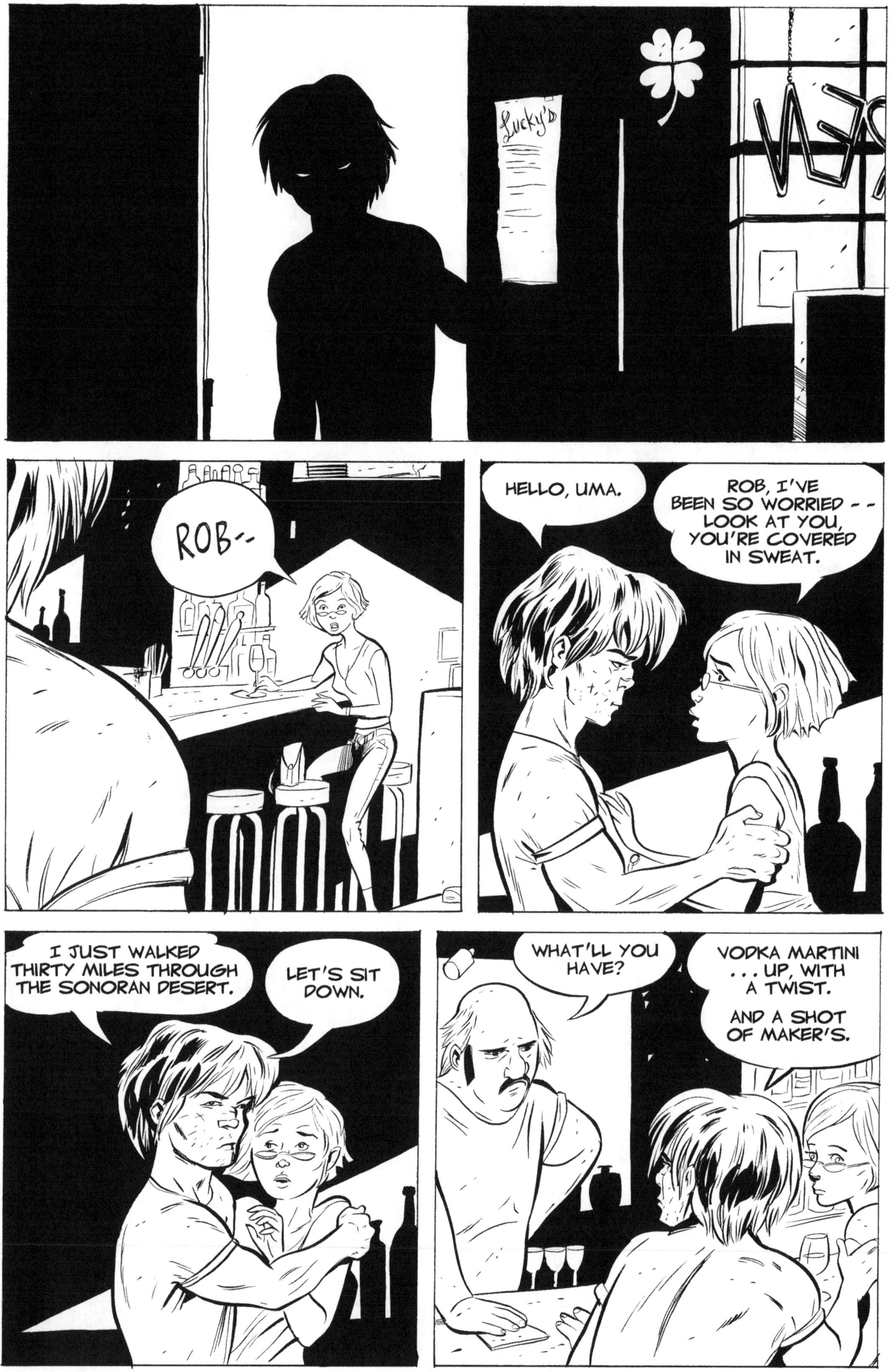
Lucky's
ROB--
HELLO, UMA.
ROB, I'VE BEEN SO WORRIED -- LOOK AT YOU, YOU'RE COVERED IN SWEAT.
I JUST WALKED THIRTY MILES THROUGH THE SONORAN DESERT.
LET'S SIT DOWN.
WHAT'LL YOU HAVE?
VODKA MARTINI . . . UP, WITH A TWIST.
AND A SHOT OF MAKER'S.

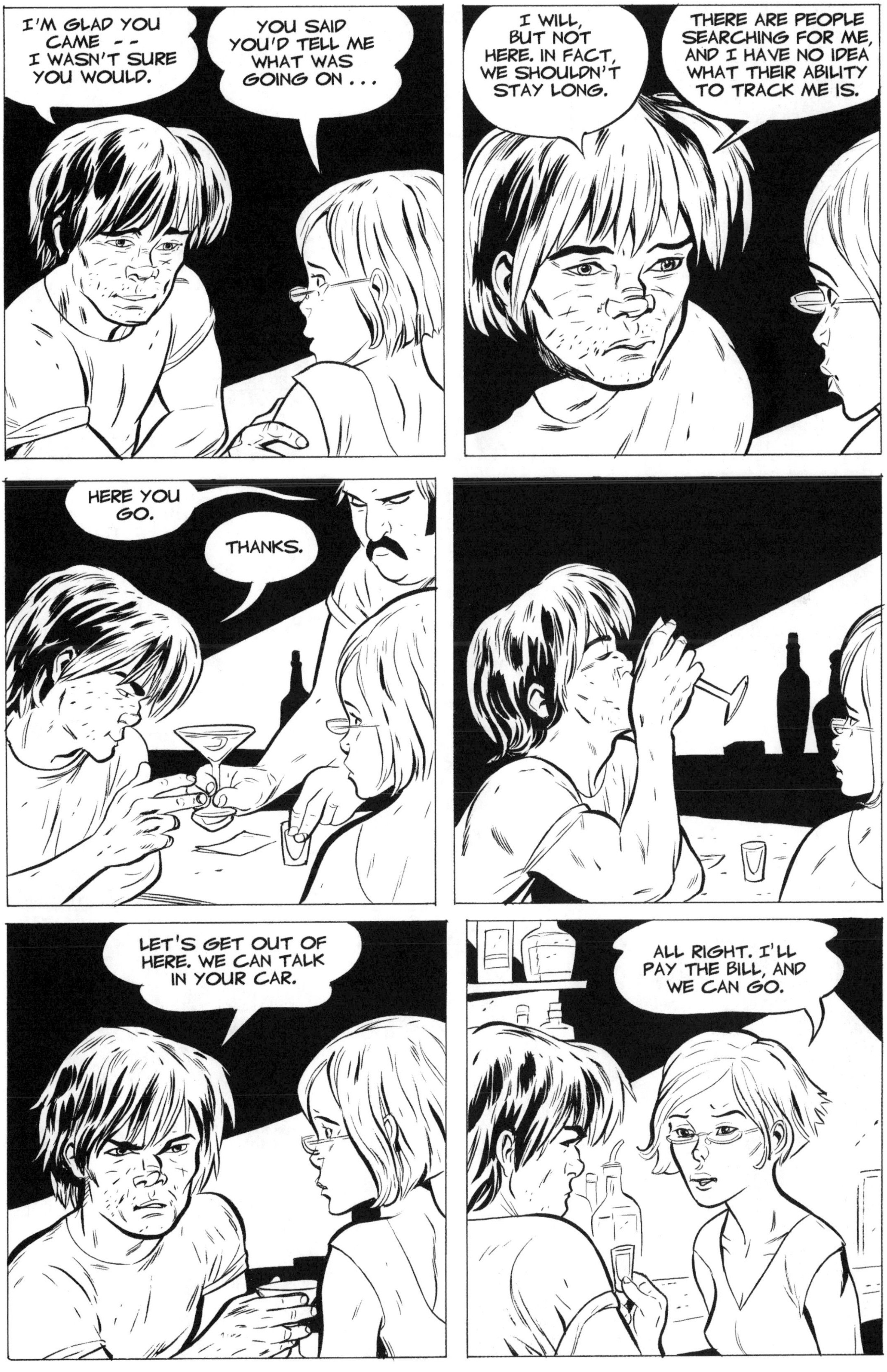
I'M GLAD YOU CAME -- I WASN'T SURE YOU WOULD.
YOU SAID YOU'D TELL ME WHAT WAS GOING ON . . .
I WILL, BUT NOT HERE. IN FACT, WE SHOULDN'T STAY LONG.
THERE ARE PEOPLE SEARCHING FOR ME, AND I HAVE NO IDEA WHAT THEIR ABILITY TO TRACK ME IS.
HERE YOU GO.
THANKS.
LET'S GET OUT OF HERE. WE CAN TALK IN YOUR CAR.
ALL RIGHT. I'LL PAY THE BILL, AND WE CAN GO.

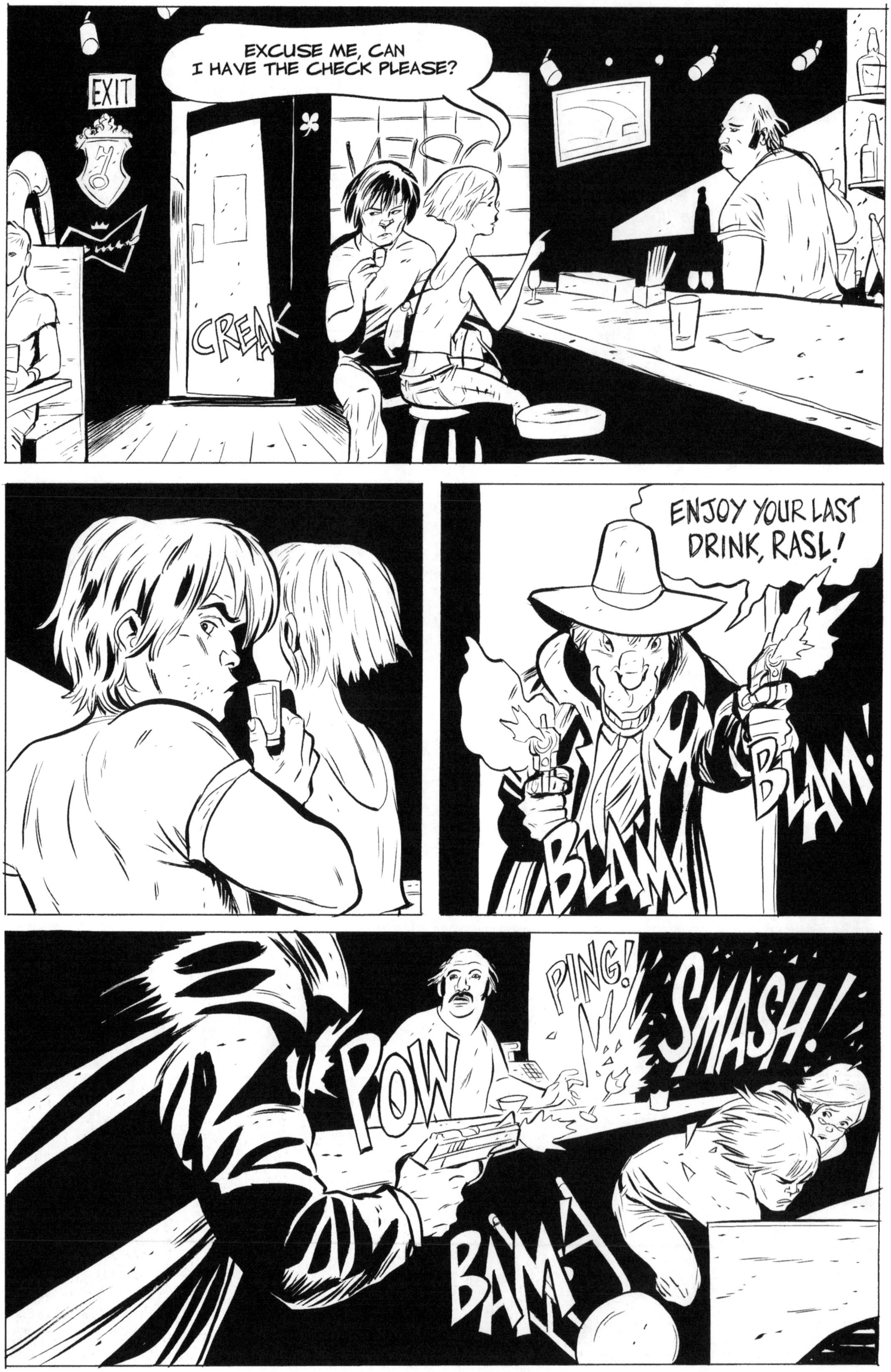
EXCUSE ME, CAN I HAVE THE CHECK PLEASE?
EXIT
CREAK
ENJOY YOUR LAST DRINK, RASL!
BLAM
BLAM!
POW
PING!
SMASH!
BAM!

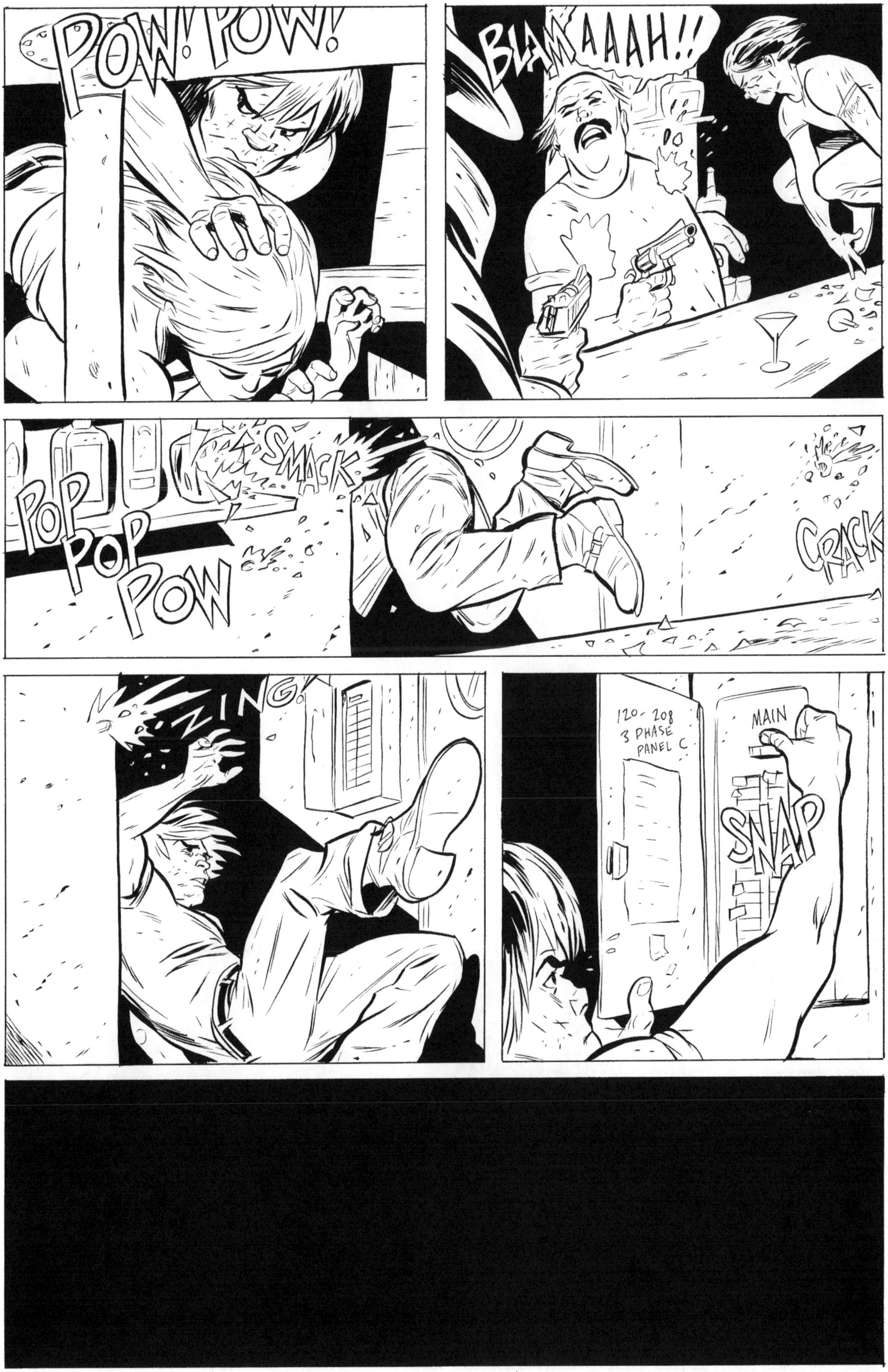
POW! POW!
BLAM
AAAH!!
SMACK
POP
POP
POW
CRACK
ZING!
120-208
3 PHASE
PANEL C
MAIN
SNAP

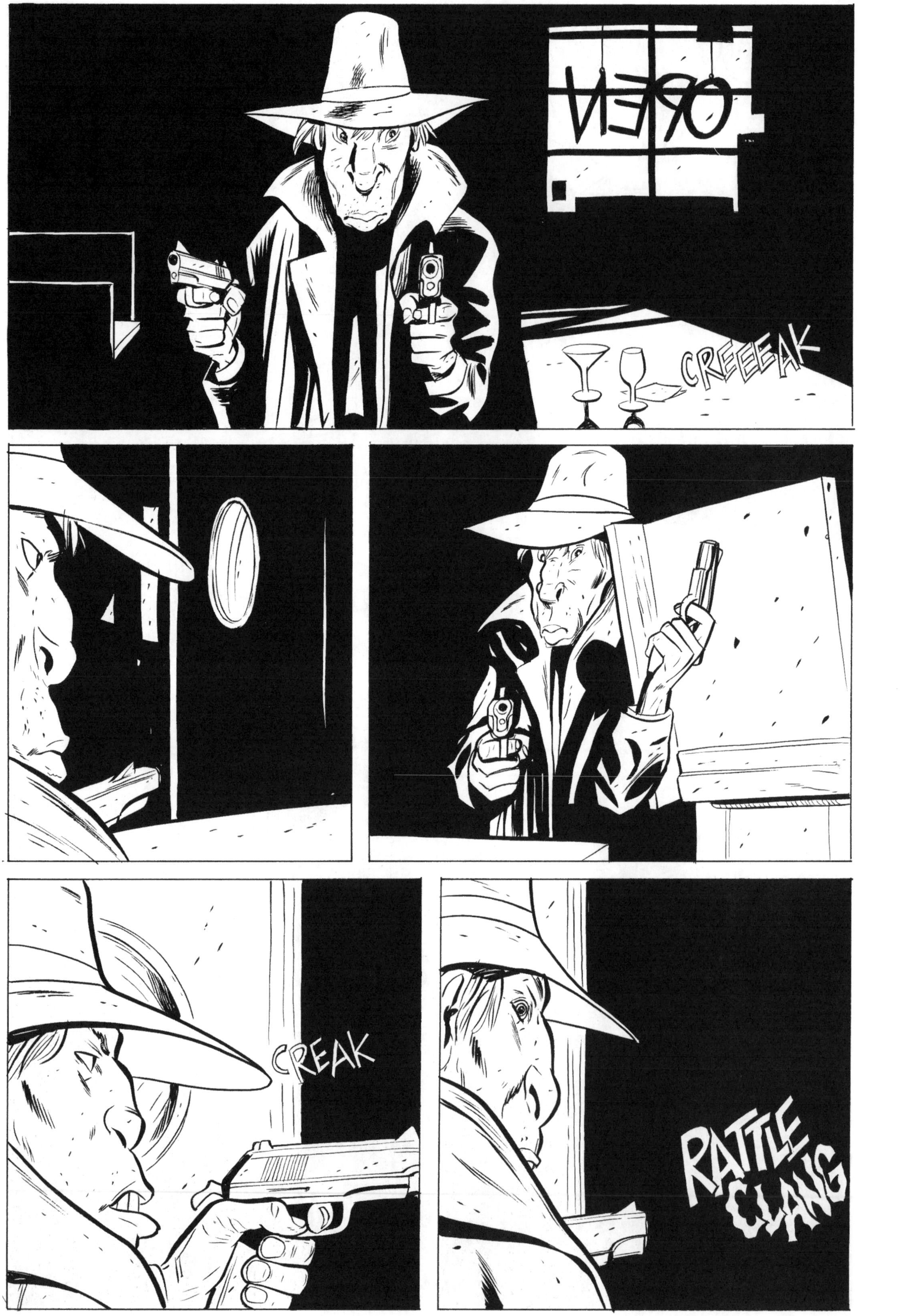
OPEN
CREEEAK
CREAK
RATTLE CLANG

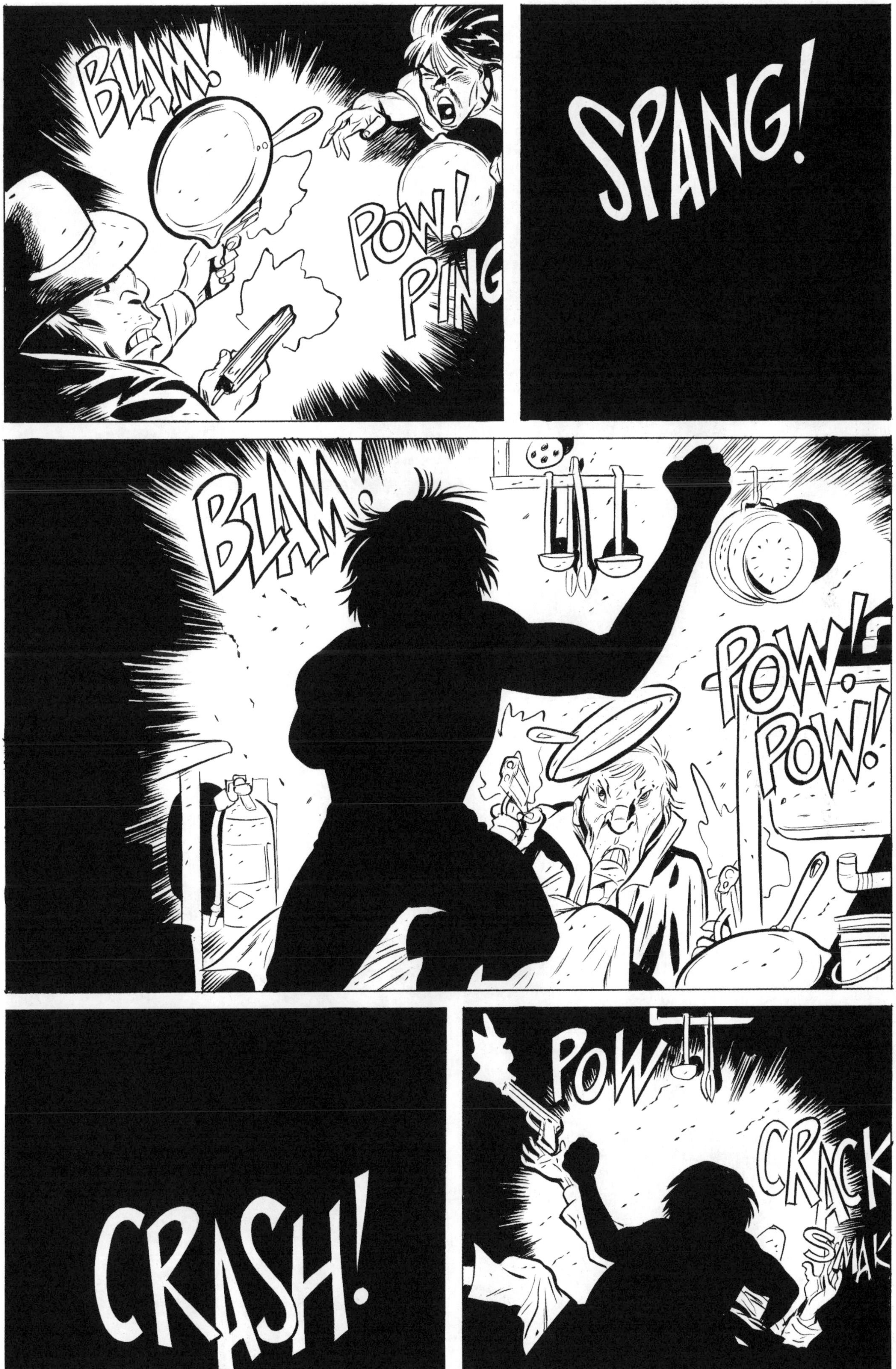
BLAM!
POW!
PING
SPANG!
BLAM!
POW!
POW!
CRASH!
POW
CRACK
SMAK

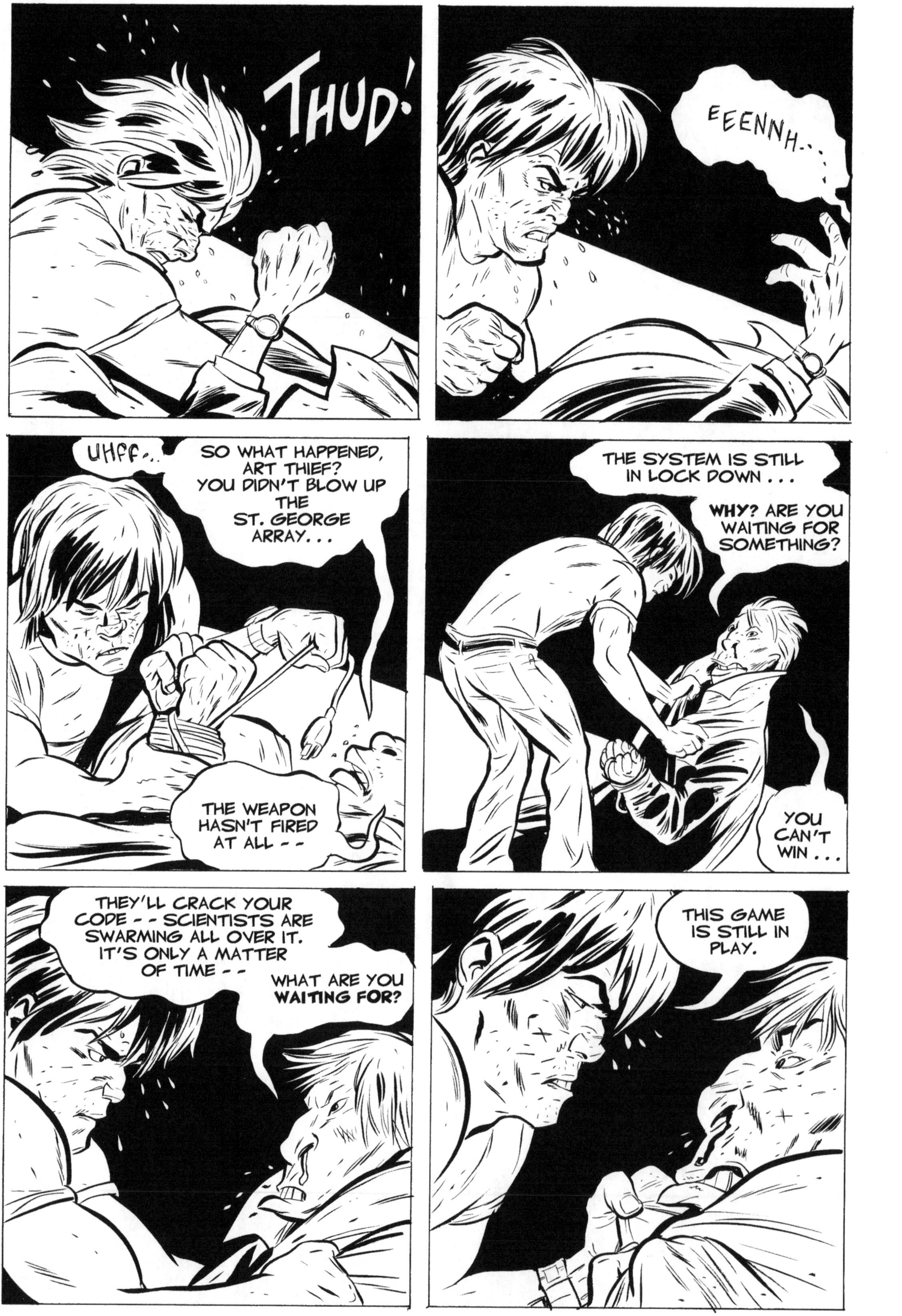
THUD!
EEENNH...
UHFF...
SO WHAT HAPPENED, ART THIEF? YOU DIDN'T BLOW UP THE ST. GEORGE ARRAY...
THE WEAPON HASN'T FIRED AT ALL --
THE SYSTEM IS STILL IN LOCK DOWN...
WHY? ARE YOU WAITING FOR SOMETHING?
YOU CAN'T WIN...
THEY'LL CRACK YOUR CODE -- SCIENTISTS ARE SWARMING ALL OVER IT. IT'S ONLY A MATTER OF TIME --
WHAT ARE YOU WAITING FOR?
THIS GAME IS STILL IN PLAY.

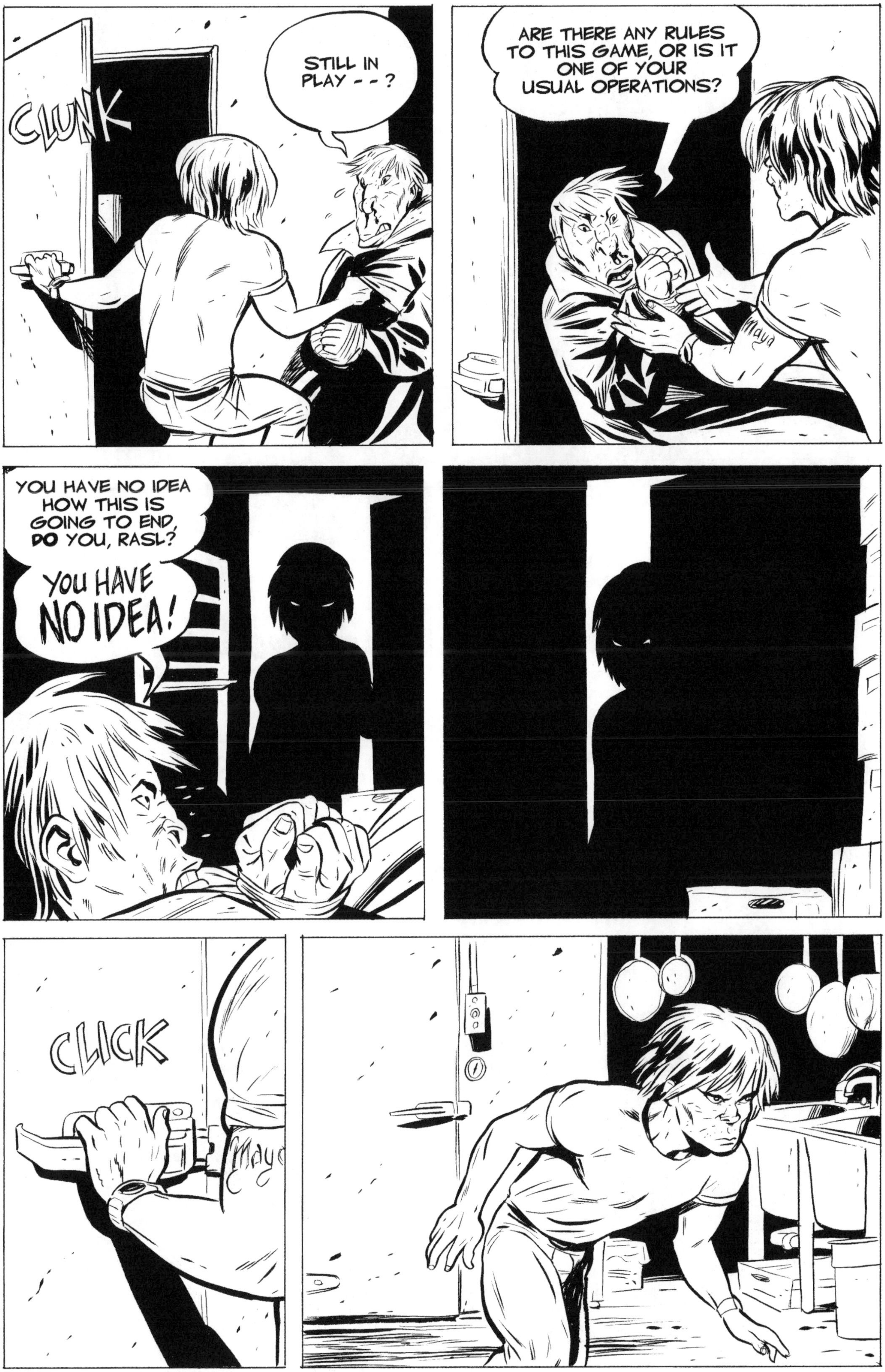
CLUNK
STILL IN PLAY - - ?
ARE THERE ANY RULES TO THIS GAME, OR IS IT ONE OF YOUR USUAL OPERATIONS?
Maya
YOU HAVE NO IDEA HOW THIS IS GOING TO END, DO YOU, RASL?
YOU HAVE NO IDEA!
CLICK
Maya

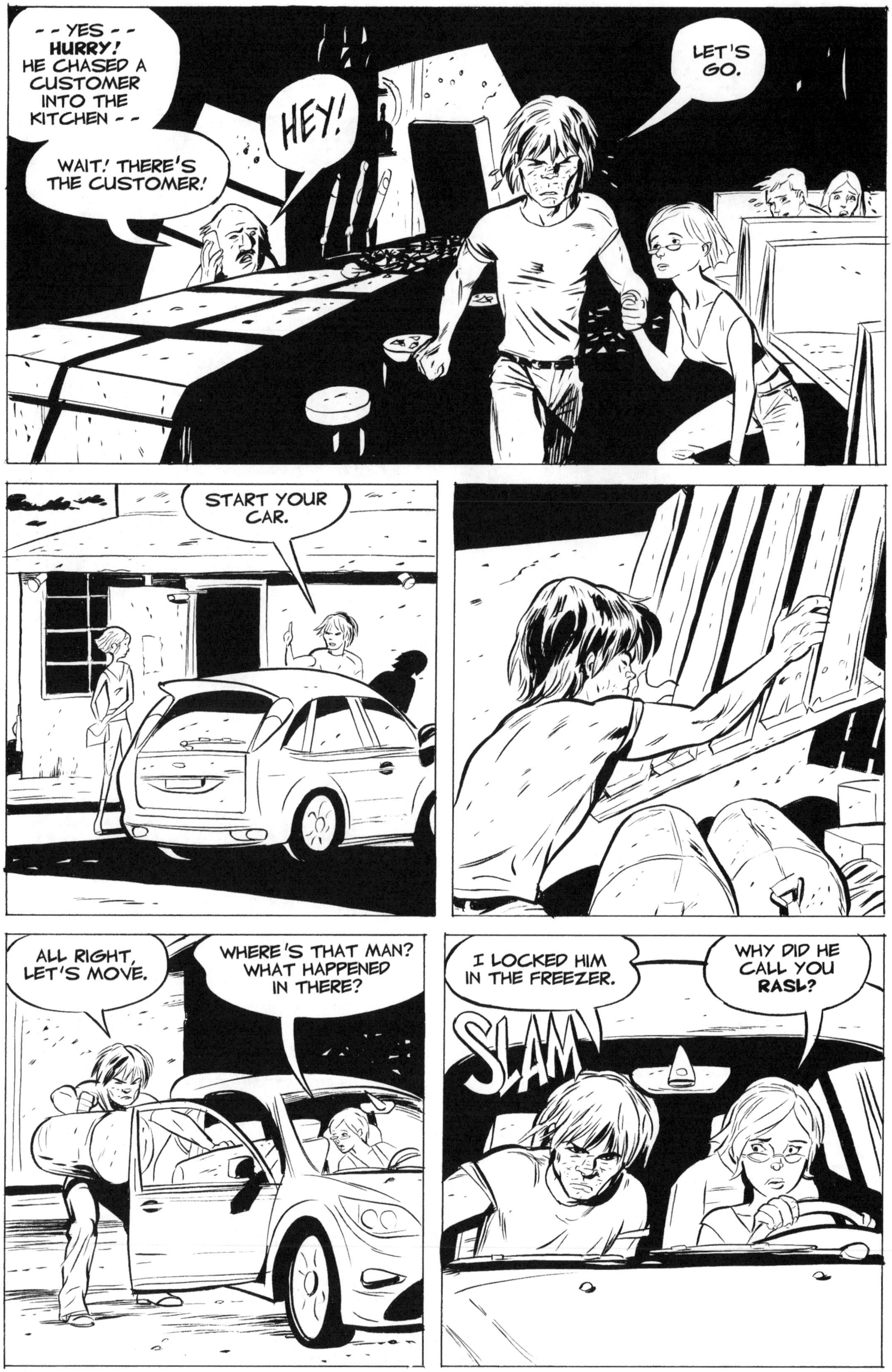

- - YES - - **HURRY!** HE CHASED A CUSTOMER INTO THE KITCHEN - -
WAIT! THERE'S THE CUSTOMER!
HEY!
LET'S GO.
START YOUR CAR.
ALL RIGHT, LET'S MOVE.
WHERE'S THAT MAN? WHAT HAPPENED IN THERE?
SLAM
I LOCKED HIM IN THE FREEZER.
WHY DID HE CALL YOU **RASL?**

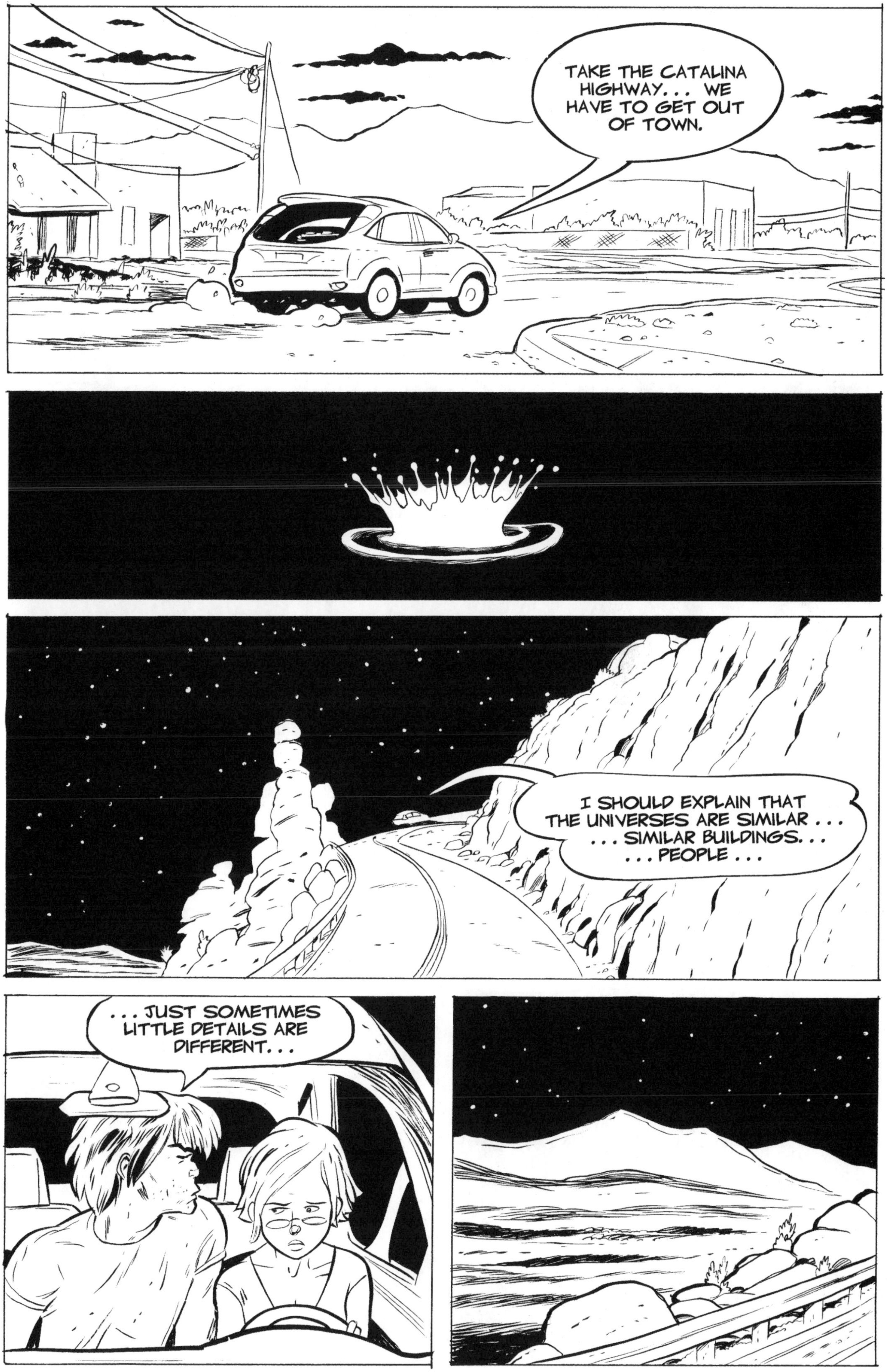
TAKE THE CATALINA HIGHWAY... WE HAVE TO GET OUT OF TOWN.
I SHOULD EXPLAIN THAT THE UNIVERSES ARE SIMILAR ... ... SIMILAR BUILDINGS... ... PEOPLE ...
... JUST SOMETIMES LITTLE DETAILS ARE DIFFERENT...

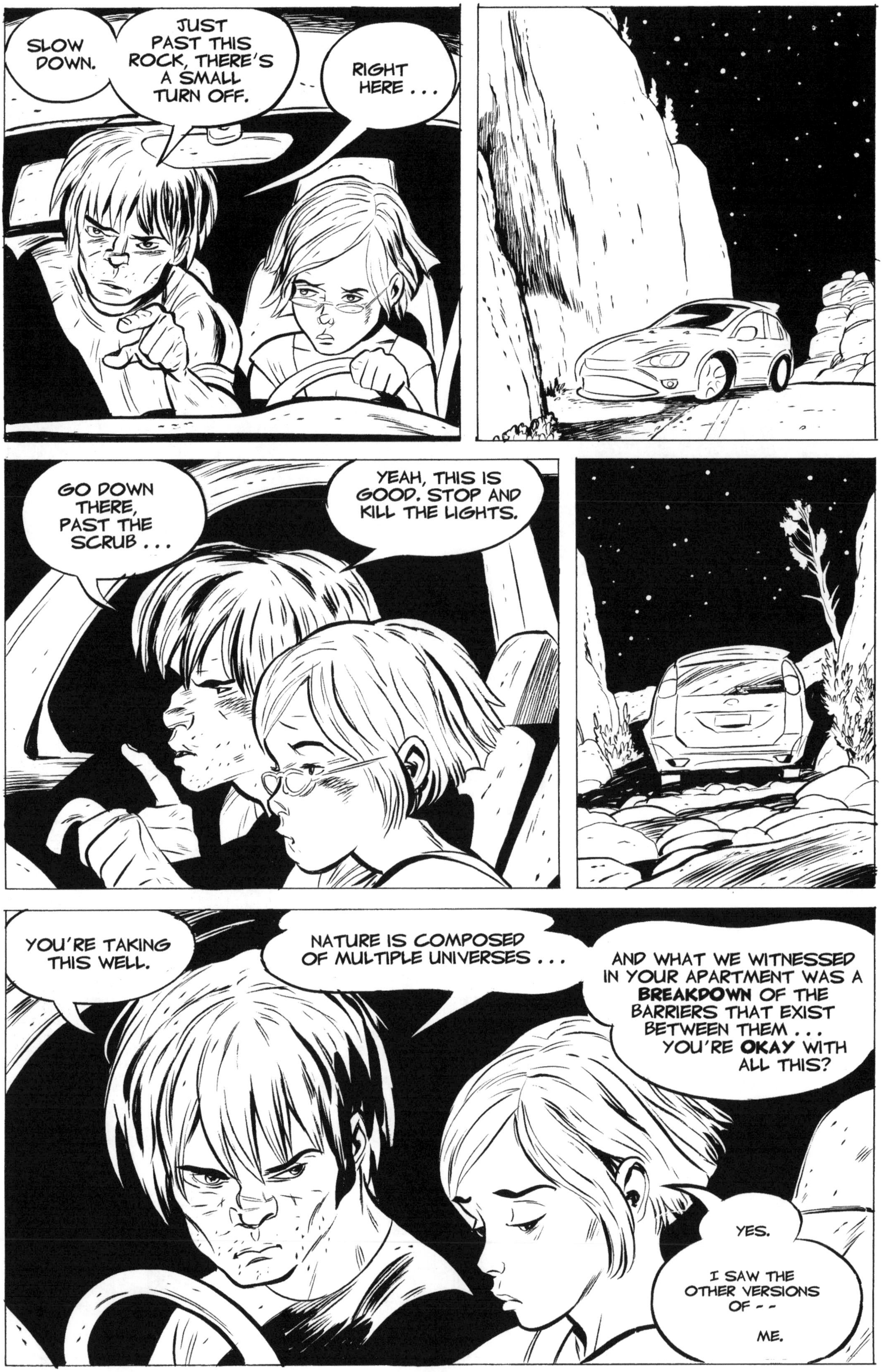
SLOW DOWN.
JUST PAST THIS ROCK, THERE'S A SMALL TURN OFF.
RIGHT HERE . . .
GO DOWN THERE, PAST THE SCRUB . . .
YEAH, THIS IS GOOD. STOP AND KILL THE LIGHTS.
YOU'RE TAKING THIS WELL.
NATURE IS COMPOSED OF MULTIPLE UNIVERSES . . .
AND WHAT WE WITNESSED IN YOUR APARTMENT WAS A **BREAKDOWN** OF THE BARRIERS THAT EXIST BETWEEN THEM . . .
YOU'RE **OKAY** WITH ALL THIS?
YES.
I SAW THE OTHER VERSIONS OF - -
ME.

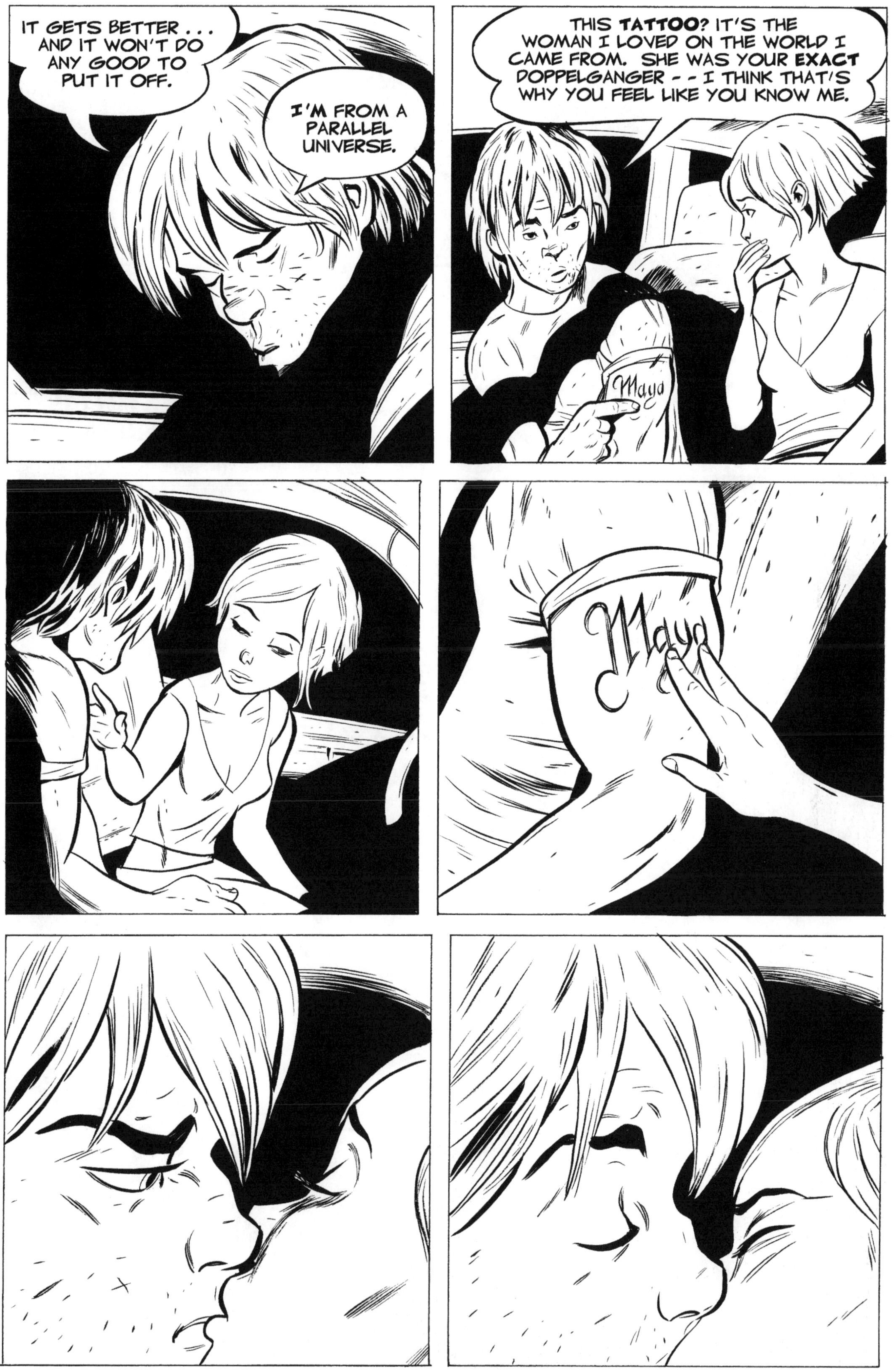
IT GETS BETTER . . . AND IT WON'T DO ANY GOOD TO PUT IT OFF.
I'M FROM A PARALLEL UNIVERSE.
THIS TATTOO? IT'S THE WOMAN I LOVED ON THE WORLD I CAME FROM. SHE WAS YOUR EXACT DOPPELGANGER - - I THINK THAT'S WHY YOU FEEL LIKE YOU KNOW ME.
Maya
Maya

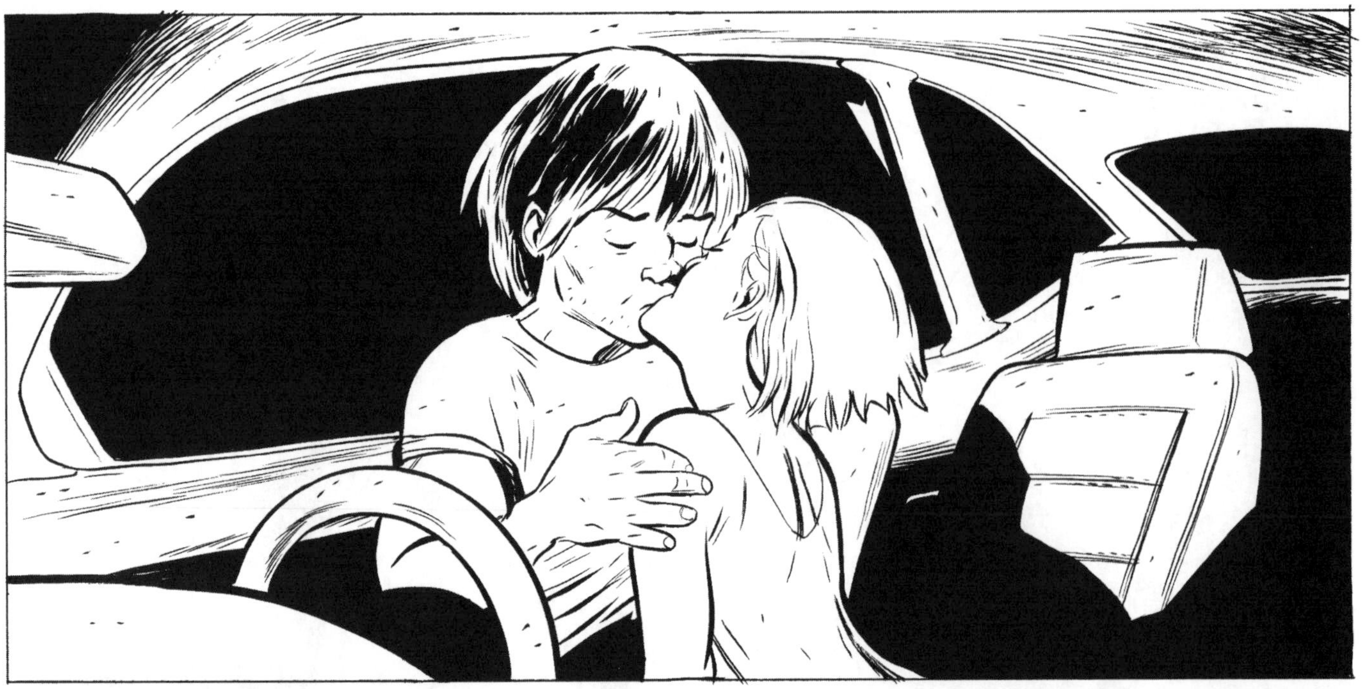

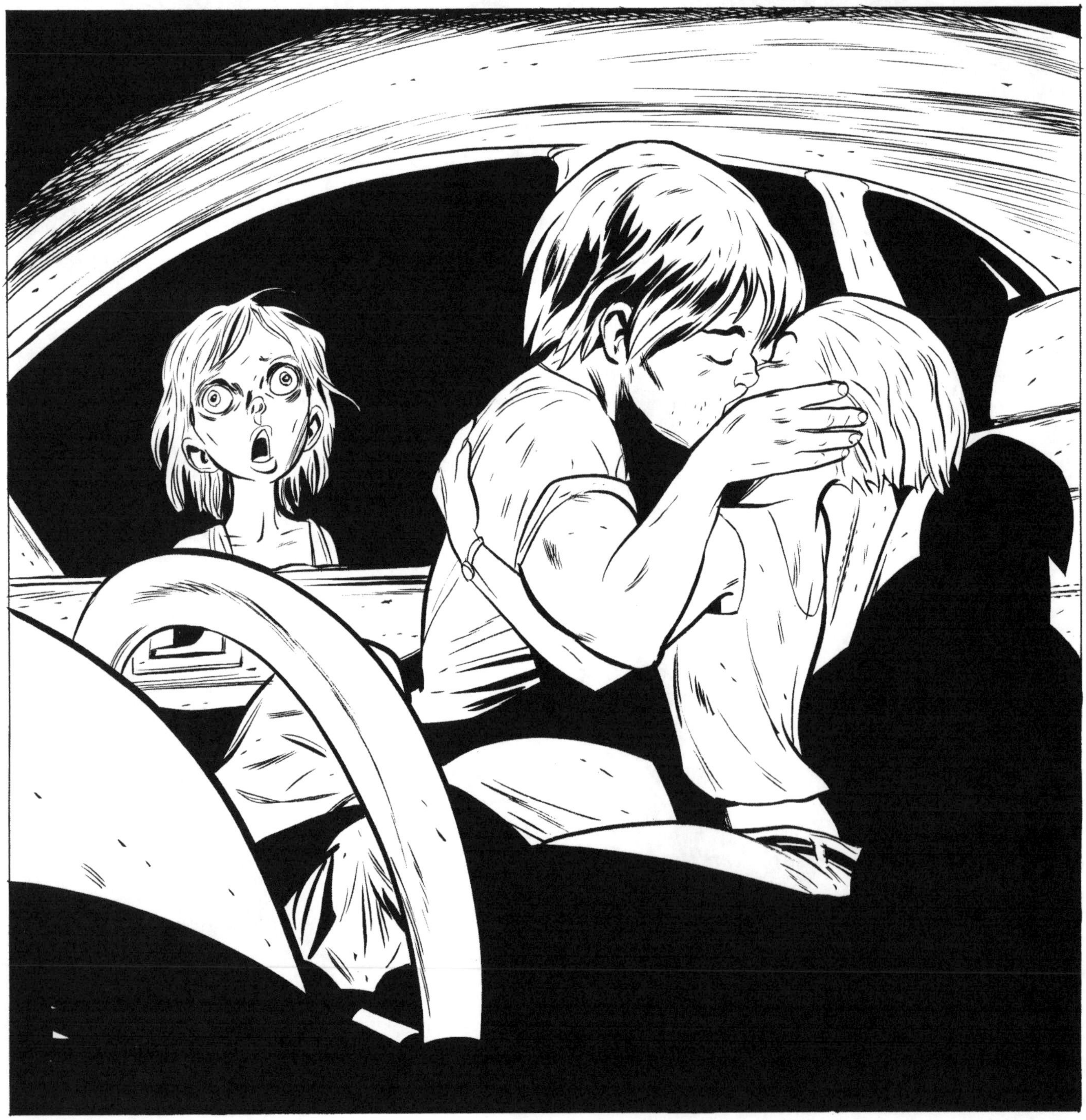

15.
TAKING THE FALL

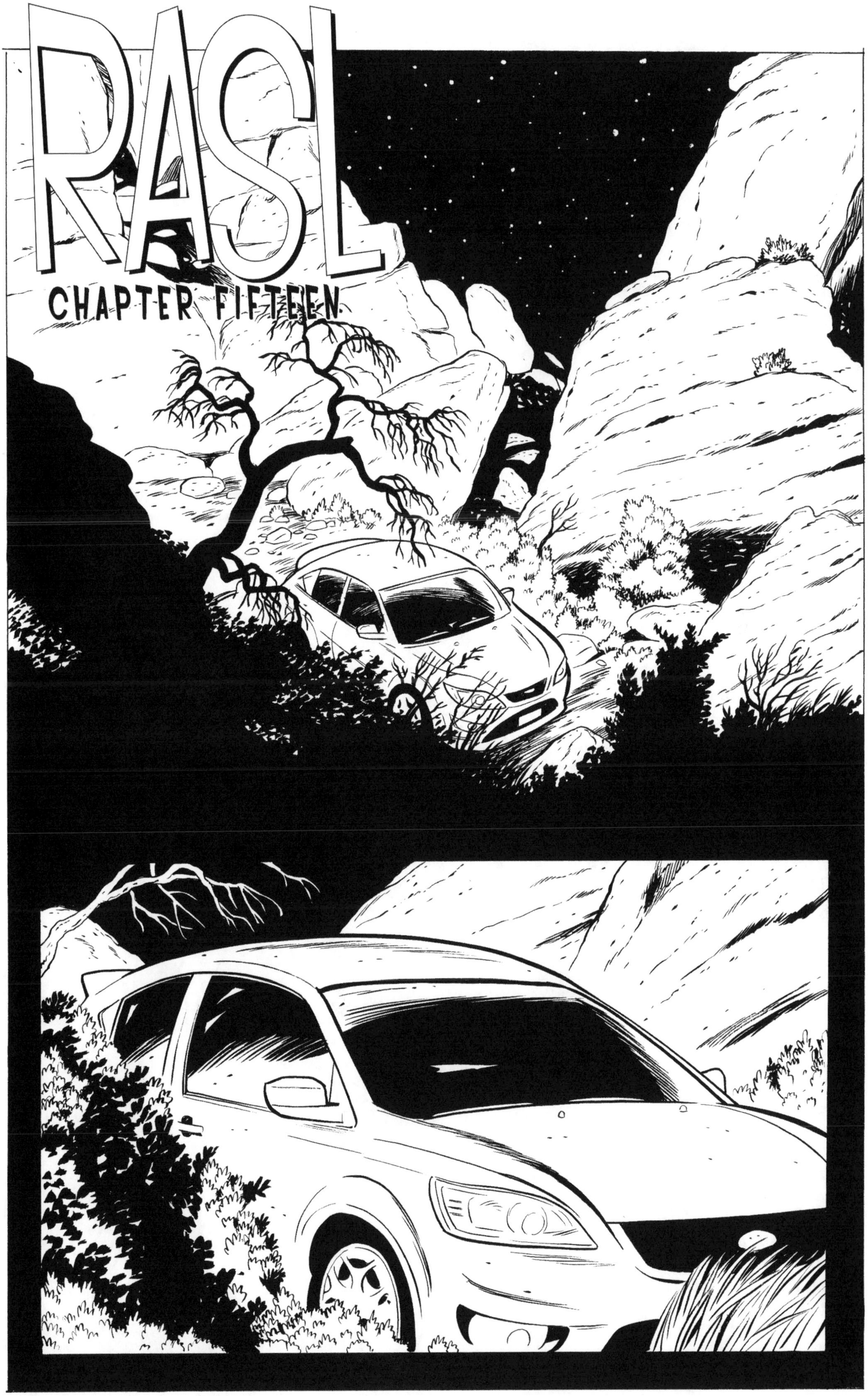
RASL
CHAPTER FIFTEEN

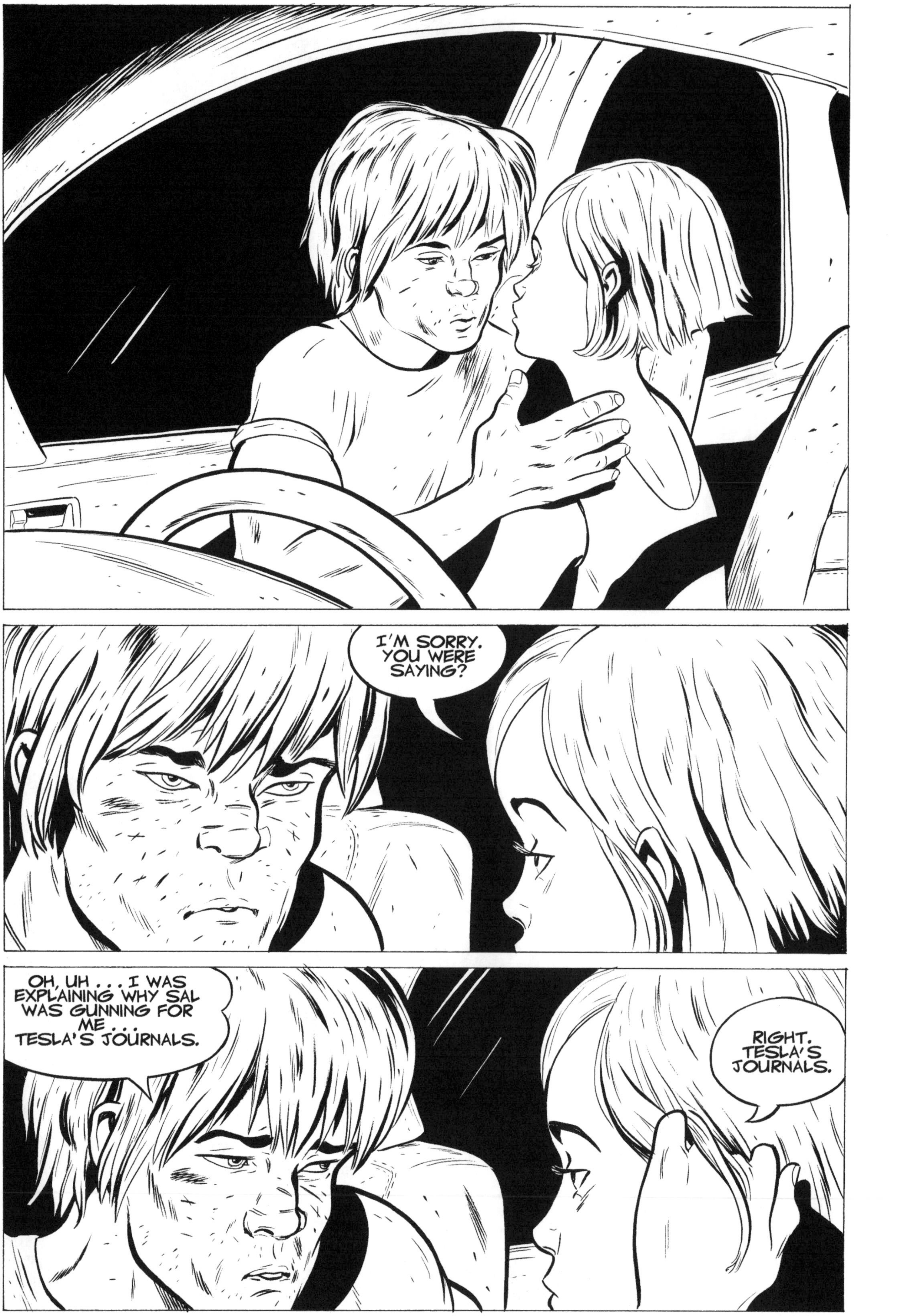
I'M SORRY. YOU WERE SAYING?
OH, UH . . . I WAS EXPLAINING WHY SAL WAS GUNNING FOR ME . . . TESLA'S JOURNALS.
RIGHT. TESLA'S JOURNALS.

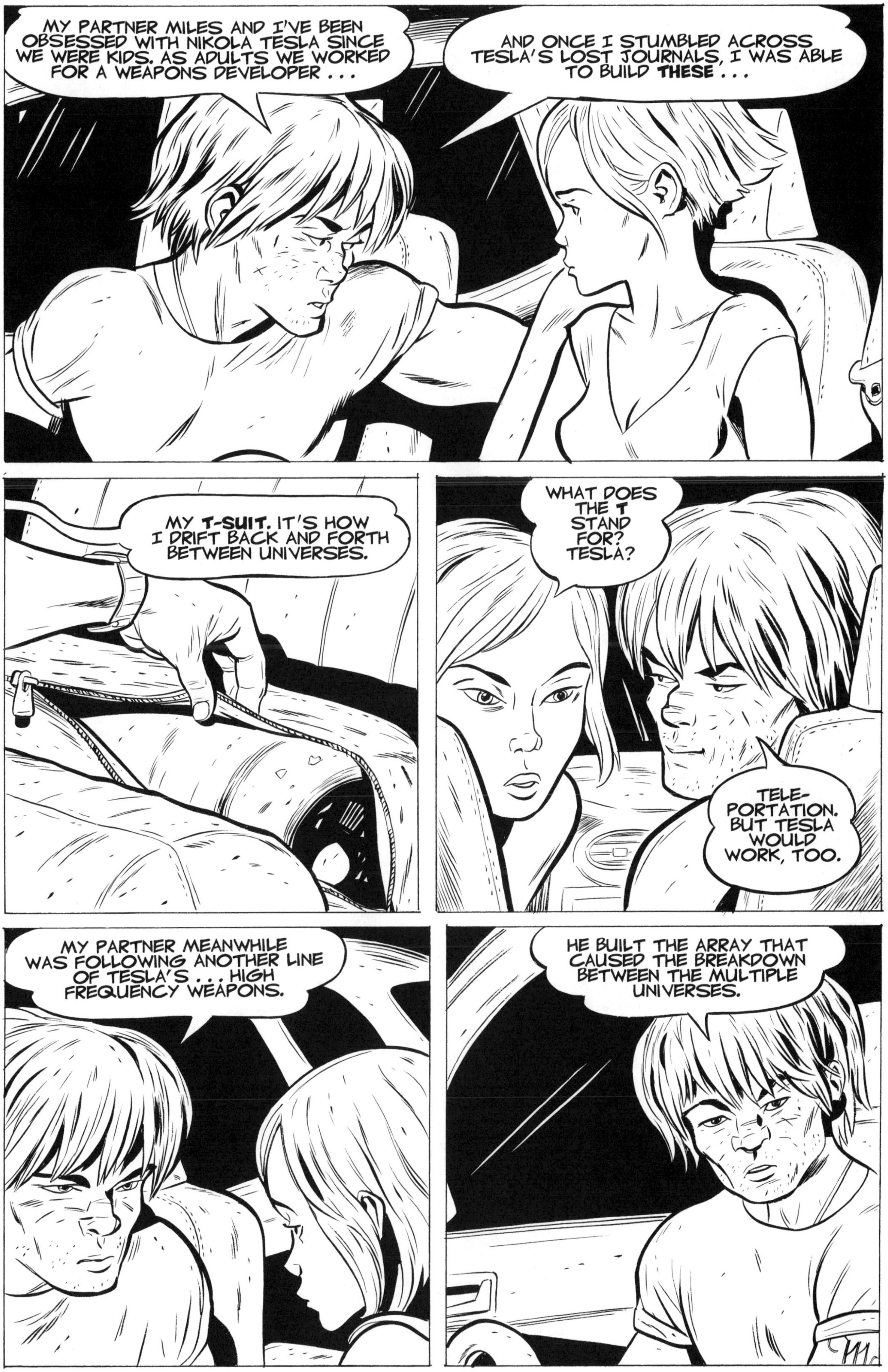
MY PARTNER MILES AND I'VE BEEN OBSESSED WITH NIKOLA TESLA SINCE WE WERE KIDS. AS ADULTS WE WORKED FOR A WEAPONS DEVELOPER . . .
AND ONCE I STUMBLED ACROSS TESLA'S LOST JOURNALS, I WAS ABLE TO BUILD **THESE** . . .
MY **T-SUIT**. IT'S HOW I DRIFT BACK AND FORTH BETWEEN UNIVERSES.
WHAT DOES THE **T** STAND FOR? TESLA?
TELE-PORTATION. BUT TESLA WOULD WORK, TOO.
MY PARTNER MEANWHILE WAS FOLLOWING ANOTHER LINE OF TESLA'S . . . HIGH FREQUENCY WEAPONS.
HE BUILT THE ARRAY THAT CAUSED THE BREAKDOWN BETWEEN THE MULTIPLE UNIVERSES.

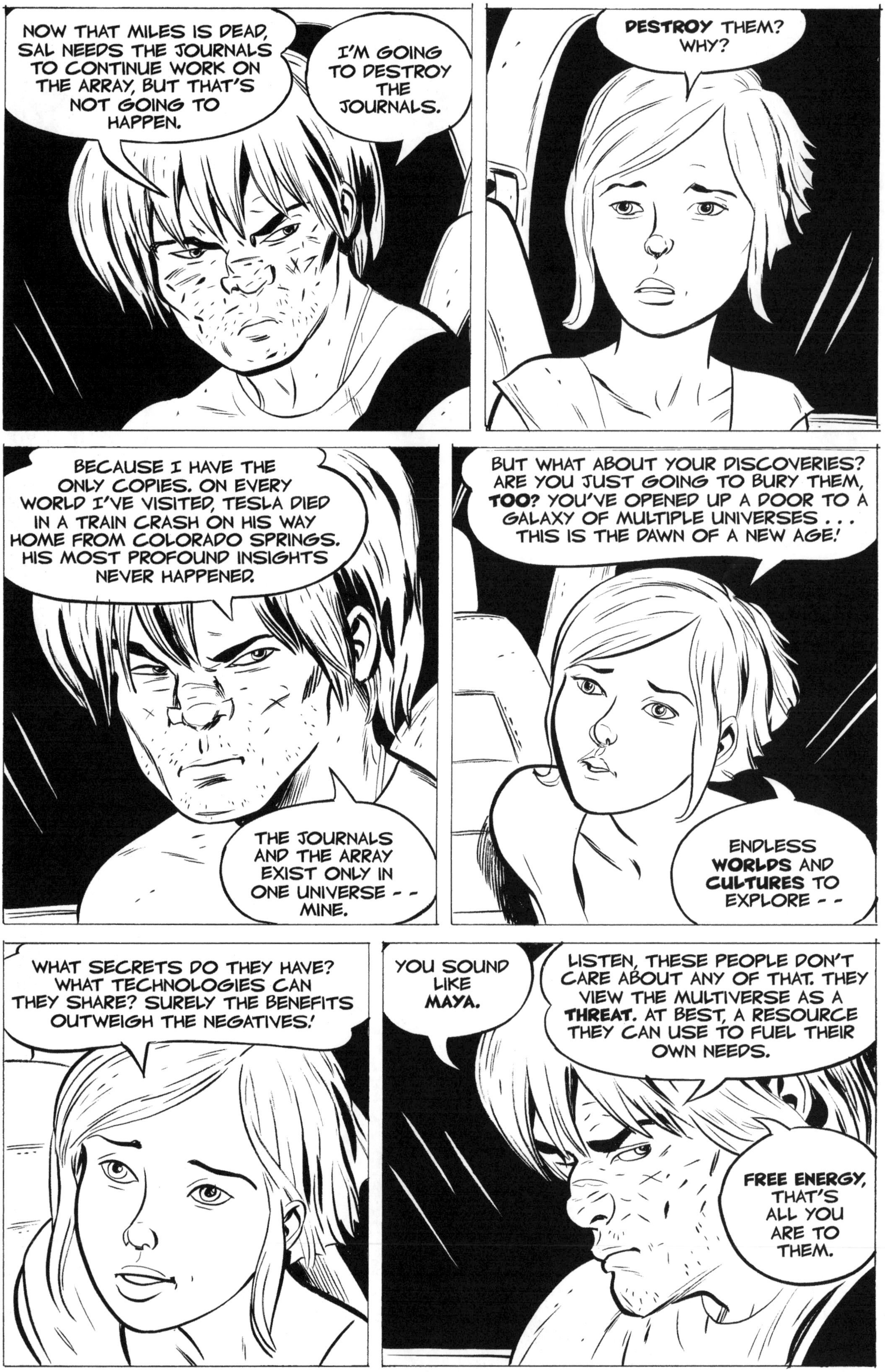
NOW THAT MILES IS DEAD, SAL NEEDS THE JOURNALS TO CONTINUE WORK ON THE ARRAY, BUT THAT'S NOT GOING TO HAPPEN.
I'M GOING TO DESTROY THE JOURNALS.
DESTROY THEM? WHY?
BECAUSE I HAVE THE ONLY COPIES. ON EVERY WORLD I'VE VISITED, TESLA DIED IN A TRAIN CRASH ON HIS WAY HOME FROM COLORADO SPRINGS. HIS MOST PROFOUND INSIGHTS NEVER HAPPENED.
THE JOURNALS AND THE ARRAY EXIST ONLY IN ONE UNIVERSE - - MINE.
BUT WHAT ABOUT YOUR DISCOVERIES? ARE YOU JUST GOING TO BURY THEM, TOO? YOU'VE OPENED UP A DOOR TO A GALAXY OF MULTIPLE UNIVERSES . . . THIS IS THE DAWN OF A NEW AGE!
ENDLESS WORLDS AND CULTURES TO EXPLORE - -
WHAT SECRETS DO THEY HAVE? WHAT TECHNOLOGIES CAN THEY SHARE? SURELY THE BENEFITS OUTWEIGH THE NEGATIVES!
YOU SOUND LIKE MAYA.
LISTEN, THESE PEOPLE DON'T CARE ABOUT ANY OF THAT. THEY VIEW THE MULTIVERSE AS A THREAT. AT BEST, A RESOURCE THEY CAN USE TO FUEL THEIR OWN NEEDS.
FREE ENERGY, THAT'S ALL YOU ARE TO THEM.

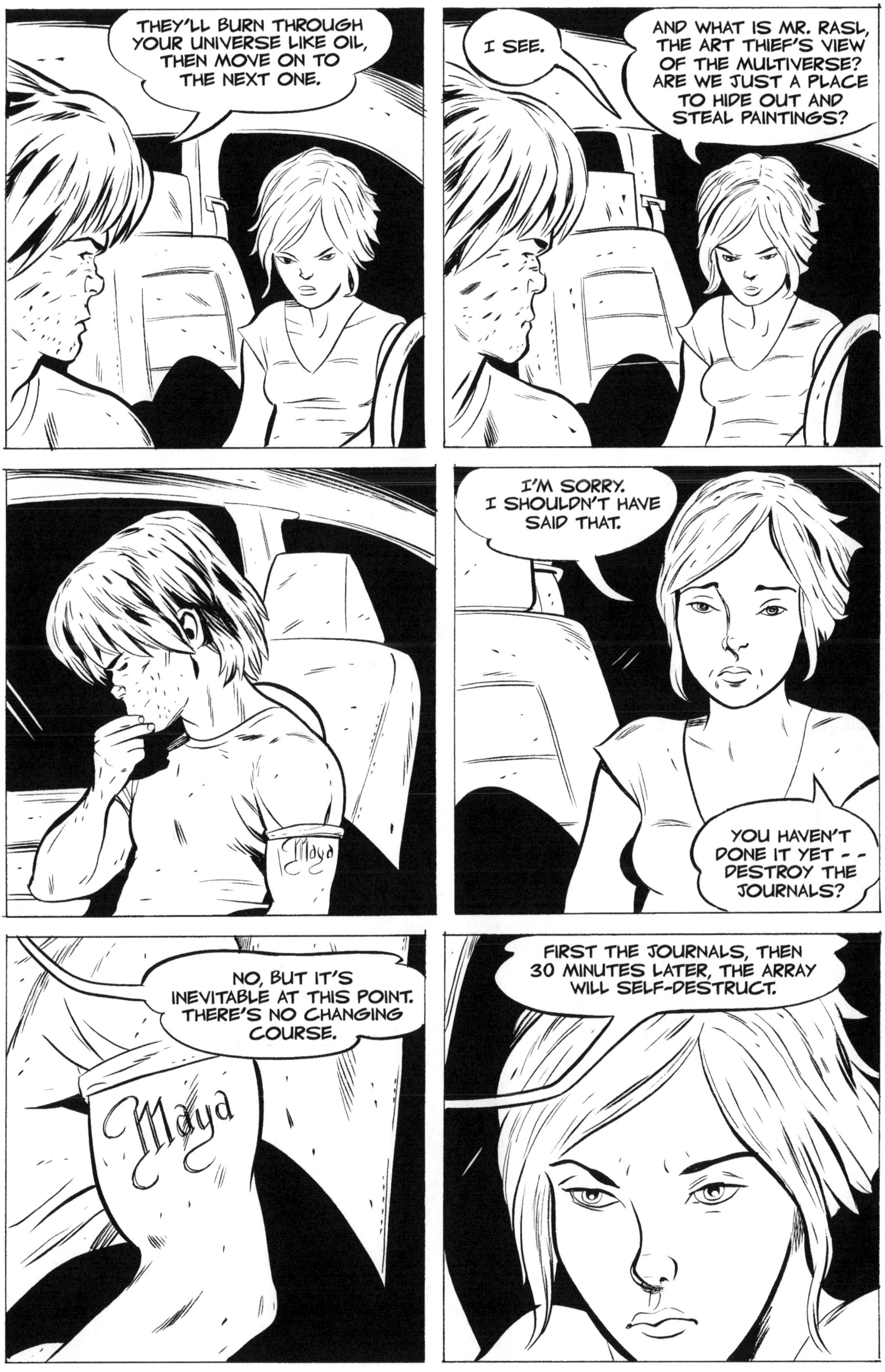
THEY'LL BURN THROUGH YOUR UNIVERSE LIKE OIL, THEN MOVE ON TO THE NEXT ONE.
I SEE.
AND WHAT IS MR. RASL, THE ART THIEF'S VIEW OF THE MULTIVERSE? ARE WE JUST A PLACE TO HIDE OUT AND STEAL PAINTINGS?
Maya
I'M SORRY. I SHOULDN'T HAVE SAID THAT.
YOU HAVEN'T DONE IT YET - - DESTROY THE JOURNALS?
NO, BUT IT'S INEVITABLE AT THIS POINT. THERE'S NO CHANGING COURSE.
Maya
FIRST THE JOURNALS, THEN 30 MINUTES LATER, THE ARRAY WILL SELF-DESTRUCT.

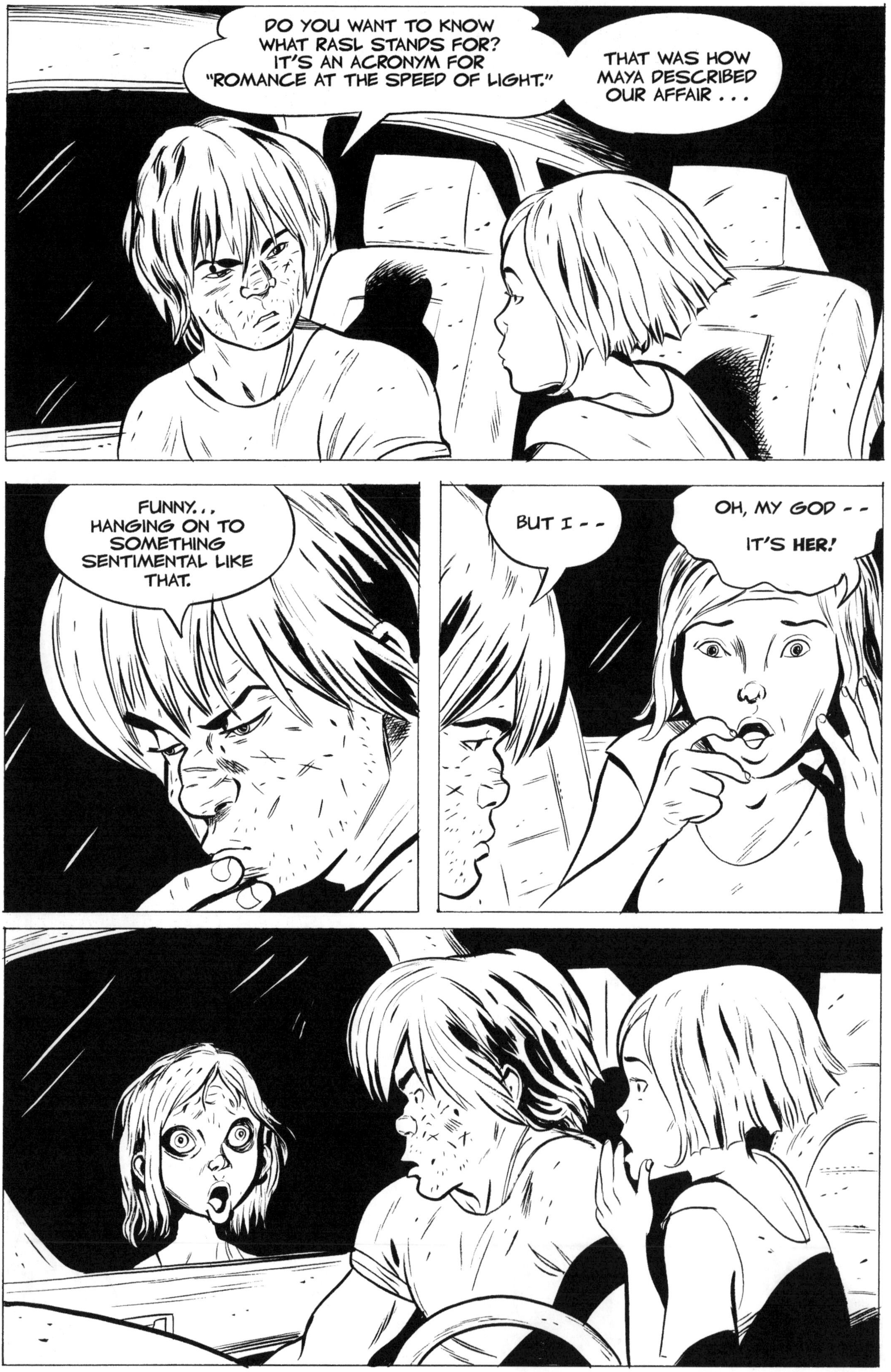
DO YOU WANT TO KNOW WHAT RASL STANDS FOR? IT'S AN ACRONYM FOR "ROMANCE AT THE SPEED OF LIGHT."
THAT WAS HOW MAYA DESCRIBED OUR AFFAIR . . .
FUNNY. . . HANGING ON TO SOMETHING SENTIMENTAL LIKE THAT.
BUT I - -
OH, MY GOD - -
IT'S **HER!**

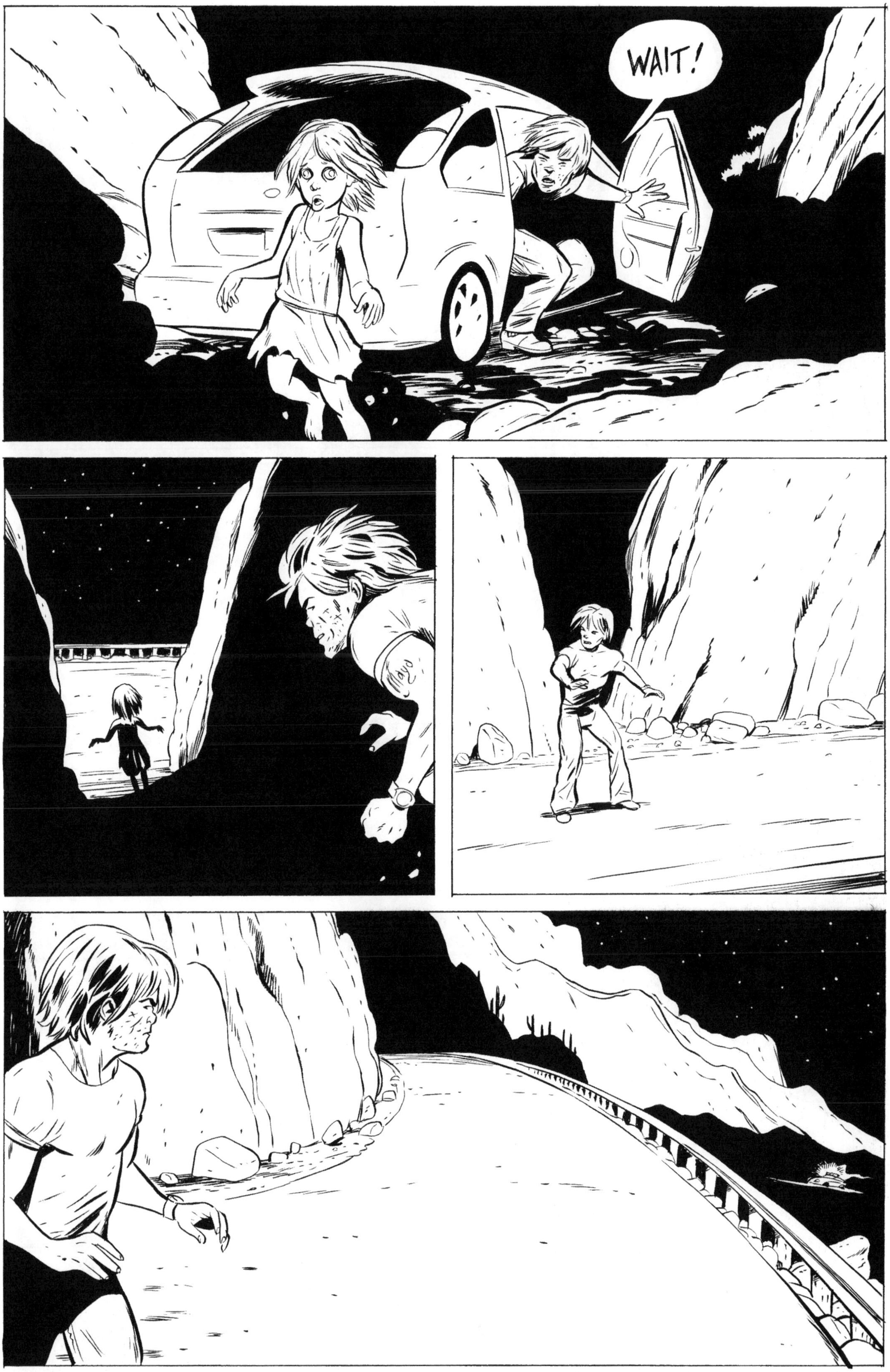
WAIT!

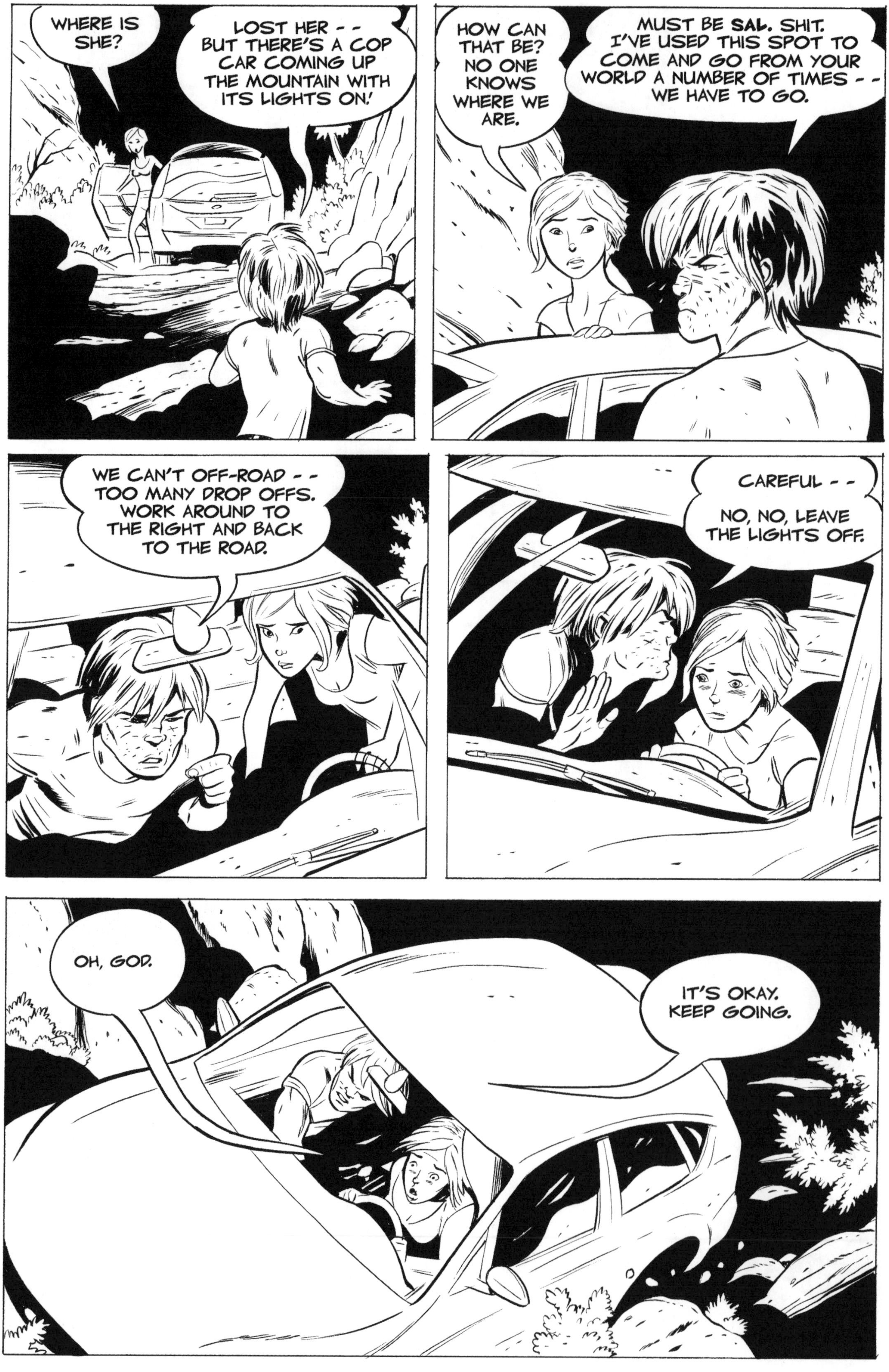
WHERE IS SHE?
LOST HER - - BUT THERE'S A COP CAR COMING UP THE MOUNTAIN WITH ITS LIGHTS ON!
HOW CAN THAT BE? NO ONE KNOWS WHERE WE ARE.
MUST BE SAL. SHIT. I'VE USED THIS SPOT TO COME AND GO FROM YOUR WORLD A NUMBER OF TIMES - - WE HAVE TO GO.
WE CAN'T OFF-ROAD - - TOO MANY DROP OFFS. WORK AROUND TO THE RIGHT AND BACK TO THE ROAD.
CAREFUL - -
NO, NO, LEAVE THE LIGHTS OFF.
OH, GOD.
IT'S OKAY. KEEP GOING.

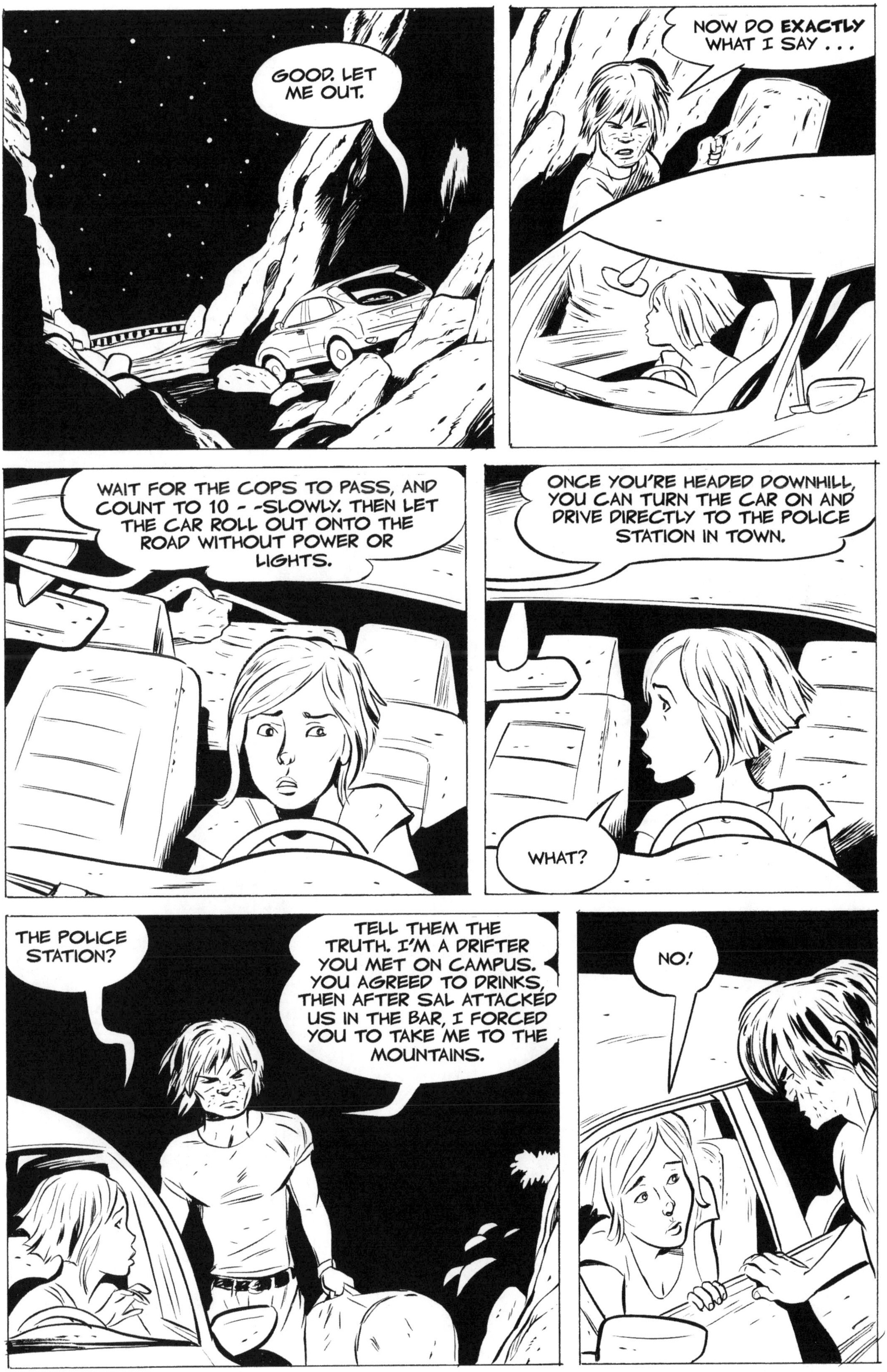
GOOD. LET ME OUT.
NOW DO **EXACTLY** WHAT I SAY . . .
WAIT FOR THE COPS TO PASS, AND COUNT TO 10 - -SLOWLY. THEN LET THE CAR ROLL OUT ONTO THE ROAD WITHOUT POWER OR LIGHTS.
ONCE YOU'RE HEADED DOWNHILL, YOU CAN TURN THE CAR ON AND DRIVE DIRECTLY TO THE POLICE STATION IN TOWN.
WHAT?
THE POLICE STATION?
TELL THEM THE TRUTH. I'M A DRIFTER YOU MET ON CAMPUS. YOU AGREED TO DRINKS, THEN AFTER SAL ATTACKED US IN THE BAR, I FORCED YOU TO TAKE ME TO THE MOUNTAINS.
NO!

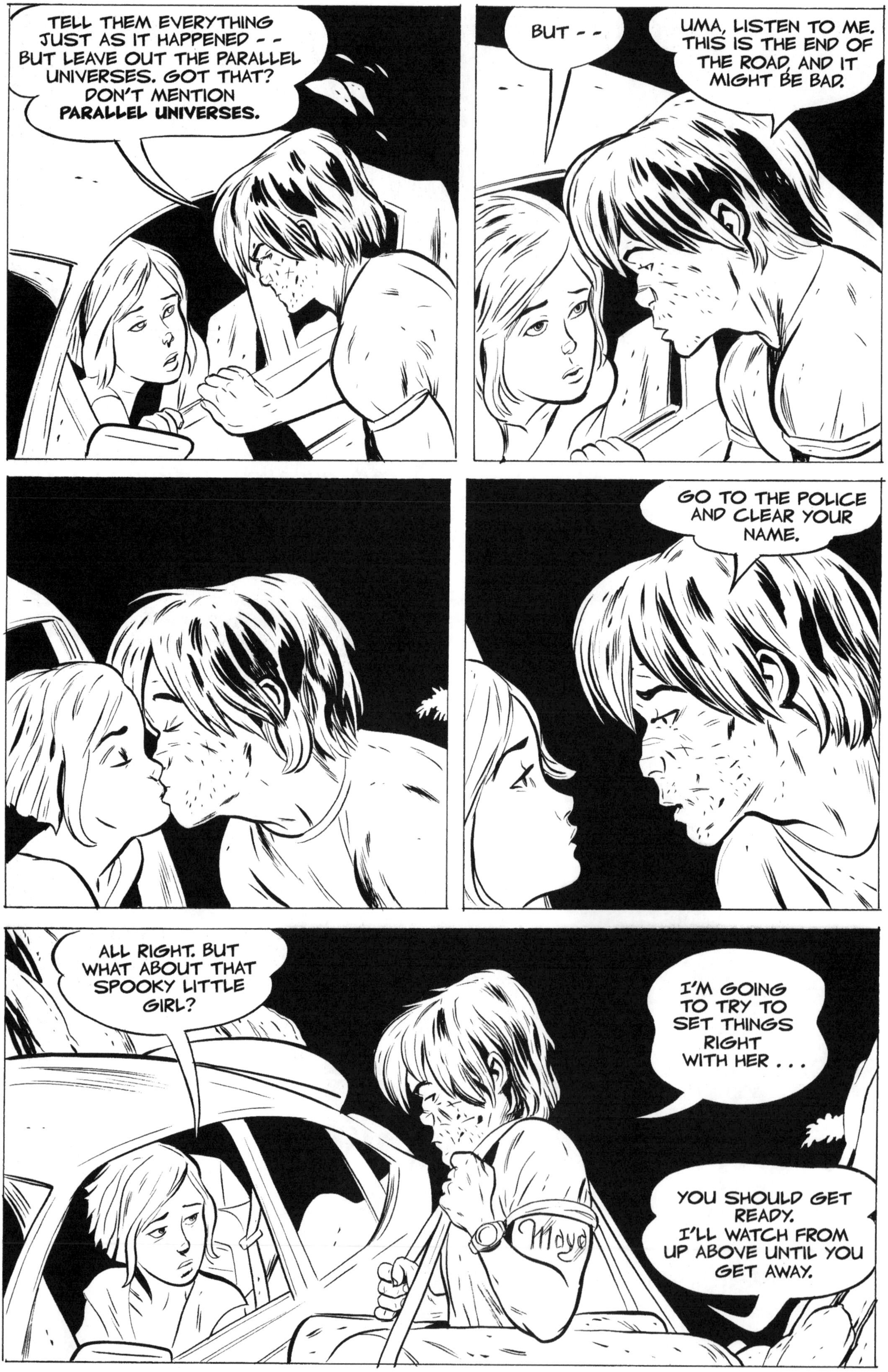
TELL THEM EVERYTHING JUST AS IT HAPPENED - - BUT LEAVE OUT THE PARALLEL UNIVERSES. GOT THAT? DON'T MENTION **PARALLEL UNIVERSES.**
- -
BUT - -
- -
UMA, LISTEN TO ME. THIS IS THE END OF THE ROAD, AND IT MIGHT BE BAD.
GO TO THE POLICE AND CLEAR YOUR NAME.
ALL RIGHT. BUT WHAT ABOUT THAT SPOOKY LITTLE GIRL?
- -
I'M GOING TO TRY TO SET THINGS RIGHT WITH HER . . .
YOU SHOULD GET READY. I'LL WATCH FROM UP ABOVE UNTIL YOU GET AWAY.

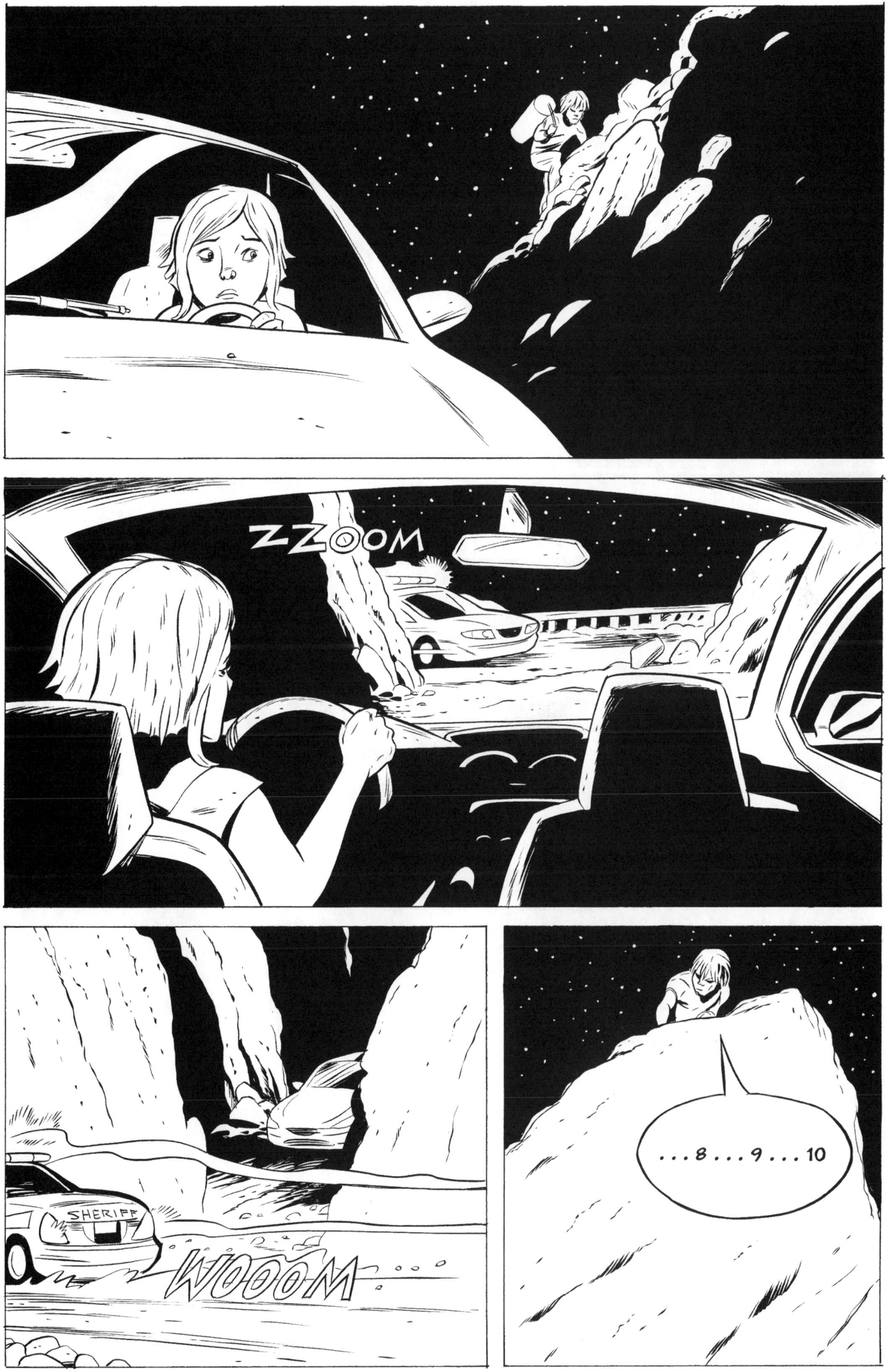
ZZOOM
SHERIFF
WOOOM
. . . 8 . . . 9 . . . 10

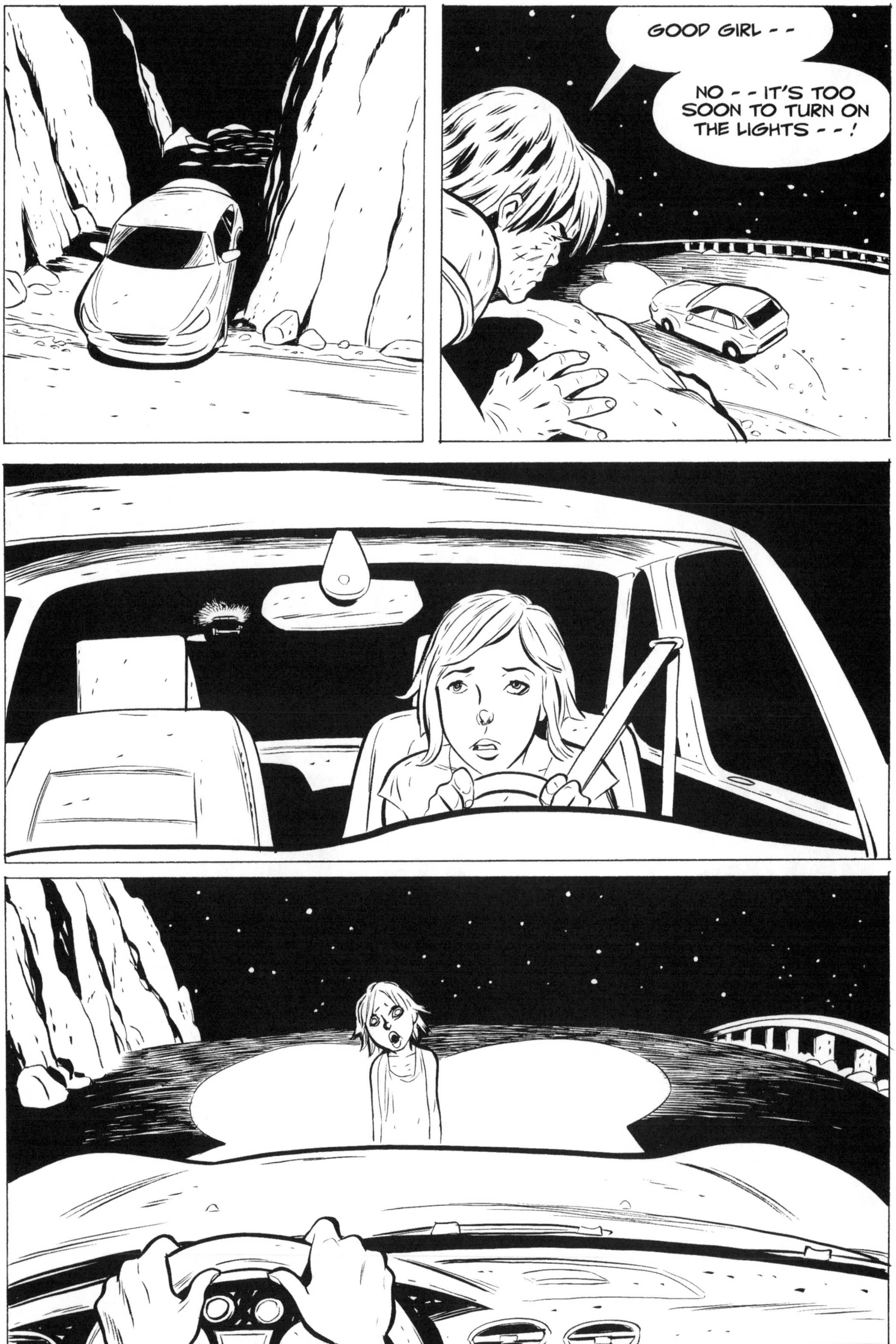
GOOD GIRL - -
NO - - IT'S TOO SOON TO TURN ON THE LIGHTS - - !

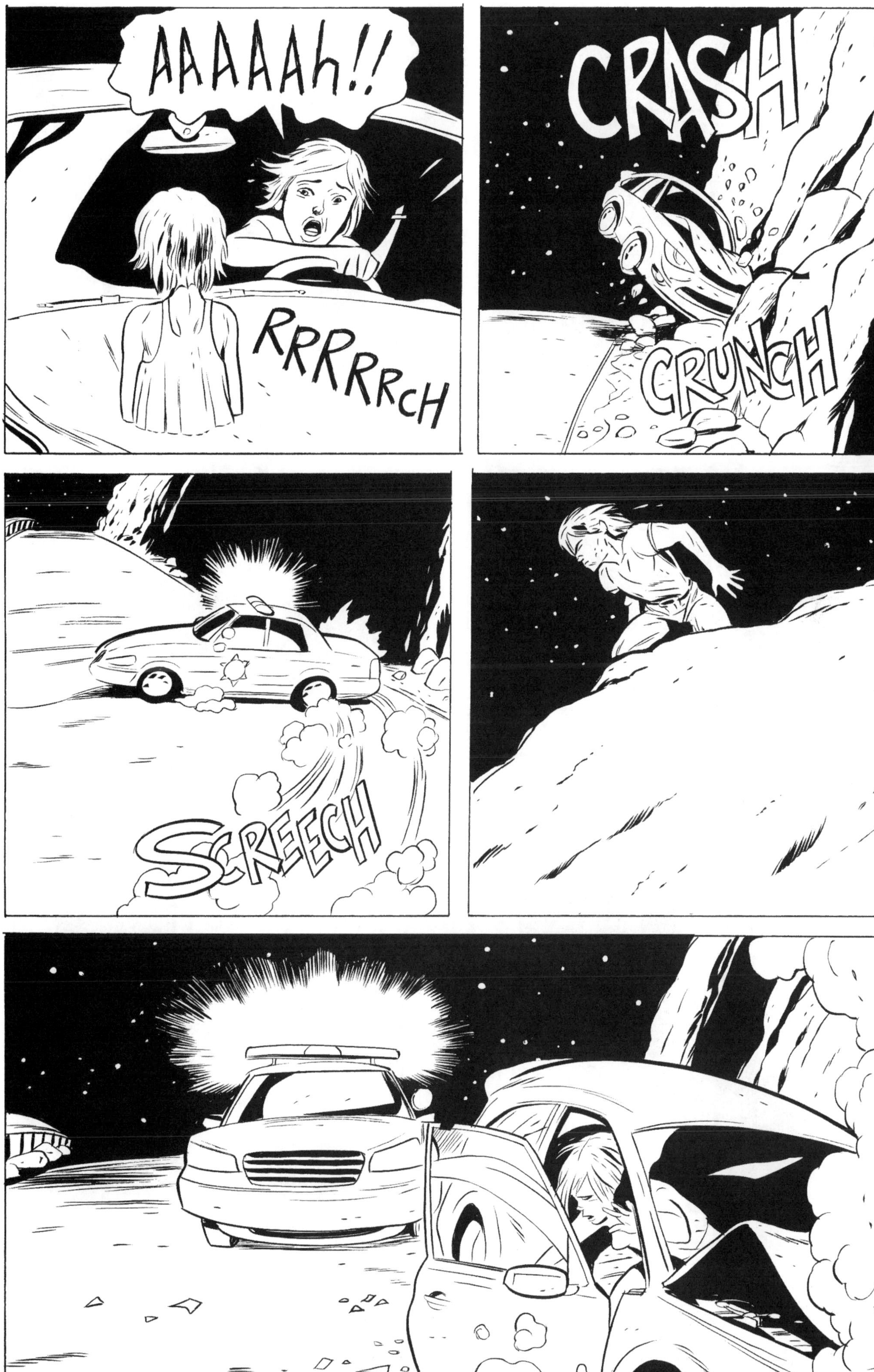
AAAAAh!!
RRRRRRCH
CRASH
CRUNCH
SCREECH

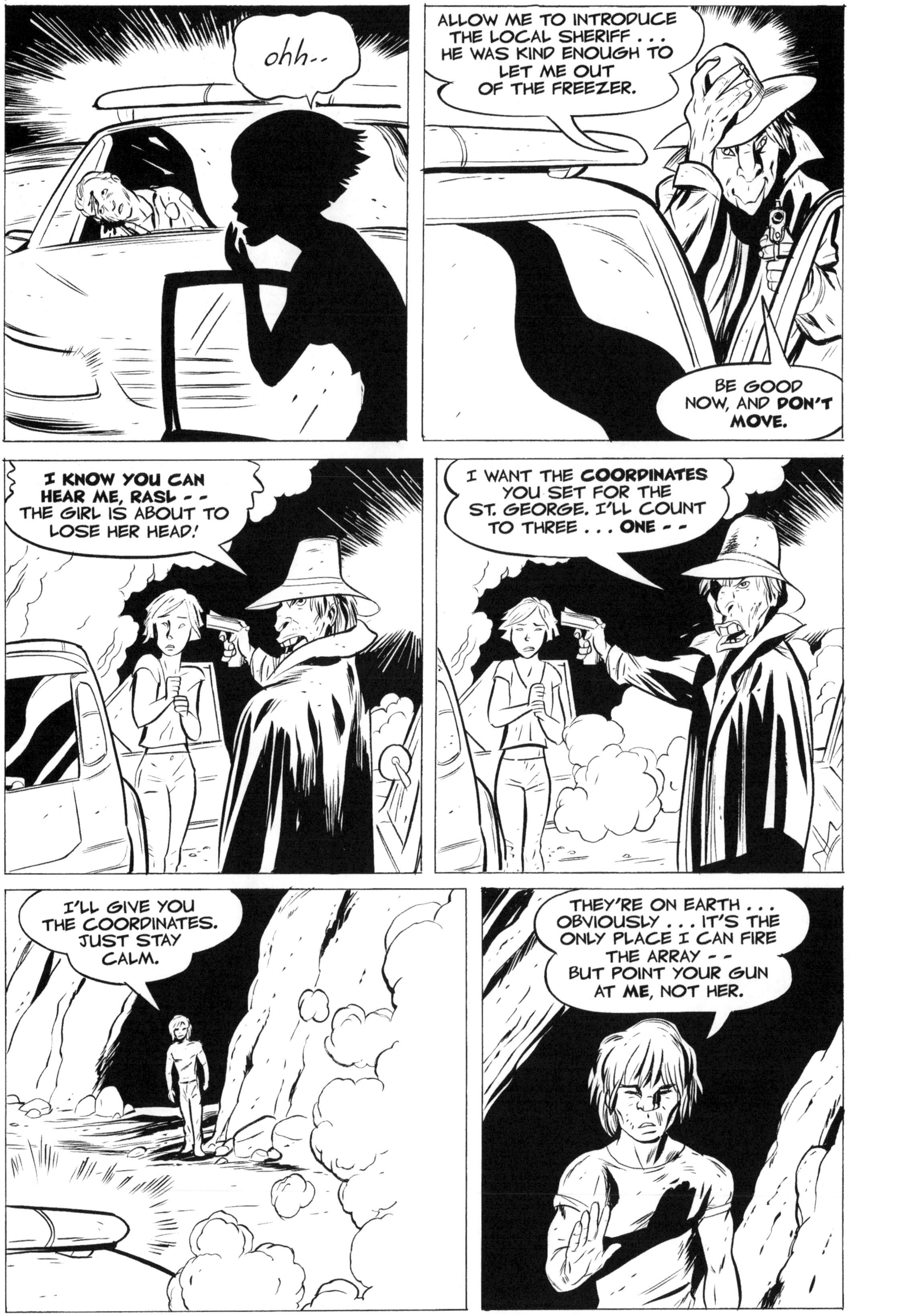
ohh..
ALLOW ME TO INTRODUCE THE LOCAL SHERIFF . . . HE WAS KIND ENOUGH TO LET ME OUT OF THE FREEZER.
BE GOOD NOW, AND DON'T MOVE.
I KNOW YOU CAN HEAR ME, RASL - - THE GIRL IS ABOUT TO LOSE HER HEAD!
I WANT THE COORDINATES YOU SET FOR THE ST. GEORGE. I'LL COUNT TO THREE . . . ONE - -
I'LL GIVE YOU THE COORDINATES. JUST STAY CALM.
THEY'RE ON EARTH . . . OBVIOUSLY . . . IT'S THE ONLY PLACE I CAN FIRE THE ARRAY - - BUT POINT YOUR GUN AT ME, NOT HER.

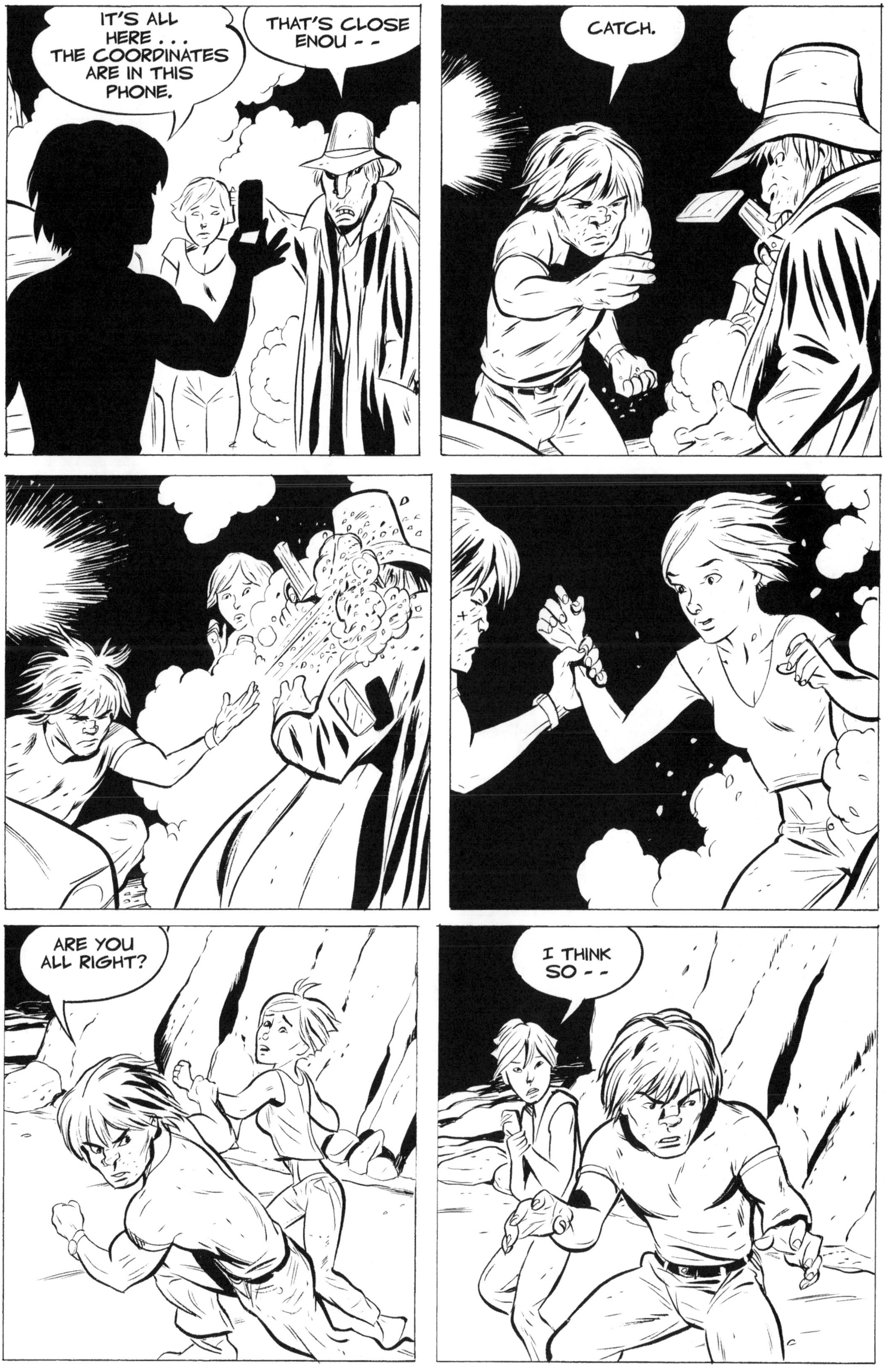
IT'S ALL HERE . . . THE COORDINATES ARE IN THIS PHONE.
THAT'S CLOSE ENOU - -
CATCH.
ARE YOU ALL RIGHT?
I THINK SO - -

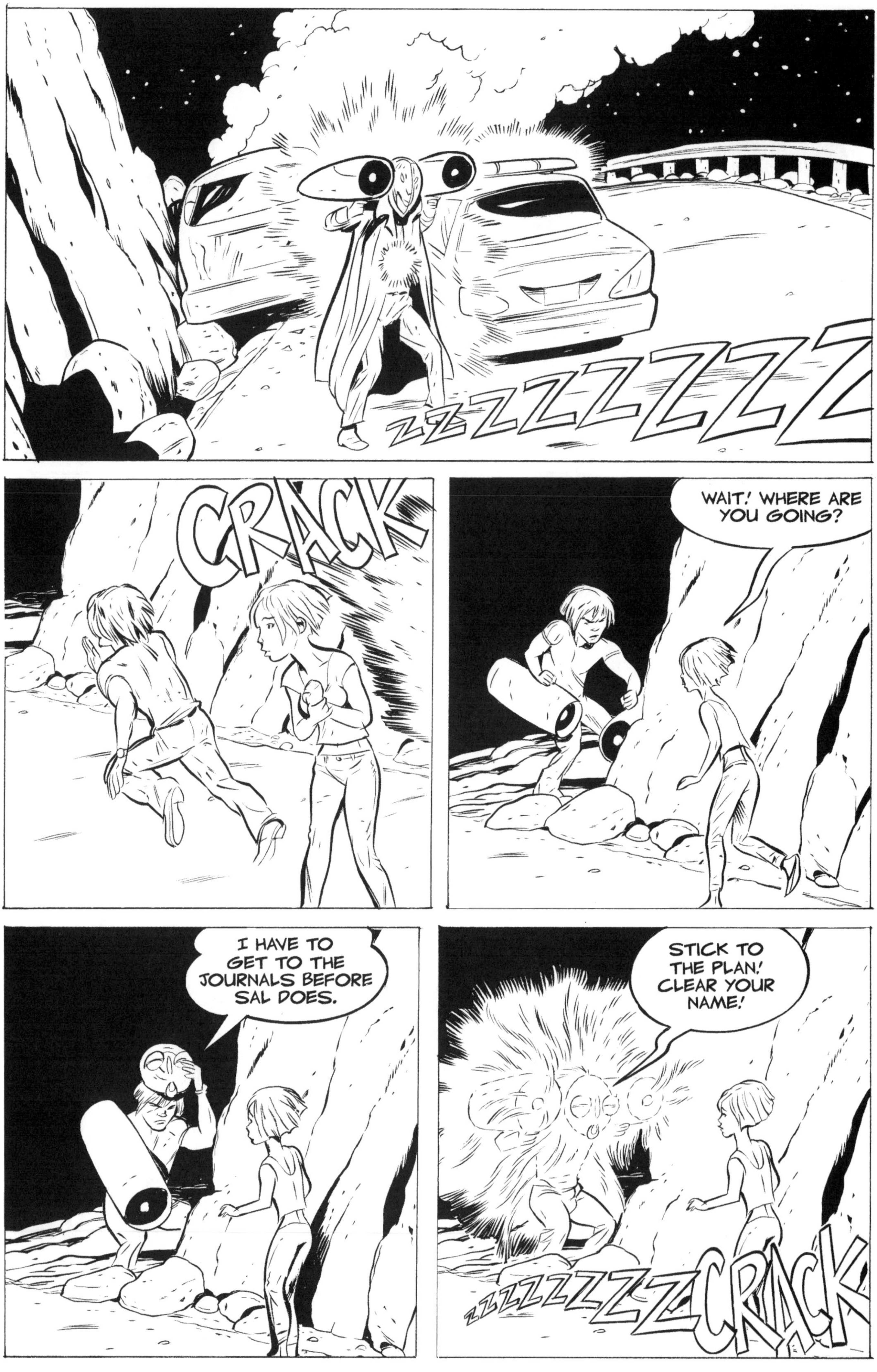
ZZZZZZZZZZZ
CRACK
WAIT! WHERE ARE YOU GOING?
I HAVE TO GET TO THE JOURNALS BEFORE SAL DOES.
STICK TO THE PLAN! CLEAR YOUR NAME!
ZZZZZZZZZZ CRACK

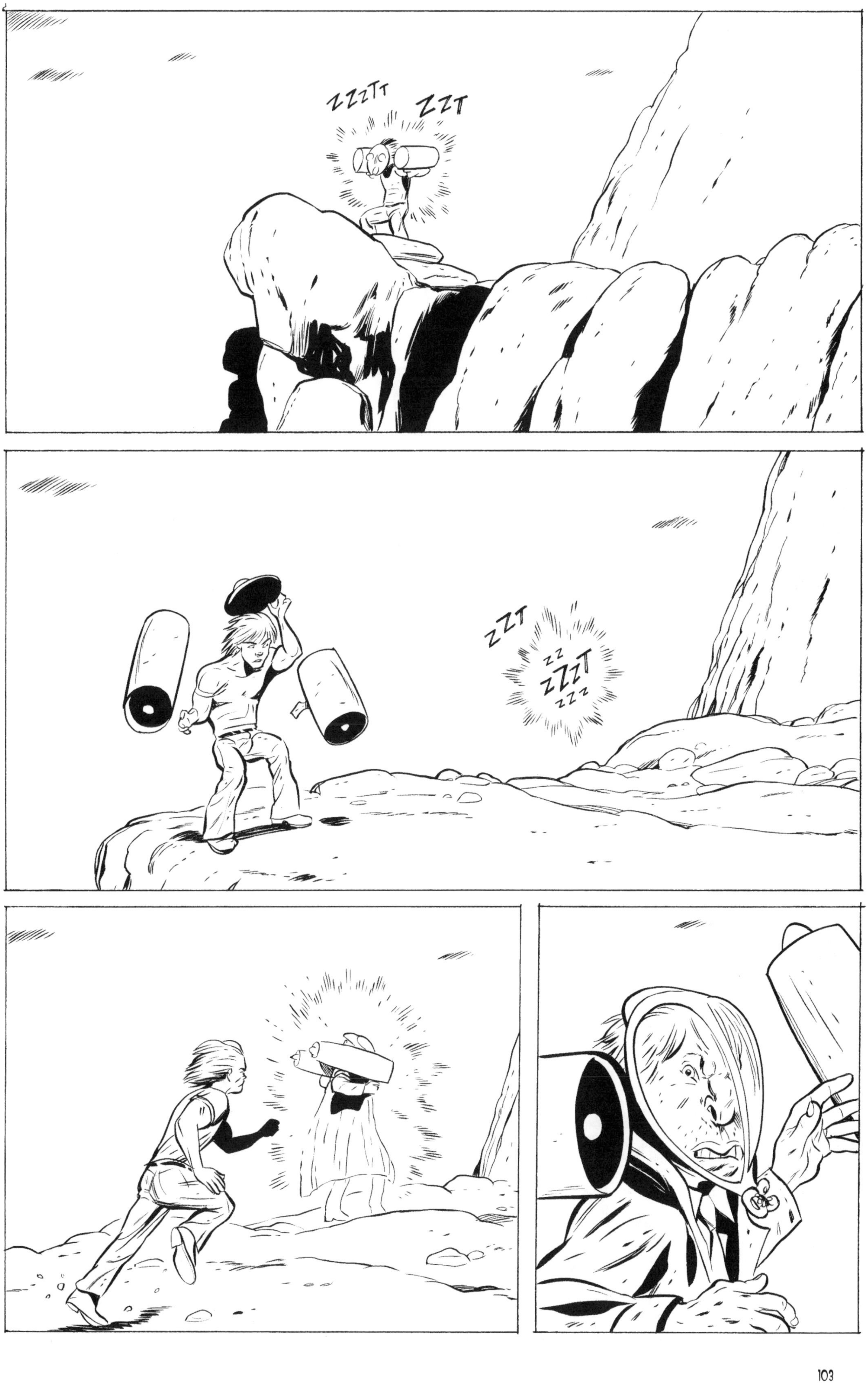
ZZZTT
ZZT
ZZT
ZZZT

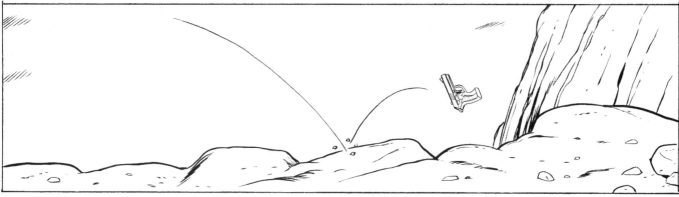

CRACK

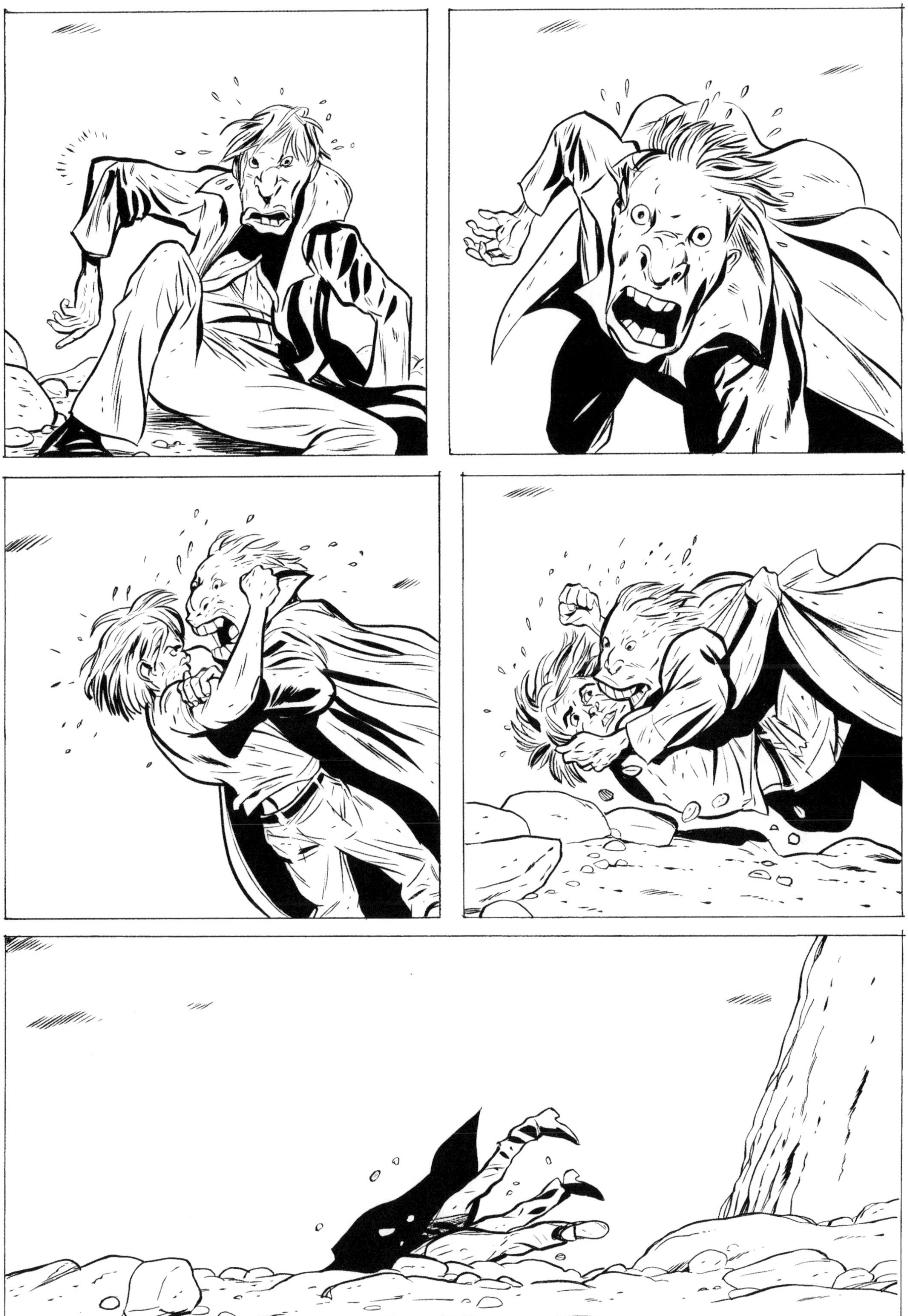

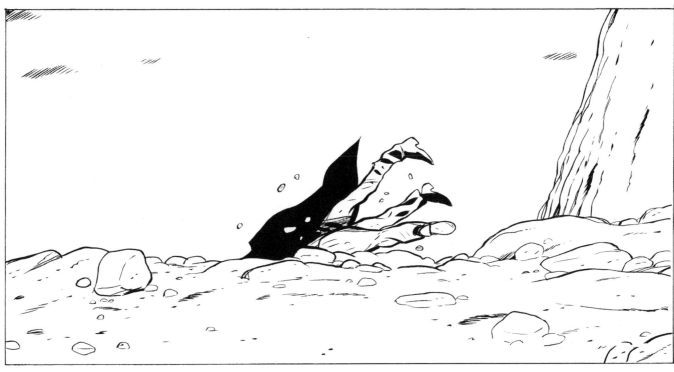

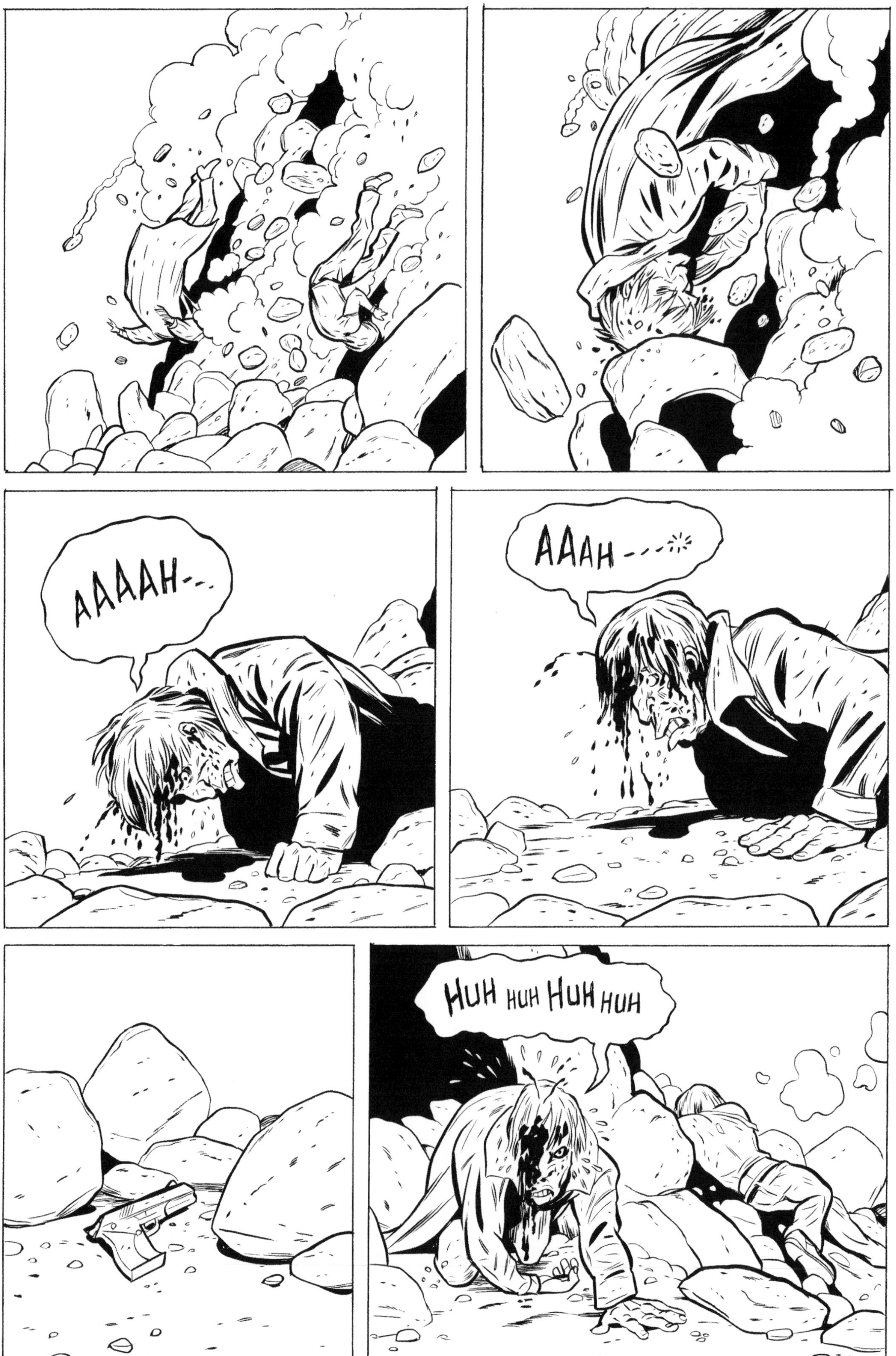
AAAAH--
AAAH---
HUH HUH HUH HUH

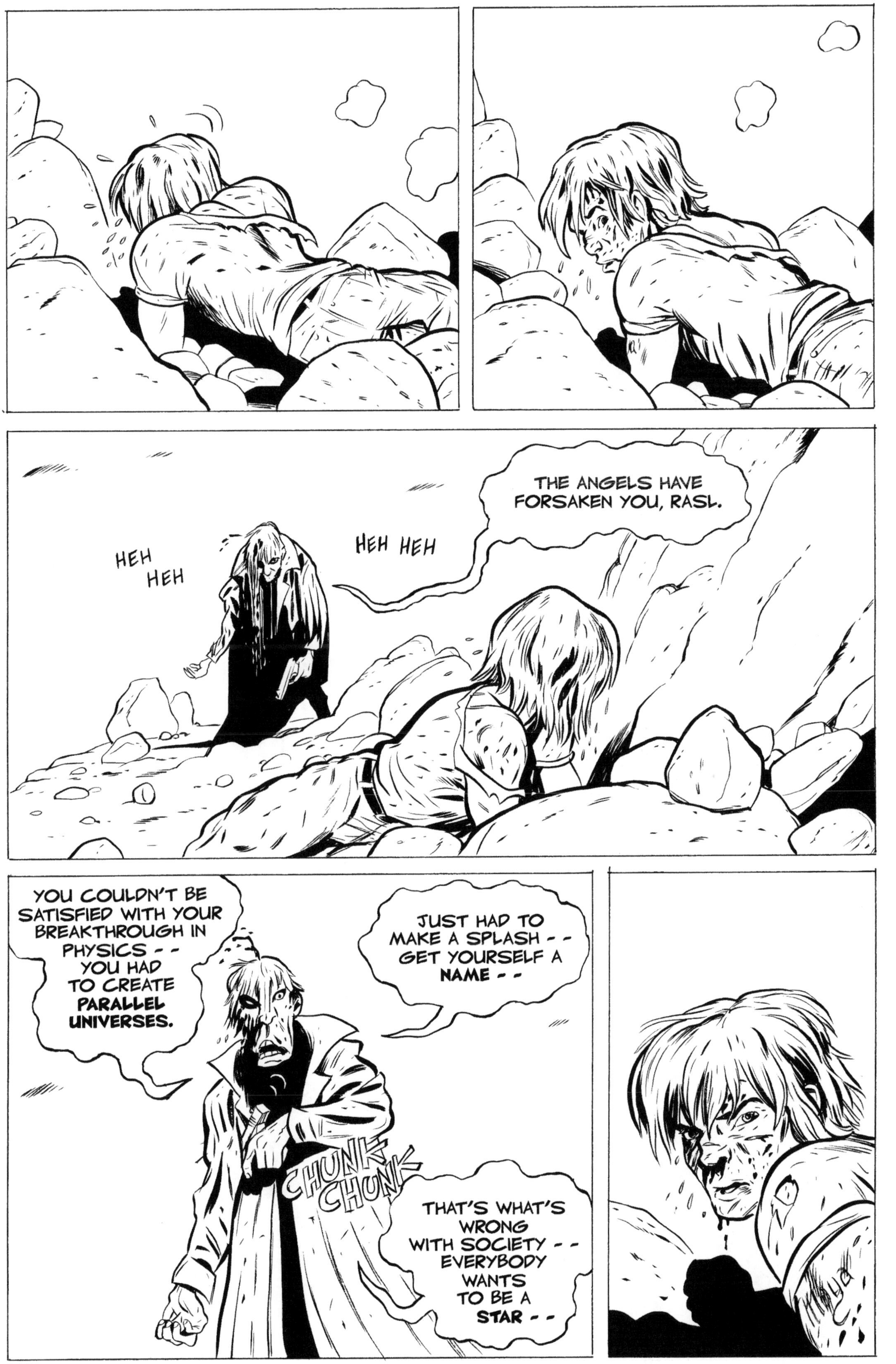
THE ANGELS HAVE FORSAKEN YOU, RASL.
HEH HEH
HEH HEH
YOU COULDN'T BE SATISFIED WITH YOUR BREAKTHROUGH IN PHYSICS - - YOU HAD TO CREATE **PARALLEL UNIVERSES.**
JUST HAD TO MAKE A SPLASH - - GET YOURSELF A **NAME** - -
CHUNK CHUNK
THAT'S WHAT'S WRONG WITH SOCIETY - - EVERYBODY WANTS TO BE A **STAR** - -

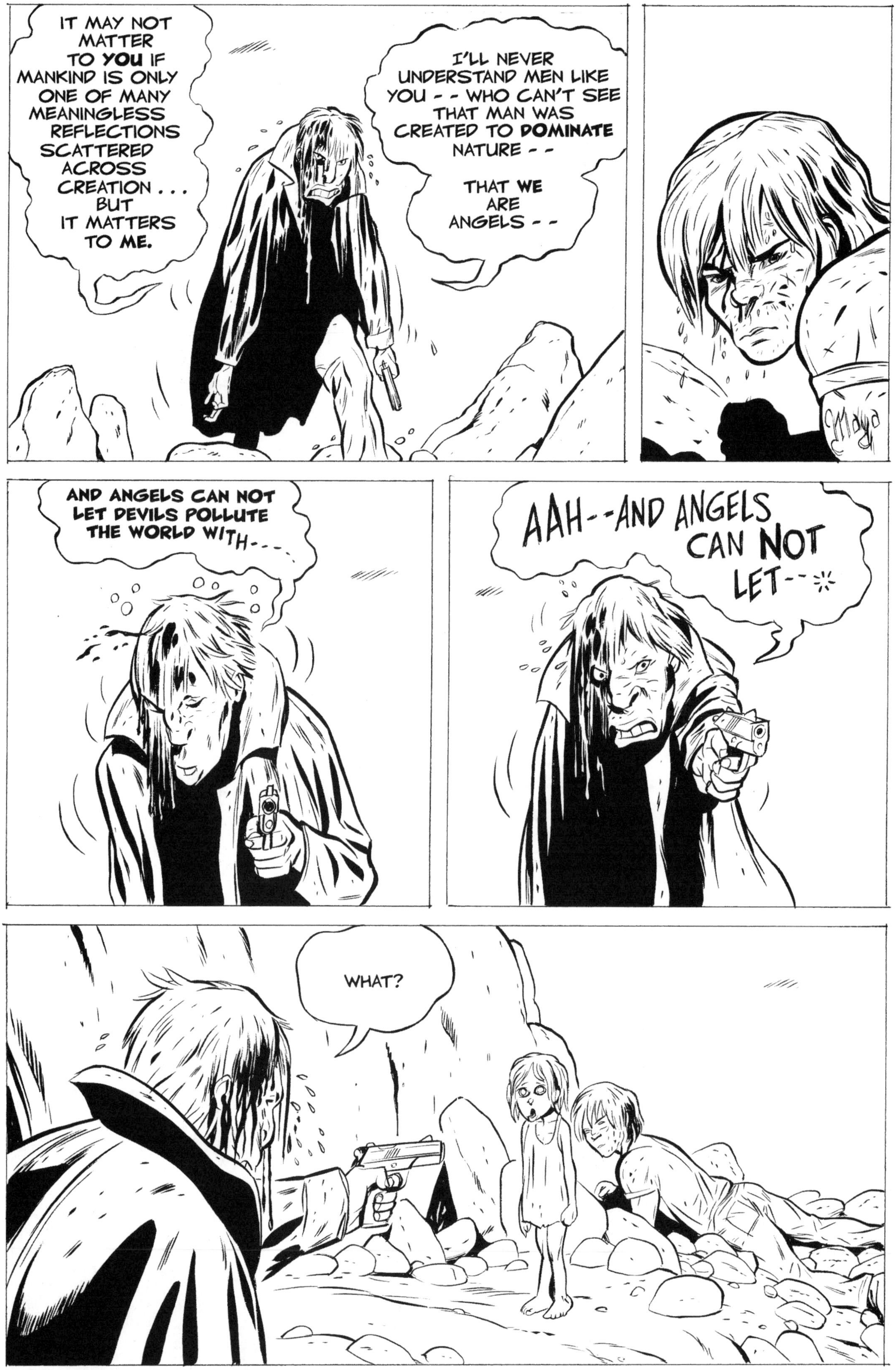
IT MAY NOT MATTER TO YOU IF MANKIND IS ONLY ONE OF MANY MEANINGLESS REFLECTIONS SCATTERED ACROSS CREATION . . . BUT IT MATTERS TO ME.
I'LL NEVER UNDERSTAND MEN LIKE YOU - - WHO CAN'T SEE THAT MAN WAS CREATED TO DOMINATE NATURE - -
THAT WE ARE ANGELS - -
AND ANGELS CAN NOT LET DEVILS POLLUTE THE WORLD WITH- - - -
AAH- -AND ANGELS CAN NOT LET- -
WHAT?

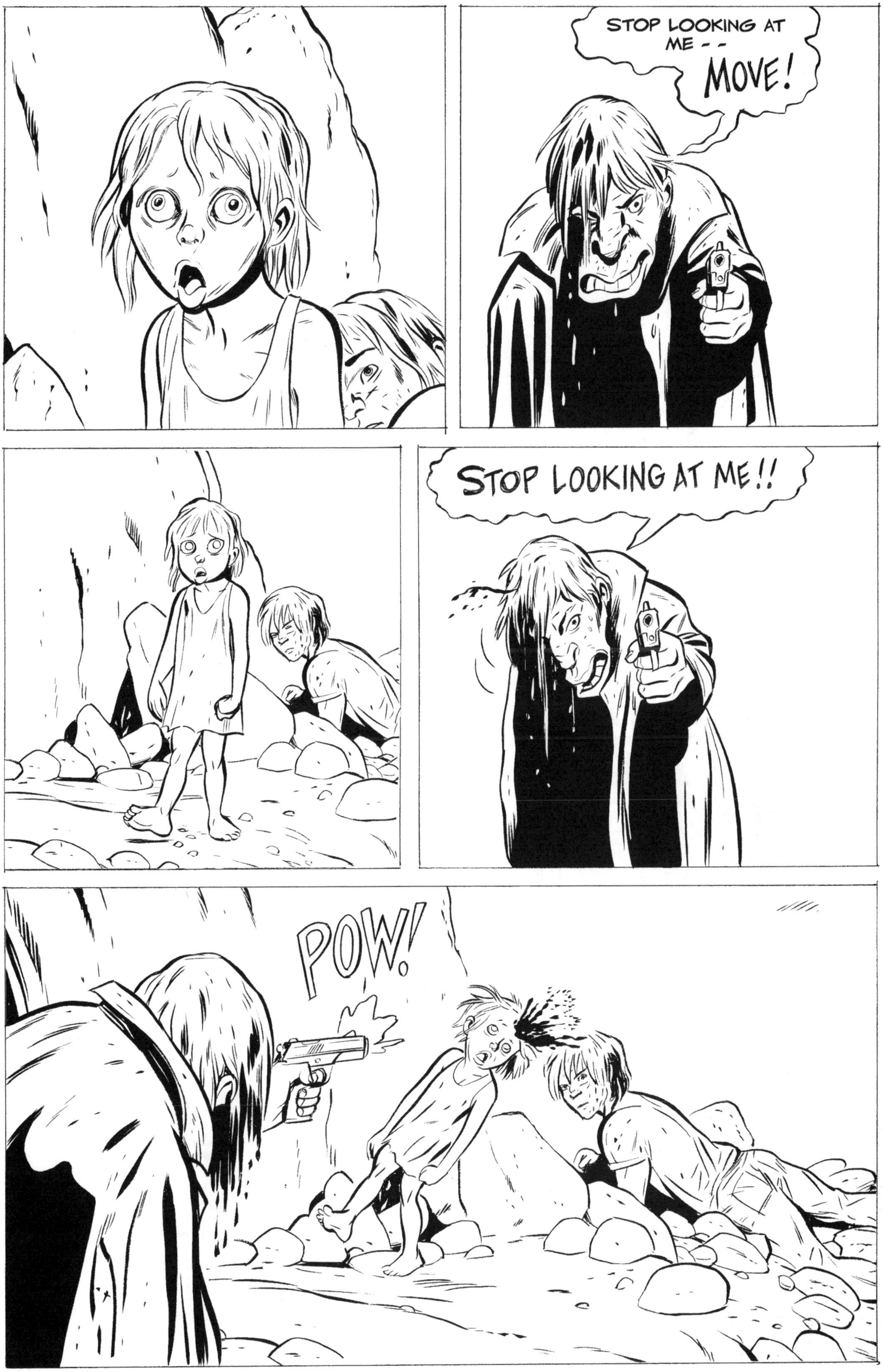
STOP LOOKING AT ME - - MOVE!
STOP LOOKING AT ME!!
POW!

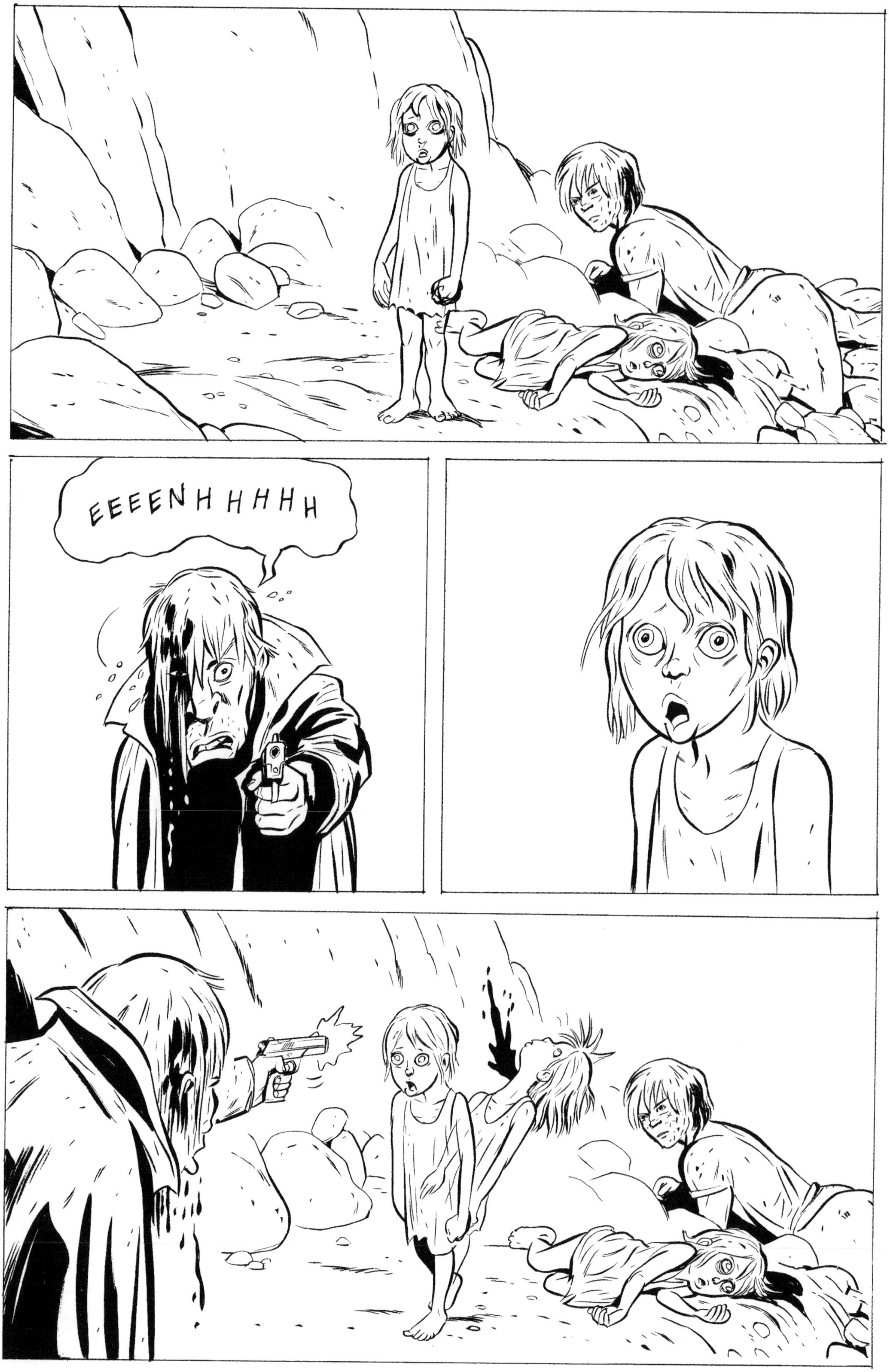
EEEENHHHHH

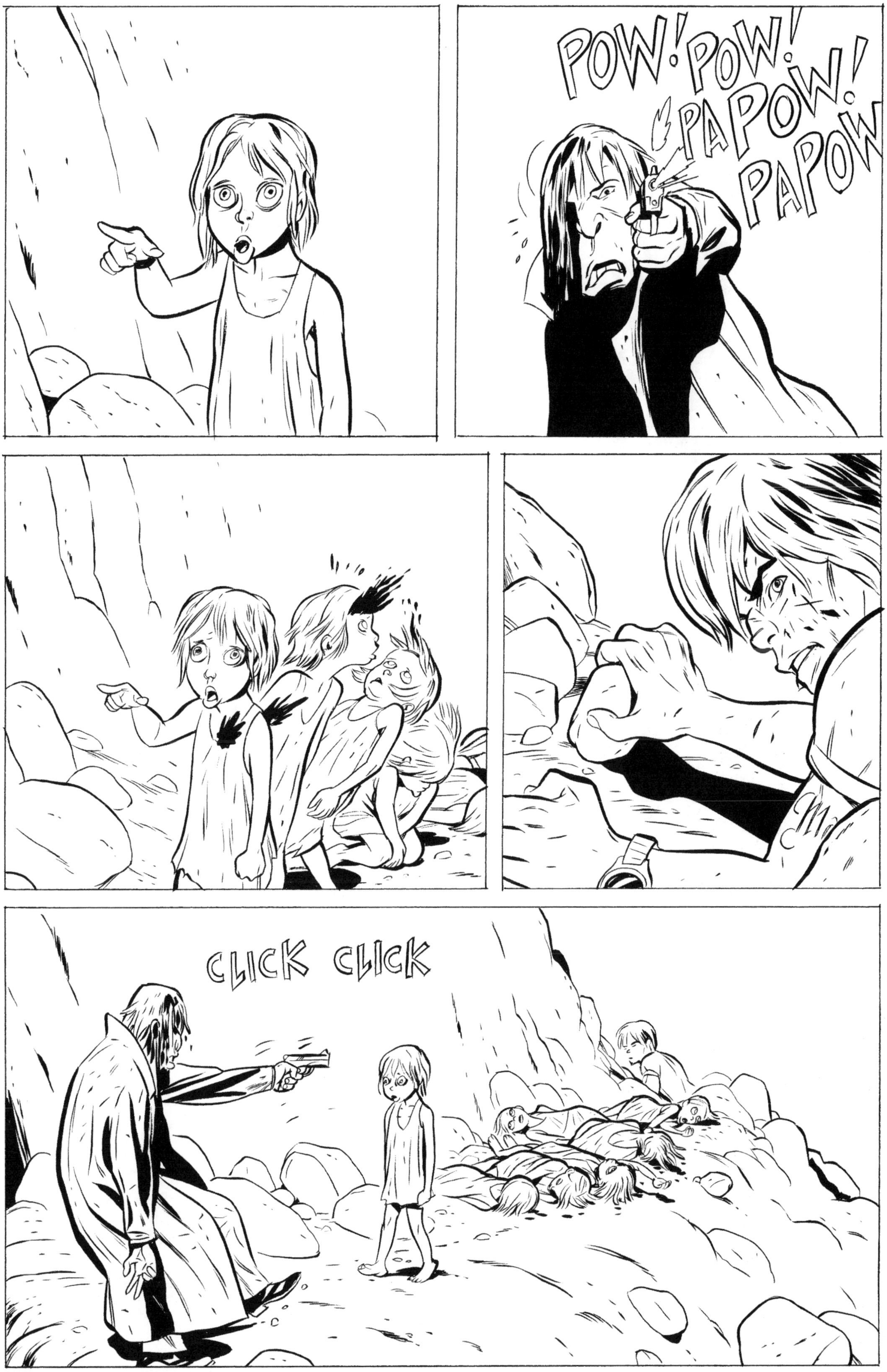
POW! POW! PAPOW! PAPOW
CLICK CLICK

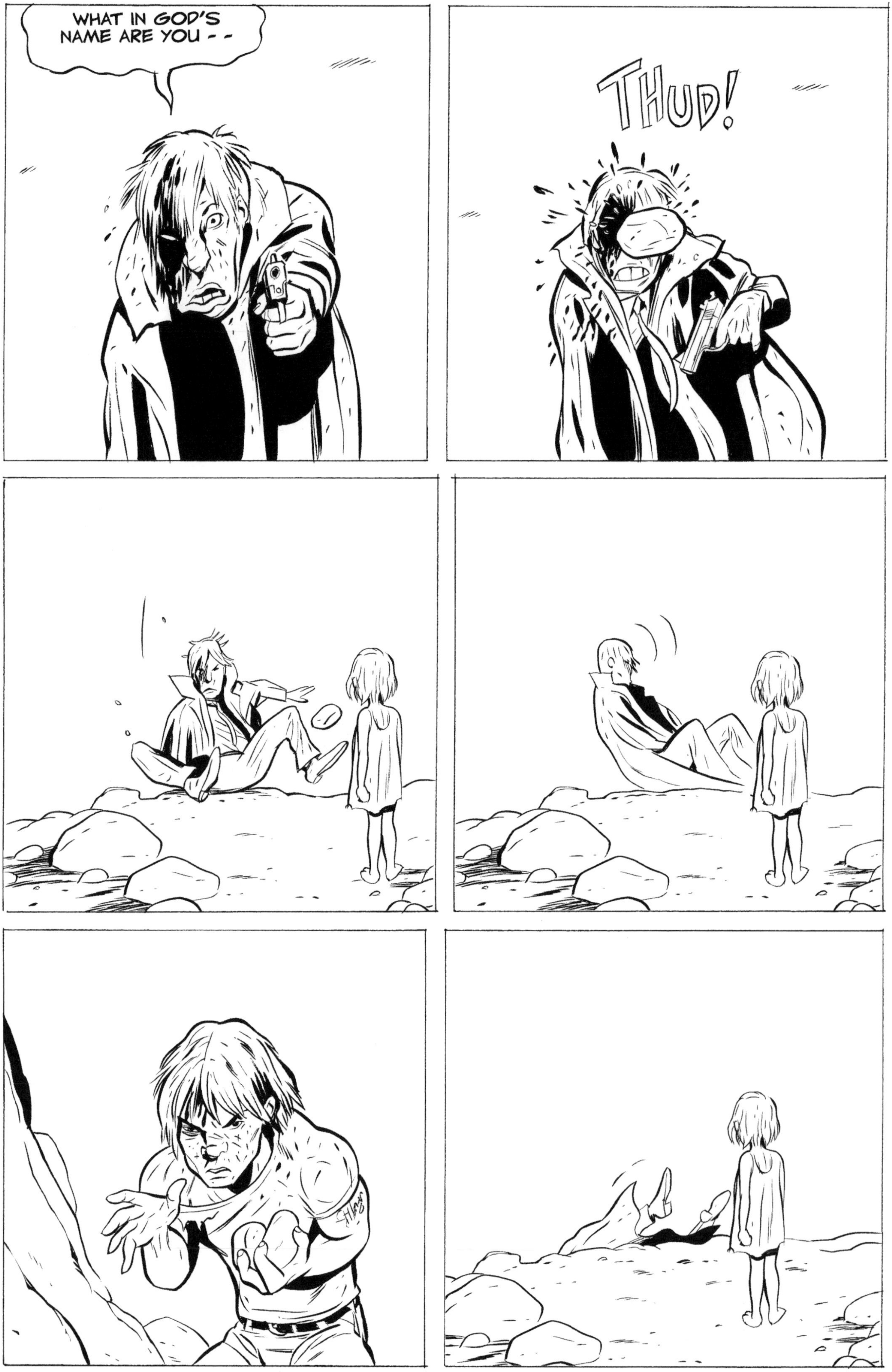
WHAT IN GOD'S NAME ARE YOU - -
THUD!

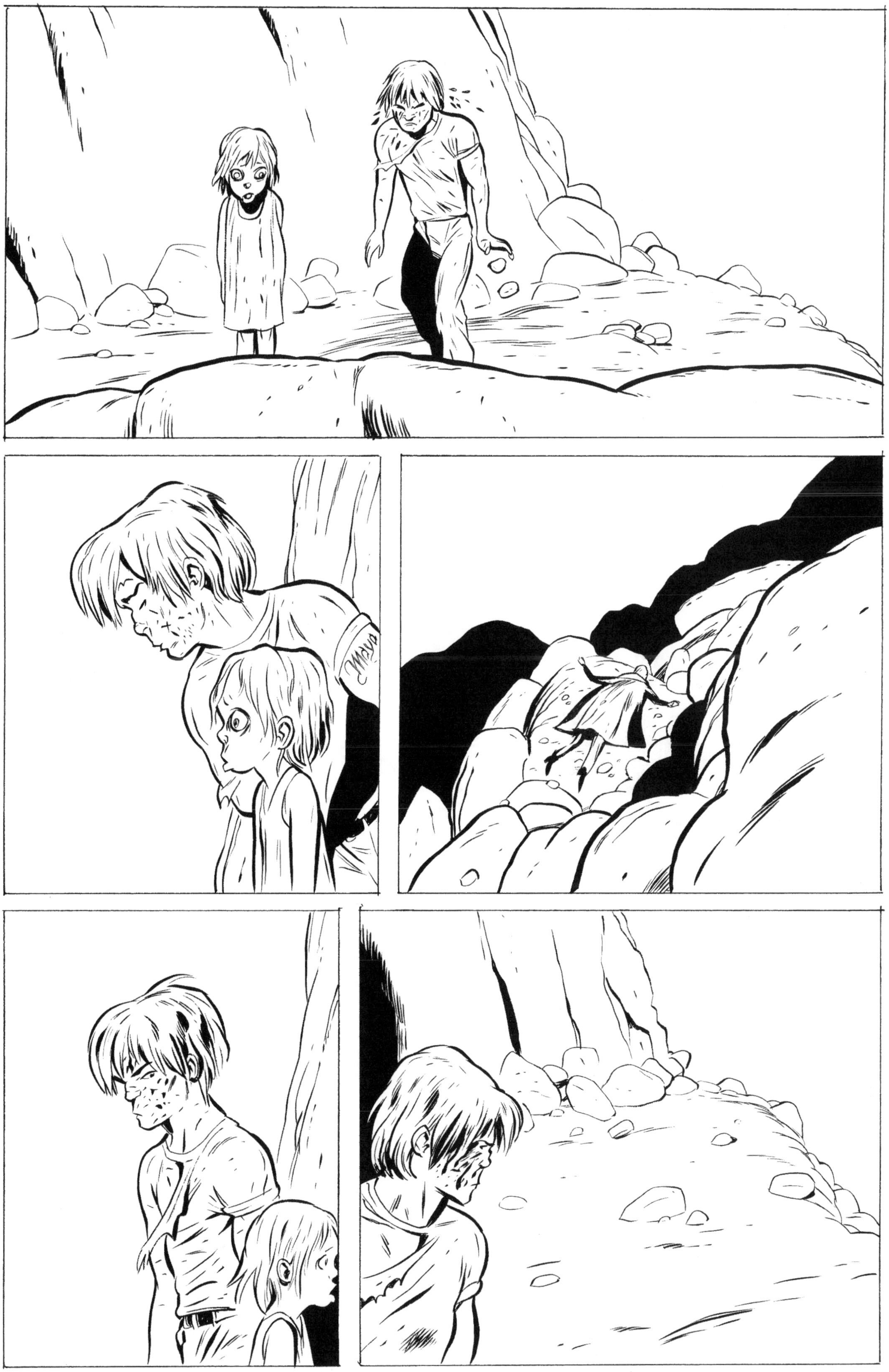

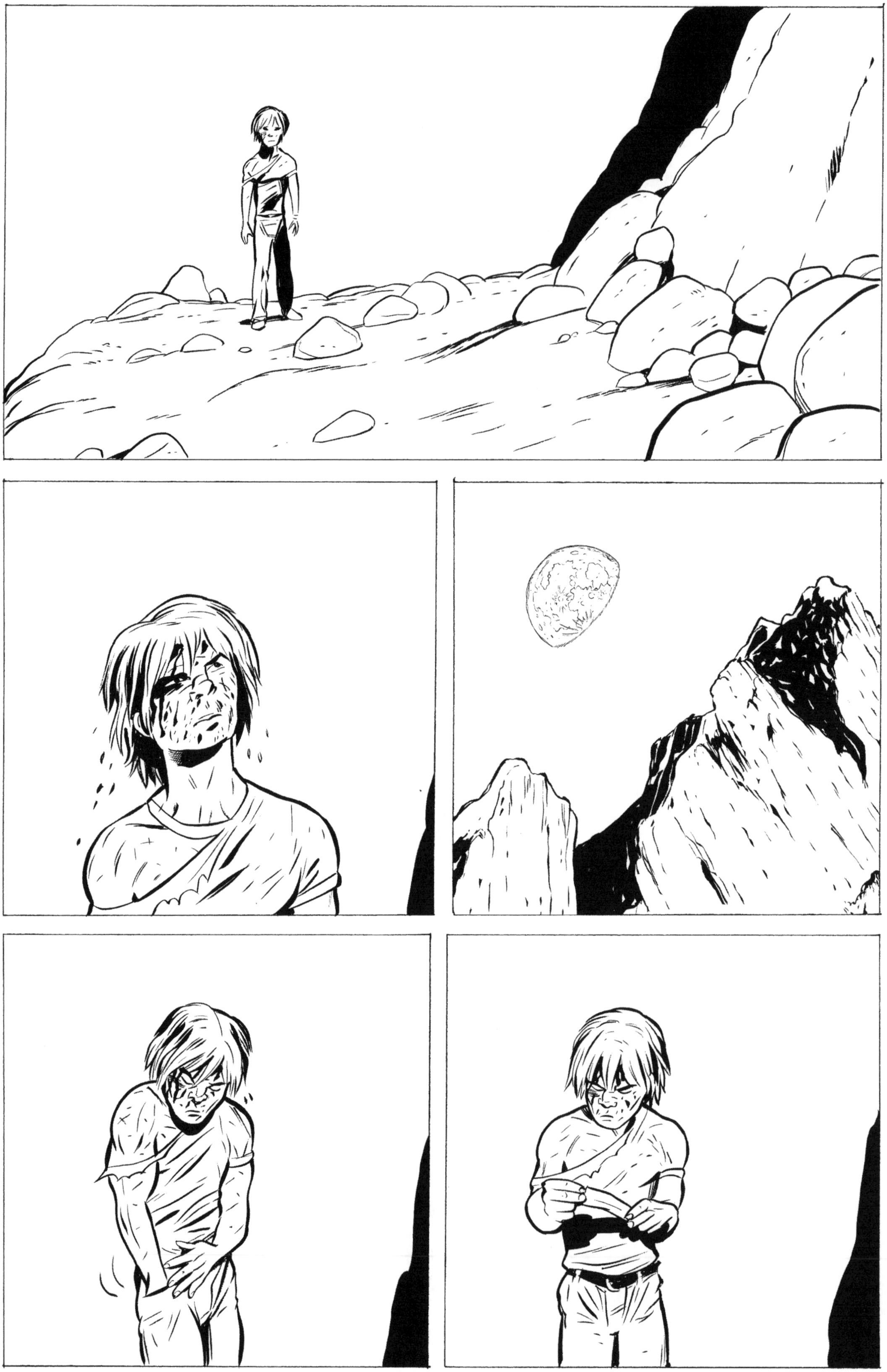

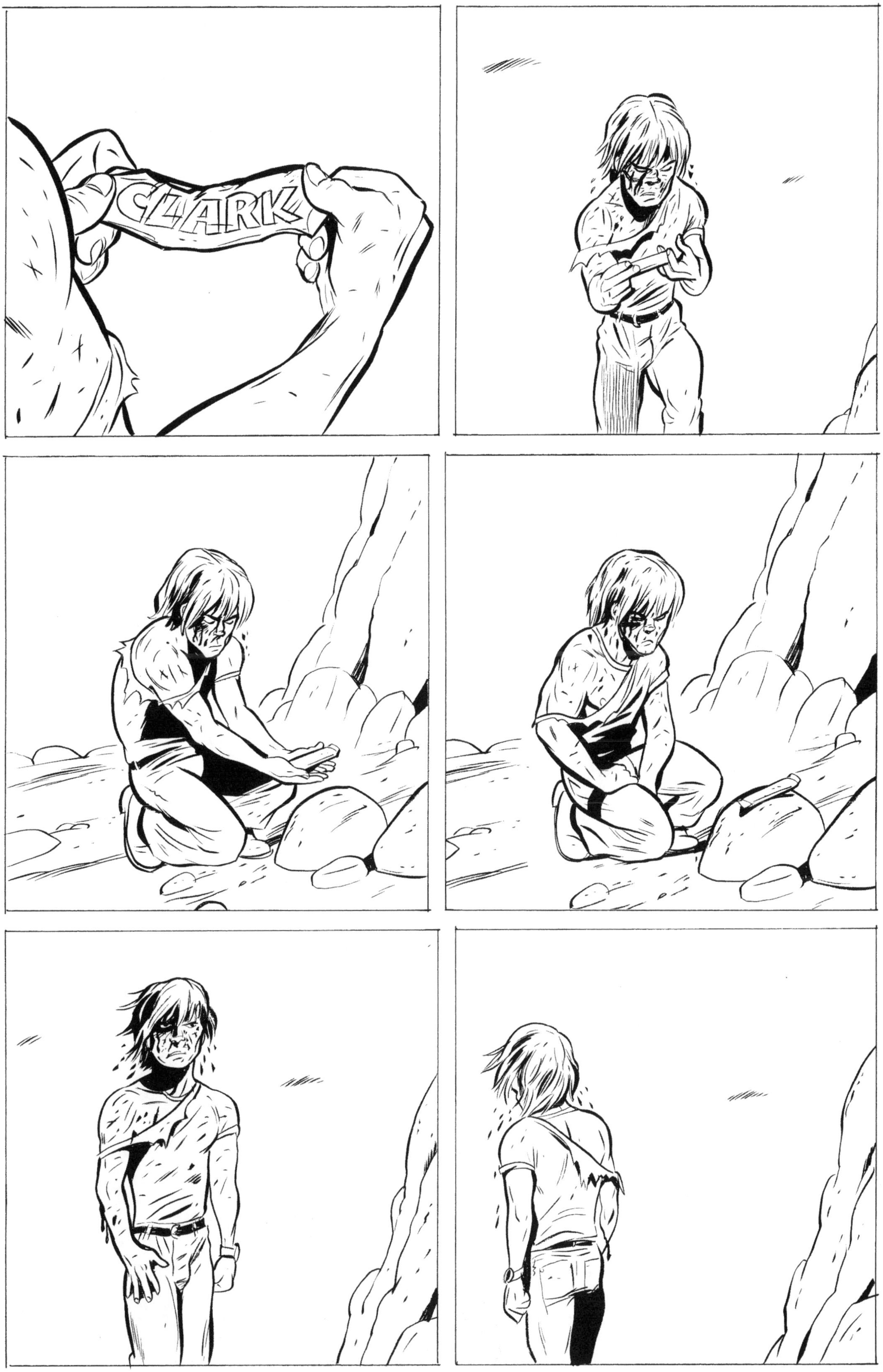
CLARK

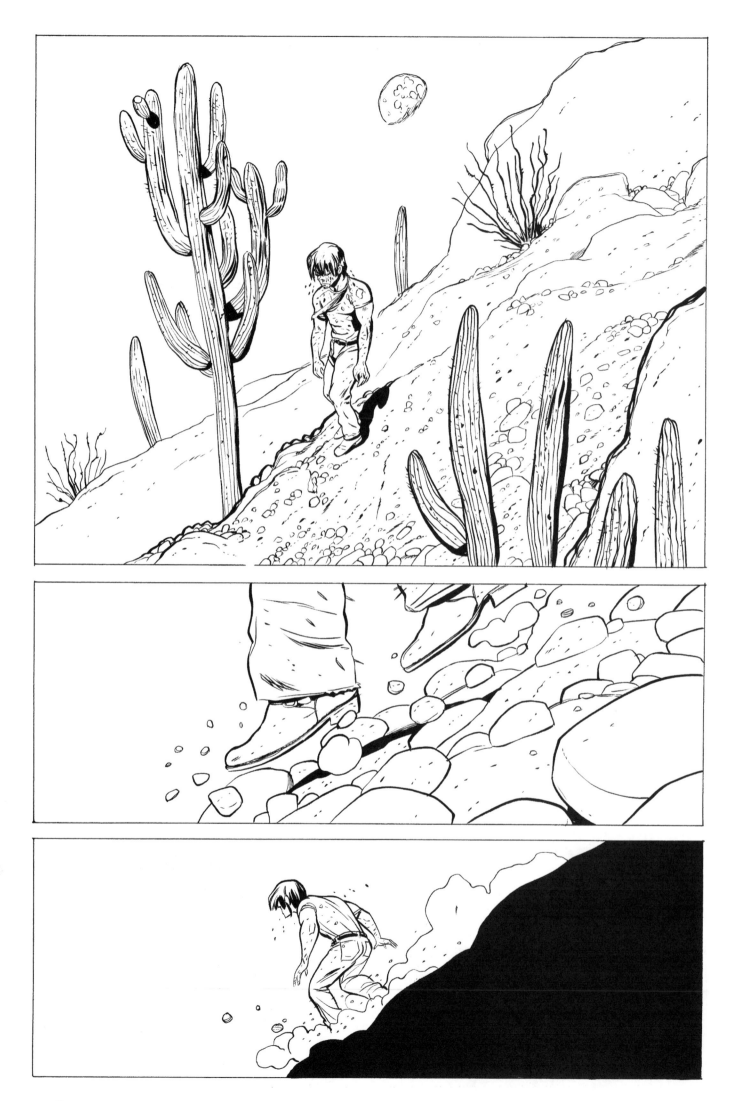

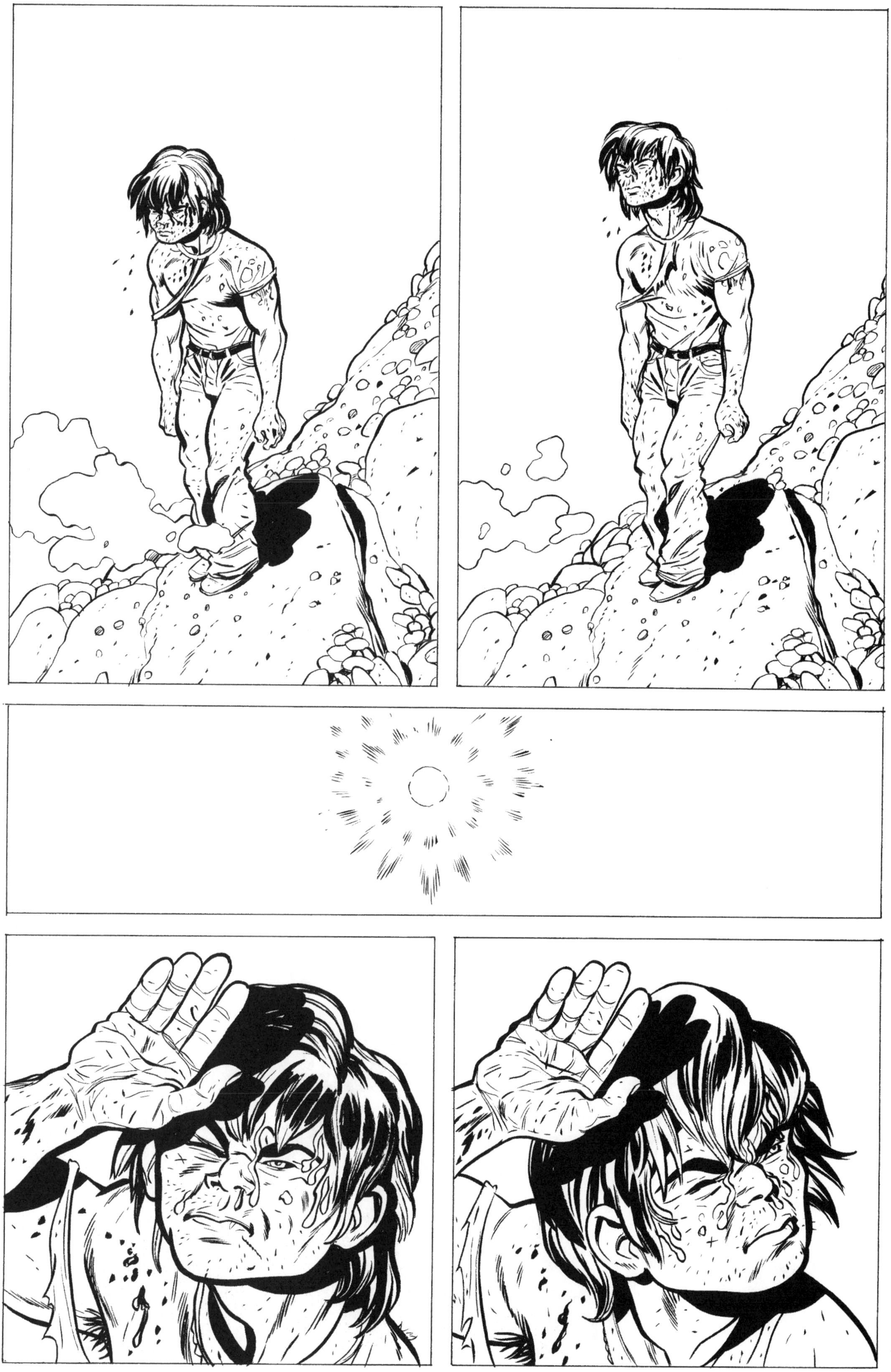

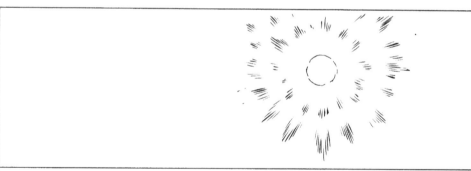

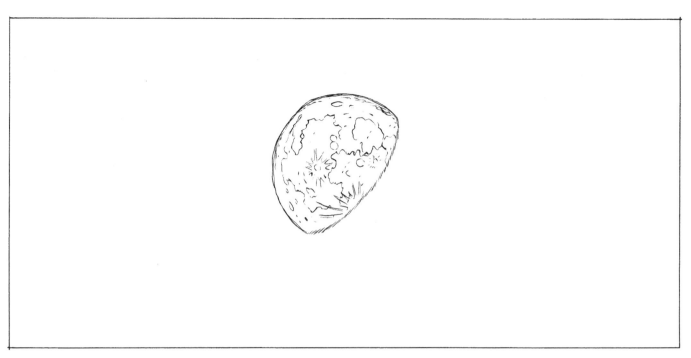

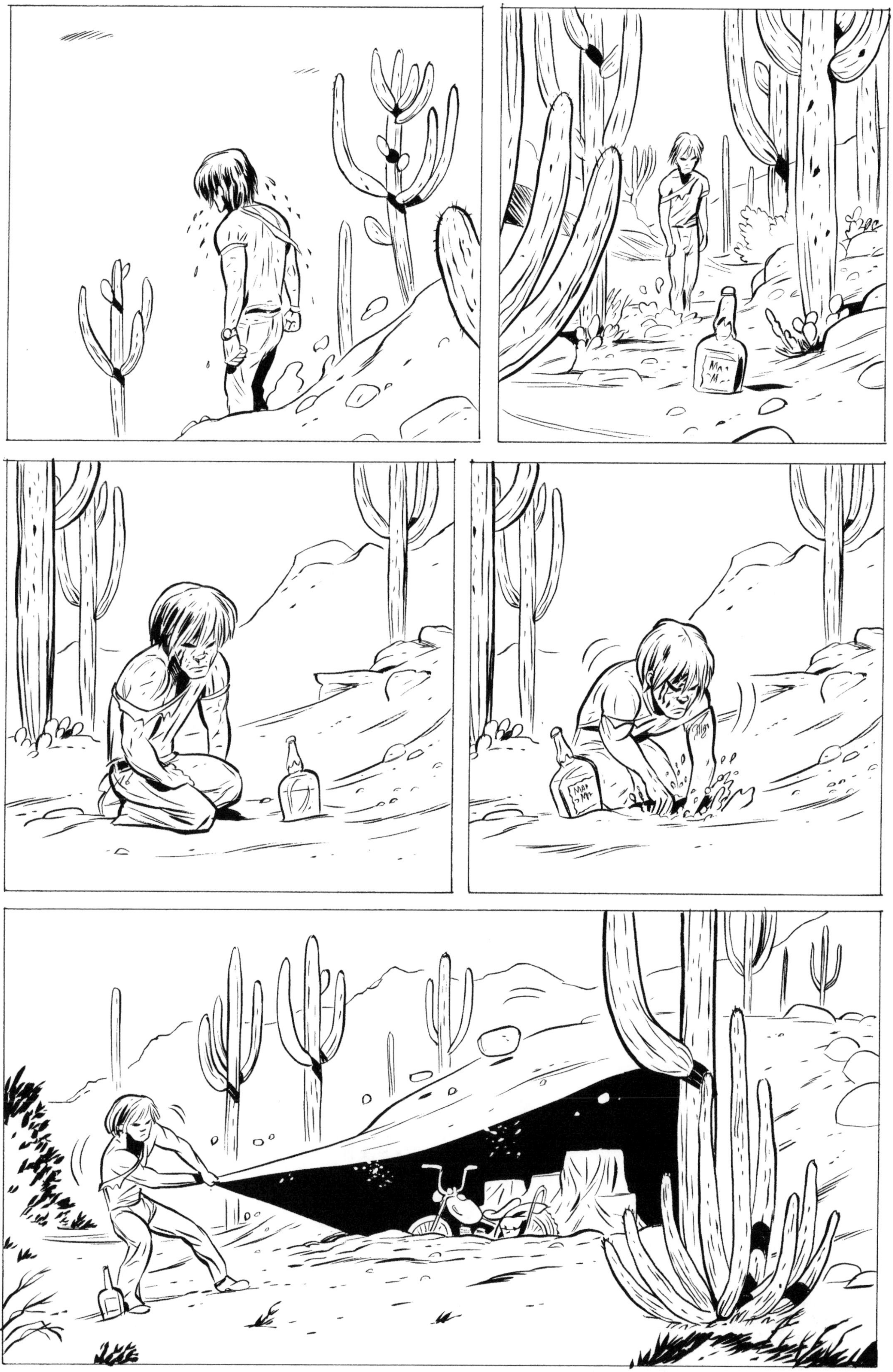

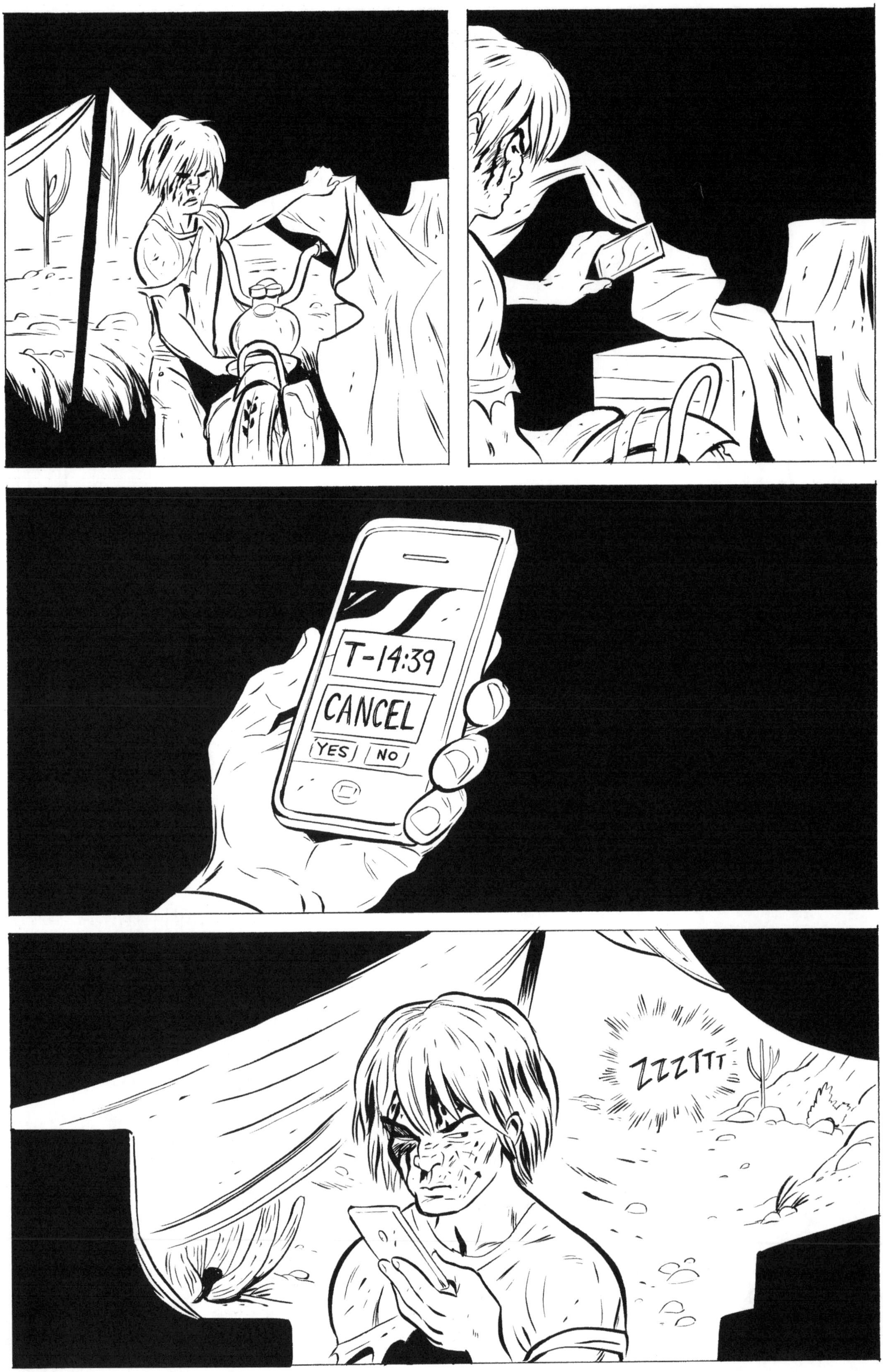
T-14:39
CANCEL
YES
NO
ZZZTTT

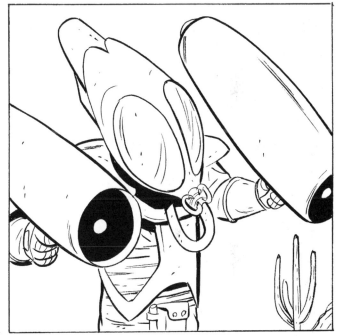

CHUNK

CHUNK

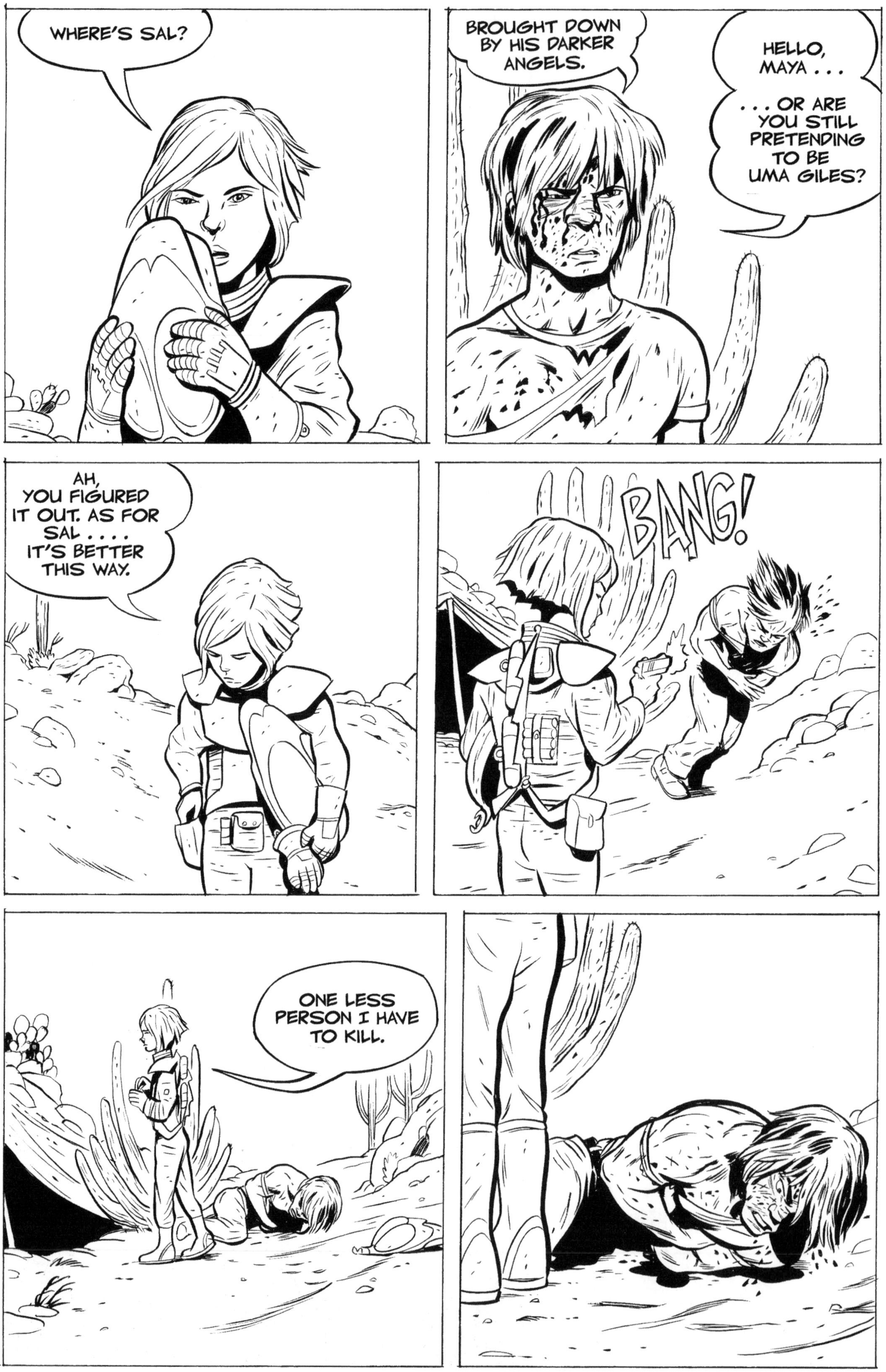
WHERE'S SAL?
BROUGHT DOWN BY HIS DARKER ANGELS.
HELLO, MAYA . . .
. . . OR ARE YOU STILL PRETENDING TO BE UMA GILES?
AH, YOU FIGURED IT OUT. AS FOR SAL . . . . IT'S BETTER THIS WAY.
BANG!
ONE LESS PERSON I HAVE TO KILL.

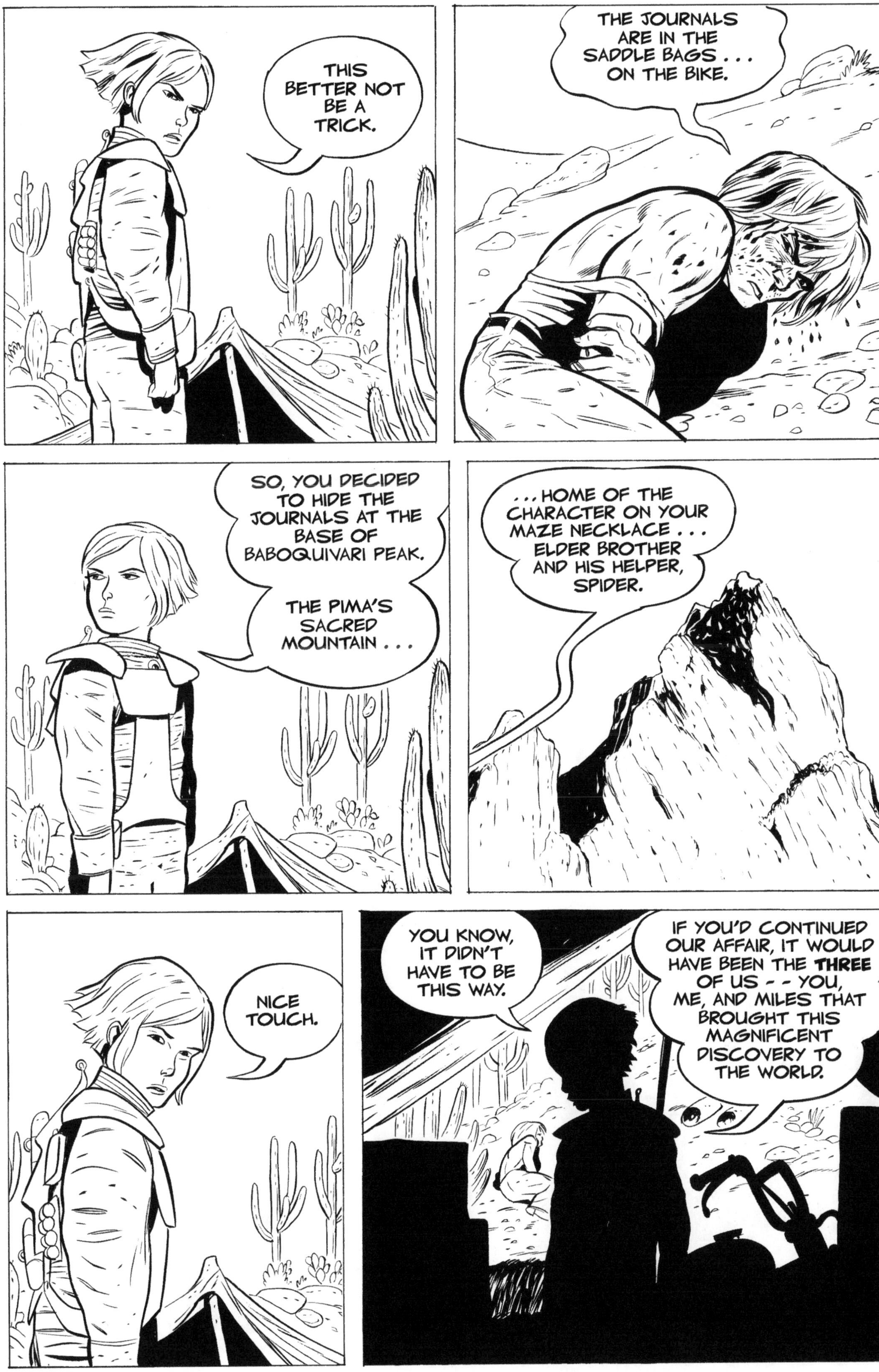
THIS BETTER NOT BE A TRICK.
THE JOURNALS ARE IN THE SADDLE BAGS . . . ON THE BIKE.
SO, YOU DECIDED TO HIDE THE JOURNALS AT THE BASE OF BABOQUIVARI PEAK.
THE PIMA'S SACRED MOUNTAIN . . .
. . . HOME OF THE CHARACTER ON YOUR MAZE NECKLACE . . . ELDER BROTHER AND HIS HELPER, SPIDER.
NICE TOUCH.
YOU KNOW, IT DIDN'T HAVE TO BE THIS WAY.
IF YOU'D CONTINUED OUR AFFAIR, IT WOULD HAVE BEEN THE **THREE** OF US - - YOU, ME, AND MILES THAT BROUGHT THIS MAGNIFICENT DISCOVERY TO THE WORLD.

TURNS OUT, YOU'RE **BOTH** BLEEDING HEARTS. THAT'S WHY I HAD TO KILL HIM.

AFTER I HELPED MILES REBUILD THE ST. GEORGE ARRAY, HE STARTED TO HAVE SECOND THOUGHTS . . .

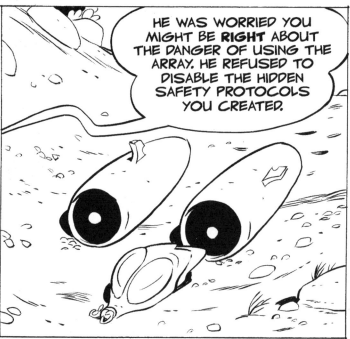

HE WAS WORRIED YOU MIGHT BE **RIGHT** ABOUT THE DANGER OF USING THE ARRAY. HE REFUSED TO DISABLE THE HIDDEN SAFETY PROTOCOLS YOU CREATED.

OF COURSE, THE REAL REASON I HAD TO KILL MILES WAS BECAUSE HE DISCOVERED PROOF THAT IT WAS **ME** WHO BLEW UP THE ORIGINAL ARRAY.

THAT'S RIGHT, I FOUND YOUR LITTLE GHOST PROGRAM MEANT TO BOG DOWN THE SYSTEM -- AND ADDED ONE OF MY OWN.

MILES WAS SUPPOSED TO DIE IN THE EXPLOSION, BUT HE SURVIVED. . . FOR ANOTHER COUPLE OF YEARS, ANYWAY.

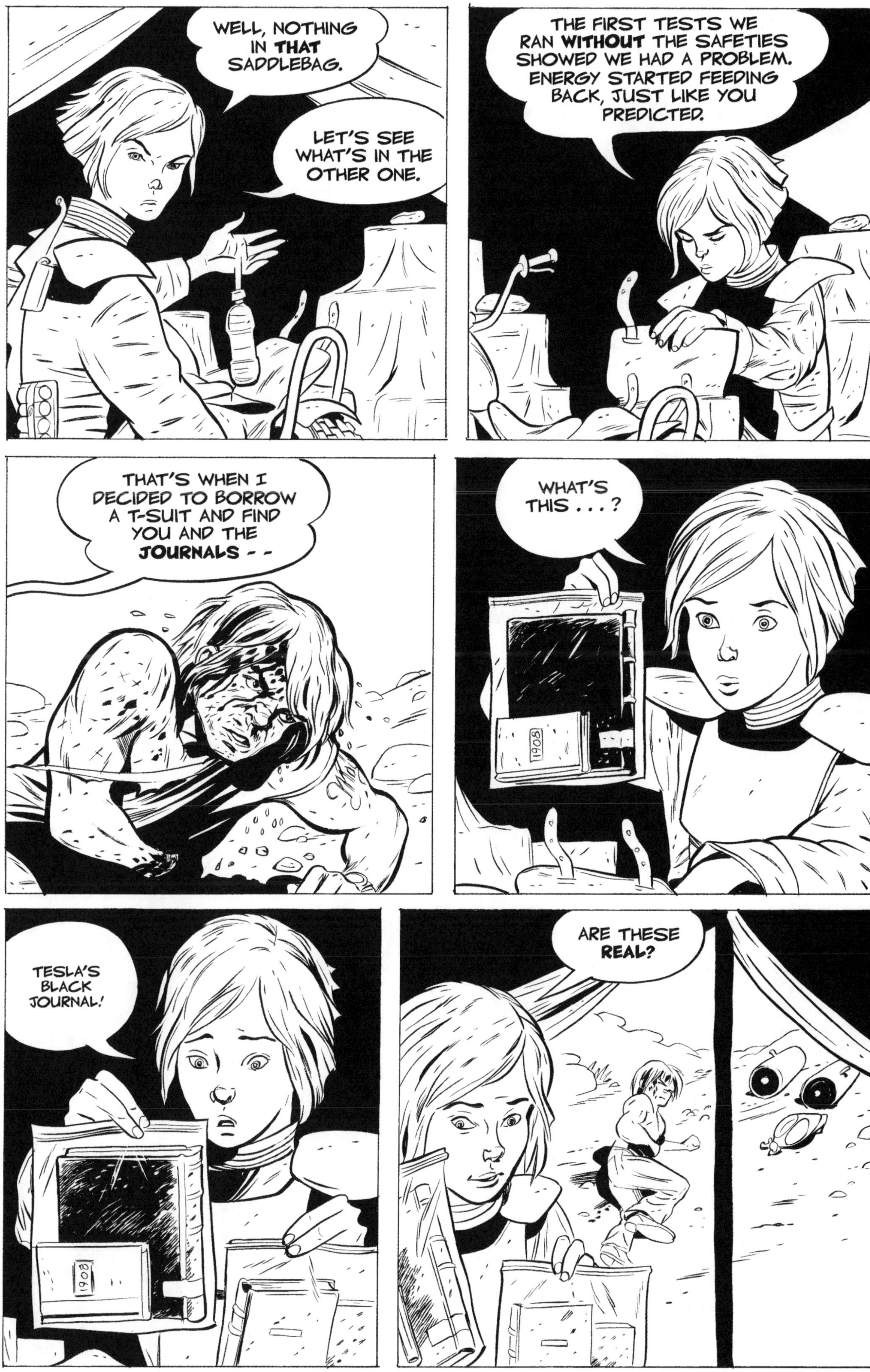
WELL, NOTHING IN THAT SADDLEBAG.
LET'S SEE WHAT'S IN THE OTHER ONE.
THE FIRST TESTS WE RAN WITHOUT THE SAFETIES SHOWED WE HAD A PROBLEM. ENERGY STARTED FEEDING BACK, JUST LIKE YOU PREDICTED.
THAT'S WHEN I DECIDED TO BORROW A T-SUIT AND FIND YOU AND THE JOURNALS - -
WHAT'S THIS . . . ?
1908
TESLA'S BLACK JOURNAL!
1908
ARE THESE REAL?

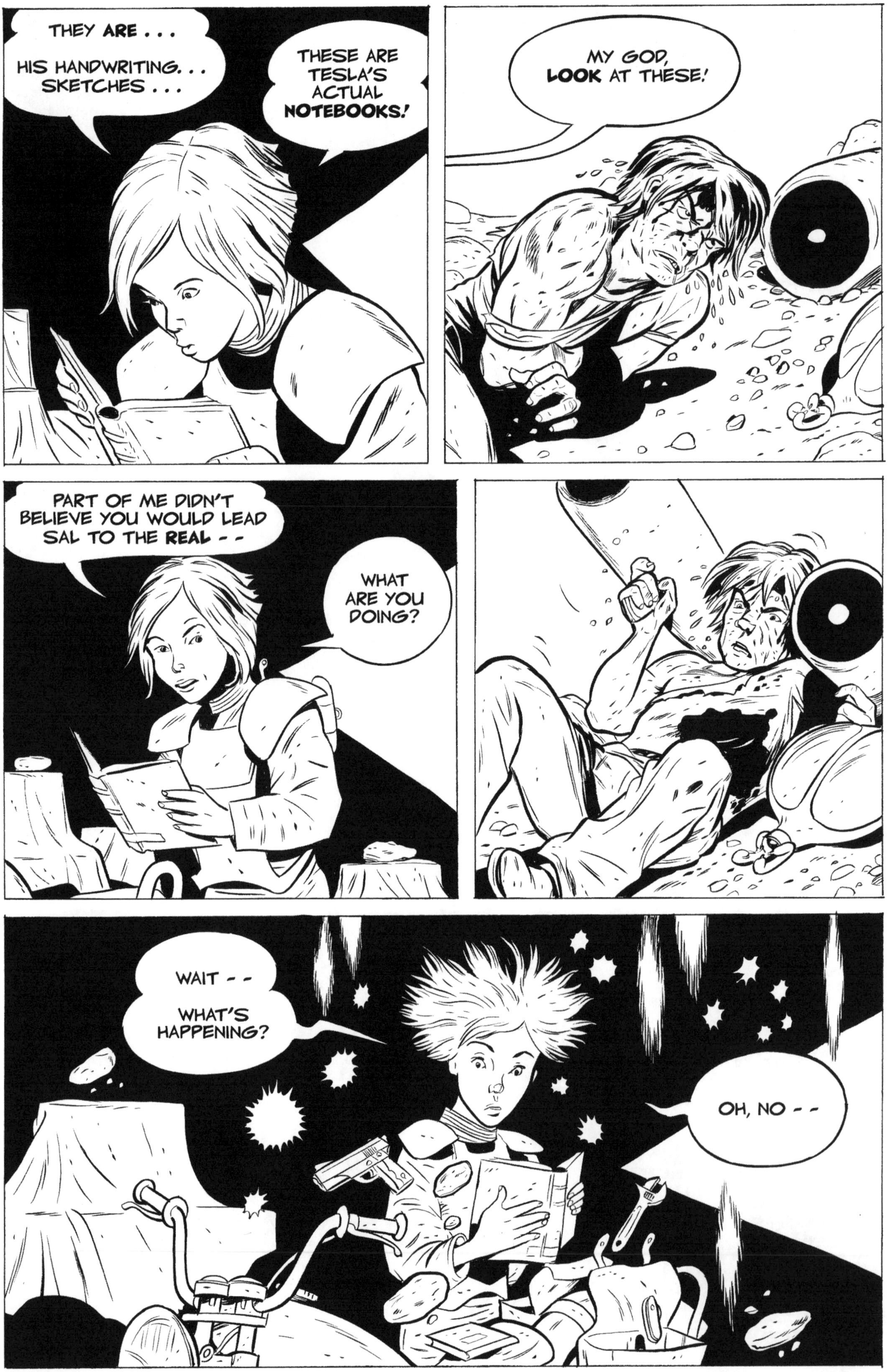
THEY ARE . . .
HIS HANDWRITING. . . SKETCHES . . .
THESE ARE TESLA'S ACTUAL NOTEBOOKS!
MY GOD, LOOK AT THESE!
PART OF ME DIDN'T BELIEVE YOU WOULD LEAD SAL TO THE REAL - -
WHAT ARE YOU DOING?
WAIT - -
WHAT'S HAPPENING?
OH, NO - -

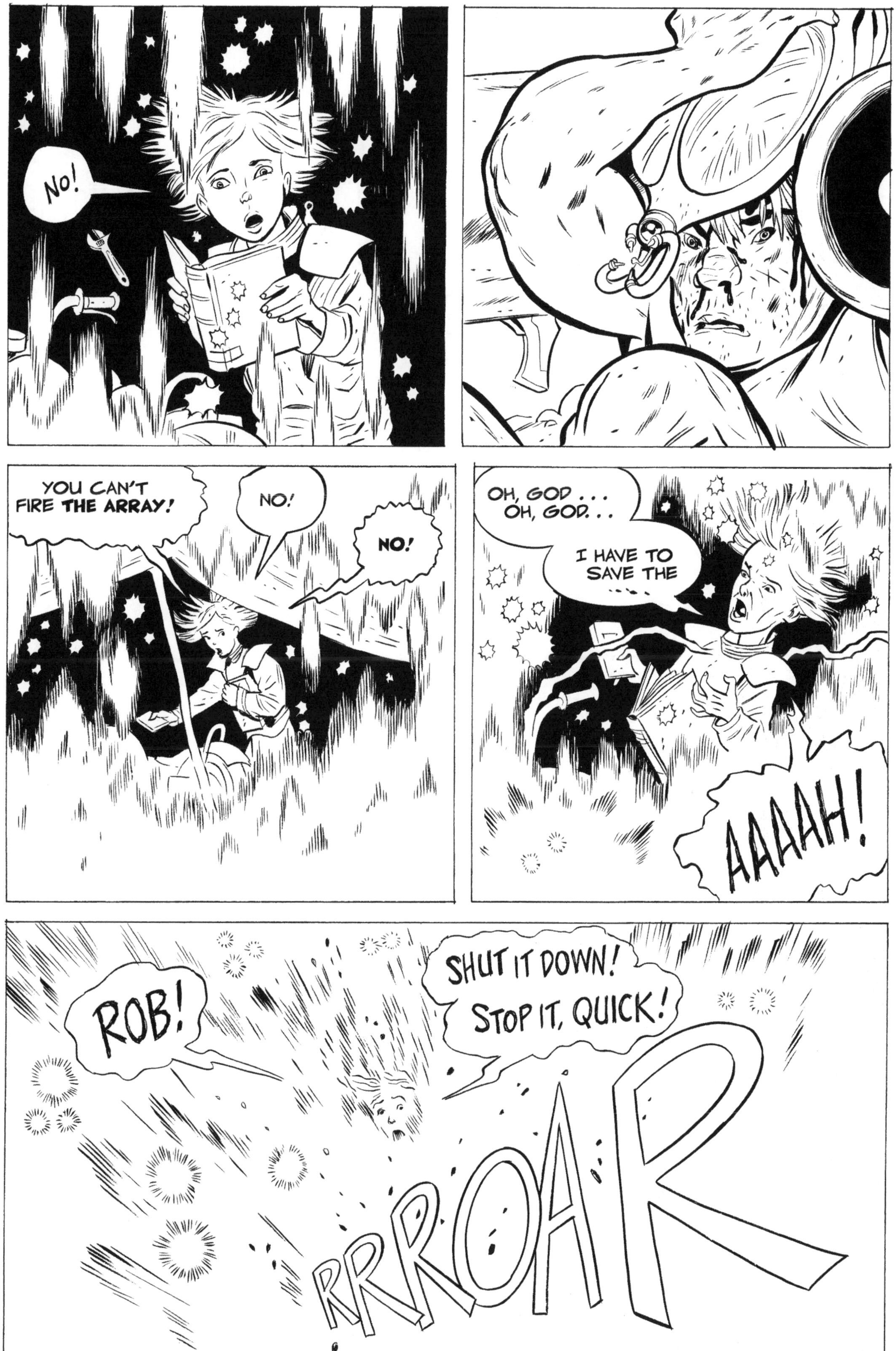
NO!
YOU CAN'T FIRE THE ARRAY!
NO!
NO!
OH, GOD . . . OH, GOD . . .
I HAVE TO SAVE THE . . .
AAAAH!
ROB!
SHUT IT DOWN! STOP IT, QUICK!
RRROAR

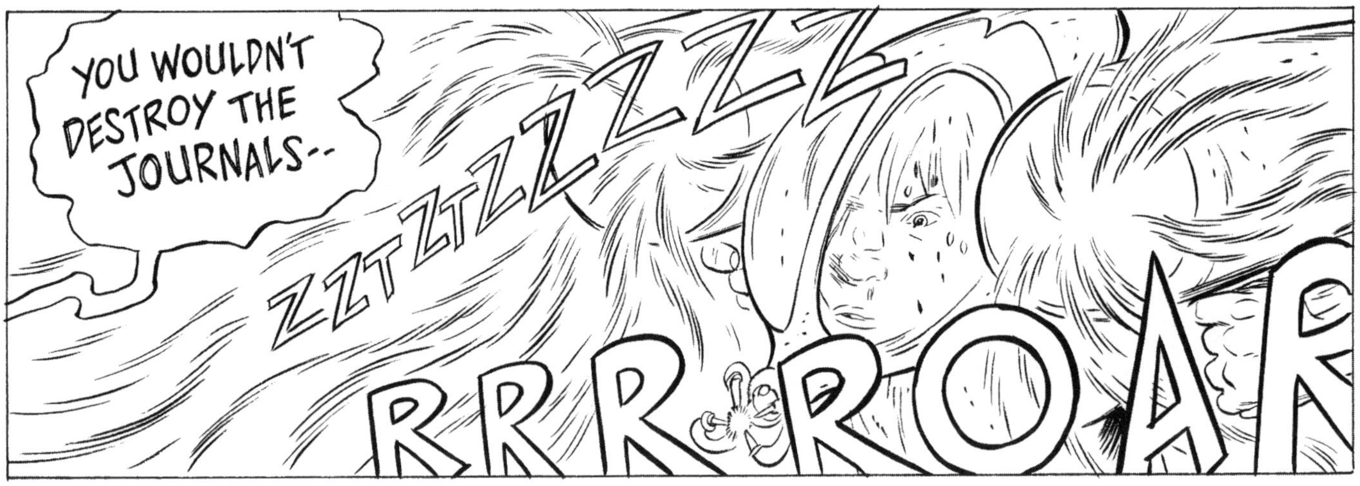
YOU WOULDN'T DESTROY THE JOURNALS--
ZZTZTZTZZZZZZ
RRR-ROAR

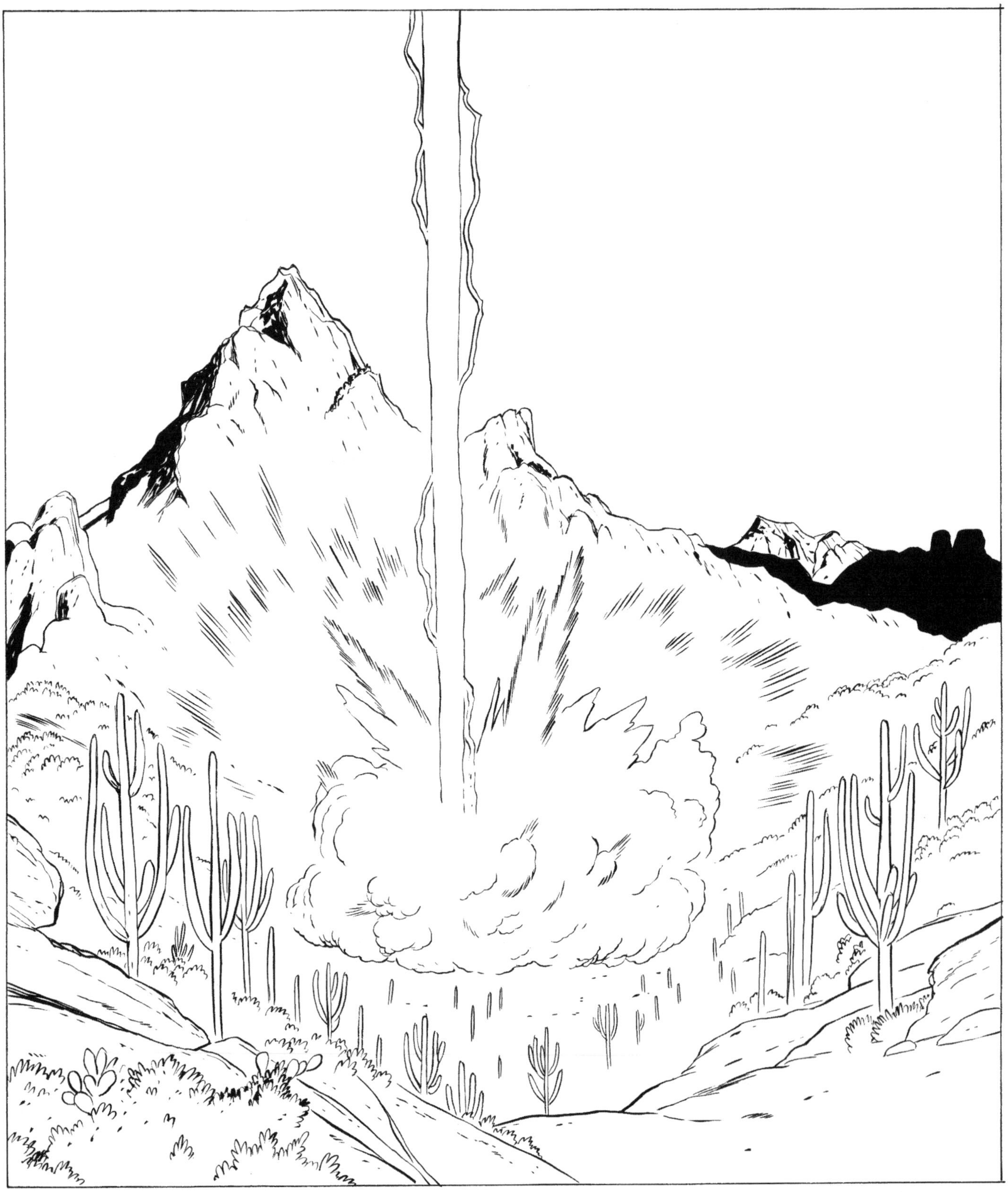

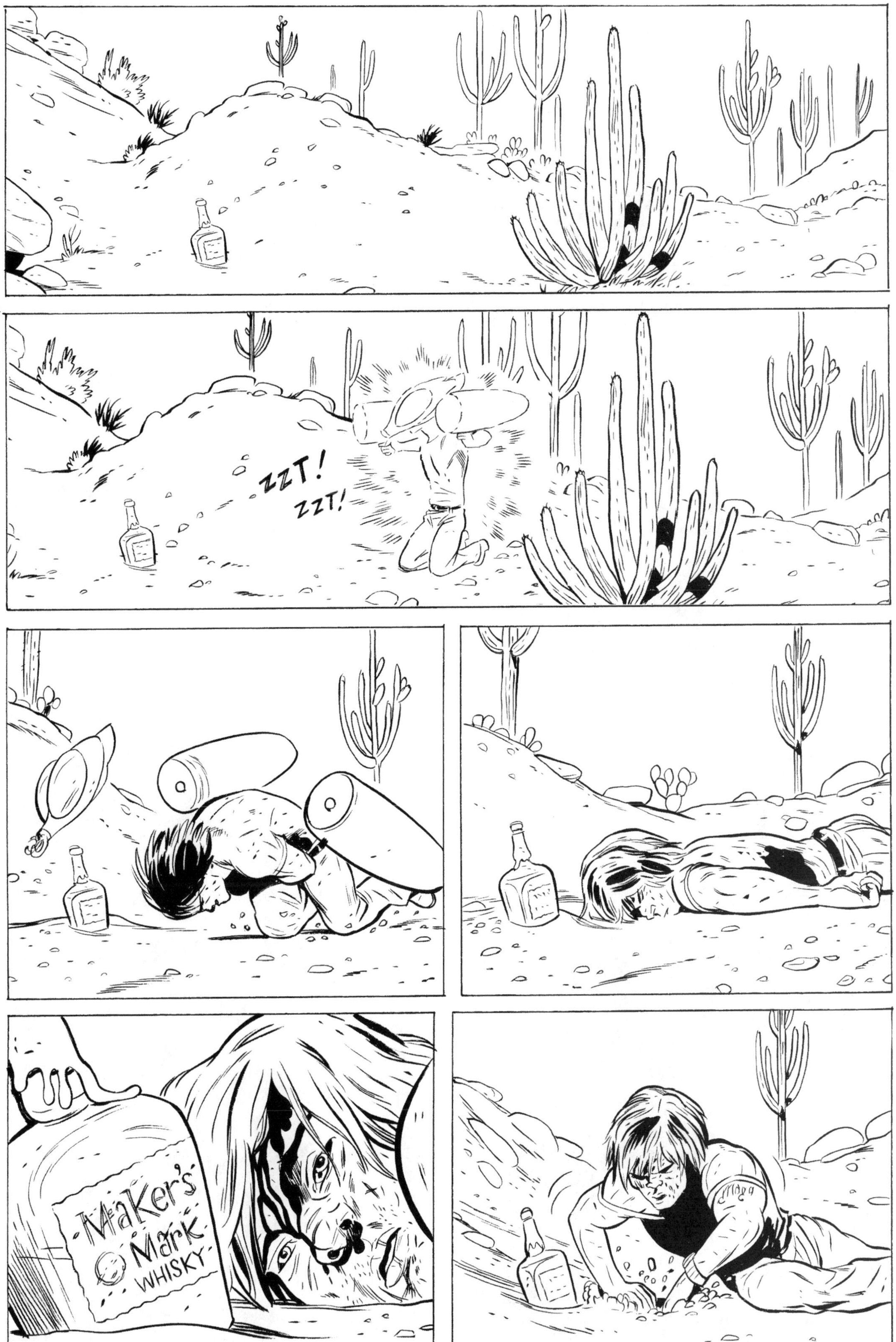
ZZT!
ZZT!
Maker's Mark WHISKY

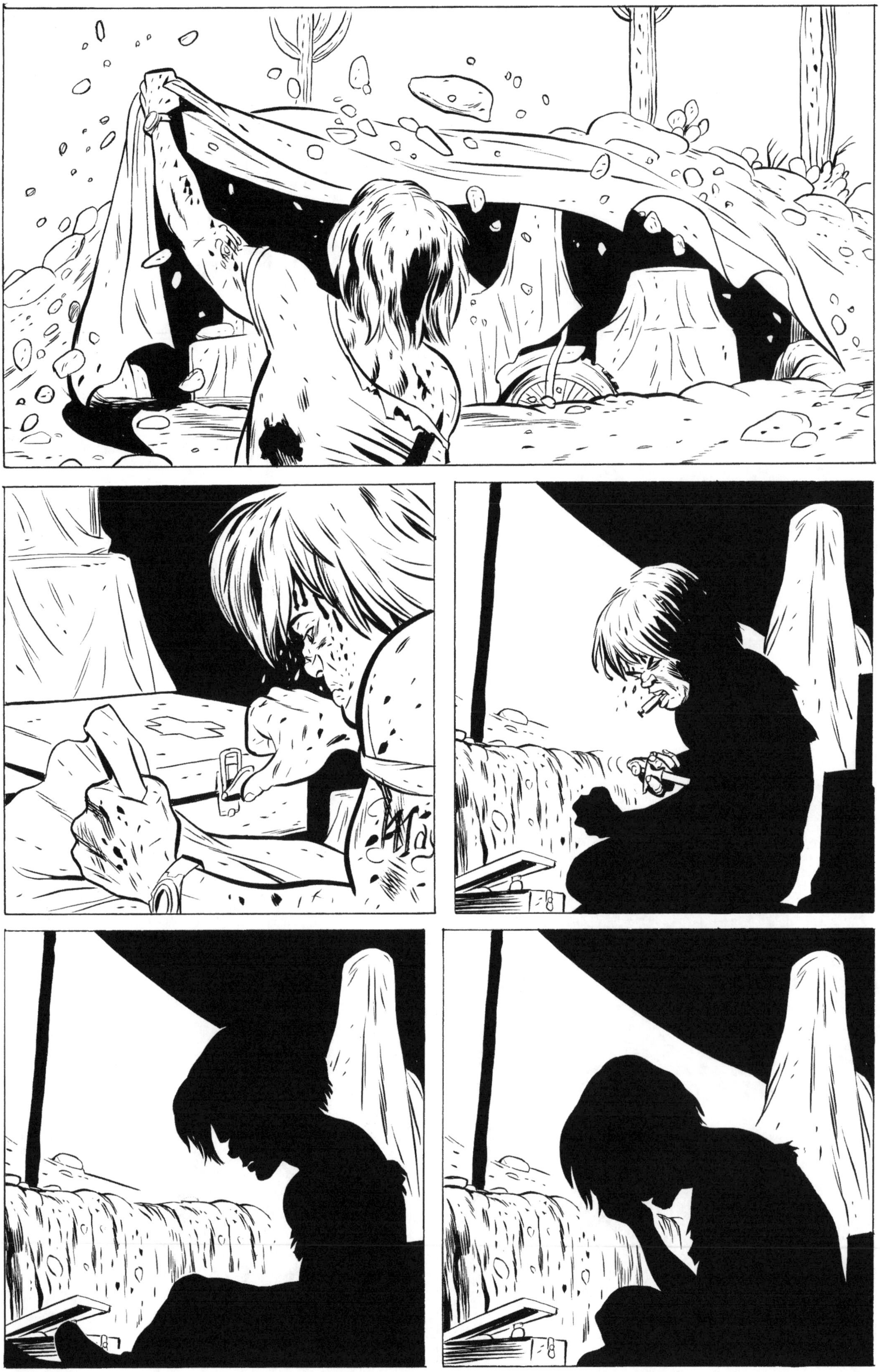

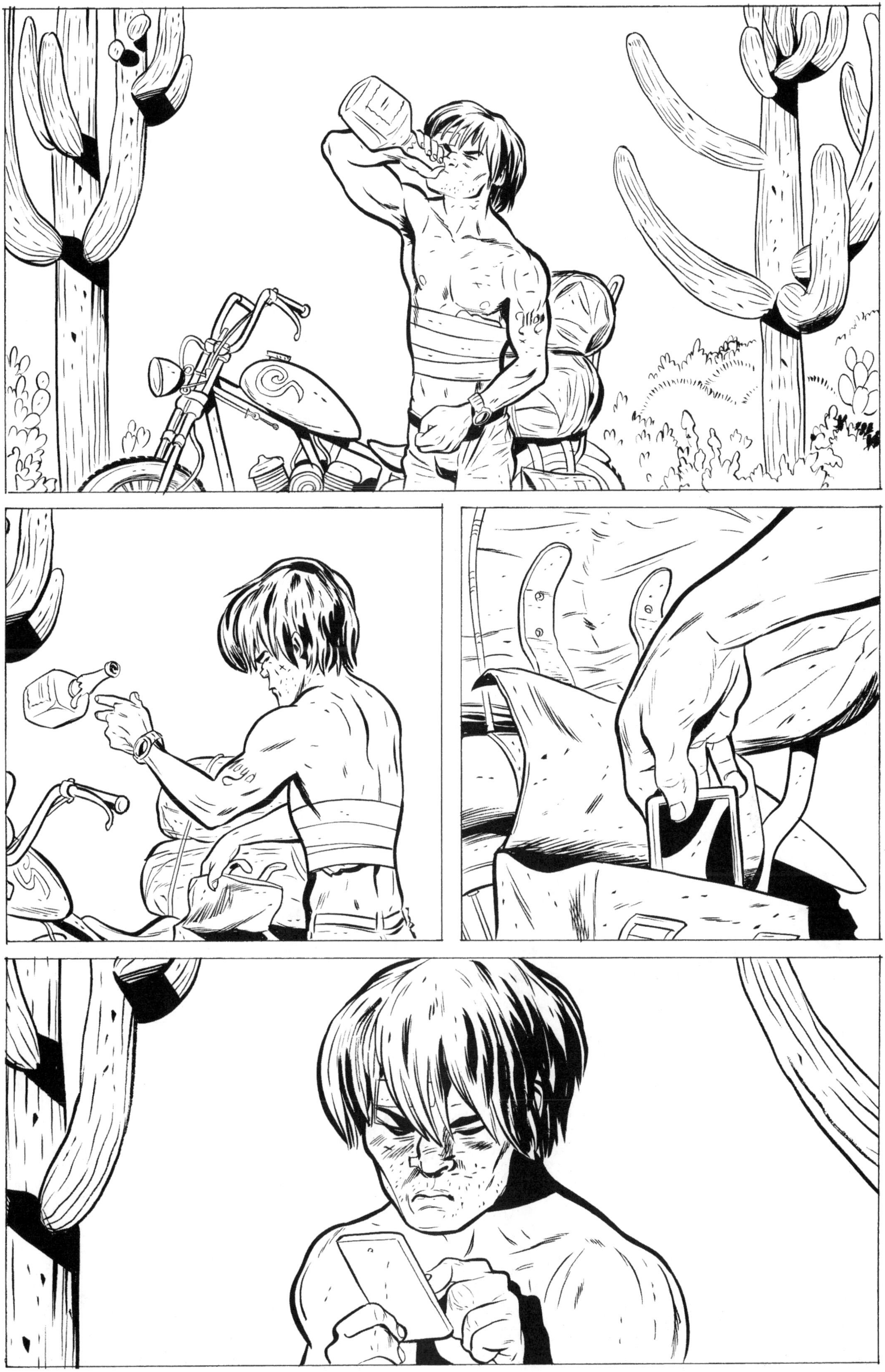

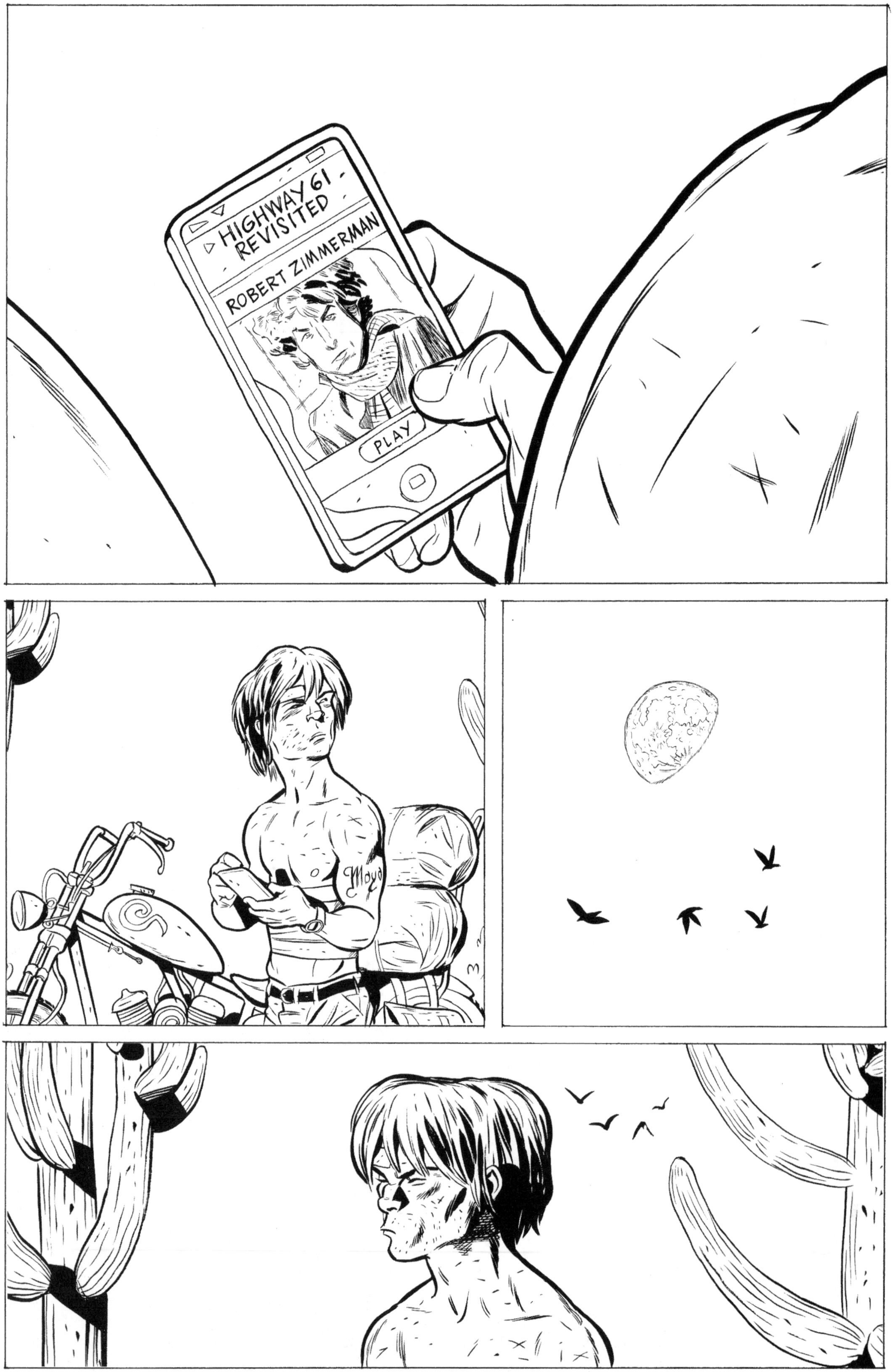
HIGHWAY 61
REVISITED
ROBERT ZIMMERMAN
PLAY
Moya

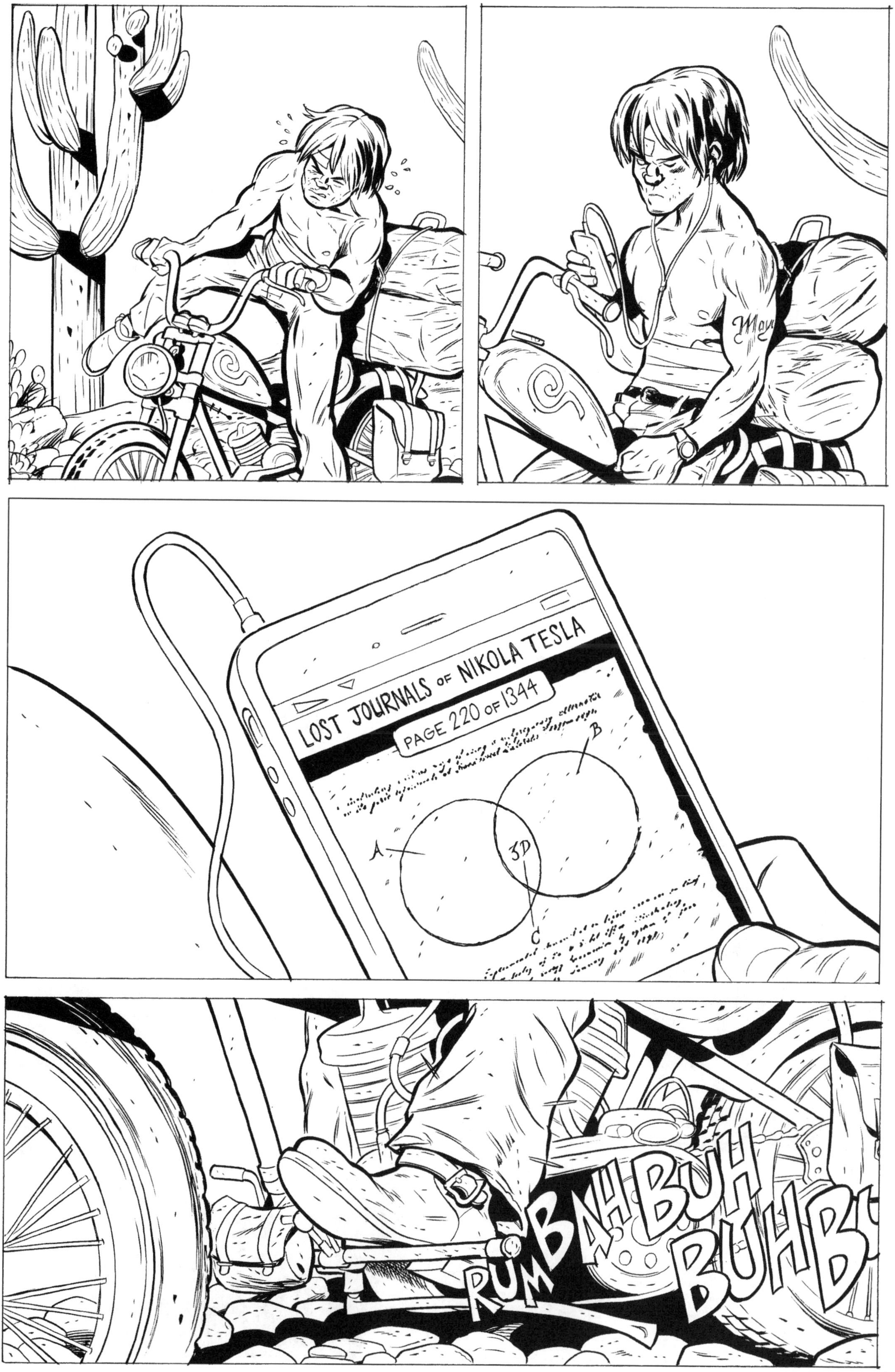
LOST JOURNALS OF NIKOLA TESLA
PAGE 220 OF 1344
A
B
3D
C
RUM BAH BUH
BUH

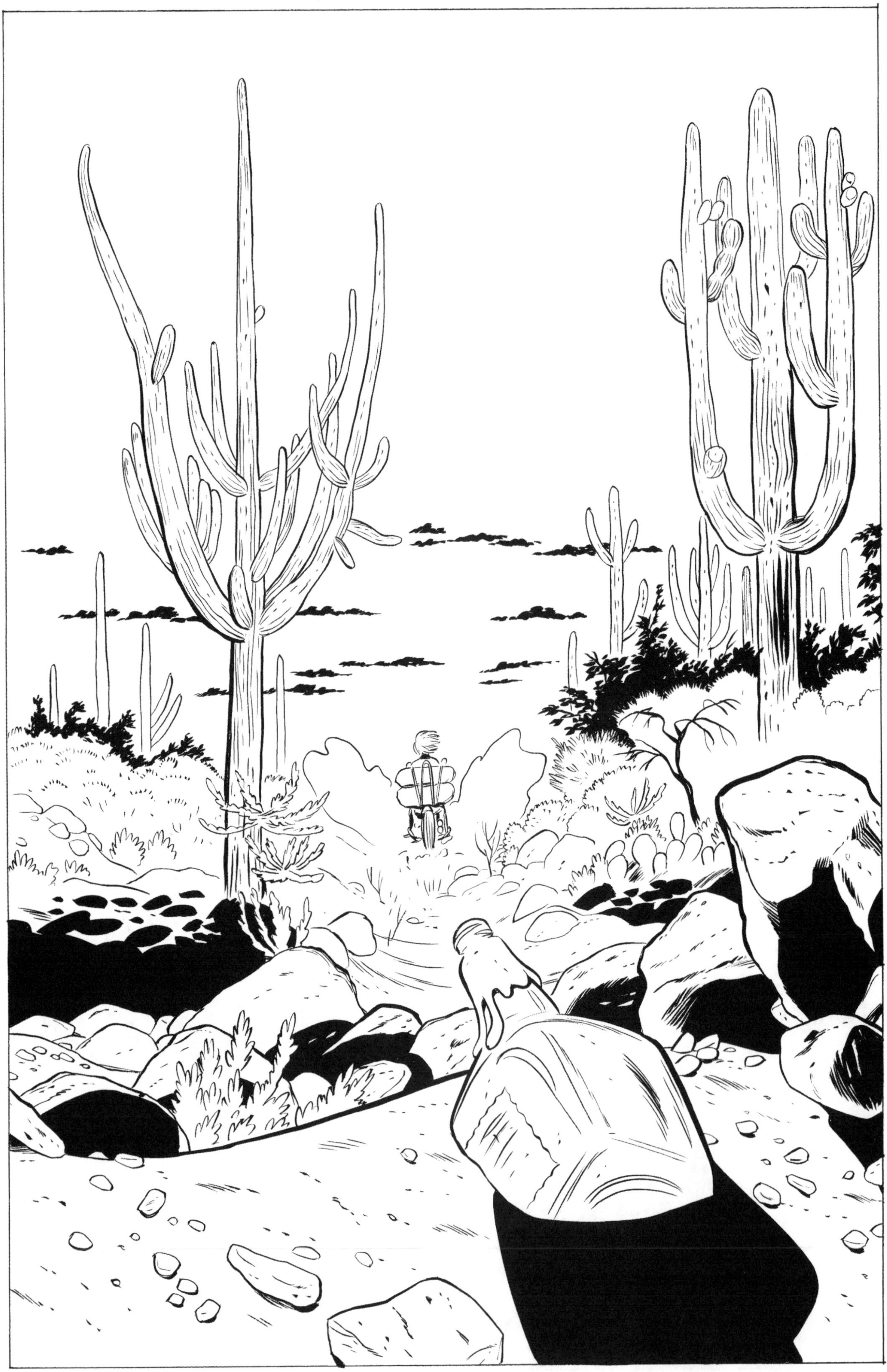

APPENDIX PART TWO

BEHIND THE SCENES OF RASL VOLUMES THREE AND FOUR

RASL
No. 8
JEFF SMITH

RASL
No. 9
JEFF SMITH

RASL
No. 10
JEFF SMITH

RASL
No. 11
JEFF SMITH

RASL
No. 12
Maker's Mark
WHISKY
JEFF SMITH

RASL
No. 13
JEFF SMITH

RASL
No. 14
JEFF SMITH

RASL
No. 15
JEFF SMITH

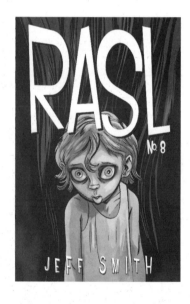

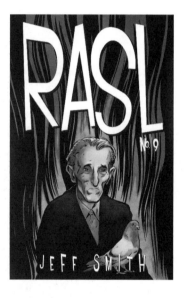

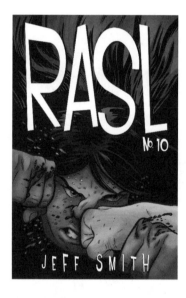

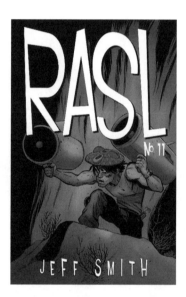

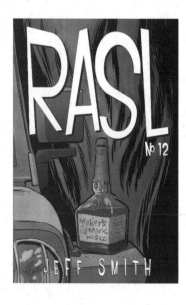

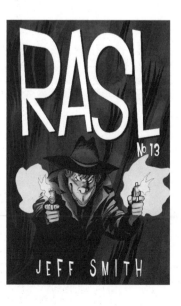

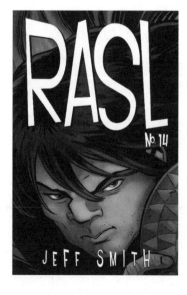

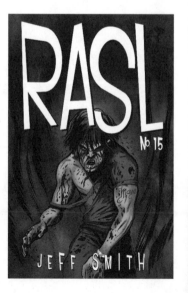

Designing Romance & Lost Journals

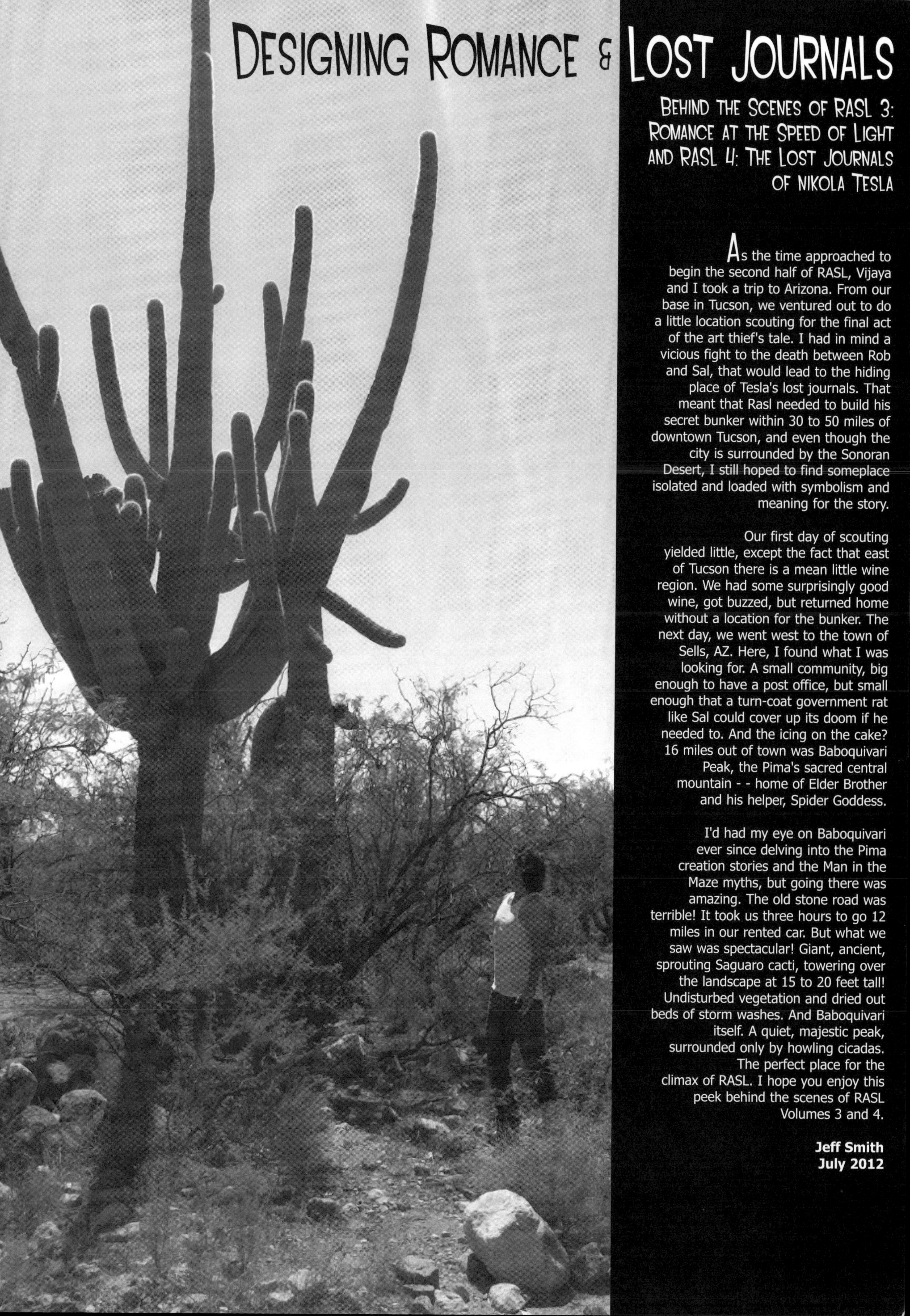

Behind the Scenes of RASL 3: Romance at the Speed of Light and RASL 4: The Lost Journals of Nikola Tesla

As the time approached to begin the second half of RASL, Vijaya and I took a trip to Arizona. From our base in Tucson, we ventured out to do a little location scouting for the final act of the art thief's tale. I had in mind a vicious fight to the death between Rob and Sal, that would lead to the hiding place of Tesla's lost journals. That meant that Rasl needed to build his secret bunker within 30 to 50 miles of downtown Tucson, and even though the city is surrounded by the Sonoran Desert, I still hoped to find someplace isolated and loaded with symbolism and meaning for the story.

Our first day of scouting yielded little, except the fact that east of Tucson there is a mean little wine region. We had some surprisingly good wine, got buzzed, but returned home without a location for the bunker. The next day, we went west to the town of Sells, AZ. Here, I found what I was looking for. A small community, big enough to have a post office, but small enough that a turn-coat government rat like Sal could cover up its doom if he needed to. And the icing on the cake? 16 miles out of town was Baboquivari Peak, the Pima's sacred central mountain - - home of Elder Brother and his helper, Spider Goddess.

I'd had my eye on Baboquivari ever since delving into the Pima creation stories and the Man in the Maze myths, but going there was amazing. The old stone road was terrible! It took us three hours to go 12 miles in our rented car. But what we saw was spectacular! Giant, ancient, sprouting Saguaro cacti, towering over the landscape at 15 to 20 feet tall! Undisturbed vegetation and dried out beds of storm washes. And Baboquivari itself. A quiet, majestic peak, surrounded only by howling cicadas. The perfect place for the climax of RASL. I hope you enjoy this peek behind the scenes of RASL Volumes 3 and 4.

Jeff Smith
July 2012

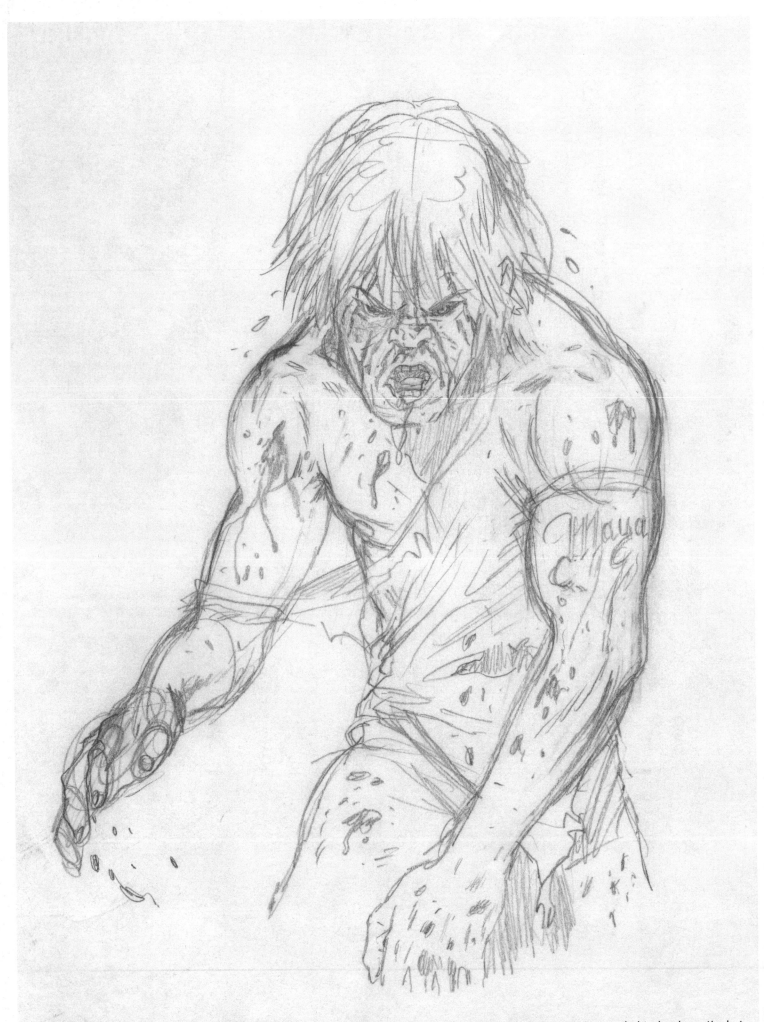

Pencil drawing for the cover of RASL #15. Done with a regular pencil, the cover of the last issue of the series needed to be dramatic, but also consistent with the situation our hero found himself in at the beginning of the tale. In issue #1, we first met Rob as he wandered through the desert, bloody and exhausted, from what we learn in the final chapter was a death-match with Sal.

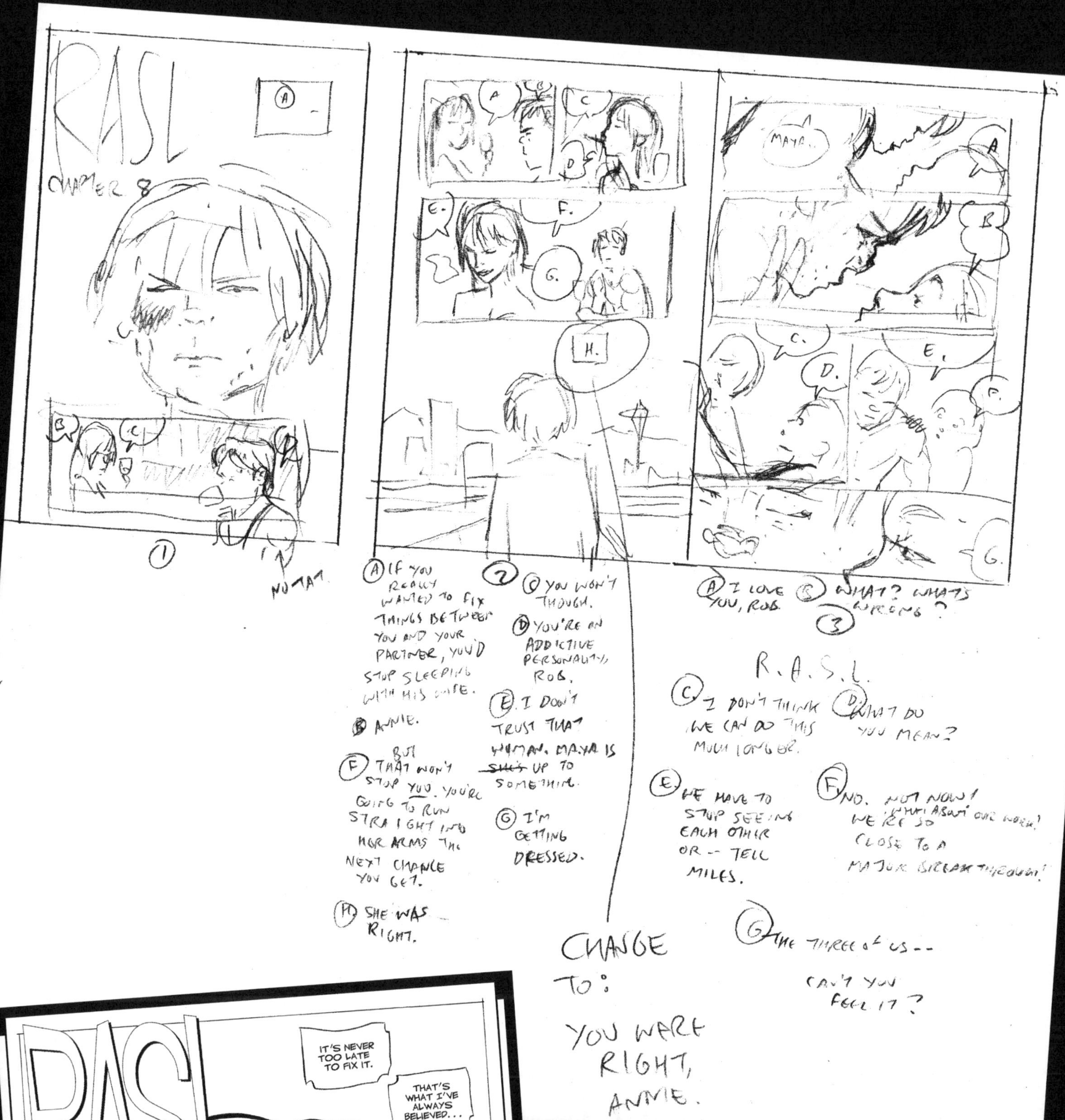
RASL
CHAPTER 8
(A) IF YOU REALLY WANTED TO FIX THINGS BETWEEN YOU AND YOUR PARTNER, YOU'D STOP SLEEPING WITH HIS WIFE.
(B) ANNIE.
(C) YOU WON'T THOUGH.
(D) YOU'RE AN ADDICTIVE PERSONALITY, ROB.
(E) I DON'T TRUST THAT WOMAN. MAYA IS UP TO SOMETHING.
(F) BUT THAT WON'T STOP YOU. YOU'RE GOING TO RUN STRAIGHT INTO HER ARMS THE NEXT CHANCE YOU GET.
(G) I'M GETTING DRESSED.
(H) SHE WAS RIGHT.
CHANGE TO: YOU WERE RIGHT, ANNIE.
MAYA...
(A) I LOVE YOU, ROB.
(B) WHAT? WHAT'S WRONG?
R.A.S.L.
(C) I DON'T THINK WE CAN DO THIS MUCH LONGER.
(D) WHAT DO YOU MEAN?
(E) WE HAVE TO STOP SEEING EACH OTHER OR -- TELL MILES.
(F) NO. NOT NOW! WHAT ABOUT OUR WORK! WE'RE SO CLOSE TO A MAJOR BREAKTHROUGH!
(G) THE THREE OF US -- CAN'T YOU FEEL IT?

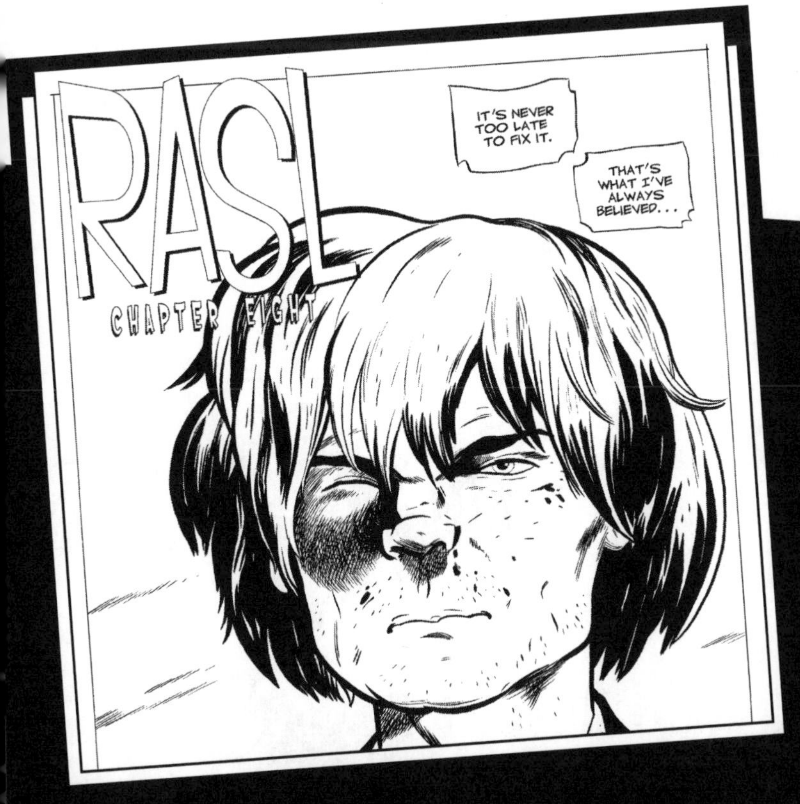
RASL
CHAPTER EIGHT
IT'S NEVER TOO LATE TO FIX IT.
THAT'S WHAT I'VE ALWAYS BELIEVED...

Script pages for the the opening of RASL Volume 3 [chapter 8]
The second half of the story begins with a warning from Rob's only confidant, Annie (seen here in a flashback):
Annie tells Rob that she doesn't trust Maya - - that woman is up to something!

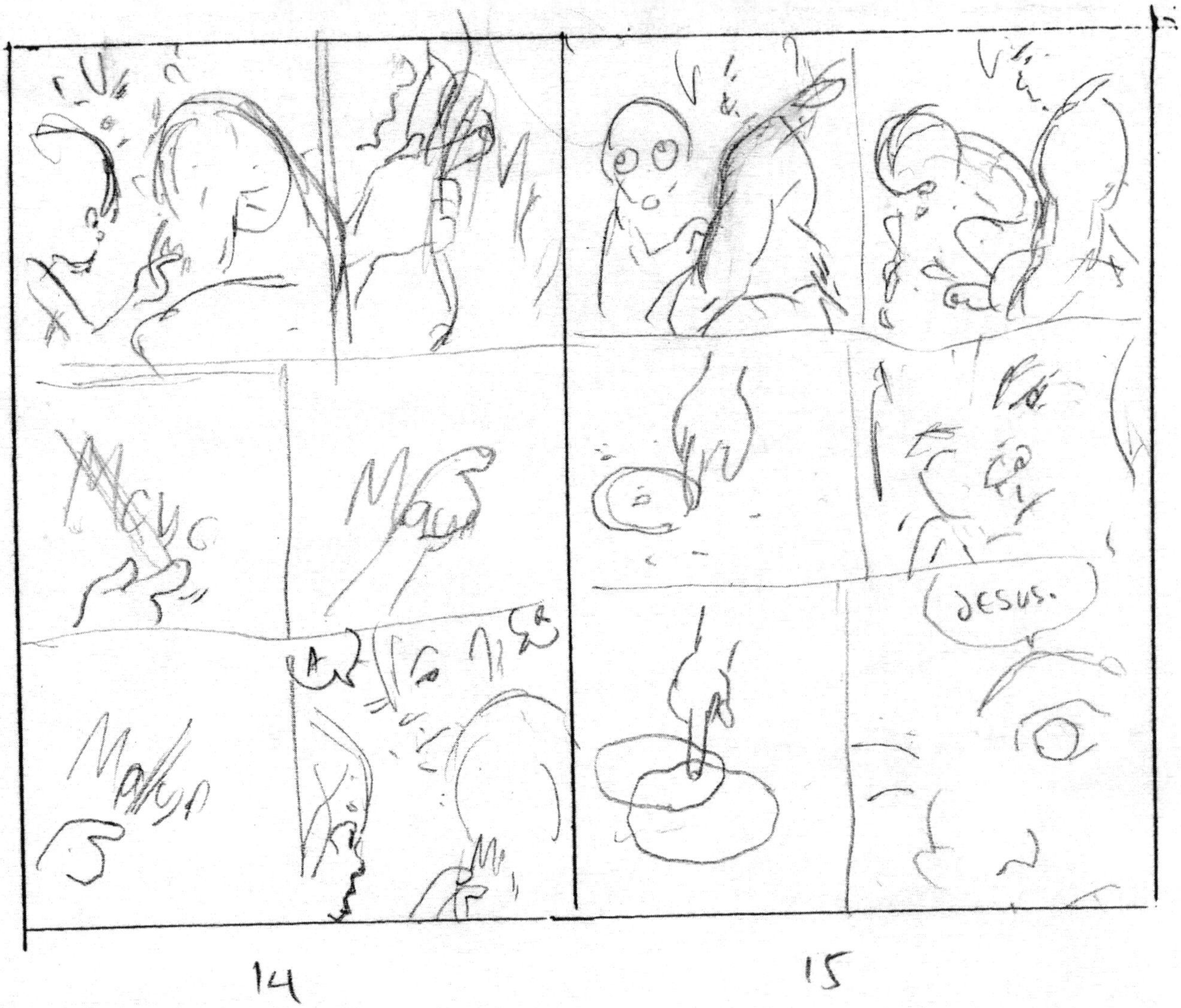
JESUS.
14
15

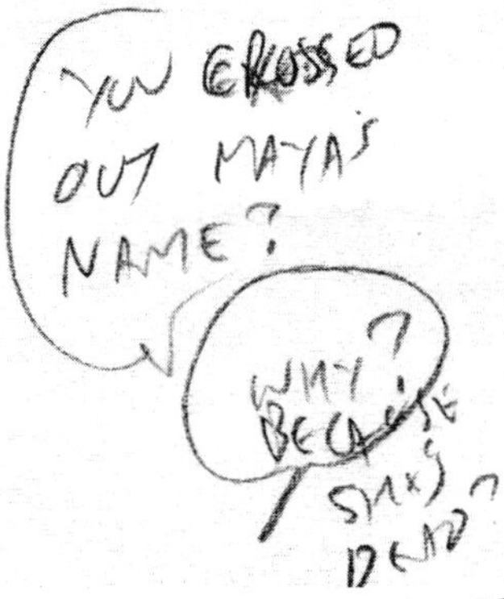
YOU CROSSED OUT MAYA'S NAME?
WHY? BECAUSE SHE'S DEAD?

This page and opposite:
Script sketches, pencils and finished inks from RASL #8. More warnings about Maya, this time from the Multiverse itself? The little girl tries to communicate through limited means, sketching out Tesla's double circle, the sign of the Multiverse inside the Lost Journals.

Opposite page:
Pencils and finished inks for the cover of RASL #8.

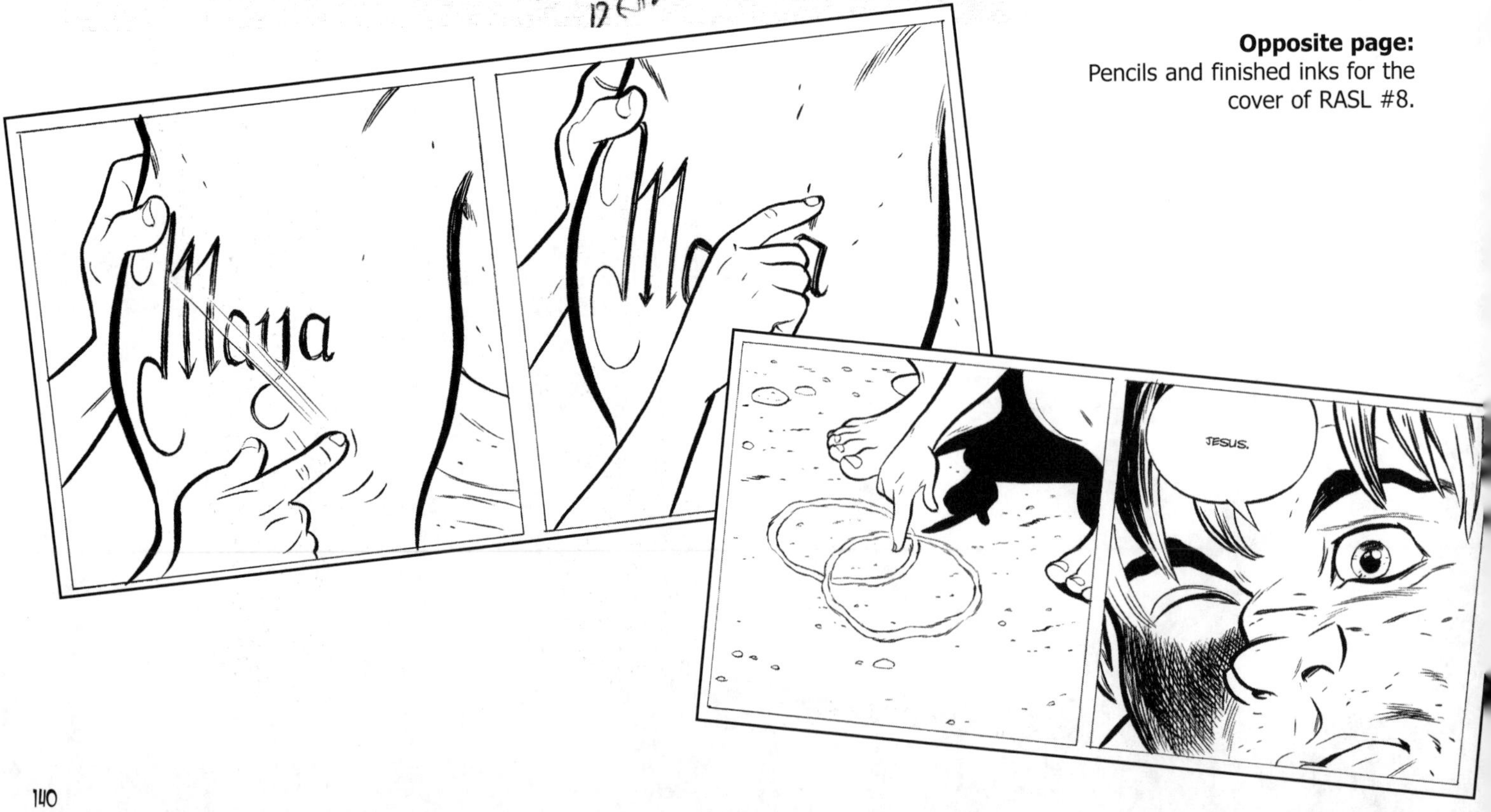
Maya
JESUS.

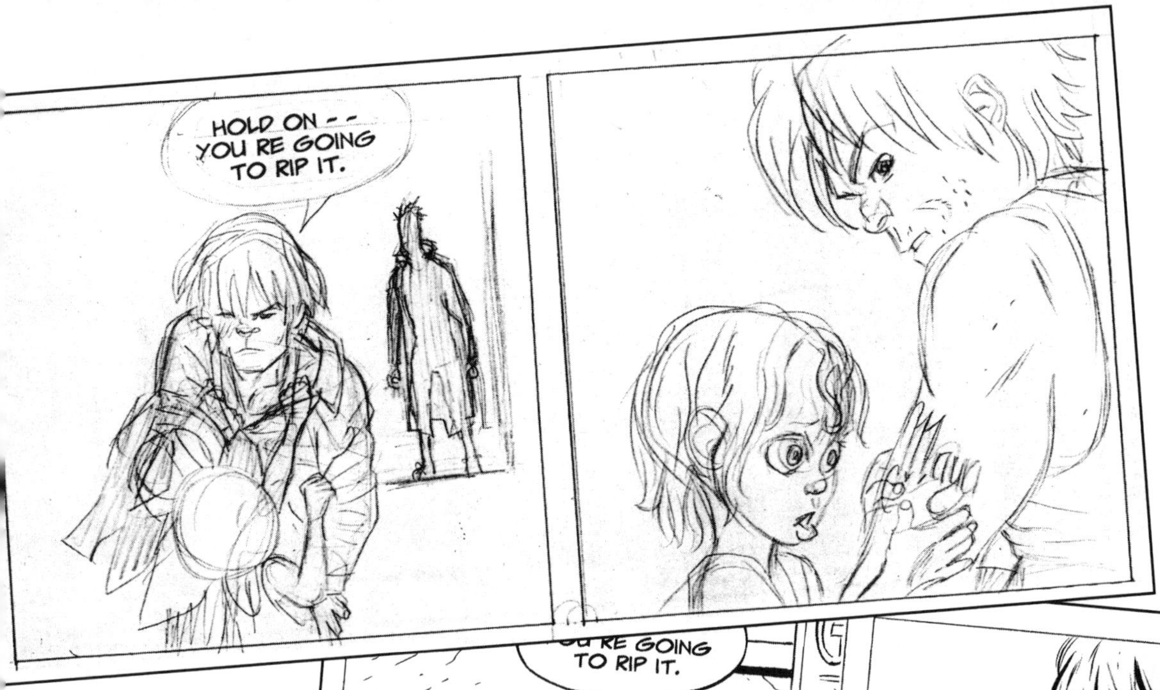
HOLD ON -- YOU RE GOING TO RIP IT.

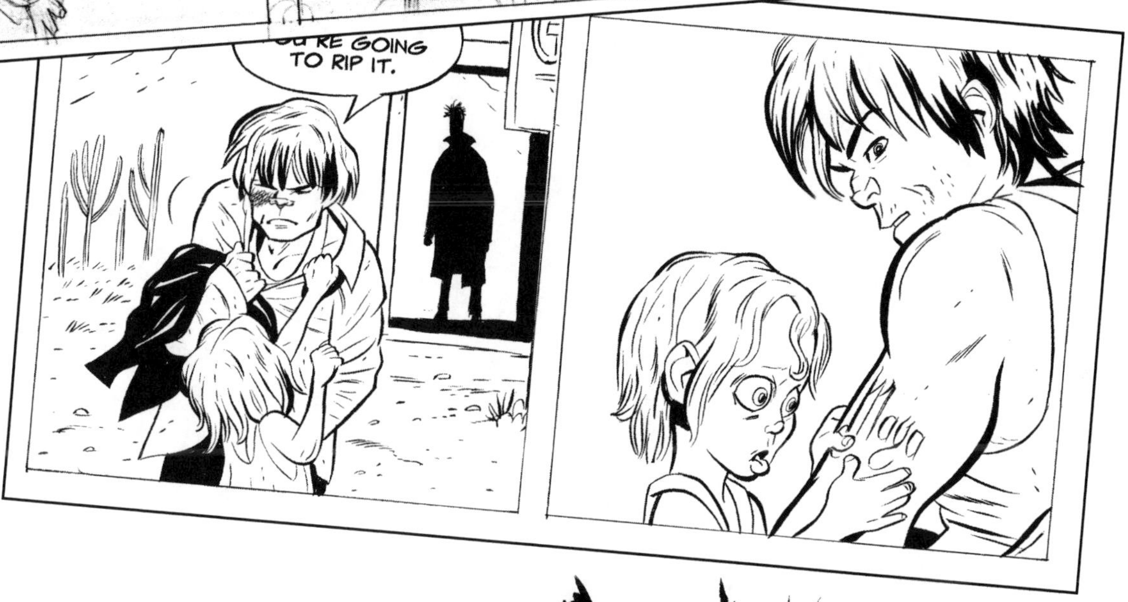
RE GOING TO RIP IT.

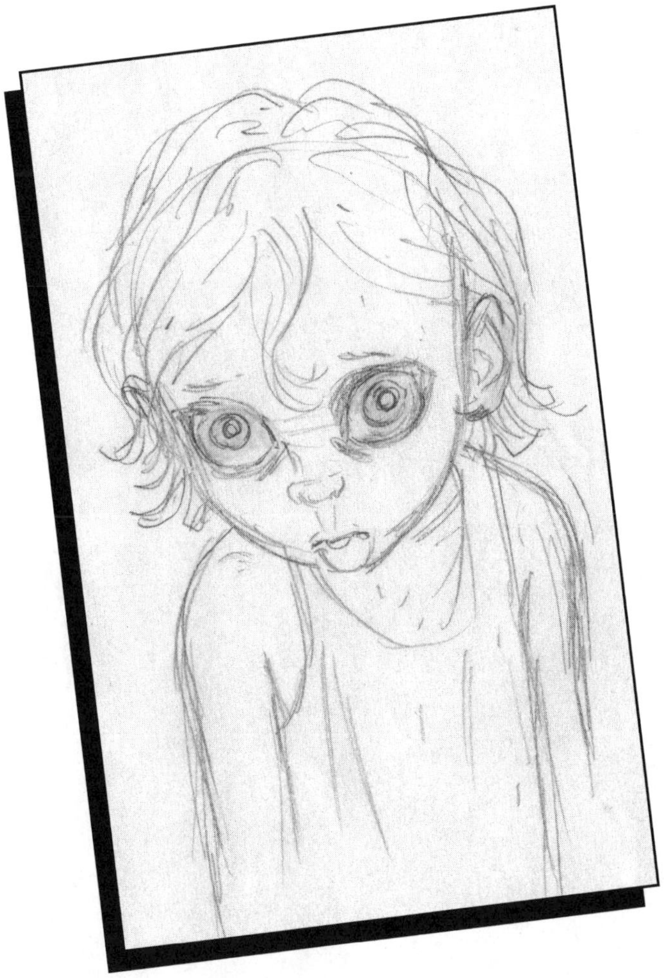

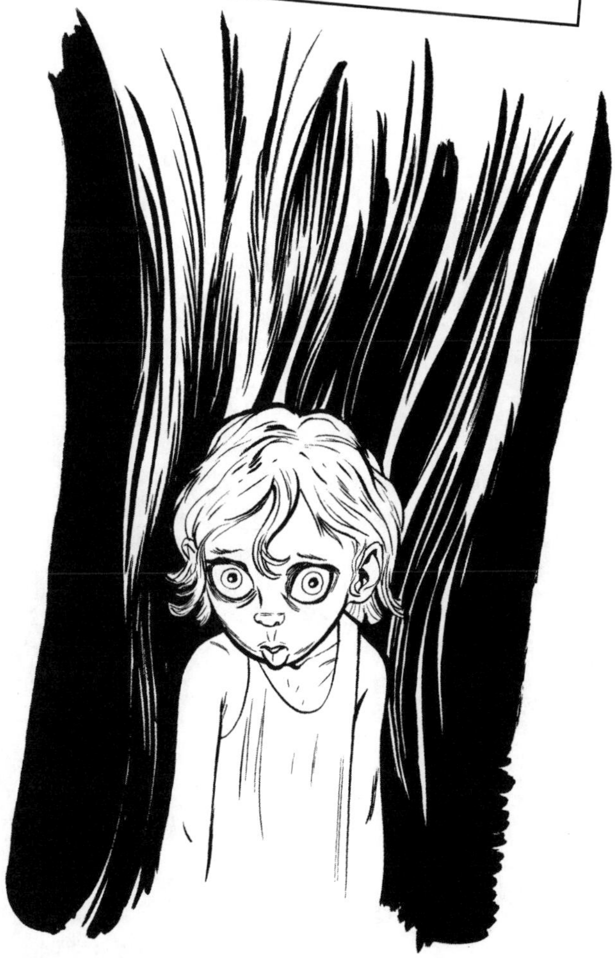

This page:
My friend Jennifer Oliver saw a space ship once. Below is a sketch of what she saw. I used it pretty much verbaitm in RASL #9.

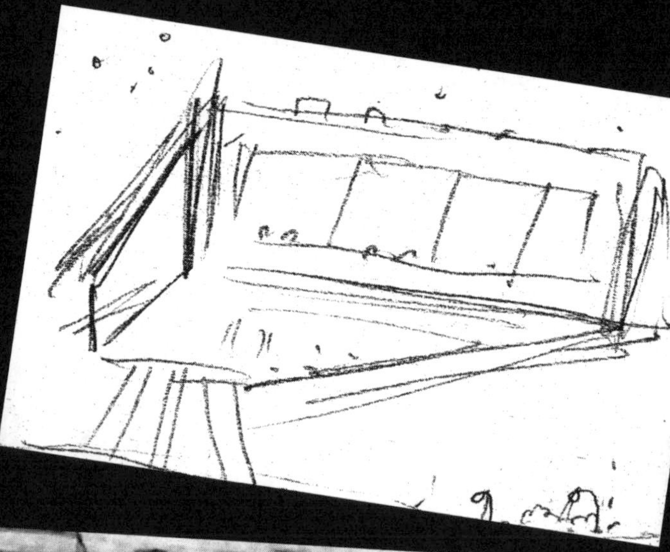

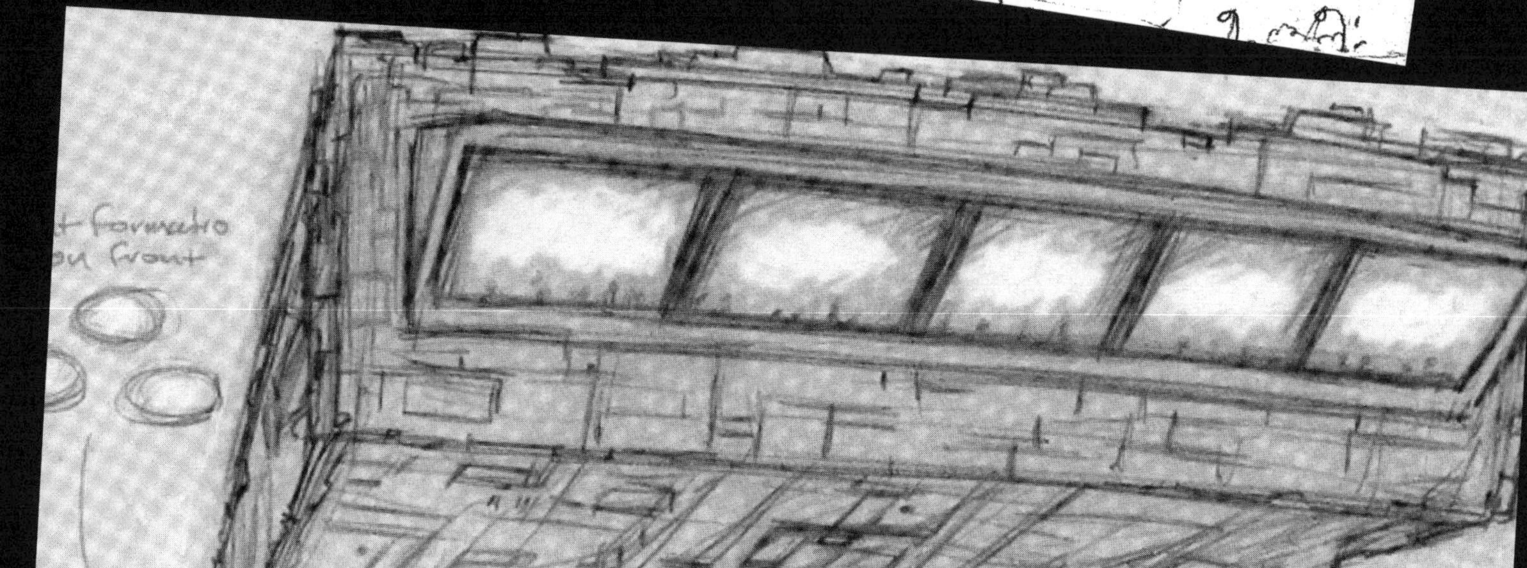

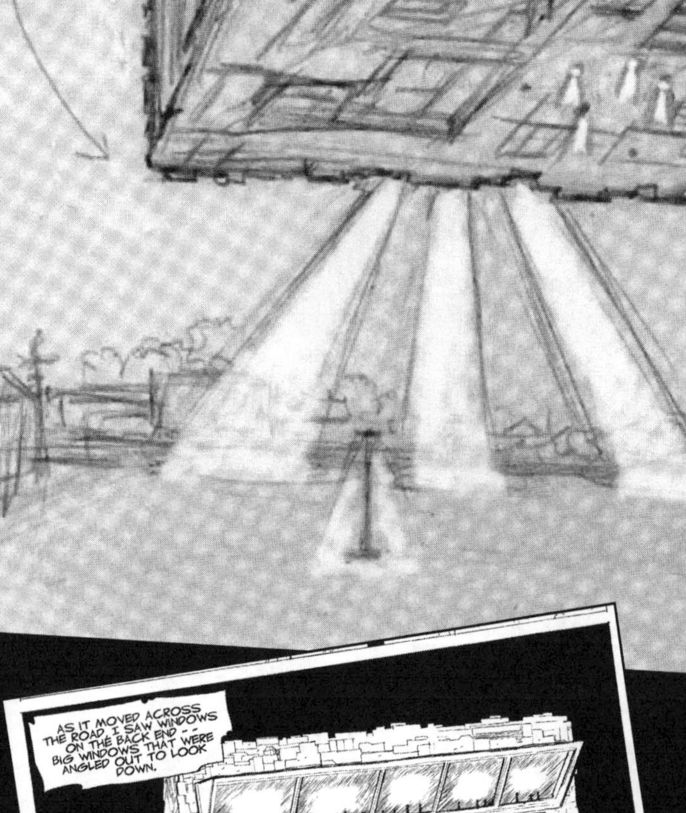
AS IT MOVED ACROSS THE ROAD, I SAW WINDOWS ON THE BACK END -- BIG WINDOWS THAT WERE ANGLED OUT TO LOOK DOWN.
THE LIGHT INSIDE WAS REAL LOW, BUT YOU COULD SEE IT WAS HUGE -- AND THERE WERE FIGURES MOVING TOWARD THE GLASS LIKE THEY WERE TRYING TO GET A LOOK AT ME.

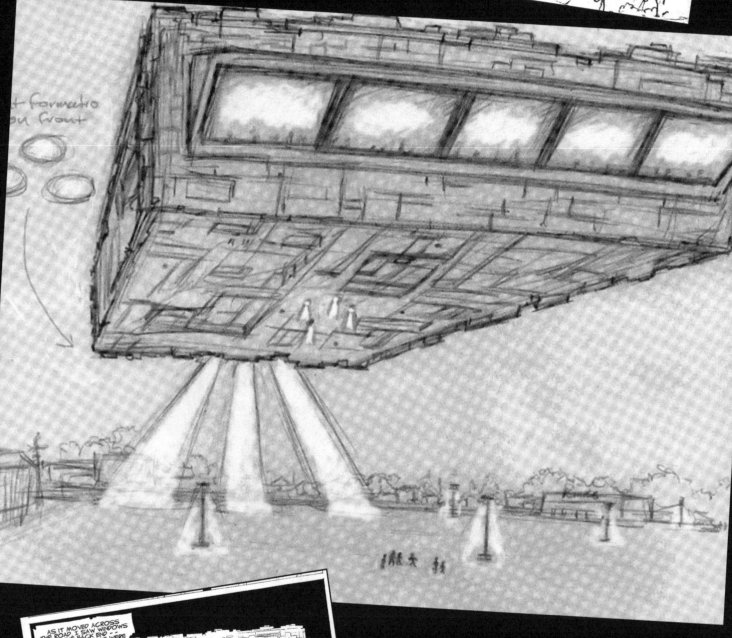

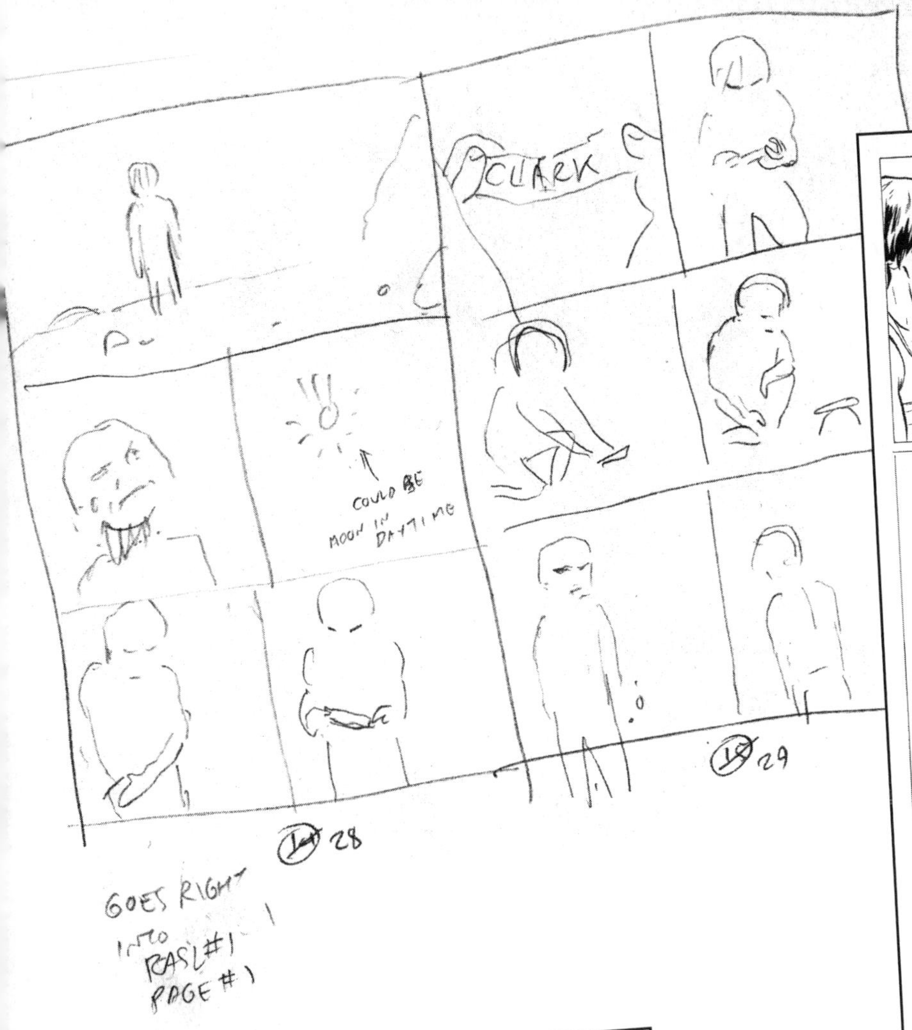
CLARK
COULD BE MOON IN DAYTIME
29
28
GOES RIGHT INTO RASL#1 PAGE#1

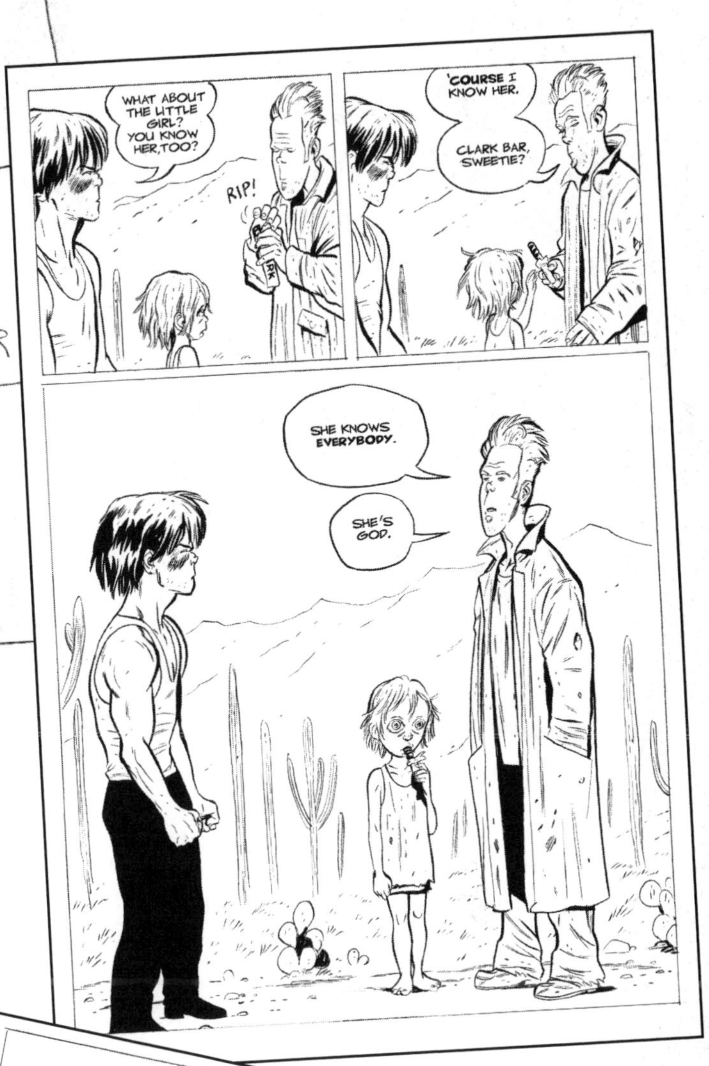
WHAT ABOUT THE LITTLE GIRL? YOU KNOW HER, TOO?
RIP!
'COURSE I KNOW HER.
CLARK BAR, SWEETIE?
SHE KNOWS EVERYBODY.
SHE'S GOD.

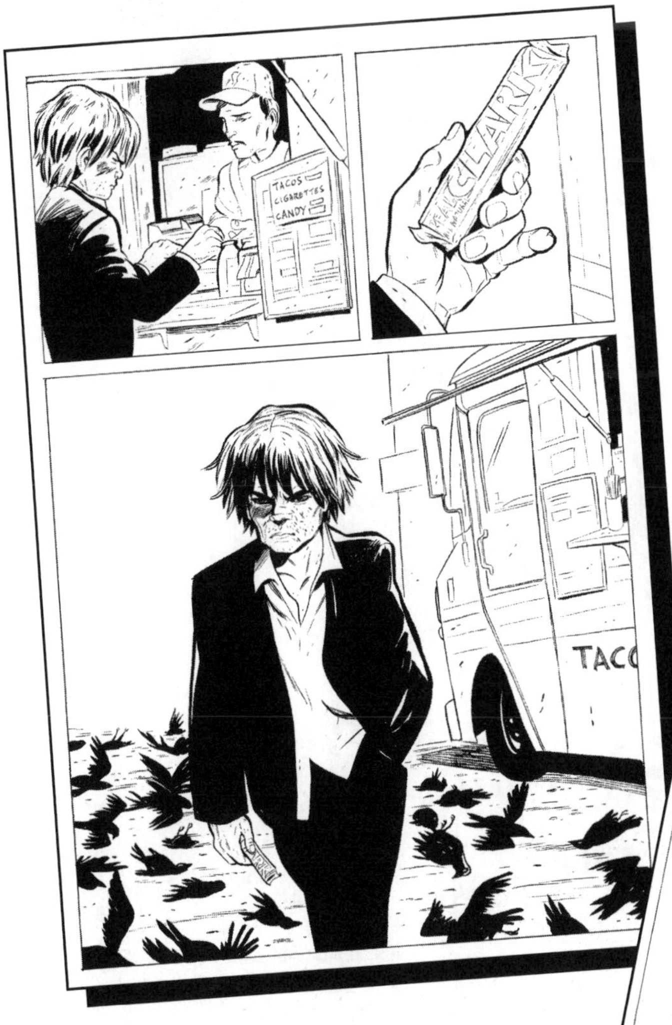
TACOS
CIGARETTES
CANDY
CLARK
TACO

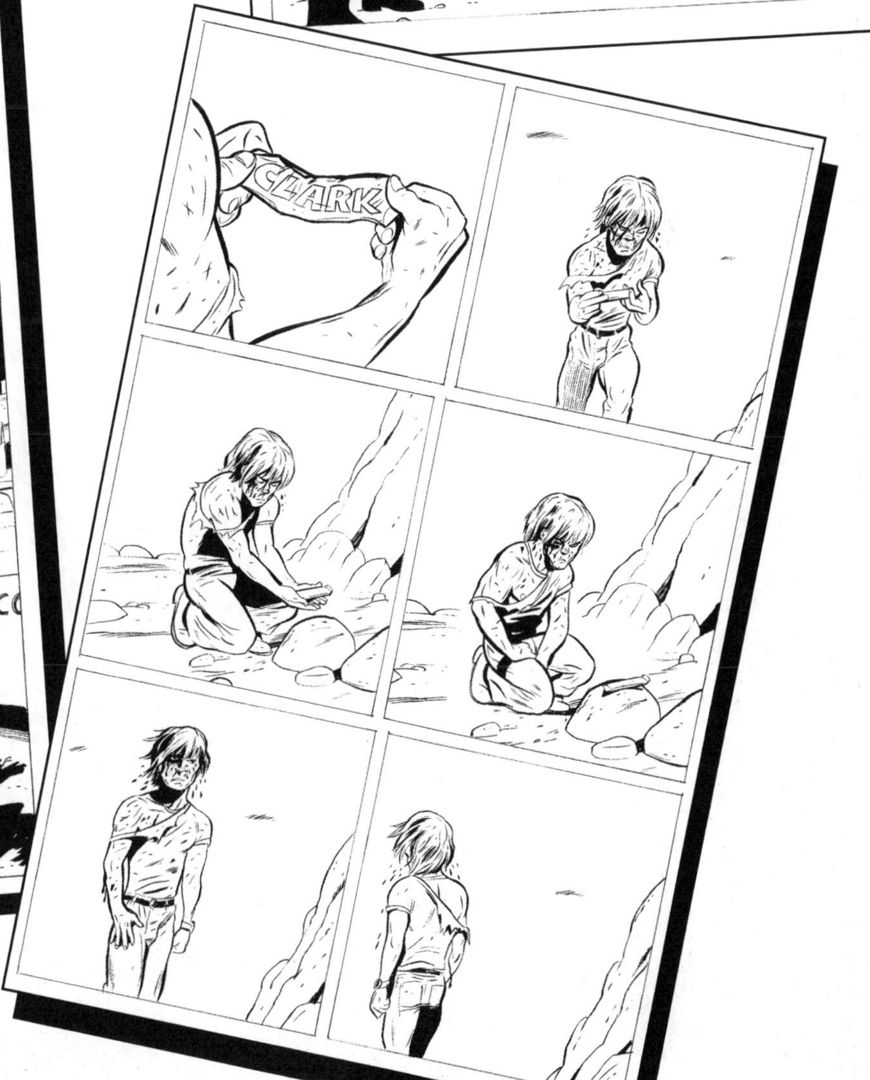
CLARK

his page:
asl, a self proclaimed believer in nothing, decides to edge his bets by purchasing a Clark Bar, the preferred andy of the gods.

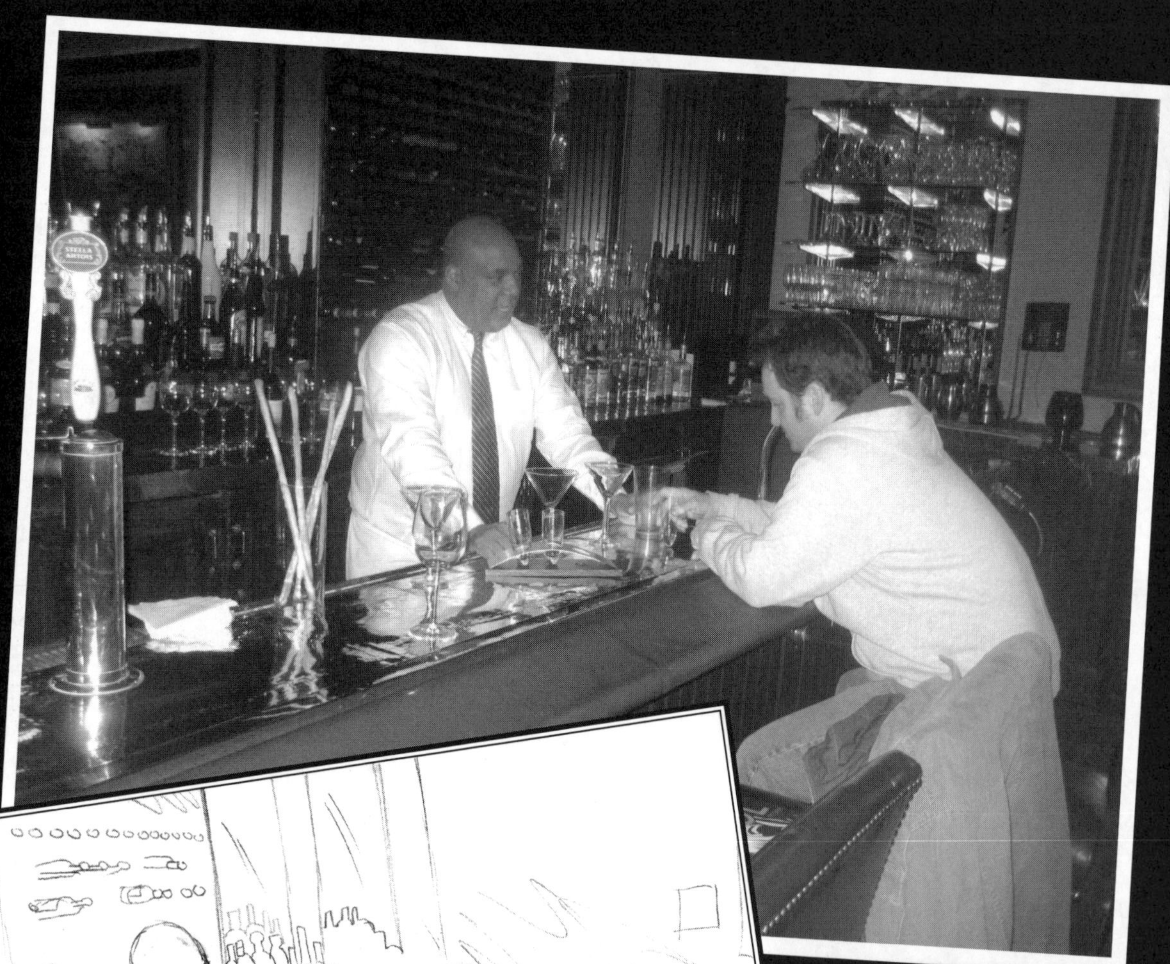

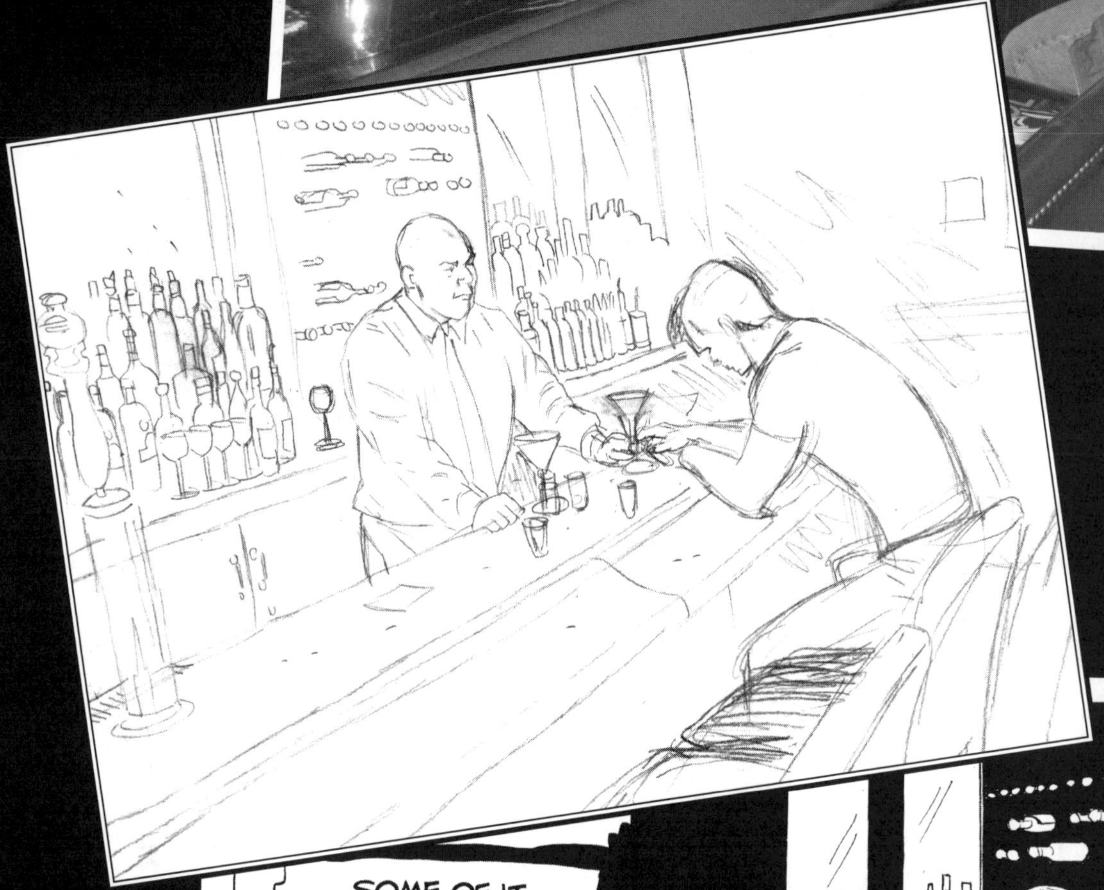

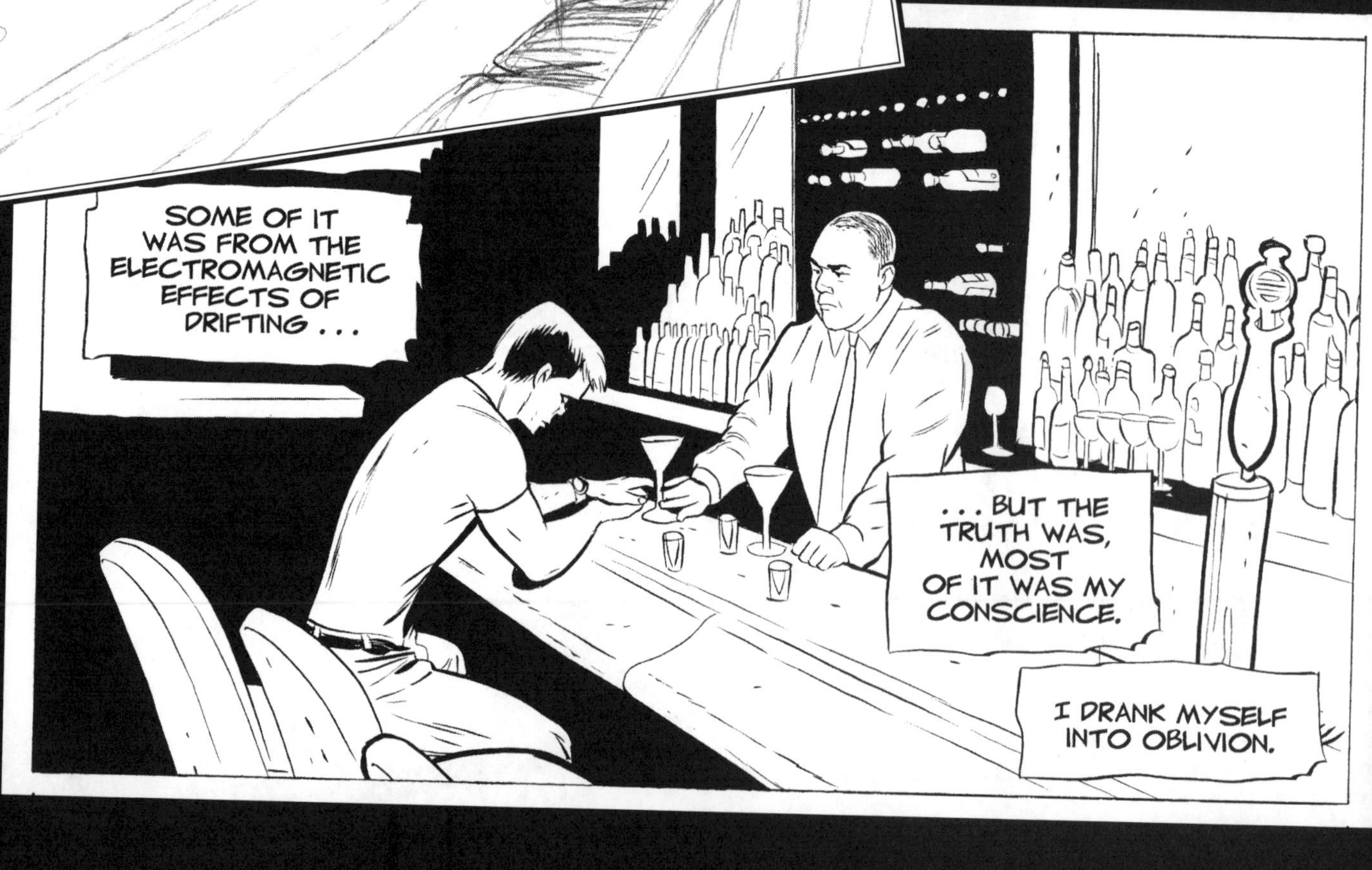
SOME OF IT WAS FROM THE ELECTROMAGNETIC EFFECTS OF DRIFTING . . .
. . . BUT THE TRUTH WAS, MOST OF IT WAS MY CONSCIENCE.
I DRANK MYSELF INTO OBLIVION.

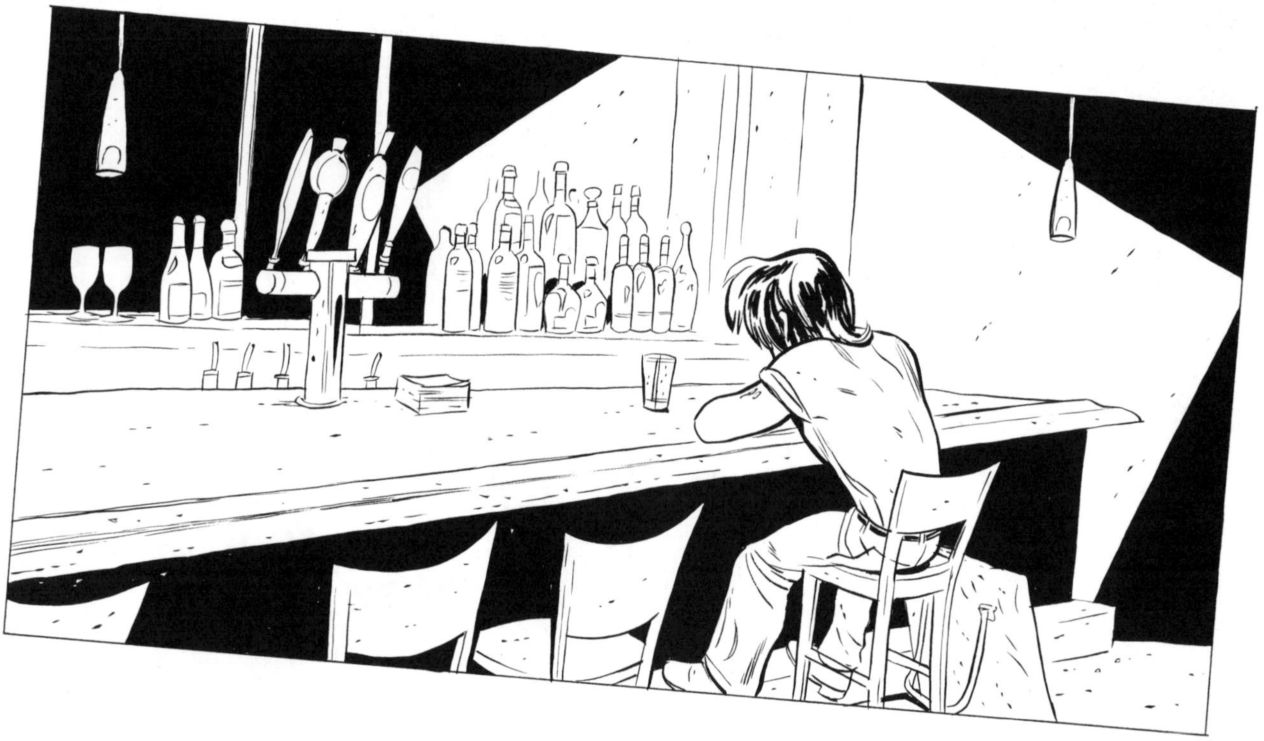

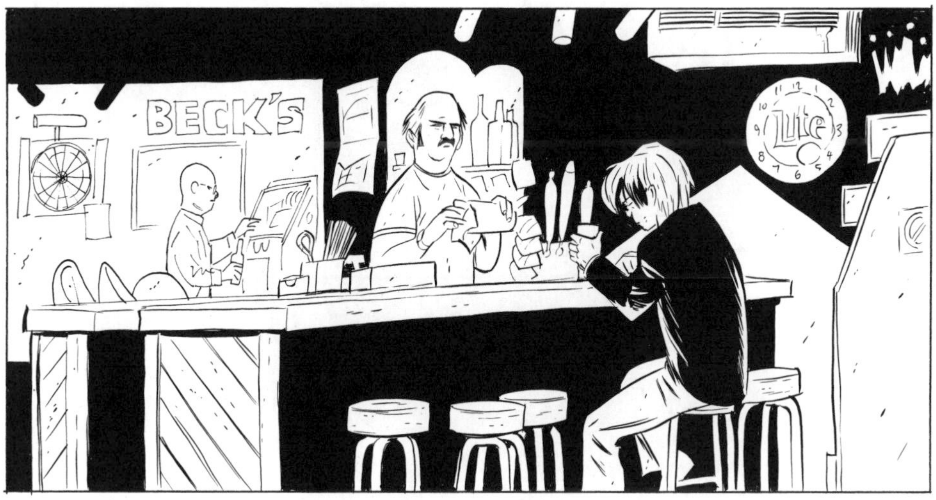

BECK'S
Lite

All the bars featured in RASL are loosely based on my local German Village watering holes in Columbus, Ohio. Opposite is Lindey's, with bartender Tony Murray. (Murray is a pal of mine, and when he opened his own establishment, T. Murray's in the Brewery District, I painted a large mural on the wall.), also represented: G. Michaels's, The Beck Tavern, and Club 185.

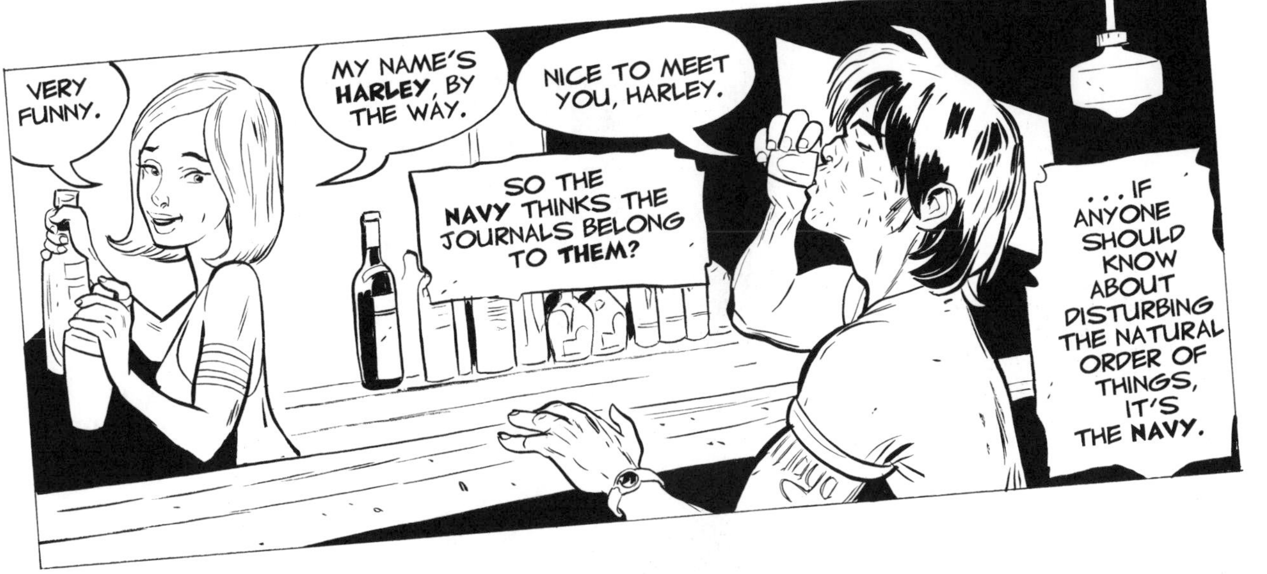

SO THE **NAVY** THINKS THE JOURNALS BELONG TO **THEM**?
. . . IF ANYONE SHOULD KNOW ABOUT DISTURBING THE NATURAL ORDER OF THINGS, IT'S THE **NAVY**.
VERY FUNNY.
MY NAME'S **HARLEY**, BY THE WAY.
NICE TO MEET YOU, HARLEY.

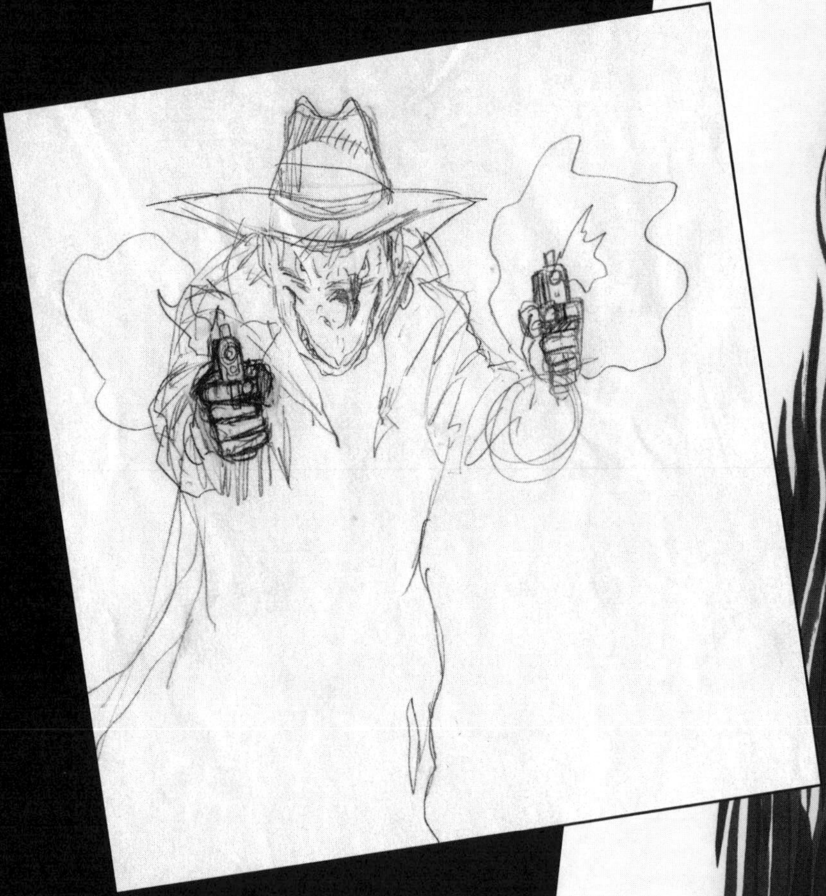

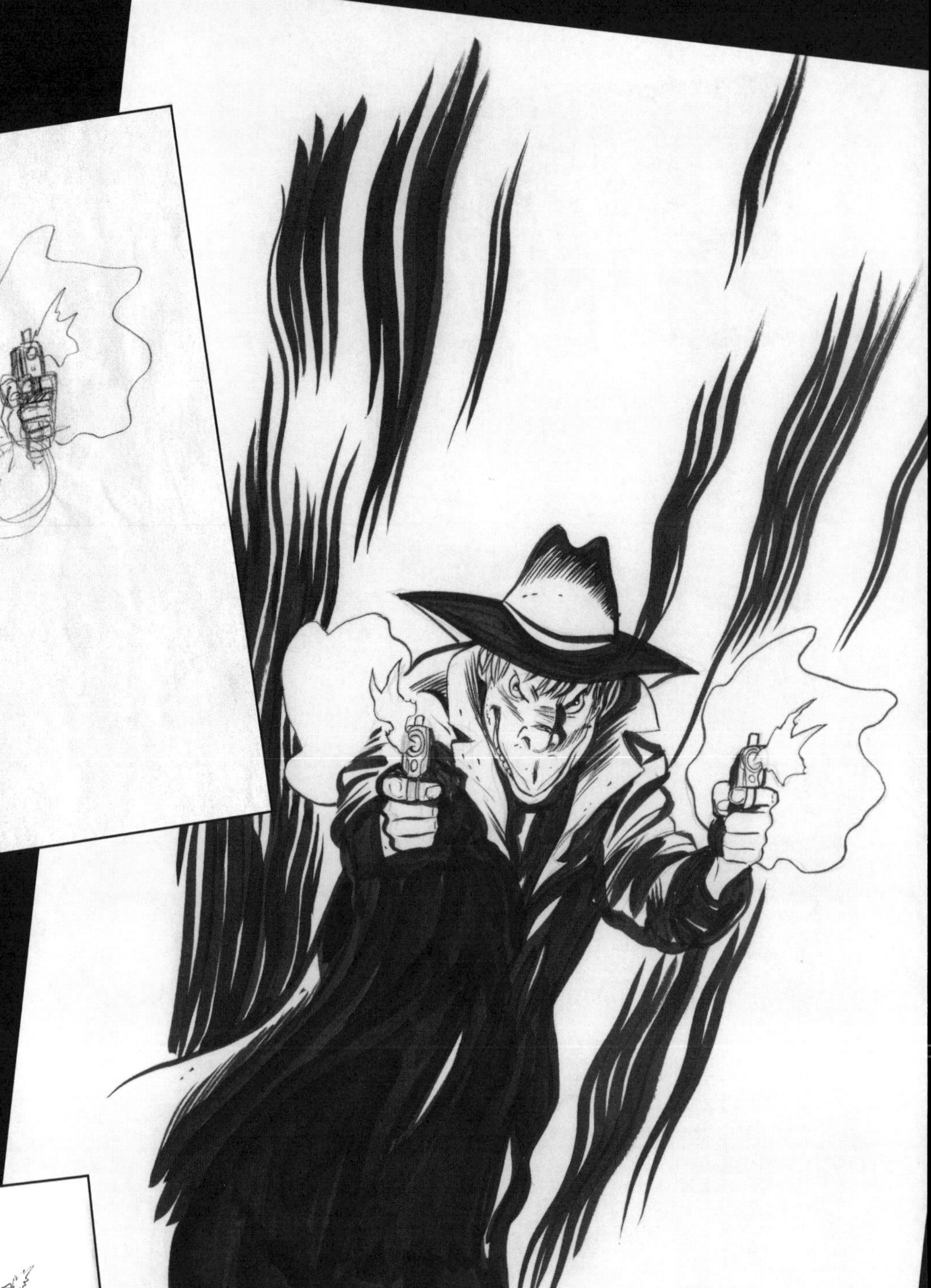
SL No. 13

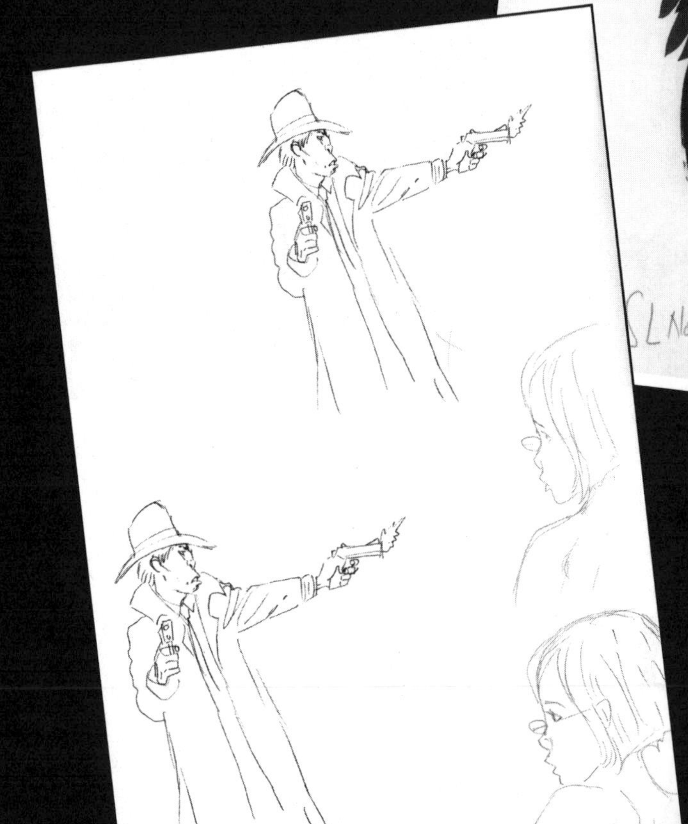

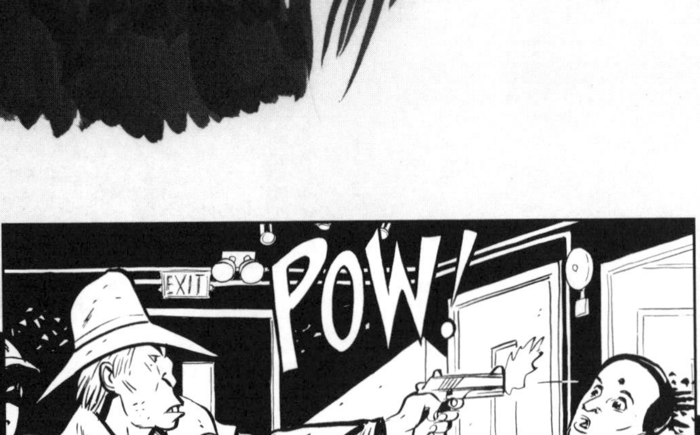
EXIT
POW!

Opposite page(top to bottom):
Sal loves his guns. Sketch and ink of cover of RASL #13,
Sal shoots Kalani in RASL #14.
Opposite page(top to bottom):
In the script, I imagined Sal smiling after the shooting rampage in #14. But then I thought a scowl would be more appropriate. In the end, Sal's creepy smile won out.

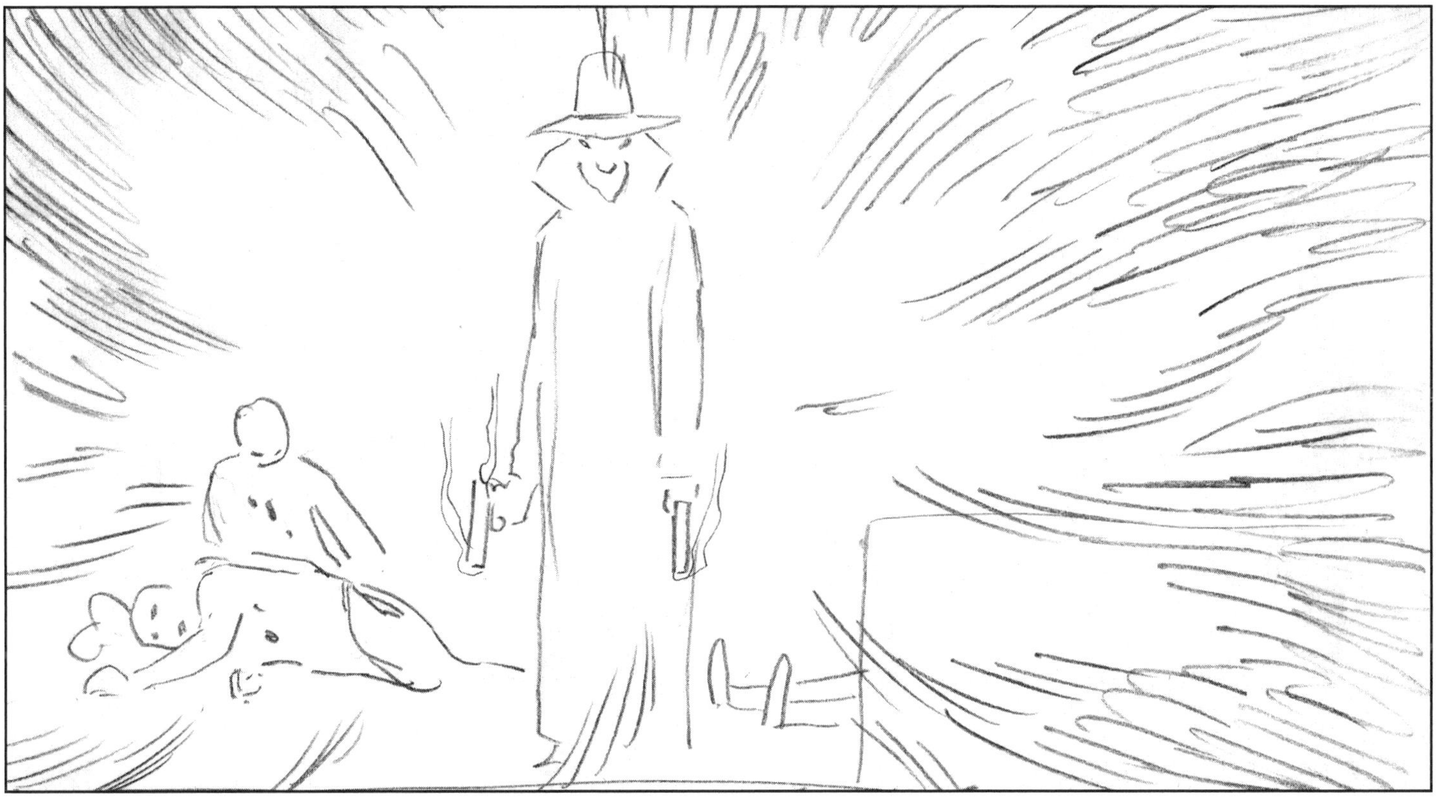

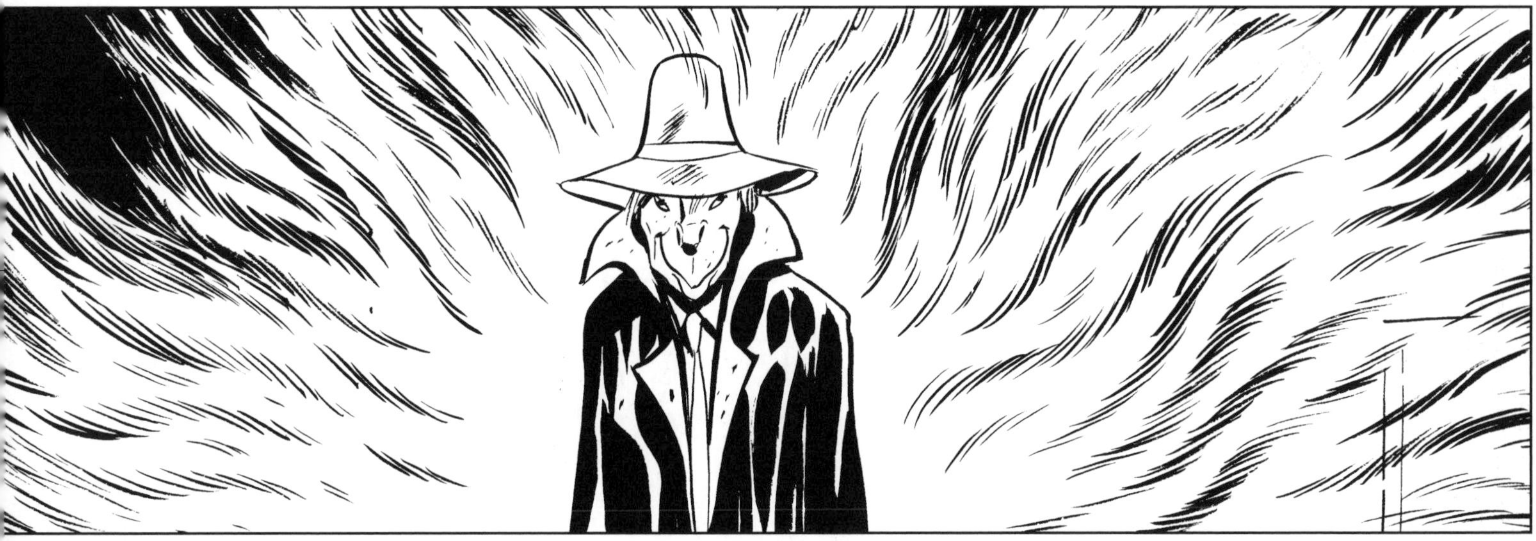

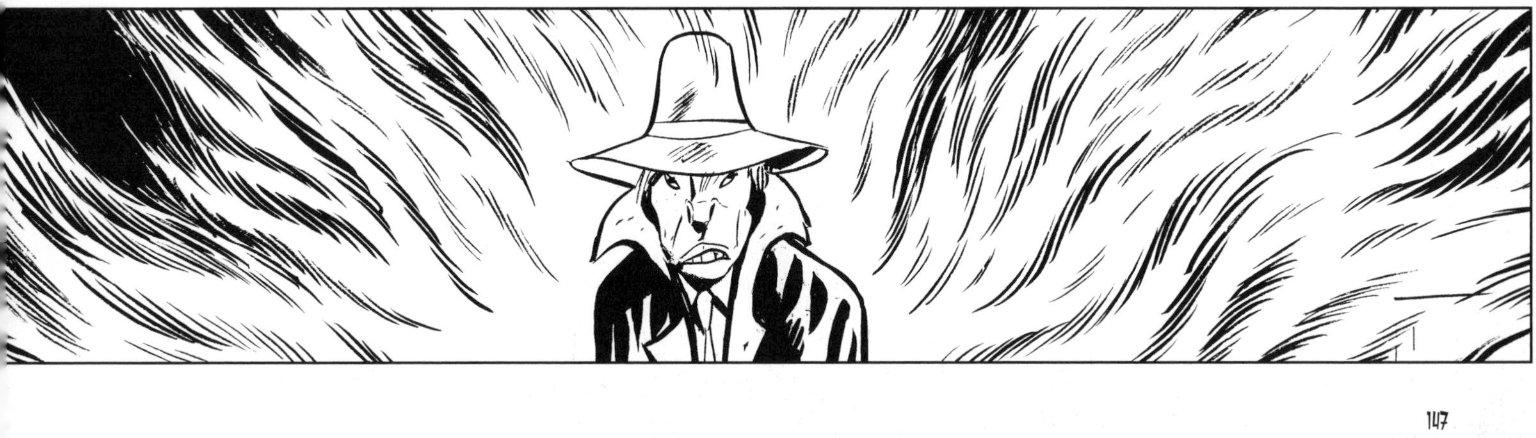

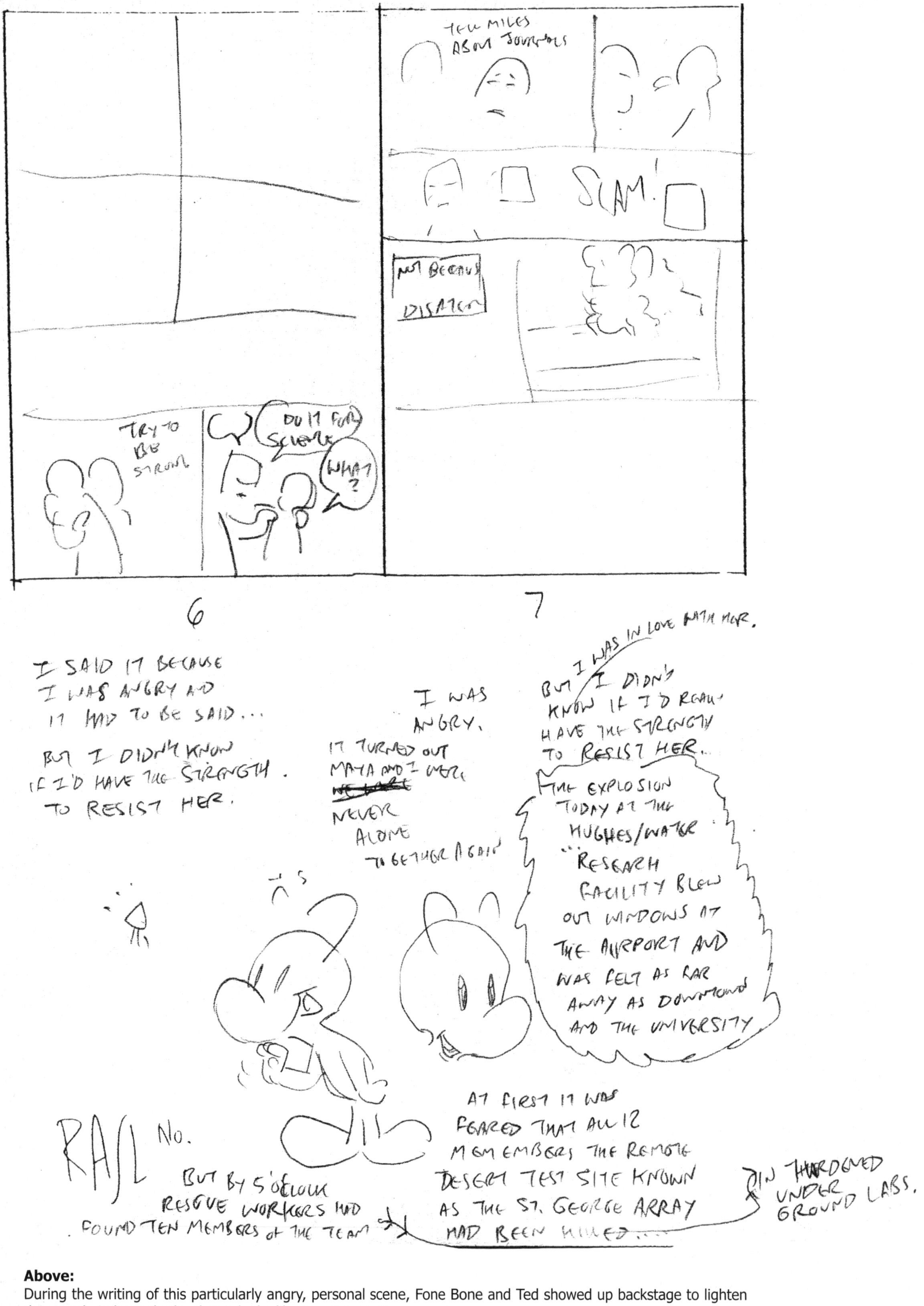
SLAM!
TRY TO BE STRONG
DO IT FOR SCIENCE
WHAT ?
6
7
I SAID IT BECAUSE I WAS ANGRY AND IT HAD TO BE SAID...
BUT I DIDN'T KNOW IF I'D HAVE THE STRENGTH TO RESIST HER.
I WAS ANGRY.
IT TURNED OUT MAYA AND I WERE NEVER ALONE TOGETHER AGAIN
BUT I WAS IN LOVE WITH HER. I DIDN'T KNOW IF I'D REALLY HAVE THE STRENGTH TO RESIST HER.
THE EXPLOSION TODAY AT THE HUGHES/WATER RESEARCH FACILITY BLEW OUT WINDOWS AT THE AIRPORT AND WAS FELT AS FAR AWAY AS DOWNTOWN AND THE UNIVERSITY
AT FIRST IT WAS FEARED THAT ALL 12 MEMBERS THE REMOTE DESERT TEST SITE KNOWN AS THE ST. GEORGE ARRAY HAD BEEN KILLED...
IN HARDENED UNDERGROUND LABS.
RASL No.
BUT BY 5 O'CLOCK RESCUE WORKERS HAD FOUND TEN MEMBERS OF THE TEAM

Above:
During the writing of this particularly angry, personal scene, Fone Bone and Ted showed up backstage to lighten the mood. At least that's what it looks like in retrospect!
Opposite page:
Inks of RASL angrily breaking up with Maya.

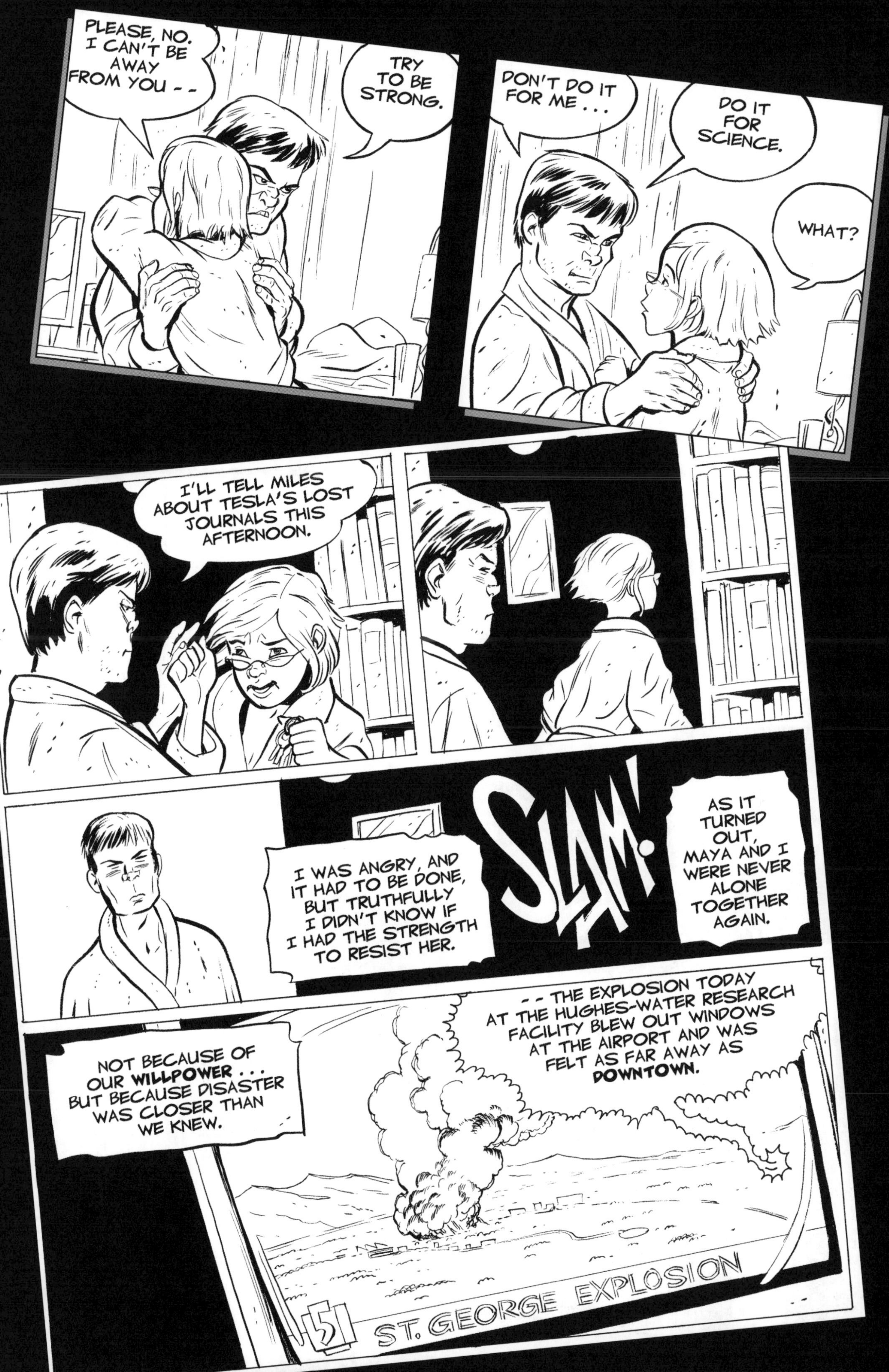
PLEASE, NO. I CAN'T BE AWAY FROM YOU - -
TRY TO BE STRONG.
DON'T DO IT FOR ME . . .
DO IT FOR SCIENCE.
WHAT?
I'LL TELL MILES ABOUT TESLA'S LOST JOURNALS THIS AFTERNOON.
I WAS ANGRY, AND IT HAD TO BE DONE, BUT TRUTHFULLY I DIDN'T KNOW IF I HAD THE STRENGTH TO RESIST HER.
SLAM!
AS IT TURNED OUT, MAYA AND I WERE NEVER ALONE TOGETHER AGAIN.
NOT BECAUSE OF OUR WILLPOWER . . . BUT BECAUSE DISASTER WAS CLOSER THAN WE KNEW.
- - THE EXPLOSION TODAY AT THE HUGHES-WATER RESEARCH FACILITY BLEW OUT WINDOWS AT THE AIRPORT AND WAS FELT AS FAR AWAY AS DOWNTOWN.
5
ST. GEORGE EXPLOSION

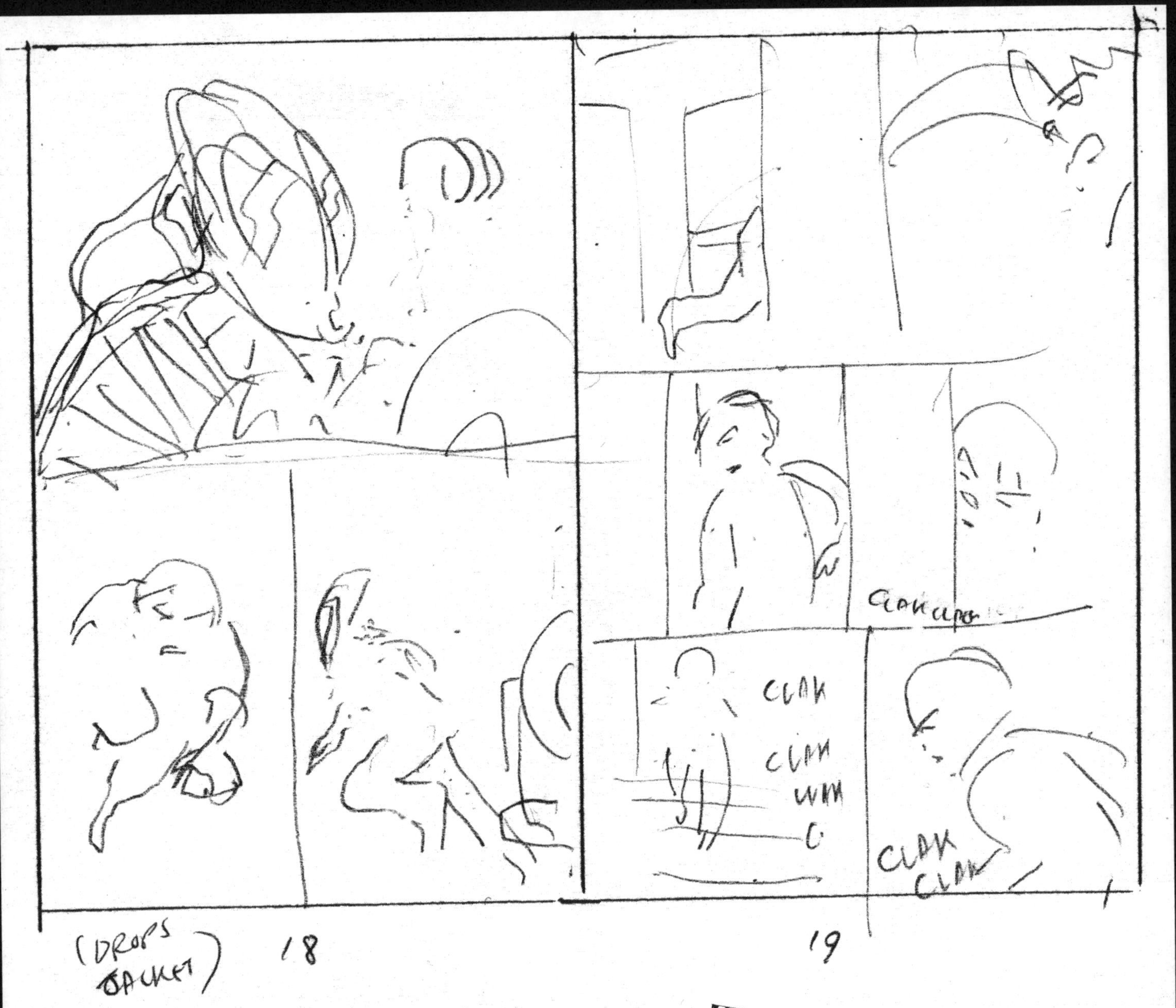
CLAK
CLAK
CLAK CLAK
(DROPS JACKET)
18
19

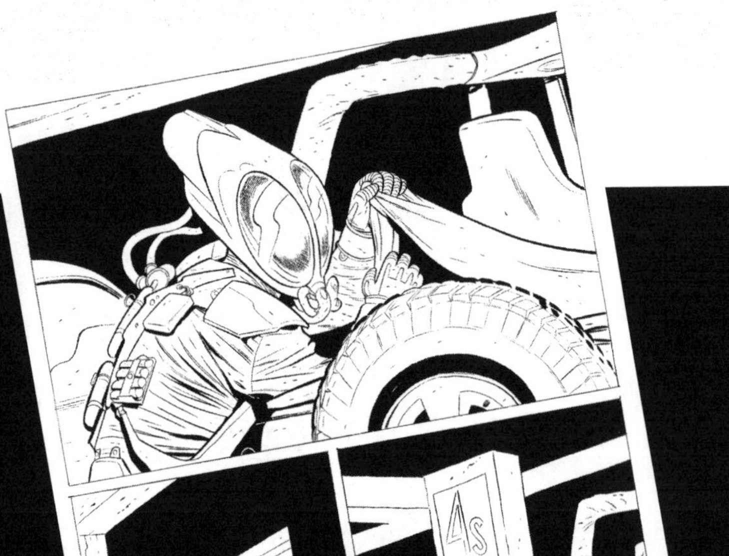
4s
4s

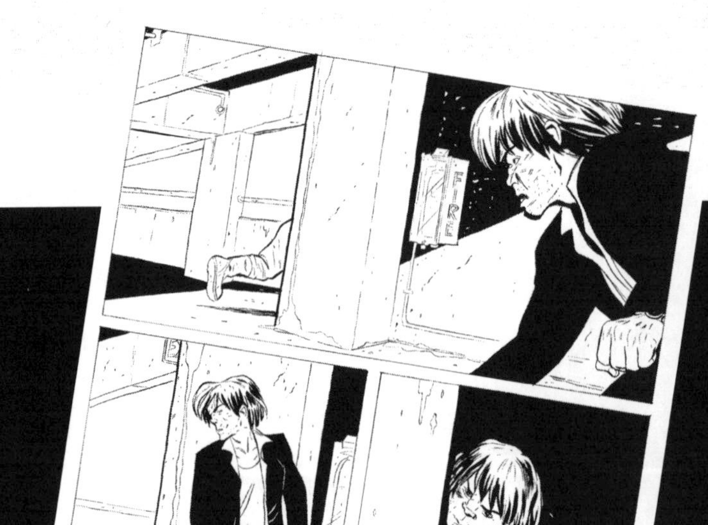
FIRE
CLAK CLAK
3s
CLAK CLAK CLAK
CLAK CLAK

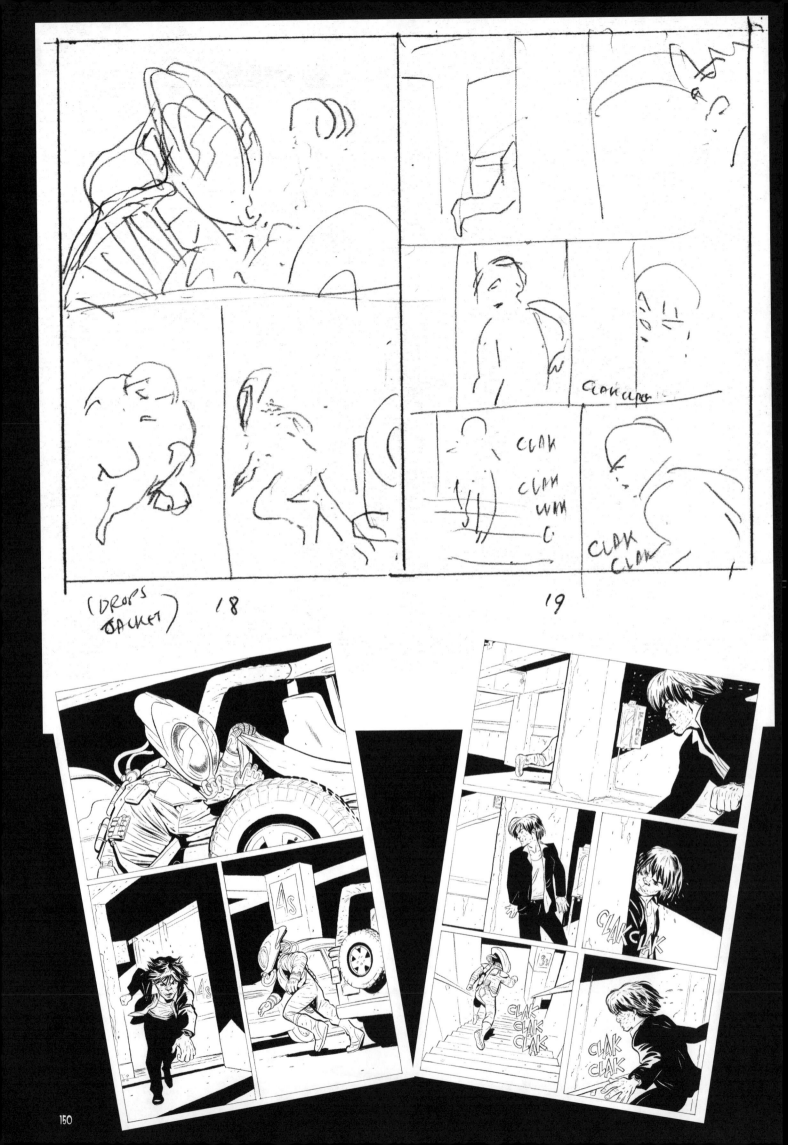

Opposite page:
Opposite page: Script pages showing an unidentified intruder; later, when this
same intruder appears at the site of RASL's desert bunker, we learn that the thief is Maya!

Above:
How to draw Maya in the Mulitiverse? I only drew her once with one additional head; Steve Hamaker
then reproduced her over and over to create the breaching event.

Below:
Despite warnings from others, Maya herself never blinks; below, three examples of Maya effortlessly lying to Rob.

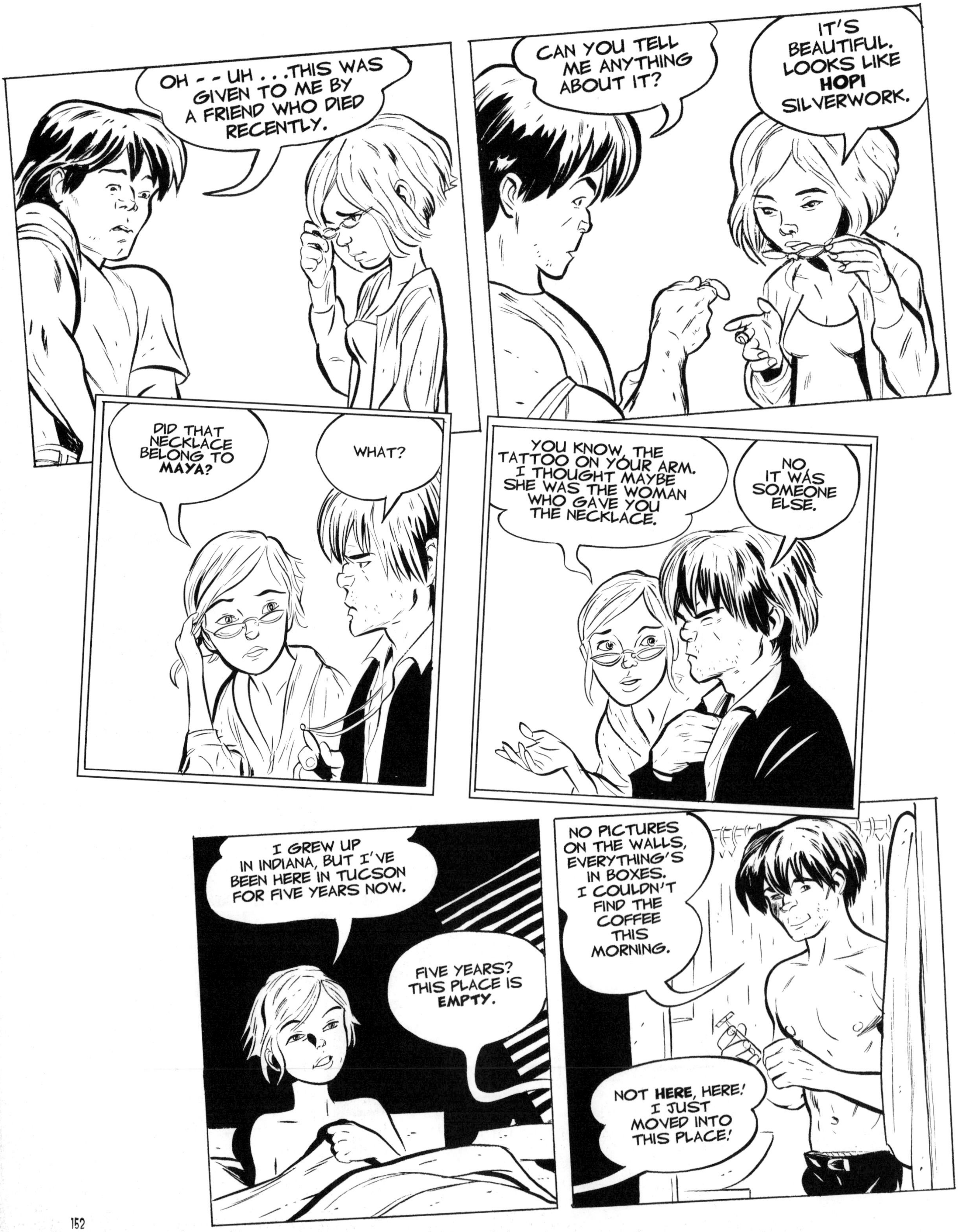

OH - - UH . . . THIS WAS GIVEN TO ME BY A FRIEND WHO DIED RECENTLY.
CAN YOU TELL ME ANYTHING ABOUT IT?
IT'S BEAUTIFUL. LOOKS LIKE **HOPI** SILVERWORK.
DID THAT NECKLACE BELONG TO **MAYA**?
WHAT?
YOU KNOW, THE TATTOO ON YOUR ARM. I THOUGHT MAYBE SHE WAS THE WOMAN WHO GAVE YOU THE NECKLACE.
NO IT WAS SOMEONE ELSE.
I GREW UP IN INDIANA, BUT I'VE BEEN HERE IN TUCSON FOR FIVE YEARS NOW.
FIVE YEARS? THIS PLACE IS **EMPTY**.
NO PICTURES ON THE WALLS, EVERYTHING'S IN BOXES. I COULDN'T FIND THE COFFEE THIS MORNING.
NOT **HERE**, HERE! I JUST MOVED INTO THIS PLACE!

Below:
These are some photo references I used to sketch Nikola Tesla.

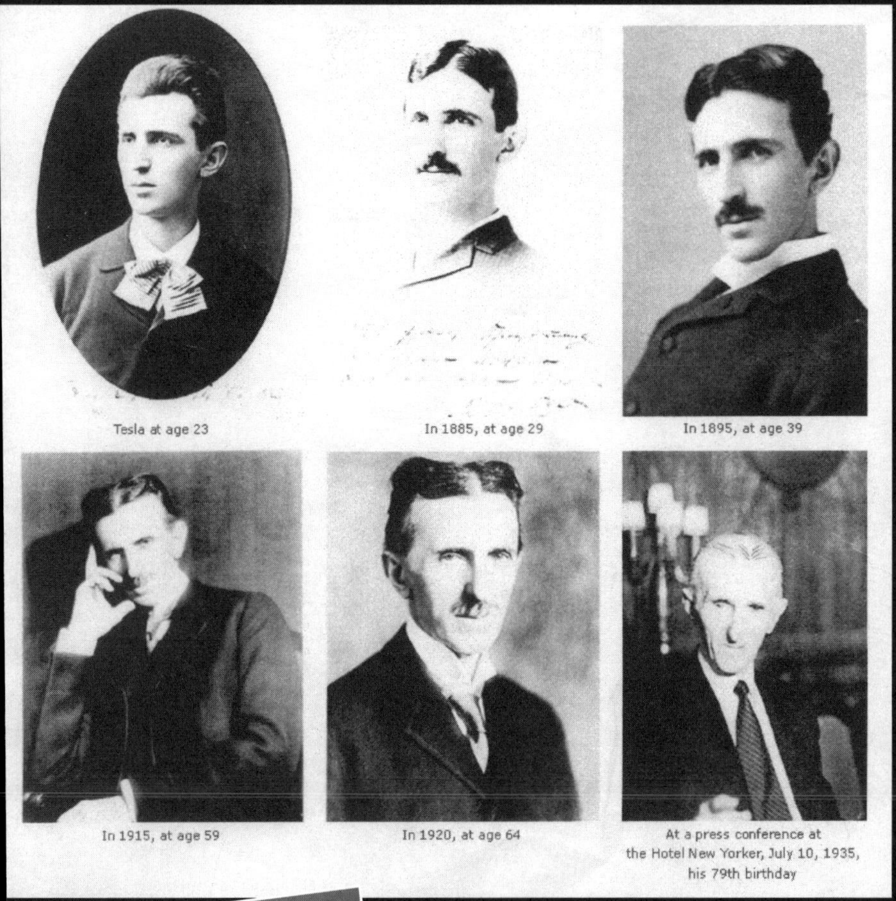

Tesla at age 23 — In 1885, at age 29 — In 1895, at age 39

In 1915, at age 59 — In 1920, at age 64 — At a press conference at the Hotel New Yorker, July 10, 1935, his 79th birthday

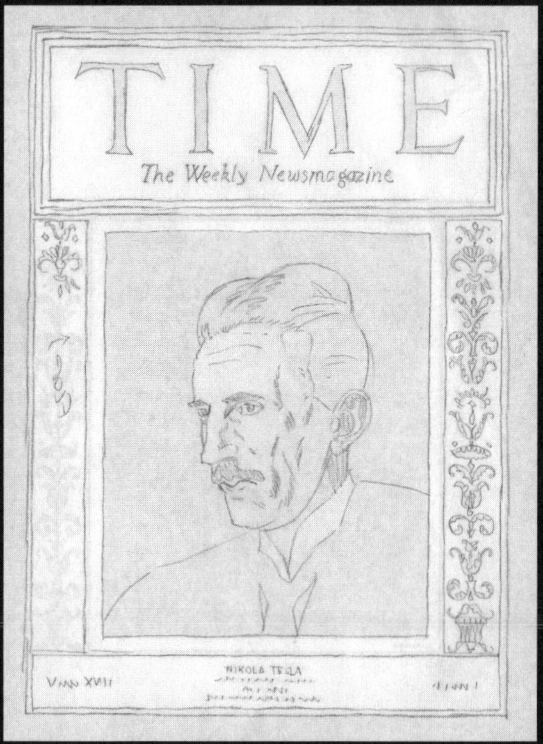

TIME
The Weekly Newsmagazine
NIKOLA TESLA

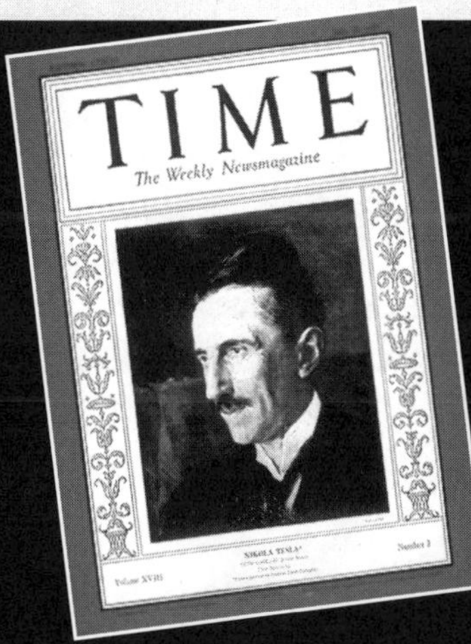

TIME
The Weekly Newsmagazine

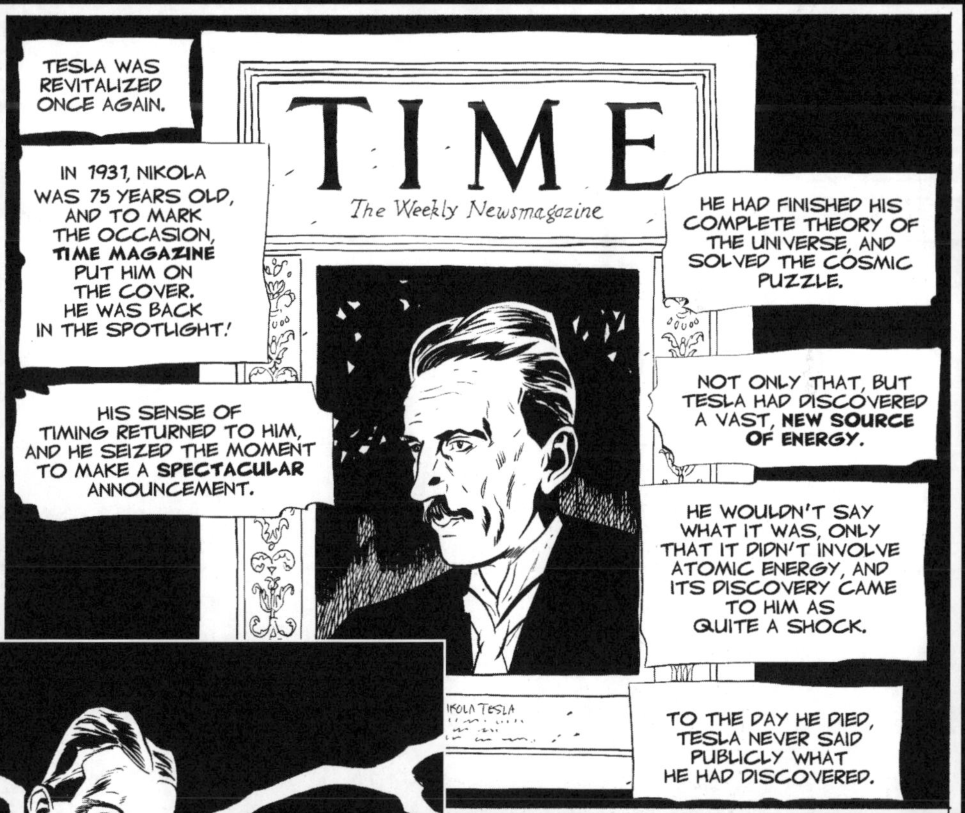

TESLA WAS REVITALIZED ONCE AGAIN.
IN 1931, NIKOLA WAS 75 YEARS OLD, AND TO MARK THE OCCASION, TIME MAGAZINE PUT HIM ON THE COVER. HE WAS BACK IN THE SPOTLIGHT!
HIS SENSE OF TIMING RETURNED TO HIM, AND HE SEIZED THE MOMENT TO MAKE A SPECTACULAR ANNOUNCEMENT.
TIME
The Weekly Newsmagazine
HE HAD FINISHED HIS COMPLETE THEORY OF THE UNIVERSE, AND SOLVED THE COSMIC PUZZLE.
NOT ONLY THAT, BUT TESLA HAD DISCOVERED A VAST, NEW SOURCE OF ENERGY.
HE WOULDN'T SAY WHAT IT WAS, ONLY THAT IT DIDN'T INVOLVE ATOMIC ENERGY, AND ITS DISCOVERY CAME TO HIM AS QUITE A SHOCK.
NIKOLA TESLA
TO THE DAY HE DIED, TESLA NEVER SAID PUBLICLY WHAT HE HAD DISCOVERED.

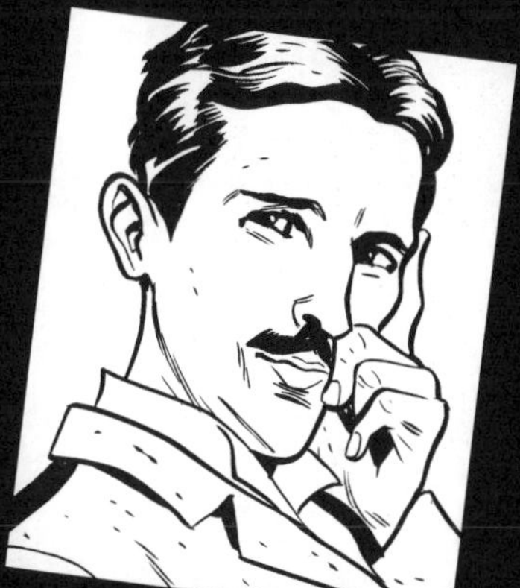

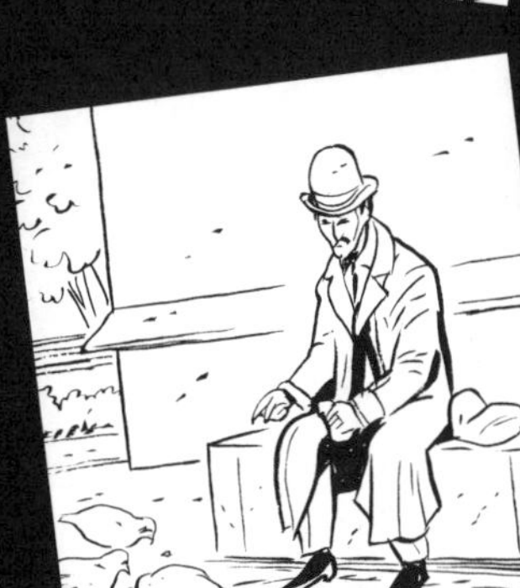

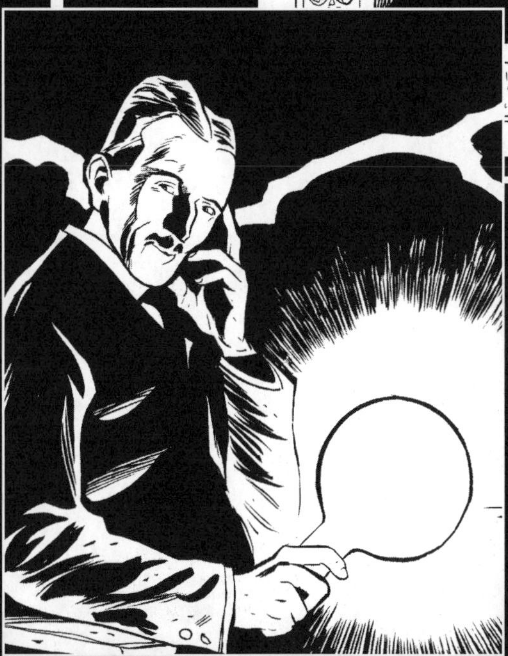

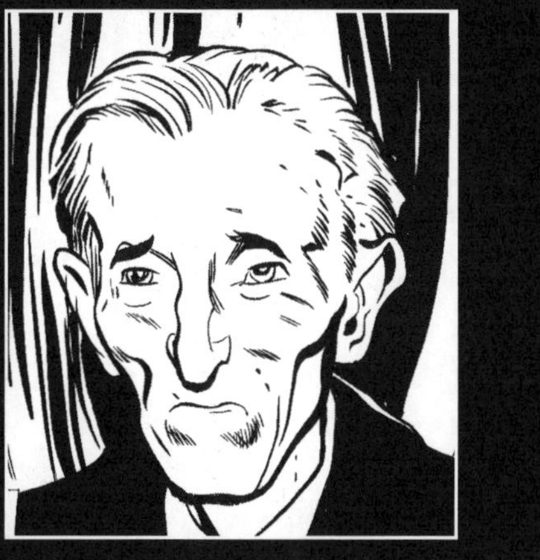

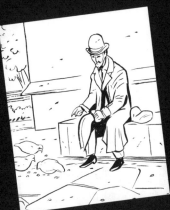

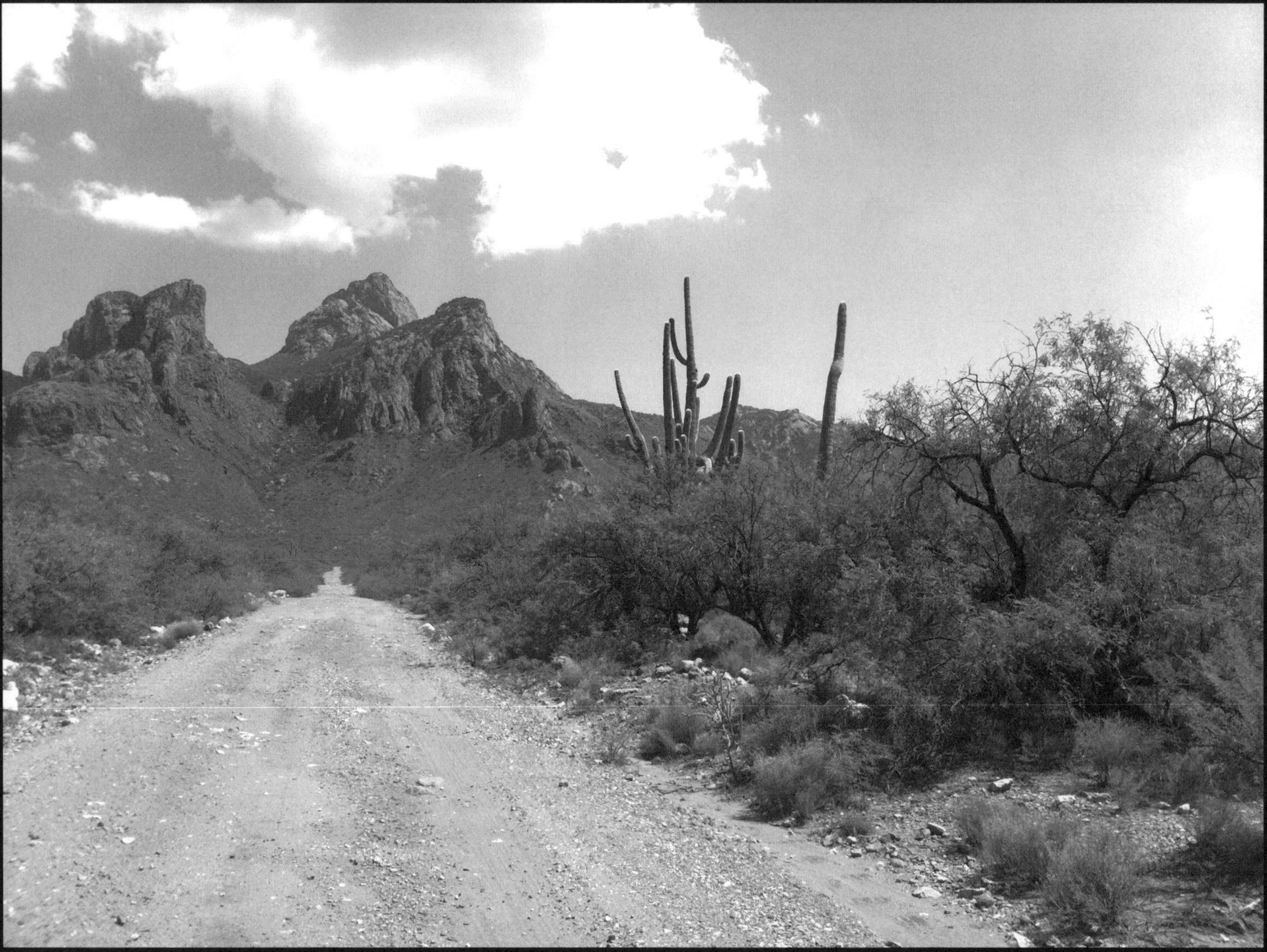

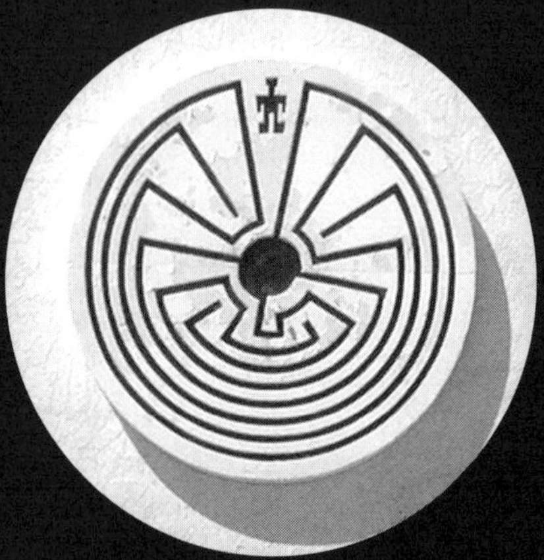

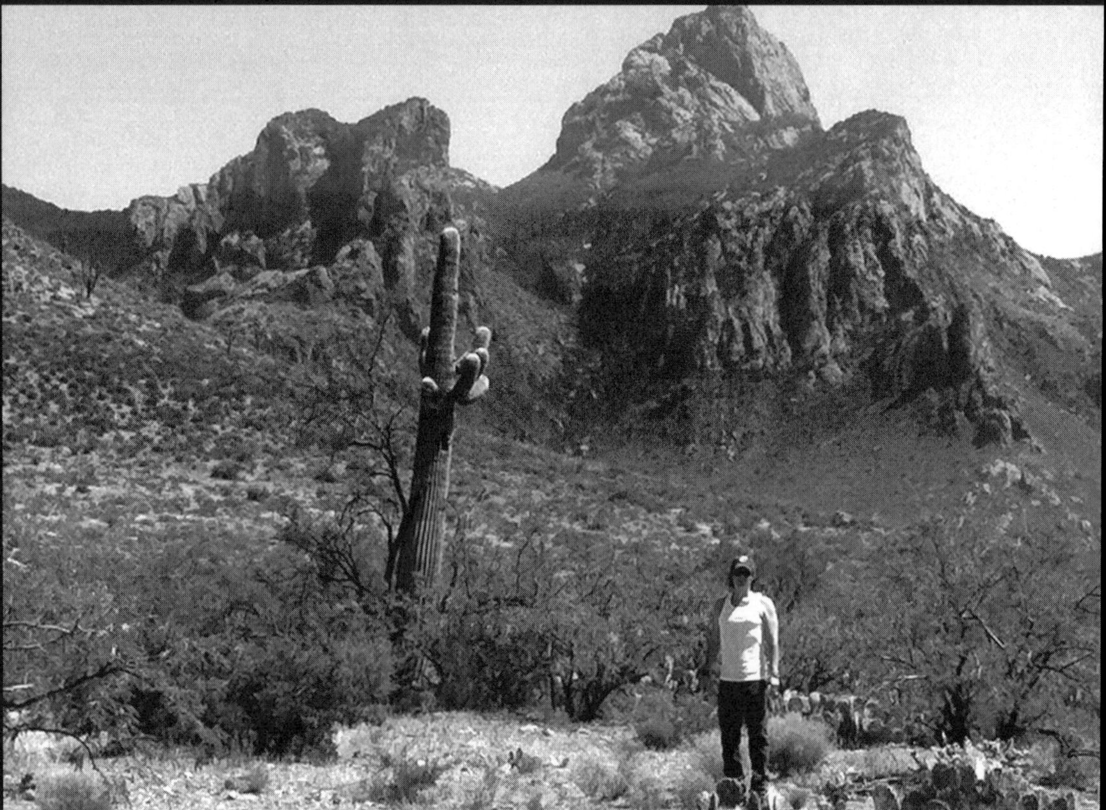

Location scouting in the Sonoran Desert. This is Baboquivari Peak on the Pima Reservation. A sacred mountain, and the perfect hiding place for the lost journals.

The place is extremely isolated; very few people venture this deep into the desert. The road, such as it is, would only allow Vijaya and I to go 10 miles per hour.

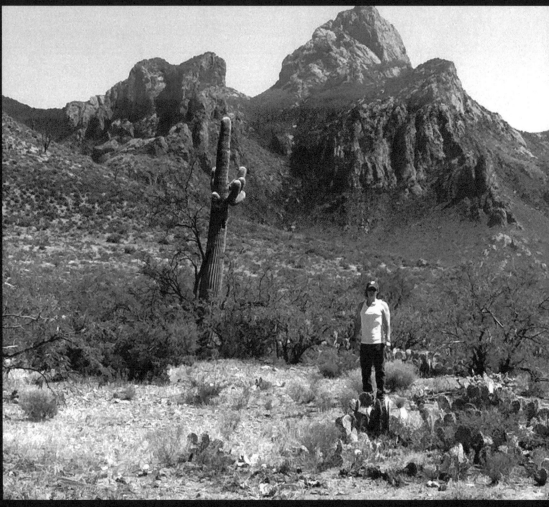

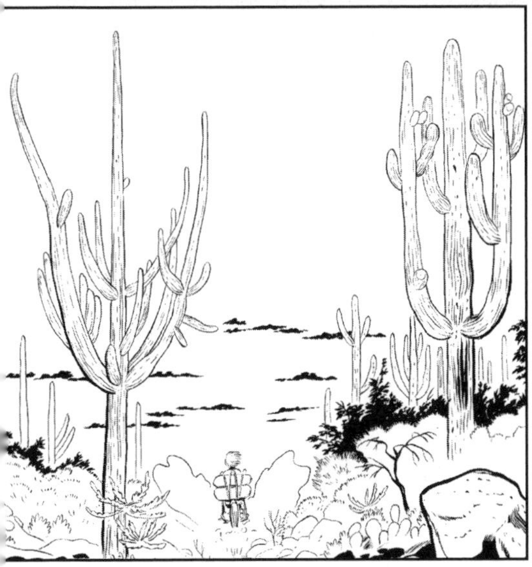
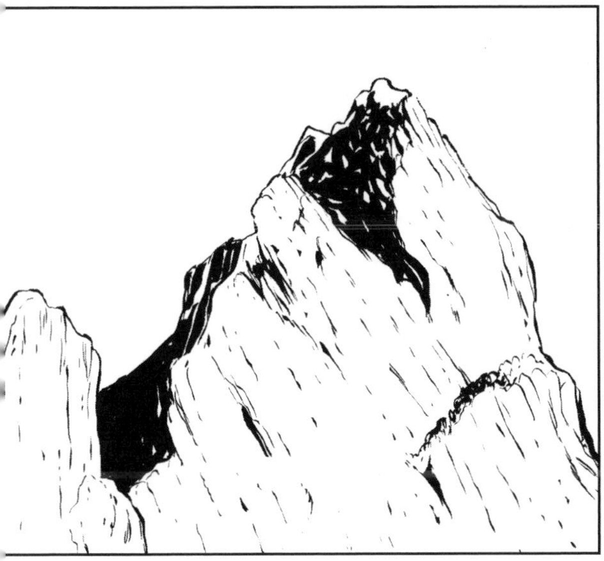
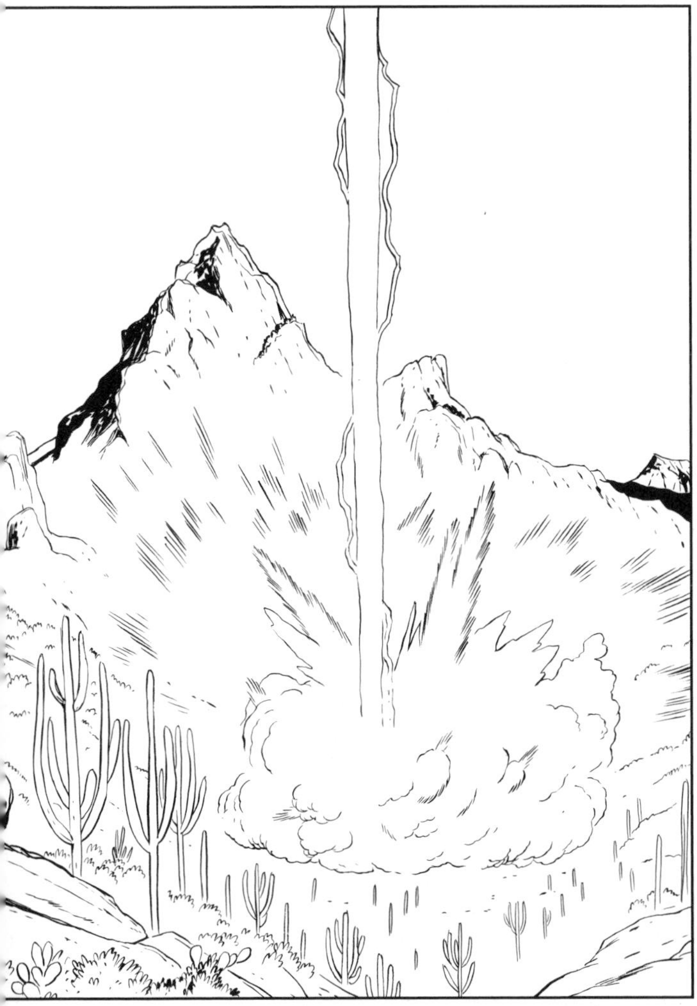
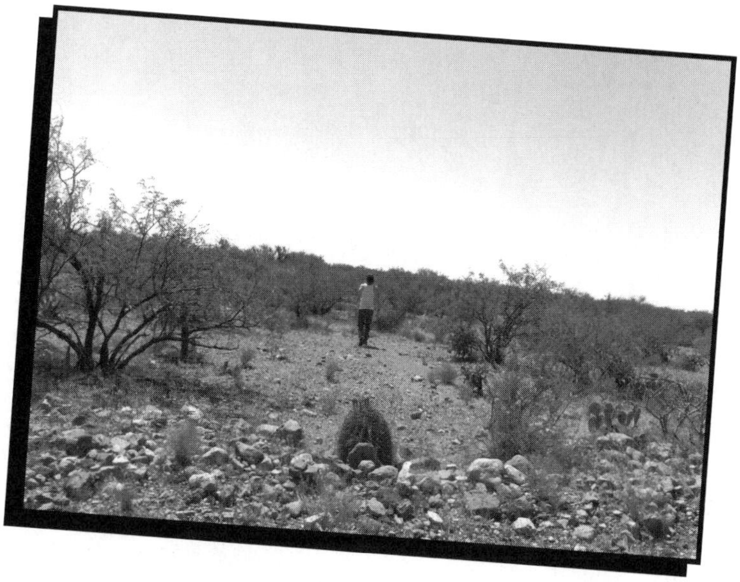
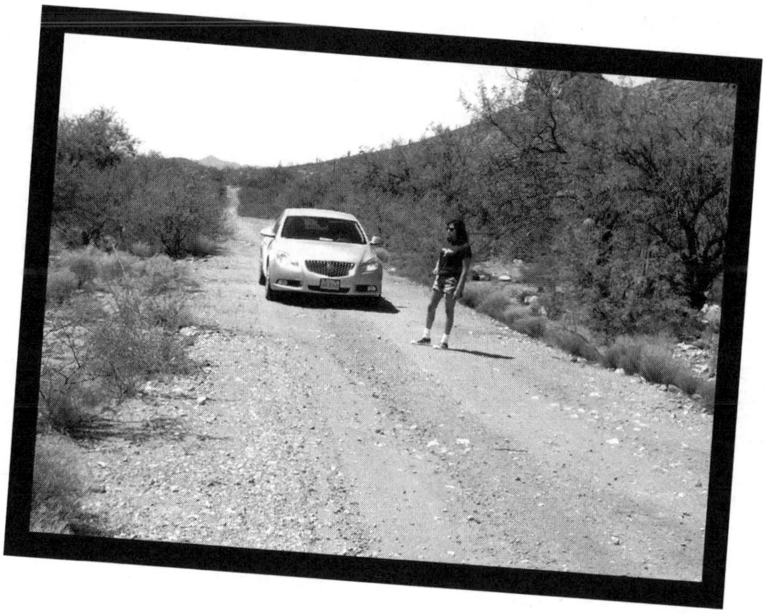
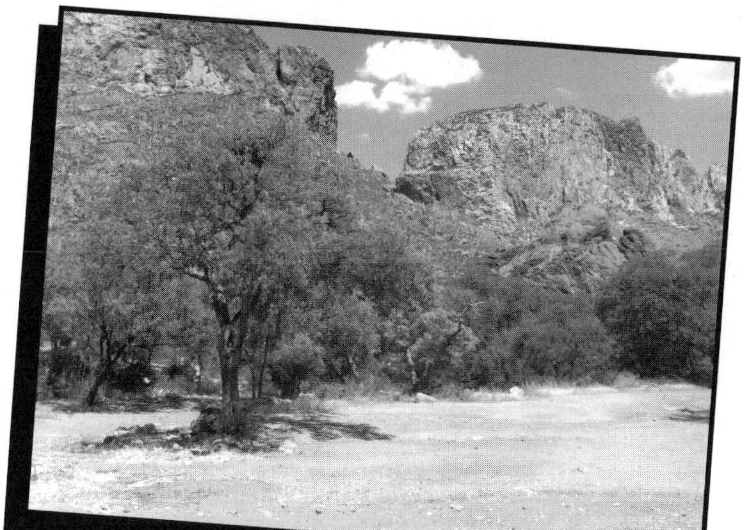

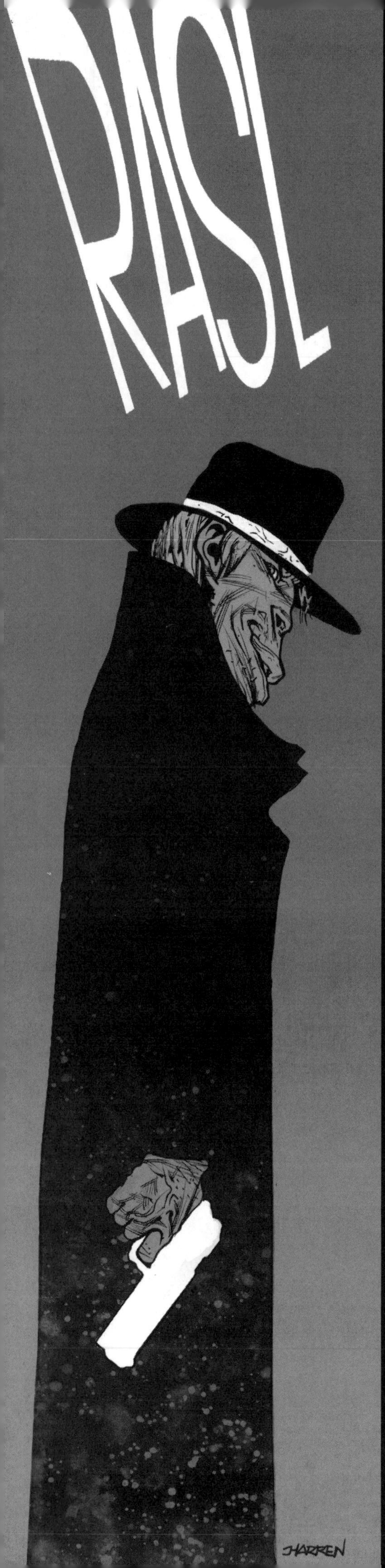
RASL
JHARREN

THE SINDIECATE
A TRIBUTE TO THE INDEPENDENT

Over the last four and half years, we've seen a lot of RASL inspired art, from fan sites to tattoos, but by far our favorite at Cartoon Books was the indie dedicated site called The Sinidecate. Here are their RASL pieces, and if you'd like to see more of their amazing drawings, visit them at thesindiecate.com.

Mike Ch

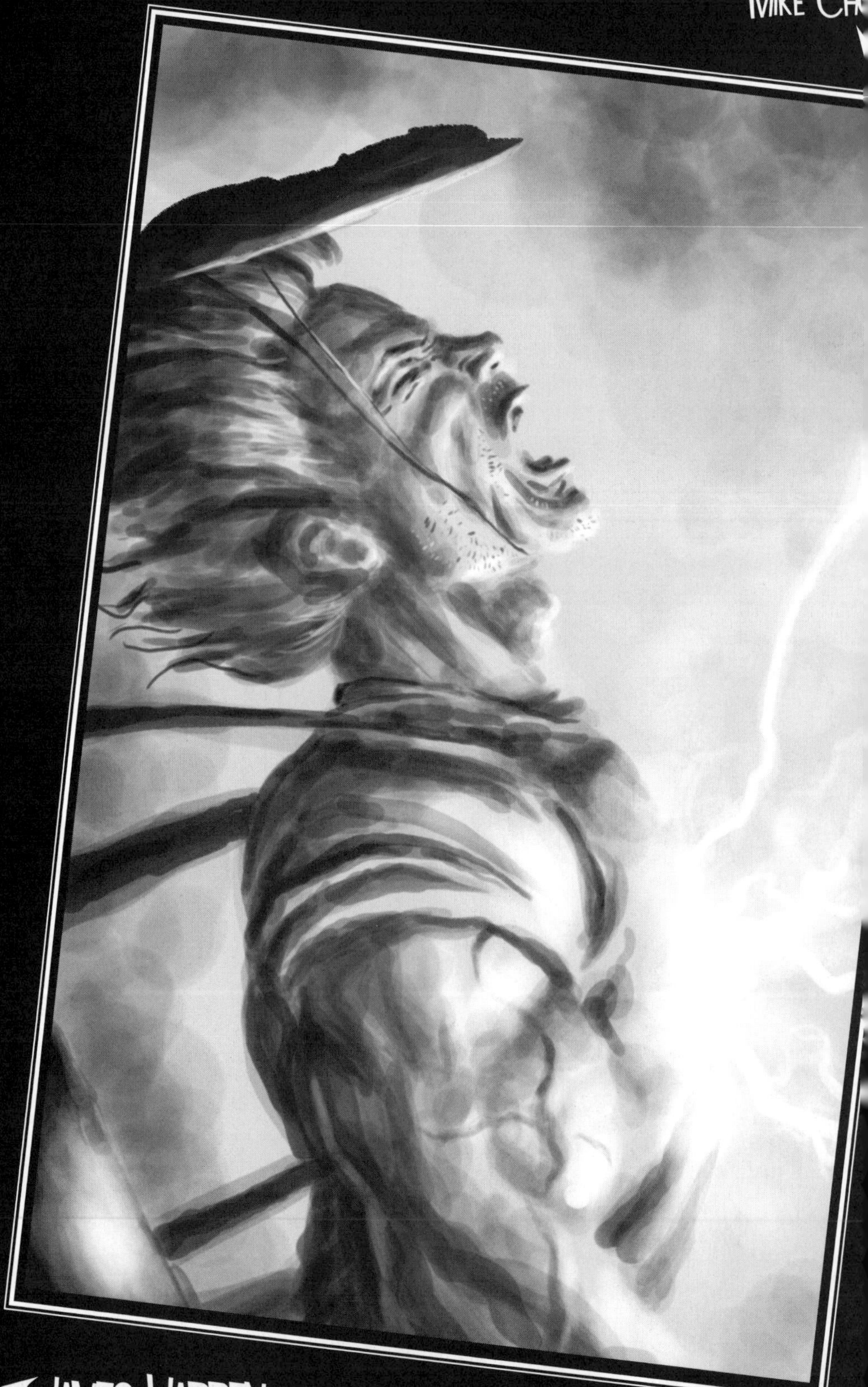

◄ James Harren

JORGE F. MUÑOZ

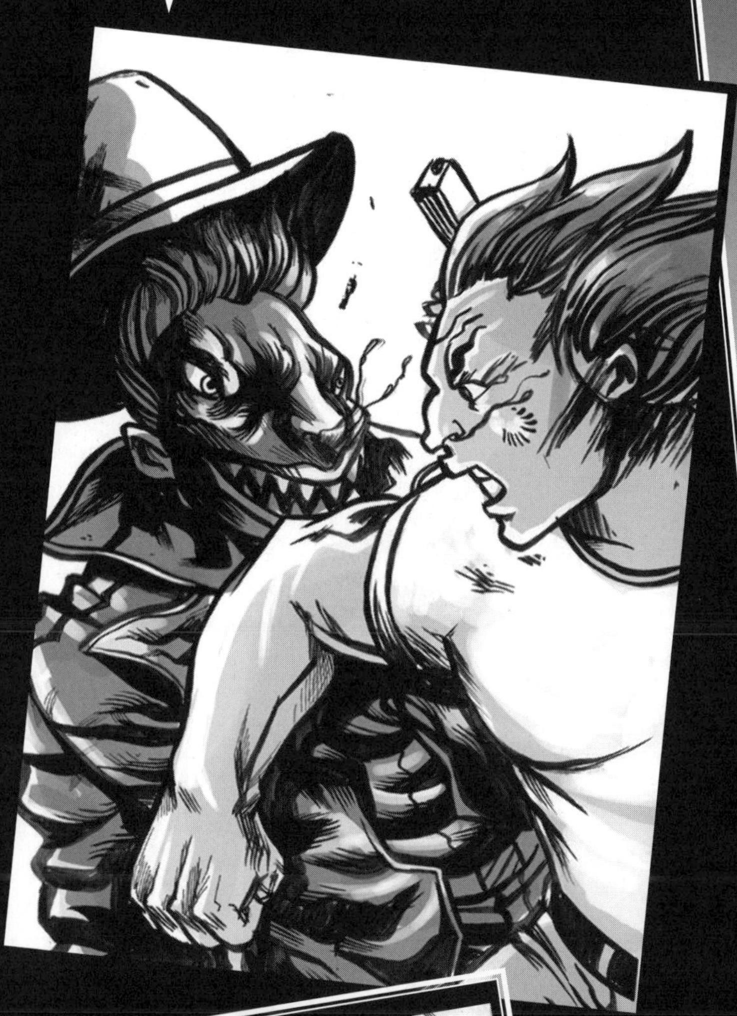

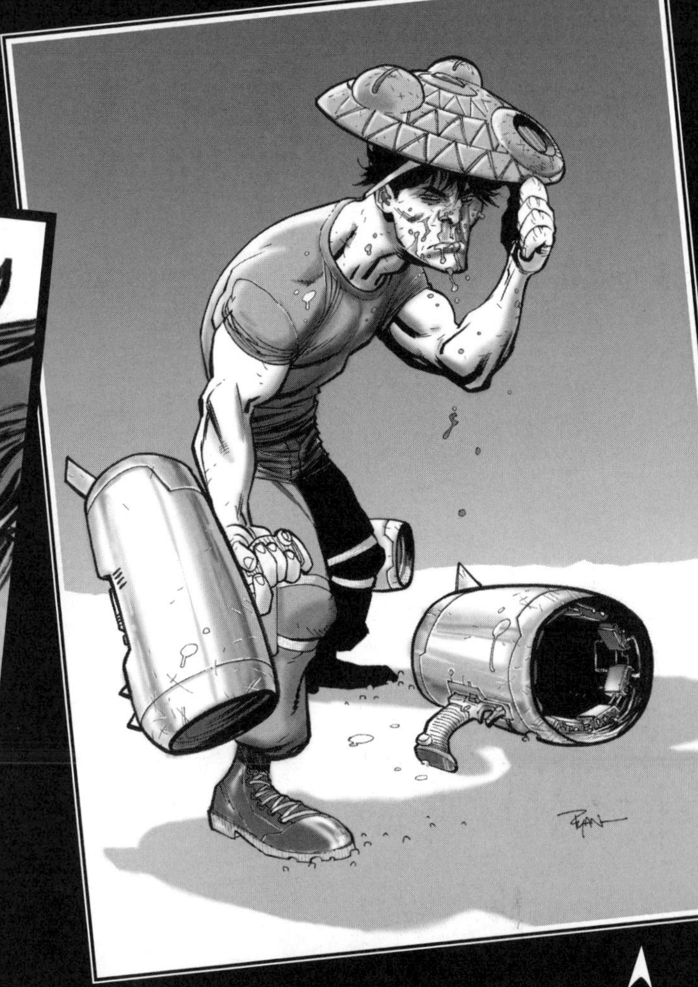

RYAN OTTLEY

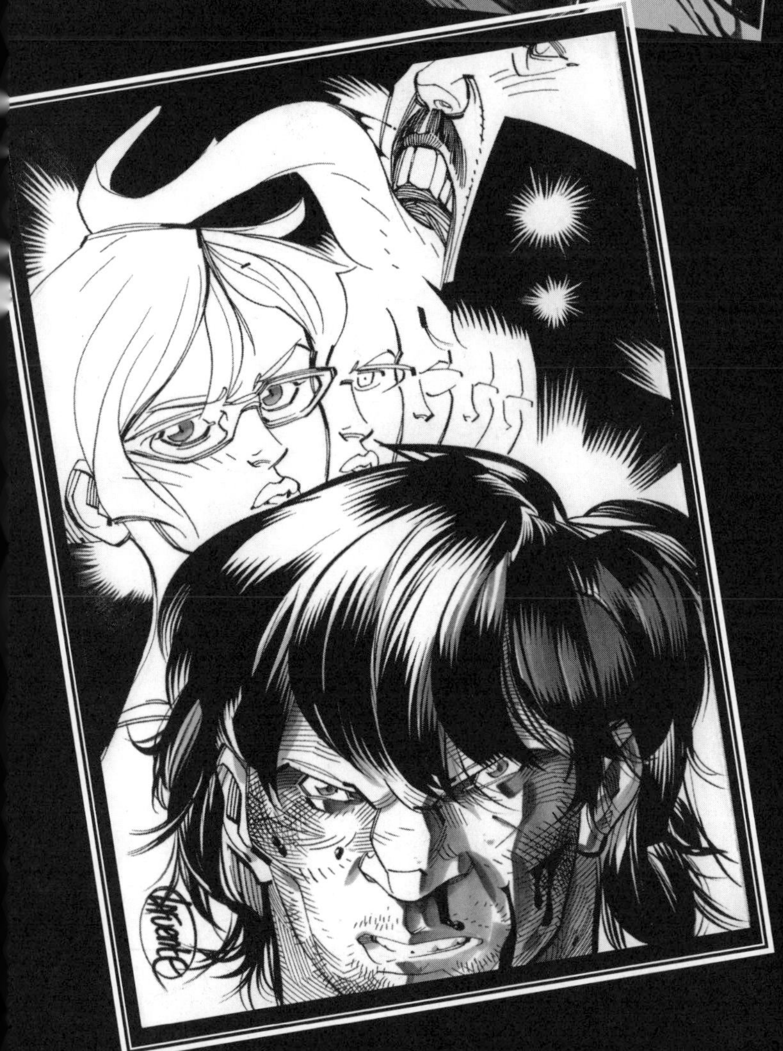

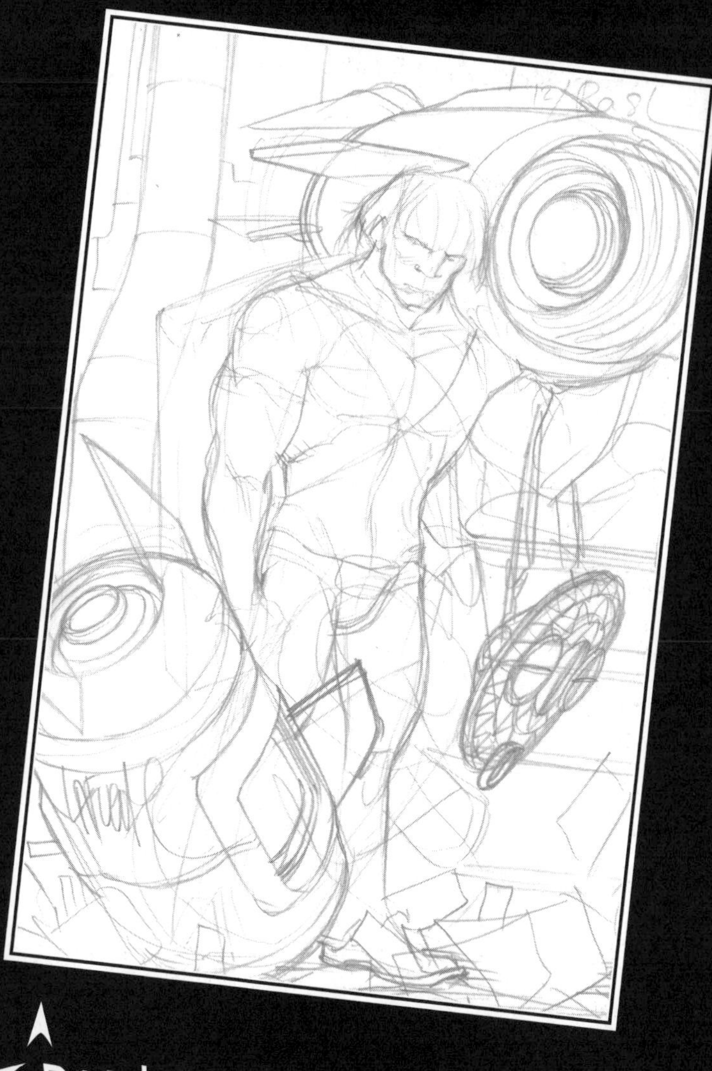

DAVID LAFUENTE

SPECIAL THANKS TO
TONY MURRAY, TOM LECKRONE,
KHARI SAFFO, HOWARD FINE,
JENNIFER OLIVER, MARTY FULLER,
SCOTT HARBIN, PHIL CORRIGAN,
VIJAYA IYER, KATHLEEN GLOSAN,
STEVE HAMAKER AND TOM GAADT
FOR SHARING THEIR KNOWLEDGE,
ADVICE AND PATIENCE.

A Brief Bibliography

Books:

Fabric of the Cosmos
by Brian Greene
(Vintage)

Parallel Worlds
by Michio Kaku
(Anchor Books)

Secrets of the Unified Field
by Joseph P. Farrell
(Adventures Unlimited Press)

Paths of Life
edited by Sheridan & Parezo
(University of Arizona Press)

The Philadelphia Experiment
by Moore & Berlitz
(Fawcett)

DVDs:

Tesla: Master of Lightning
(PBS Home Videos)

Nova: The Elegant Universe
(WGBH Boston Video)

Cosmos by Carl Sagan
(Cosmos Studios)

*Holes in Heaven? H.A.A.R.P. and
Advances in Tesla Technology*
(NSI)

Frankenstein
directed by James Whale
(Universal Studio)

Google:

Key words: Tesla, H.A.A.R.P.,
Philadelphia Experiment, Tunguska.
Enter any combination of these words
and hold on to your hat!

About the Author:

A co-founder of the 90's Self-Publishing
Movement, and an early adopter of the
graphic novel format, Jeff Smith is best
known as the writer and artist of *BONE*,
an award winning adventure about three
cartoon cousins lost in a world of myth
and ancient mysteries. In 2009, Smith
was the subject of a documentary
called *The Cartoonist: Jeff Smith, BONE,
and the Changing Face of Comics*.

Besides *BONE* and *RASL*, his other
books include *Shazam: The Monster
Society of Evil*, and *Little Mouse
Gets Ready*!

boneville.com